T0374678

Religious Politics and Secular States

# Religious Politics and Secular States

*Egypt, India, and the United States*

Scott W. Hibbard

The Johns Hopkins University Press
*Baltimore*

Johns Hopkins Paperback edition, 2012
9  8  7  6  5  4  3  2  1

The Johns Hopkins University Press
2715 North Charles Street
Baltimore, Maryland 21218-4363
www.press.jhu.edu

*The Library of Congress has catalogued the hardcover edition
of this book as follows:*

Hibbard, Scott W., 1962–
    Religious politics and secular states : Egypt, India, and the United
States / Scott W. Hibbard.
        p. cm.
    Includes bibliographical references and index.
    ISBN-13: 978-0-8018-9669-9 (hardcover : alk. paper)
    ISBN-10: 0-8018-9669-X (hardcover)
    1. Religion and politics—Egypt. 2. Religion and politics—India.
3. Religion and politics—United States. 4. Conservatism—Egypt.
5. Conservatism—India. 6. Conservatism—United States. 7. Egypt—
Politics and government. 8. India—Politics and government.
9. United States—Politics and government. I. Title.
    BL65.P7H53 2010
    322′1—dc22        2009052694

A catalog record for this book is available from the British Library.

ISBN-13: 978-1-4214-0577-3
ISBN-10: 1-4214-0577-6

*Special discounts are available for bulk purchases of this book. For more
information, please contact Special Sales at 410-516-6936 or specialsales@
press.jhu.edu.*

*To the memory of Arthur Williams and Duncan Littlefair—two men who demonstrated that religion and free thought are not only compatible but complementary.*

At some point, the manipulator of [a] symbol becomes manipulated by the symbol. Those who start out using religious symbols instrumentally to gain power or other benefits end up becoming servants of those symbols psychologically. 

MICHAEL SELLS

# Contents

# Preface

This book is the product of many years' work. The origins of the research go back to the early 1990s, when I was following Islamist politics at the U.S. Institute of Peace. It was during this period (1992–97) that many of the events chronicled in chapter 3 were unfolding. At that time, there was a spike in Islamist violence in the Middle East, North Africa, and South Asia, as the former *mujahedin* (holy warriors) from the U.S.-backed war in Afghanistan returned to their home countries and continued their *jihad*. What was particularly intriguing about the case of Egypt was how the conflict between the state and its Islamist opposition unfolded. Even as the government security forces were eradicating the militant opposition groups in the field, the discourse of Islamic fundamentalism became increasingly entrenched in Egyptian public life. The assaults on intellectual freedom and religious diversity in Egypt that characterized this period provided the paradox that prompted the initial research for this book. Why was the Egyptian government winning the battles against Islamist militancy, while losing the ideological war?

The answer to this question became apparent in the subsequent fieldwork that informs this study. The efforts of successive state actors to coopt conservative religion in Egypt were central to the normalization of the Islamist discourse in that society. Instead of offering a genuine ideological alternative, state actors consistently sought to use a *salafist* (or illiberal) interpretation of Islamic tradition for their own purposes. While the promotion of religious fundamentalisms (as I call them) in Egypt was very much influenced by Saudi Arabia and its newfound oil wealth, this strategy also reflected a fundamentally different attitude toward conservative religion among state elites than was the case during the Nasser period. This changing attitude toward fundamentalist religion, moreover, was unique neither to Egypt nor to the region. On the contrary, state support for conservative or illiberal renderings of religious tradition was ubiquitous throughout the 1970s and 1980s. It was a central feature of the Cold War strategy of the United States in the Middle East and South Asia, which culminated in the 1980s war in Afghanistan. It was also evident in the domestic politics of countries around the world. The invocation of illiberal renderings of religious tradition provided state actors with a cultural basis for their claims to rule and an effective means of mobilizing popular sentiment behind traditional patterns of social and political hierarchy. Conservative religion, in short, served as a bulwark against the ideas and activists associated with the political left.

This book examines this trend in the context of three societies in which commitments to secular norms were displaced by exclusive forms of religious politics: Egypt, India, and the United States. The point of departure is this question, Why have conservative or illiberal interpretations of religion been so common—and so effective—in the politics of three ostensibly secular societies? In other words, why have exclusive interpretations of religious tradition retained such strong political resonance, particularly in light of their earlier marginalization? As the following pages will demonstrate, the answer can be found in three interrelated issues. First, religion is an essential part of the construction of collective identities and hence provides an important basis of social solidarity and political mobilization. As a result, religion has been central to the contemporary discourse of modern nationalism and other variants of political communalism. Second, religion provides a moral framework for interpreting modern politics and articulating collective purpose. In other words, it is the normative and traditional elements of religion that make it relevant to modern political life. Finally, state actors, along with other political operatives, have consistently manipulated such identities and, more so in recent years, found utility in promoting a theologically conservative interpretation of religion as a basis of populist legitimacy. It is this last part of the explanation that is the primary focus of each case in this study.

This emphasis on state actors as an explanatory variable represents a novel approach to the study of contemporary religious politics. It runs counter to the assumptions of modernization theory, which holds that states (and modernity) were firmly secular and committed to a particular vision of development. It also differs from the framework offered by the World Values Survey, which has reaffirmed many of the earlier claims made by modernization theory. The focus on state actors also marks a sharp departure from much of the recent academic work that has informed the flourishing field of religion and politics. This research has tended to focus on the social movements and ideologies associated with religious fundamentalisms. While this mode of inquiry has contributed enormously to our understanding of religious politics in the post–Cold War era, it has tended to overlook the broader ideological context in which these movements emerged. The emphasis on religious activism has also neglected the complicity of state actors in the rise of illiberal religious ideologies. This book fills both of these gaps by providing a more comprehensive account of the historical record in question. As such, it highlights the effort of state actors to co-opt illiberal religion and the corresponding ideological transformation that attended the rise of modern religious fundamentalisms.

To be clear, I do not argue that the religious ideologies and movements associated with fundamentalisms are in any way unimportant. That is clearly not the case. Nor do I argue that state manipulation of religion was the only factor contributing to the resurgence of religious politics in the three case studies, or that state actors somehow created religious fundamentalisms. There are obviously other important factors at work as well. Rather, the key point of this research is to highlight a third variable that is often overlooked. In case after case, ostensibly secular state leaders and other mainstream political actors worked to normalize illiberal religious ideologies and helped to bring the ideas and activists associated with fundamentalist movements into the ideological mainstream. The theoretical framework that informs this study, then, provides a more nuanced understanding of contemporary religious politics, one that accounts for the agency of religious activists, the changing orientation of state actors, and the significance of ideas themselves. It also emphasizes the political importance of the competition for cultural authenticity but does not assume that competing political actors necessarily offer genuine alternatives on questions of religion, ideology, or secularism.

Some of the material in the cases may be familiar to readers, especially those who have a longstanding interest in the study of religion and politics. However, the reader will encounter a distinctly different "take" on these issues than is found in more conventional explanations for the rise of religious politics. This includes often surprising material from the historical record that is not widely known or otherwise disregarded as anomalous. This is particularly true of the case of the United States. While most readers will have a familiarity with recent American history, many will be surprised to learn that Richard Nixon held religious services in the East Wing of the White House. Similarly, few may realize that George McGovern's critique of the Nixon administration had its own religious moorings with a rich history in the American tradition, or that the "culture wars" of the 1990s find their roots in debates over the role of religion in public life that go back to the country's founding. The point is that the emphasis of the U.S. case study on the religious roots of American secularism and the *intra*-religious debates of American politics is fundamentally different from the more simplistic secular-religious framework that is commonly used to characterize contemporary American politics. Moreover, like the other cases in this study, the emphasis of the U.S. chapters is on the instrumental manipulation of illiberal religious ideas (and activists) by mainstream political actors. From this perspective, the resurgence of religious politics was not simply the reaction of a traditional population to the excesses of the 1960s and 1970s but was very much a byproduct of the Republican Party's strategy of positive polarization. The rise of the religious right, in short, did not emerge autonomously from the realm of civil society. Rather, it was abetted by a group of party operatives and moneyed interests who sought to use Christian churches, ideas, and organizations to minimize the salience of economic considerations as a basis for voting by working-class Americans.

Although this argument may be unconventional, it is very much informed by my own experiences in government throughout the 1980s and 1990s. During that time, I served as a congressional staff member for three different members of Congress and later worked in an independent federal agency. It was in this context that I saw firsthand the conscious manipulation of religious sentiments and the right-wing populism that informed both the Reagan era and the Republican takeover of the House and Senate in the early 1990s. It was evident to me at the time that the country was less divided than its politics and that the polarization of the American electorate that defined this period was the result of conscious strategies developed by public affairs firms, think tanks, and other elements of the conservative movement's political machinery. These groups had learned well the art of obfuscation and mass mobilization. More to the point, they had tapped into the anxiety of working Americans with great effectiveness, convincing many in this demographic that the problems with American society were the result of liberal culture, not postindustrial capitalism.

I am solely responsible for the work presented in this book, but a great many people aided me throughout this endeavor. I would like to thank David Little, a mentor, friend and esteemed colleague. He was kind enough to read several drafts of the manuscript in its various iterations and has been enormously helpful throughout the writing of this book. More to the point, his own research greatly influenced my thinking on the relationship between religion and politics, thus it informs much of this text. I also owe a debt of gratitude to Scott Appleby, whom I had the good fortune to know during my time at the U.S. Institute of Peace. His appreciation for the variation of religion, as with Little's emphasis on ideology and identity, influenced my thinking on these issues. Special thanks also go to my advisors at the Johns Hopkins University, Mark Blyth and Mimi Keck, who read earlier drafts of this manuscript when it formed the basis of my dissertation. Their comments, patience, and support made this a much better study and made my time at Johns Hopkins enormously rewarding. A note of appreciation also goes to Veena Das and Waleed Hazbun, members of my dissertation committee who provided extremely helpful feedback on the earlier work.

In Egypt, I had the invaluable help of Hossam El-Hamalawy, without whom serious research would literally have been impossible. It is also with fond memories that I acknowledge Tahsin Bashir's insights and advice. There were many others with whom I had a chance to speak in Egypt, and their thoughts have shaped my thinking on the politics of this most fascinating of societies. This group includes Emad Shahin, Mohamed Kamal, Gehad Auda, Said Al-Ashmawy, Sayed Al-Quimni, Essam El-Erian, Milad Hanna, Hasan Hanafi, Bahey al-Din Hussain, Walid Kazziha, Samir Ruca, among many others. I have also been greatly aided by the work, insights, and comments of Nabil Abdel Fatah and Fouad Ajami. Particular thanks also go to Saad Eddin Ibrahim and his wife Barbara; they helped get me started in my research and extended me a warm welcome to the country during my last visit.

In India, I had the good fortune of speaking with such individuals as Zoya Hasan, Asghar Ali Engineer, Achin Vanaik, Raj Mohan, Sujit Dutta, Ashis Nandy, Nandini Sandar, Romila Thapar, among others. I am particularly indebted to Pasha Anwer of Delhi University (and his wife, Pam), both for his friendship and his insights. And, of course, there are Avnish and Ushi Puri, who made my time in India so rewarding, memorable, and genuinely enriching. I extend a note of particular appreciation to the various outside reviewers who helped me with this manuscript, including Joseph Margulies, Aziz Huq, Tim Sisk, John Tirman, and the anonymous external reviewer from the Johns Hopkins University Press; their comments and critiques made this a much better work. I would also like to thank Ashref El Sharif, Nina Mohseni, and Damir Kozlica for their able and enormously helpful research assistance as well as the National Security Education Program (NSEP) for funding much of the research. Finally, I owe special thanks to my mother, my father, and (especially) my wife, Tara, who have so patiently supported me throughout this project. *Shukran.*

Religious Politics and Secular States

# Rethinking the Secular State

On October 6, 1981, Anwar Sadat stood on a ceremonial platform and observed a military procession commemorate Egypt's victory in the 1973 war with Israel. In what was known as the Great Crossing, the Egyptian army seized the Israeli military positions on the east bank of the Suez Canal and pushed into the Sinai Peninsula. Although the conflict ended inconclusively, the 1973 war was Sadat's finest hour. The "Hero of the Crossing" redeemed, to some extent, the 1967 military defeat that had so tarnished the legacy of his predecessor, Gamal Abdel Nasser. It also helped to confer legitimacy upon Sadat's rule. It was ironic, then, that, just as Egypt's leader was marking the 1973 victory with foreign dignitaries and other government officials, his presidency was about to come to an abrupt end. During the parade, as jets roared overhead, an army truck veered out of line and stopped abruptly in front of the presidential entourage. Four soldiers leapt out, hurling grenades and firing automatic rifles. Sadat was killed almost instantly. As the presidential security scrambled to react, the lead assassin shouted: "I am Khalid Islambouli. I have killed Pharaoh, and I do not fear death."[1]

Three years later, in October 1984, a similar event transpired a continent away. Indira Gandhi, the prime minister of India, walked from her official residence toward an office on the grounds of the ministerial estate. She was scheduled to give a television interview to the British actor and documentary producer, Peter Ustinov. As she proceeded through the gardens, two of her Sikh bodyguards drew their weapons and fired at the leader they were charged to protect. She was hit by more than thirty bullets and mortally wounded. Other members of Mrs. Gandhi's security detail responded to the gunfire. One of the assassins was killed at the scene; the other was wounded and subsequently tried, convicted, and hanged, along with a co-conspirator. In the days that followed the assassination, Hindu mobs rampaged through Delhi and other cities, attacking Sikhs and burning their homes and businesses. More than three thousand Sikh men, women, and children were killed in the course of a week, and their property destroyed. Tens of thousands were forced to flee their homes.

The conventional explanation for these events reflects a common understanding of religious politics writ large. Both Sadat and Gandhi are typically seen as secular leaders gunned down by religious fanatics. The assassinations, moreover, are said to reflect a broader struggle between religious opposition groups and secular state elites. At issue is not just a competition for power but also a fundamental conflict between tradition and modernity, between religion and secularism.[2] Similarly, the attack on the Sikh community in the aftermath of Mrs. Gandhi's assassination is attributed to the communal passions latent in traditional society. The religious nature of traditional populations, it is argued, predisposes them to the kind of collective violence—and irrationality—not typically associated with modern political life. At face value, this interpretation of events appears self-evident. Sadat's assassins were members of Islamic Jihad, an underground militant group that had penetrated the Egyptian army. They were committed to the establishment of an Islamic state and were critical of Sadat's overtures to both the West and Israel. Similarly, the assassination of Mrs. Gandhi was retribution for a bloody encounter that had transpired a few months earlier in the Indian state of the Punjab. A militant group led by Sikh fundamentalist Sant Bhindranwale had barricaded itself in the Golden Temple of Amritsar, the Sikh religion's holiest shrine. The militants were only expelled—and killed—after a bloody assault by the Indian army acting under orders from Mrs. Gandhi.

The reality behind these events, however, differs in significant ways from the account offered above. In the case of Egypt, the policies of Anwar Sadat were far from secular. His tenure in office was defined by the active promotion of

Islamic fundamentalism through the institutions of the modern state. He greatly expanded religious education, increased Islamic programming on state-run television, and built mosques with government funds. The regime also cooperated with—and actively sought to coopt—Egypt's Muslim Brotherhood. In the same vein, Sadat's domestic intelligence services throughout the 1970s supported an array of Islamist student groups on Egypt's university campuses. On the one hand, the goal of these policies was to provide a new basis of authority for the regime, one rooted in religious tradition, not Arab (or secular) nationalism. On the other hand, the effort to coopt Islamic ideas and activists was intended to provide a counterweight to the continuing influence of the secular left in Egyptian politics. It was the unreconstructed Nasserists and communists that Sadat feared, not the fundamentalists. The regime's ability to control the forces it unleashed, however, was limited. After Sadat's historic trip to Jerusalem in 1977, the Islamists turned on the "believing president" with deadly results.

Similarly, Indira Gandhi's assassination was an unintended consequence of her own manipulation of religious politics. Gandhi's son, Sanjay, and other Congress Party officials (most notably Zail Singh, the future president of India) had supported the militant Bhindranwale in an effort to isolate more moderate Sikh leaders in the Punjab. These moderate Sikhs, affiliated with the Akali Dal political party, were Mrs. Gandhi's main rivals in the region. In an effort to split the Sikh vote and undermine the Akali Dal, Congress Party operatives supported Bhindranwale and turned a blind eye toward his many excesses. Whatever control they had over the militant sant, however, was gone by the time that he and his followers barricaded themselves in the Golden Temple. This instrumental manipulation of religious politics was also linked to the Congress Party's own communalist tendencies and its efforts to use religion to court the Hindu vote. The anti-Sikh violence that followed Mrs. Gandhi's assassination, for example, was not a spontaneous outpouring of grief; rather, it was a coordinated response by Congress Party leaders who sought to remind the Sikh community of their subordinate position in Indian society. Similarly, the party used the threat of terrorism and minority separatism for much of the following decade to mobilize Hindu support behind their continued rule. Fear, religion, and a thinly veiled Hindu nationalism came to define the Congress Party's electoral strategy throughout this period.

What is particularly interesting about this history is that the events in question are not anomalous, nor was the promotion of religious ideologies by modern states limited to the cases discussed above. On the contrary, the conscious manipulation of conservative or illiberal religion by state elites throughout the 1970s and 1980s was widespread.[3] In countries as diverse as Malaysia, Pakistan, Turkey, Israel, Sudan, Sri Lanka, Algeria, and the United States,[4] ostensibly secular state actors consciously sought to coopt the ideas and activists associated with religious fundamentalisms.[5] In each of these cases, illiberal or exclusive interpretations of religion were used to provide a "priestly" affirmation for existing patterns of social and political power and provide a popular basis for politically conservative governments. In this context, theologically conservative interpretations of religion were a central feature of the ideological debates of the period and were used to challenge liberal visions of social order.[6] Religious "fundamentalisms," in short, were invoked by state elites to sanction a new era of conservative politics.

Although it is not surprising that state actors would appeal to religion—politicians rely on a variety of means to secure and maintain power—it is significant that they consistently gravitated toward an illiberal rendering of religious tradition. This is counterintuitive, for a variety of reasons. First, it was state elites who, during the mid-twentieth century, had been the lead proponents of a secular vision of national development. In this earlier period, leaders such as Nasser in Egypt and Jawaharlal Nehru in India had vehemently opposed the kind of illiberal religious ideologies that were later taken up in the 1970s and 1980s. It is not that religion was absent from the politics of the mid-twentieth century but rather that state actors tended to eschew the more intolerant interpretations of religion that later became so prevalent. Second, the trend contradicts the widely held assumptions that states—and modernity—were fundamentally secular in nature and that the influence of religion was irrevocably on the wane. As the events above illustrate, religion remained not only relevant to modern politics but was also central to the construction of an alternative vision of modernity. It is ironic, then, that it was secular elites who so readily embraced this religious vision of modern social life.

The following chapters examine this trend in comparative perspective. The book reviews the resurgence of religious politics in the context of three ostensibly secular societies: Egypt, India, and the United States. In each case, commitments to secular norms were embedded in the institutions of nation and state during the mid-twentieth century and disembedded in later decades. The particular focus of the cases, though, is on the role of state actors in facilitating this transition and their contribution to the emergence of an exclusive religious politics. The central argument of the book is that the changing orientation of state elites toward religion had an enormous, and yet largely overlooked, impact on the ideological transformation that defined this period.[7] The book also examines the consequences of the instrumental manipulation of religion. By abandoning earlier commitments to secular norms—and consciously invoking exclusive religious themes—state actors reopened longstanding debates over the nature and basis of the national community. They also privileged conservative religious activists at the expense of their liberal counterparts. It was mainstream political elites, in short, who helped to normalize illiberal religious ideologies and brought these ideas into the political mainstream.[8]

## Religious Politics Reconsidered

### *The Rise and Fall of Secularism*

A defining feature of the post–Cold War period has been the resurgence of religious politics in countries and regions around the world. The Bosnian genocide, the rise of the Christian Right in the United States, and the dominance of Hindu nationalism in India are all examples of this broader phenomenon. So, too, is the spread of Islamic fundamentalism throughout the Middle East and South Asia. Explaining this phenomenon, however, has remained a challenge. The enduring relevance of religion to contemporary politics contradicts the basic assumptions of modernization theory and its corollary, the secularization thesis.[9] These theories argued that the influence of traditional belief systems would diminish with the onset of economic and political development. As the secular institutions of states and markets came to dominate modern life, many assumed that traditional influences such as the church would be simply less relevant. Similarly, as science and reason became intellectually predominant, the salience of religion for individuals would decline. It was secular norms and ideas that would shape the future, not religion.[10]

The three cases examined in this study reflect this paradox. In each instance, the post–World War II period was defined by a commitment to a secular vision of modernity and an inclusive national identity. These commitments, however, were displaced in subsequent years by a wave of illiberal, and communal, religious politics. In Egypt, the modernist ideas of Nasser gave way to a conservative or *salafist* interpretation of Islam during the tenure of his successors, Anwar Sadat and Hosni Mubarak.[11] In this latter period, the vernacular of political discourse came to be defined by an austere interpretation of Islam influenced by Saudi Wahhabism.[12] In India, the inclusive norms of Indian nationalism that characterized the post-Independence period were similarly replaced by the more assertive and chauvinistic ideals of Hindu nationalism. This was accompanied by an increase in violence against religious minorities. Similarly, the rise of the religious right in the United States marked an ideological retrenchment in American public life and an end to the secular consensus of the post-World War II period.

The question, then, is how does one explain the resurgence of religious politics in these three cases, particularly given the marginalization of illiberal religious ideologies in the mid-twentieth century? In other words, why has religion—and particularly a conservative and often illiberal rendering of religious tradition—remained so influential in the politics of these three ostensibly secular societies?

The answer to these questions can be found in four interrelated issues. To begin with, religion remains relevant to modern politics because of its close association with communal identities and moral legitimacy. Even if religious *institutions* are less central to modern social life, religion remains enormously influential in the construction and mobilization of collective identities. This is especially relevant for modern nationalisms and other forms of political communalism. By communalism I am referring to a belief that those who share a common religious or ethnic identity have similar economic and political interests (despite class or other considerations), while those of different ethnic or religious groups are assumed to have divergent "secular" interests. Hence, the satisfaction of one community's interests is seen as necessarily coming at the expense of another. (In the West, this ethic normally goes by the name *sectarianism*.) Nationalist ideologies draw on religious motifs and symbols in order to reinforce this type of social solidarity and mobilize populations along communal lines. Within this context, religion becomes deeply intertwined with patriotism and is invoked to demonstrate cultural authenticity. Second, the moral language inherent in religious tradition makes it a uniquely effective means of sanctioning modern political views and policies. By linking human existence to a transcendent realm, religion provides a framework for interpreting political events and articulating moral purpose. In this way, religion provides a normative language for public life and helps to legitimize—and sacralize—political authority or claims to authority.

Third, political actors of all stripes regularly manipulate religion (and religious identities) for political ends. This includes modern state elites. Although religion is commonly used to critique the status quo (in what is called the "prophetic" function of religion), state actors have never been reluctant to appropriate religion for their own purposes. On the contrary, state actors have long used religion to sanctify political power and to imbue relationships of dominance with an aura of legitimate authority. The intent of this "priestly" function of religion is to situate an ephemeral set of power relations within a broader, and enduring, moral framework. In either instance—prophetic or priestly—the ultimate goal is to link the narrow political interests of a particular group with a broader vision of moral, national, and religious purpose.

Although these first three issues help to explain the continuing relevance of religion to modern politics writ large, the question remains why a conservative or illiberal rendering of religious tradition has been so prominent, and not a more inclusive or liberal interpretation. The explanation for this can be found in the particular historical context, specifically in the changing orientation of state elites toward an exclusive vision of religion and society. It is this last aspect of contemporary religious politics that is the primary focus of this book.

As I demonstrate in the following volume, the attitude of state elites toward religion in the second half of the twentieth century fluctuated dramatically. In the 1950s and 1960s, state actors were the articulators of a progressive conception of national development. They promoted an inclusive vision of religion and society and sought to embed secular norms in the institutions of nation and state. Government policy during this period was commonly associated with such issues as poverty alleviation, state-led economic development, and social justice. It was this historical moment that informed modernization theory and the belief that modernity was, by its very definition, secular and progressive. Secularism in this context did not necessarily entail the removal of religion from the public sphere (although many advocated this alternative). Rather, secularism in the mid-twentieth century was seen as providing a basis of citizenship that was not rooted in a particular religious identity. Secular norms and identities were thus perceived as an important mechanism for integrating diverse populations into a common political framework. Conservative social forces, on the other hand, and the illiberal religious ideas they espoused were typically associated with a reactionary past and seen as an obstacle to the kind of economic and political reform promoted by modern states.

In the 1970s and 1980s, however, the commitment of state elites to social change diminished, and along with it their dedication to a secular vision of national life. State leaders and other mainstream political actors subsequently abandoned their support for a liberal vision of religion and society in favor of

conservative or illiberal religious ideologies. During this period, illiberal interpretations of religious traditions were used to counter leftist politics and
legitimize hierarchical patterns of social order. Exclusive visions of national
identity were also used to heighten communal loyalties and appeal to a homog-
enized notion of group identity. This was an important means of diminishing
the salience of class in national politics and of generating popular support for
a conservative political agenda. It was also an important part of the Cold War
dynamic. In this context, state elites either took a weak stand against religious
communalism—not wishing to oppose conservative cultural forces—or actively
sought to coopt such forces for their own purposes. This changing attitude of
state actors toward illiberal religion marked a sharp break from previous practice. Although conservative religious activists had long advocated an explicitly
religious vision of social life, their influence had been curbed by the repression
of state leaders in the 1950s and 1960s. This changed dramatically, however, in
the 1970s and 1980s, as state elites came to see conservative religious actors as a
constituency to be courted, not a movement to be suppressed. The subsequent
embrace of exclusive religious ideas thus reflected a new set of priorities. Rather
than serve as an agent of social change, state policy sought to reify existing patterns of social hierarchy. In this new era, state and religion would be used to
maintain the status quo, not transform it.

## Competing Visions of the Nation

What is at issue in each of these cases is a struggle *not* between tradition and
modernity—nor between secular elites and a religious opposition—but rather
between competing visions of modern social life. In other words, it reflects
a continuing struggle to define the nation. As the ideological conflicts of the
twentieth century illustrate, modernization was never, by definition, rational,
individualist, or liberal. On the contrary, the competing modes of social organization—fascism, liberal democratic capitalism, communist totalitarianism—
were defined by an ongoing struggle between "open" and "closed" conceptions
of society.[13] None of these represented a retreat into tradition; rather, each
embodied a different vision of modern social life. The open society was committed to the Enlightenment values of individual freedom, reason, and the rule
of law, while the closed society was characterized by hierarchical patterns of
social order and the centralization of political authority. Whether it was fascism,
communism, or ethnic nationalism, *political unity* from this perspective was premised on a high degree of *cultural uniformity*. Although this illiberal vision of

social life may be antithetical to the Enlightenment norms of a liberal society, it was nonetheless a product of the modern era.

The debates between these inclusive and exclusive visions of social life had a powerful impact on the religious politics of the last fifty years. In each of the cases of this study, debates over social order have hinged on the question of whether the nation ought to be defined in secular or religious terms. In other words, should one religion be given precedence in the institutions of nation and state, or ought these institutions be nondiscriminatory in regard to matters of faith? On its face, this appears to be a religious dispute over the compatibility of secular and religious norms. As such, it taps into longstanding disagreements over the relative merits of creating an autonomous space in the public sphere where organized religion does not intrude. Those who support a more central role for religion in public life—and argue against an autonomous public sphere—believe that religion is essential for the self-actualization of the dominant community. Religion is perceived as a source of morality and a symbol of the community's commitment to a transcendent moral order. Opponents of such an expansive role of religion in public life worry about the corrupting influence that politics will have on religion and believe that secularism is an important means of protecting religion from the negative effects of politicization. Similarly, religious minorities tend to oppose a close association of religion and government because they fear marginalization, the chance that they will become second-class citizens. Hence, the argument is made that only a secular order—one that delinks religious identities from civil status—can provide a nondiscriminatory basis to the governance of multiethnic, multireligious societies.

At a deeper level, however, this debate over religion in public life reflects the aforementioned division between liberal and illiberal conceptions of society. Like the open society, civic conceptions of nationalism are premised on a nondiscriminatory cosmopolitanism that extends membership to all within the territorial boundaries of a given nation-state. Ethnic nationalism or religious communalism, on the other hand, explicitly links political standing to membership in one faith community or another. As such, it gives priority to the dominant religious or ethnic communities at the expense of minorities. What is ultimately at issue in these debates, then, is whether the society (and, hence, the nation) ought to be defined by the values of inclusion and tolerance, or whether the will (and ethnic motifs) of a particular segment of the majority population ought to be predominant. In other words, must the dominant community—and its religious identity—be given preference in the political realm, or is there an obligation for state authorities to protect minority rights and cultural diversity? Should public life, in short, be governed by the majoritarian tendencies of the closed society, or ought it be tolerant of diversity and thus reflect the Enlightenment values of the open society?

Religion is central to these debates because it provides a moral basis to *both* of these differing visions of community. This paradox reflects what Appleby calls religion's fundamental ambiguity: the continuing tension between competing interpretations of a given religious tradition and the pattern of social life that each envisions.[14] Liberal or "modernist" interpretations of religion, for example, provide a foundation for civic forms of nationalism and other forms of inclusive social life. By tolerating diverse peoples and opinions, it provides the basis for the kind of primordial compromise essential to the smooth functioning of multiethnic, multireligious societies.[15] In this context, each individual (and community) forsakes its right to religious and ethnic preference in exchange for others relinquishing similar claims. Conversely, illiberal interpretations of religion (or fundamentalisms) commonly inform ethnic nationalism and other exclusive visions of social life. Those who support an explicit religious nationalism argue that collective self-actualization requires a public sphere defined by the ethnic and religious motifs of the majority community. From this perspective, freedom is a collective affair that requires a more central role for *their* religion in public life. The tolerance of diversity, then, is neither meritorious nor expedient if it comes at the expense of majority interests or contradicts God's will.

The struggle to define the nation, then, is in essence a debate over how to construct modernity: inclusive or exclusive, liberal or illiberal. As such, it reflects both religious and political differences over how to interpret a shared tradition. What is particularly surprising about the cases in question is the changing role of the state on precisely these issues. Although state leaders were the primary defenders of pluralist conceptions of social order in the mid-twentieth century—and embraced the liberal or modernist religion prevalent at the time—this changed in subsequent decades when state actors abandoned their opposition to communalist ideas and embraced a more explicit religious nationalism. Liberal and secular norms were subsequently delegitimized, and an illiberal vision of society became embedded in state institutions. Although the competition between state elites and conservative religious activists reemerged in the 1980s and 1990s, there was little difference in their respective visions of the nation (at least in Egypt and India). Rather, these opposing political interests vied with one another for the mantle of cultural legitimacy, with each side appealing to the communal tendencies of the majority population as a basis of its claim to rule. As a result, illiberal interpretations of religion benefited enormously from the changing orientation of state elites, while advocates of liberal religion (and pluralist secularism) were relegated to near-obscurity. The instrumental manipulation of religion by state actors, in short, had an enormous impact on popular perceptions of religious and cultural authenticity and, hence, on the prevailing definition of the nation.

## *The Framework of the Study*

The purpose of this study is twofold. First, it seeks to get the story straight. It reexamines the religious politics of Egypt, India, and the United States and highlights elements of the historical record that are not commonly known or are otherwise disregarded as anomalous. The promotion of illiberal religion by state actors is a largely overlooked phenomenon, and yet it is central to understanding the resurgence of religious politics in recent decades. The empirical chapters, consequently, rely on thick description to provide a comprehensive account of the events in question and include material not readily found elsewhere. As such, the study tells a side of the story that is not typically accounted for in the conventional narratives about the rise of religious fundamentalisms. This emphasis on the historical narrative is evident in the methodological approach of the study. It uses a comparative historical analysis, which focuses on several cases that are defined by a common sequence of events from roughly the same time period.[16] The cases were selected, moreover, to highlight religious and cultural diversity, thus making common trends more significant.

A second goal of this project is to provide a more nuanced theoretical framework for interpreting modern religious politics.[17] This is the basis of chapter 1. The first part of the chapter explains the continuing relevance of religion to modern political life and institutions. Its central claims are that religious politics occur within the ideological context of the nation-state and that religion is fundamentally intertwined with nationalist or communal identities. As such, religious ideologies (and fundamentalisms) reflect not a return to tradition per se but rather an ideological reconstruction of tradition for a modern context.[18] A second theme of this chapter is the complexity of modern religious politics. Although the symbols and rhetoric of religious tradition may be a common feature of contemporary political life, the variable nature of religion means that both the interpretation of religion and the ends to which it is used are varied. In other words, differing interpretations of religions inform competing visions of society and hence are alternatively mobilized in support of, or in opposition to, an existing social order.

Although most explanations of contemporary religious politics tend to focus on the social movements associated with religious fundamentalisms, the key variable in this analysis is the changing orientation of state elites toward illiberal religion. As I argue in this book, the ideas associated with religious fundamentalisms were not new, nor were many of the organizations. Although these movements were using new means to promote their message after 1970 or so, the underlying vision and rhetoric had not significantly altered from earlier decades. What did change, however, was the context. Specifically, the attitude of state leaders (and other mainstream political actors) toward exclusive visions of religion and society changed dramatically in the 1970s and 1980s. This is not to argue that state actors *created* religious fundamentalisms or that other factors are unimportant. Rather, the central claim is that the efforts to draw on—to exploit—illiberal interpretations of religion had an enormous impact on the political fortunes of the ideas and activists associated with them. Religious fundamentalisms, in short, were greatly abetted by the modern state and the secular elites who sought to coopt religion for their own purposes.

The focus of the empirical chapters, then, is on the ideological transformation that characterizes each case. As such, the emphasis is on the differing interpretations of religion and how these inform differing visions of society. The chapters also highlight the changing attitude of state elites toward illiberal conceptions of religious politics and its impact on the debates over how to define the nation. Each case is subsequently broken into two parts that are addressed in separate chapters. The first chapter of each case study examines the embedding of a liberal, secular vision of modernity in the immediate post–World War II period and the subsequent disembedding of the secular vision. This first part of the historical narrative emphasizes the connection between state policy toward religion and the corresponding rise and fall of the secular order. The second chapter of each case study examines the fallout from these policies. In each instance, the effort of state elites to coopt an exclusive vision of religion and society—and otherwise to fan the flames of sectarianism for political gain—undermined earlier efforts to build an inclusive national identity. It also contributed to the communalization of public life and the corresponding polarization of society. What emerges is a deeply divisive politics, with religious differences informing the fault lines of political conflict.

Chapter 2 is the first of the empirical chapters. It traces the origins and the subsequent downfall of Egypt's secular nationalism. The central focus of the chapter is the long-running dispute over whether a secular vision of social order ought to predominate in Egypt, or whether religion—specifically Islam—ought to govern both state and nation.[19] During the Nasser era, state institutions promoted a liberal variant of Islam that supported the regime's secular vision of Arab nationalism and socialism. This liberal rendering of Islamic tradition was used to support a program of social revolution and to discredit political rivals who advocated a more *salafist* or literal reading of Islamic tradition. These competing interpretations of Islam were subsequently enmeshed in the political (and ideological) struggle between the Arab nationalists and their opponents in the Muslim Brotherhood, Saudi Arabia, and other bastions of religious and political orthodoxy. Nasser's control of the state greatly influenced the outcome of this debate and helped to embed a secular vision of nationalist development in Egyptian public life.

Egypt's defeat in the June 1967 war with Israel greatly damaged the credibility of the Nasserist project. It also sparked a reevaluation of the ideals of the 1952 Egyptian revolution. Although the underlying issues were economic and political, the vernacular was religious. It was in this context that the secular-Islamist debate was resurrected. This time, however, the outcome was different. Nasser's successor, Anwar Sadat, and other state leaders abandoned the secular position in favor of a Saudi-influenced *salafist* Islam. Sadat's "Corrective Revolution" sought to coopt, not confront, the Islamist vision and used it to build a new basis of state power. This strategy entailed alliances with those who had opposed Nasser in earlier years, such as the Muslim Brotherhood, Egypt's landowners, and the leaders of Saudi Arabia. It also involved the use of conservative religion to stigmatize the political left and to mobilize popular sentiment behind state authority. These policies marked a significant break with the Nasserist legacy, an abandonment of the secular orientation of Egypt's 1952 revolution.

Chapter 3 examines the long-term consequences of Sadat's policies. Although Nasser had promoted an inclusive variant of Islam, a more illiberal interpretation became pervasive under Sadat. Along with it came an exclusive vision of social life that stigmatized Egypt's Coptic Christian minority, denigrated secular norms, and precipitated a backlash against the societal progress secured by women. These changes were due in large measure to the influence of Saudi Arabia in the post-1967 era. It was also due, however, to the inability of either Sadat or his successor, Hosni Mubarak, to control the forces they had unleashed. Although the Mubarak regime has been more nuanced in its approach to religion, it has never challenged the centrality of Islam in Egyptian public life. On the contrary, the regime has sought to portray itself as the authentic defender of religious orthodoxy in Egyptian society. Moreover, Mubarak's alliance with the official religious establishment in the 1990s further entrenched an illiberal interpretation of Islam in the institutions of the Egyptian state. In an effort to counter the ideological challenge of Islamist militants, the Mubarak regime granted a high degree of autonomy to religious clerics whose vision of society differed little from that of the Islamist opposition. The result was a cultural milieu in which assaults on intellectual freedom, minority populations, and creative expression occurred with official sanction. As one analyst put it, the regime became "a prisoner of Islam."[20]

Chapter 4 examines the rise and fall of Nehruvian secularism in post-Independence India. A central feature of this case is the manner in which different interpretations of religion have historically informed competing visions of politics and the nation. This was evident in the tensions between the inclusive interpretation of Indian identity advocated by Mahatma Gandhi and the exclusive Hindu nationalism of the Rashtriya Swayemsavek Sangh (RSS) and other communal organizations. Each perspective embodied a fundamentally different rendering of Hindu tradition and a correspondingly different vision of social order. Gandhi, for example, viewed tolerance and nonviolence as central to Hinduism, and this was the basis for his inclusive vision of Indian society. Nehru's secular nationalism built on these ideas, despite his own religious differences with Gandhi. Both, however, advocated extending membership of the nation to all who lived within the territorial boundaries of the country. The RSS, on the other hand, rejected both Gandhi's conception of Hindu tradition and his inclusive vision of the nation. From the perspective of the RSS, Hinduism needed to be reformed and reshaped as a more militant, assertive, and unitary tradition. Similarly, members of the RSS and later organizations advocated an ethnic nationalism that limited membership to Hindus. These differences over religion and society formed the fault lines of Indian politics for much of the twentieth century.

Although the historically dominant Congress Party was largely committed to a secular political order—and opposed Hindu communalism during the Nehru era—this changed in the post-Emergency period (1977 onward). During this latter period, Indira Gandhi, and later her son Rajiv, sought to coopt the discourse of Hindu nationalism as a basis of populist mobilization. This was evident in the party's majoritarian electoral strategy of the 1980s, which exploited the fear of minority separatism and appeals to religious identity to garner support among Hindu voters in the "Hindi Belt," the Hindi-speaking heartland of north and central India. This politicization of religion by Congress Party operatives also entailed an abandonment of the secular vision of Indian nationalism. By coopting Hindu communalism, however, Indira and Rajiv Gandhi effectively ceded the ideological debate to their political opponents in the Sangh Parivar (a family of Hindu organizations that included the RSS) and helped to disembed secularism as a norm of the Indian state.

Although the Congress Party's manipulation of religious politics was effective in the short term, there were unintended consequences that undermined its utility in the long term. The assassination of Mrs. Gandhi was one such side effect. So, too, were the rise in communal tensions and the normalization of Hindu nationalism as an ideological discourse. This is the focus of chapter 5. As a competing ideology, the notion of *Hindutva* (literally, Hindu-ness) had been in retreat since Mahatma Gandhi's assassination by a Hindu extremist in 1948. Although this communalist ideology retained support at the grassroots level—even among Congress Party activists—a secular Indian nationalism was dominant at the national level. The Congress Party's effort to coopt these themes in the 1980s was important in bringing the communal ideas of Hindu nationalism into the ideological mainstream. The main beneficiary of this transformation, however, was not the Congress Party but rather the Hindu nationalist Bharatia Janata Party (BJP) and other elements of the Sangh Parivar. This changing ideological context helps to explain the BJP's precipitous rise in the early 1990s, which went from near-obscurity to the heights of state power in just ten years.

Chapter 6 examines similar trends in the context of the United States. Like the other cases of this study, the resurgence of religious politics in the 1980s and 1990s occurred in the context of longstanding debates over the proper role of religion in public life. Although the founding of the United States was rooted in a basic commitment to religious tolerance, American history is replete with examples of religious discrimination and messianic visions of American nationalism. This reflects the fact that American nationalism is rooted in a religious narrative, albeit one that exhibits competing tendencies. At its best, America's "civil religion" has been based upon an interpretation of Christian belief that is nonsectarian and compatible with America's secular tradition.[21] However, an exclusive and often chauvinistic religious nationalism has also been a common feature of the American experience. This interpretation of American nationalism is tied to an illiberal rendering of Christian tradition and an exclusive understanding of American identity.

Similarly, the role of state actors in facilitating the rise of an exclusive vision of religion and society at the expense of a liberal alternative was considerable. This was evident during the tenure of Richard Nixon, who used a thinly veiled religious politics as part of his 1968 and 1972 presidential campaigns. Nixon's cultural politics was part of a broader effort—the so-called Southern Strategy—to split the Democratic Party's New Deal coalition and form a new conservative majority by reaching out to Southern and working-class whites. This majoritarian electoral strategy relied on a mix of religion, patriotism, and race to appeal to traditionally Democratic constituencies. By blurring religion and nationalism into an amorphous "idea of America," Republican strategists sought to stigmatize liberal norms, minorities, and dissent as unpatriotic. It was also intended to use religion and "cultural issues" to displace economic considerations as a basis of voting among working-class Americans.

The success of Nixon's majoritarian strategy set the stage for the Reagan Revolution of the 1980s and came to define Republican electoral campaigns in the following decades. This is the focus of chapter 7. In a manner similar to Egypt and India, the political fortunes of illiberal religious ideas and activists were greatly aided by the support of key state elites from Ronald Reagan to George W. Bush. Republican Party operatives, for example, helped to bring individuals like Jerry Falwell and other members of the Christian Right into the party and into the ideological mainstream. In doing so, however, they changed the nature of their party as well as the tenor of American politics. The realignment that started under Nixon came to fruition in later years, fundamentally transforming both the Republican *and* the Democratic parties in the process. Although Democrats lost their support among conservative Southerners, liberal Republicans were marginalized, as the center of gravity in their party shifted to religious conservatives.

The emphasis on communal—and majoritarian—politics that defined the Reagan-Bush era also affected longstanding divisions between the cosmopolitanism embodied in the social contract origins of the American republic and the Christian nationalism of the Puritan tradition. These tensions between inclusive and exclusive conceptions of both faith and nation were embodied in the culture wars of the 1990s. The religious politics of this era, however, was not simply the reaction of a traditional population to secular modernity but also reflected the continuing effort by political operatives to polarize the American electorate for partisan gain. It was in this context that the liberal-conservative divide in America took on strong religious overtones, as Republican Party activists invoked conservative religion to claim the mantle of God and Country as their own. As in the Indian case, however, the excesses associated with this strategy bred its own demise. The Bush presidential victories in 2000 and 2004 may have appeared to vindicate his party's religious turn, but it ultimately led to a dangerous overreach. Empowered by the electoral victories and a misguided religious certitude, the Bush administration pursued a set of policies—including two failed wars—that proved disastrous for the party and the nation alike. The election of Barack Obama in 2008, then, represented a repudiation of the Bush administration and a return to a more centrist vision of both religion *and* politics. The ability of the Obama administration to reverse the legacy of messianic nationalism and return America to its Enlightenment roots, however, is far from assured. Nonetheless, it remains a key challenge. The resurrection of a more tolerant public sphere is essential for the well-being of the American political system and is a prerequisite for healing the deep social divisions created during the culture wars of recent decades.

# CHAPTER ONE

# Reinterpreting Modern Religious Politics

The resurgence of religious politics in recent years has been a challenge for social scientists and policymakers alike. Since the end of the Cold War, the effort to understand religious fundamentalisms and their role in contemporary politics has been a central feature of American academic and policy debates. This challenge became even more pronounced in the aftermath of the terrorist attacks of September 11, 2001. Religious extremism, however, is not an Islamic phenomenon, nor is intolerance and violence limited to one tradition or another. On the contrary, the most intriguing feature of contemporary religious politics is its ubiquity. The proliferation of religio-political movements and the politicization of religion are phenomena that cut across regions and traditions and can be found in any number of countries around the world. This trend is all the more perplexing given the (once) widely held view that religious beliefs and identities would diminish as new modes of social organization transformed traditional societies. How, then, does one explain the continuing influence of religion—particularly exclusive interpretations of religion—in modern politics? Does this reflect a genuine return to religion—a "de-secularization of the world," as Berger and others have argued—or is it simply a useful vernacular to criticize the failures of the modern state?

The amount of scholarly research dedicated to these questions is impressive. There are many studies on religion and politics writ large as well as case studies examining individual countries and movements.[2] Much of this interest, however, has focused on illiberal religious opposition groups, particularly those that advocate violence. The priority given to religious, and particularly Islamist, militancy has been fueled by the heated policy debates of the post-9/11 era. This trend is problematic for a variety of reasons. On the one hand, it has reinforced a number of misleading assumptions about the nature of modern religious politics. This includes, for example, a tendency to view contemporary religious politics as *either* political *or* religious in orientation. Religious activists are consequently seen as either messianic (and antimodern) or as unscrupulous operatives who manipulate religion for purely political ends. On the other hand, it has also contributed to a belief that religion, or at least particular religions (usually Islam), are hostile to reason and modernity and hence antithetical to the Enlightenment norms that define a free society. According to this view, the primary challenge for contemporary political leaders is the danger of antimodern fundamentalisms.[3] This perspective is enormously misleading, yet it was reflected in the Bush administration's characterization of its "war on terror" as a conflict between freedom and tyranny, modernity and tradition, states and terrorists.[4]

In this chapter I present an alternative framework for understanding contemporary religious politics. A central premise of this alternative is that the prevalence of religion in modern political life is very much intertwined with the discourse and policies of the nation-state. As such, modern religious ideologies are just that: modern. Religion is integral to the construction of nationalist or communal ideologies and is a common feature of populist (and nationalist) mobilization. Religion, moreover, is uniquely able to provide a moral sanction for political action. As a result, it is central to the legitimation of modern state institutions and the claims made by those who seek to control (or overthrow) such institutions. A second feature of this alternative is its rejection of the dichotomous understanding of religious politics noted above. The focus, instead, is on the interaction of these two phenomena and the ways in which religion informs—and is informed by—differing visions of modernity. As such, the following chapter argues that religious fundamentalisms do not reflect a conflict between tradition and modernity, nor do they represent a "return" to tradition. Rather, these are ideologies that embody a selective interpretation of religious tradition and were explicitly developed for a modern political context.

This alternative understanding of contemporary religious politics also argues that the resurgence of illiberal religious activism after the Cold War did not arise as precipitously—or as spontaneously—as many assume. As the cases in this book illustrate, the demise of the secular order was well under way in the late 1960s and early 1970s, as state actors abandoned earlier commitments to secular norms and turned toward conservative religion. The implication is two-fold. First, the broader trend goes back further than is commonly recognized and is greatly informed by the ideological debates that defined earlier parts of the twentieth century. Second, the orientation of state actors toward religion is a key variable in explaining the rise of religious fundamentalisms. The resurgence of religious politics after the Cold War, in short, was facilitated by the actions of ostensibly secular state actors who found political gain by fanning the flames of religious division. The broader trend, then, cannot simply be ascribed to a failed modernity project (it is not simply politics), nor is it due solely to the efforts of religious revivalists (it is not just religion). These are important factors, but on their own they do not explain the ideological transformation that characterized the period. The role of secular political elites in promoting an overtly religious discourse is a third, and largely overlooked, variable that also needs to be examined. This is not to argue that religious revivalism is simply a matter of elite manipulation or that social movements are unimportant. It is also not to argue that religion is devoid of causal properties. Rather, the claim here is simply that the political fortunes of fundamentalist ideas and activists were greatly abetted when state actors chose to support, instead of repress, them.

## Is It Religion or Is It Politics?

### *The Clash of Civilizations? An Essentialist Vision of Religious Politics*

Much of the conventional wisdom about religious politics finds its roots in the idea that the contemporary resurgence of religion represents a popular reaction to the modernizing tendencies of the secular state. Juergensmeyer's *Global Rebellion* and Berger's *The Desecularization of the World*, among others, typify this understanding of revivalism as an opposition to secularism.[5] From this perspective, the religious mobilization of the post–Cold War era embodies a rebellion of religious populations against secular elites. At the heart of this issue is a dispute between those who seek to infuse public life with the "traditional values" of religion and a state that (theoretically) embodies the irreligious values of secular modernity. Although religious activists call for a return to an imaginary golden era when religion played a greater role in public life and all was in harmony, secular elites ostensibly seek to modernize their societies and eradicate religion from the public sphere. As Juergensmeyer has argued, "Like the Cold War, the contest between these new forms of culture-based politics and the secular state is global in its scope, binary in its opposition, . . . and essentially a difference of ideologies."[6]

Writers such as Huntington and Kaplan similarly perceive the issue in largely religious terms.[7] This is evident in the "Clash of Civilizations" thesis, which argues that contemporary political conflicts are defined increasingly along cultural lines. Huntington's argument is based on an assumption that religious and cultural affinity will play a greater role in determining cooperation and conflict in the post–Cold War world than strategic considerations. The basis for his argument is the belief that those who live in particular civilizations hold similar views on such issues as man's relationship to God, to the community, and to one another. Moreover, different religious traditions (and, hence, civilizations) are defined and differentiated from one another by a question of values. As Huntington argues, different religious traditions have divergent positions on such issues as inclusion, tolerance of diversity, and acceptance of alternative belief systems. From this perspective, communalism, hierarchy, and an emphasis on social control are tied closely to the Islamic and Asian traditions (Hindu and Confucian), while liberal democracy, constitutionalism, equality, and individual freedom are rooted in the Western (Judeo-Christian) tradition. These differences are, according to Huntington, "not only real; they are basic."[8]

Although many have rejected Huntington's thesis and Juergensmeyer's claim of a "new Cold War," these ideas remain enormously influential. This is particularly true with the Bush administration's war on terror. Supporters of the Bush administration regularly depicted the conflict as a struggle for the future of human civilization and hence characterized it as World War IV.[9] The basis of this argument is that Islamic radicalism (or "Islamofascism") represents an ideological challenge to the West akin to that of the fascism and communism in the mid- to late twentieth century. In this context, Islamic extremism and Islam more broadly are typically characterized as inherently violent and hostile to such values as freedom, reason and, tolerance.[10] What drives the war on terror, then, is the opposition of Islam and Islamofascism to Enlightenment values. As such, the Western vision of an open society is said to be under assault by the tribal, or closed, society advocated by Islamic activists.[11] Islamic fundamentalism is consequently seen as antithetical to progress and modernity, and remains "*the* threat to a [liberal democratic] New World Order."[12] As President George W. Bush argued, "These people hate freedom, and we love freedom, and that's where the clash occurs."[13]

The self-understanding of many religious activists reinforces this view of religious politics as an ideological conflict between competing value systems. Islamist thinkers such as Sayyid Qutb, Hasan al-Bana, Hasan al-Turabi, and, more recent writers as well, have all made similar arguments about the relevance of Western values to their societies.[14] Islamists commonly argue that the contemporary social ills of Muslim society are rooted in the fragmentation of society and in the loss of a moral community that has attended efforts to impose an alien modernity. From their perspective, the separation of religion from public life and the undue emphasis on the individual is inimical to their understanding of Islam. It is also seen as breeding immorality. Sexual licentiousness, the emancipation of women, and the elevation of private interest over public good are all said to characterize the excesses of secular life. The concern of Islamist writers, however, is not that these trends have a negative effect upon Western society but that they will produce a similar result in the Islamic world. To avoid this, they argue for a "return" to a more authentic vision of social order governed by Islamic law and the values of unity and community. Thus, like Huntington, contemporary Islamic activists perceive the conflicts in the Middle East and South Asia as religious in orientation, and driven by a competition between different value systems.[15]

There are several problems, however, with this understanding of religious politics. The first issue is the credence given to illiberal religious activists, and the assumption that their understanding of religious tradition is uniquely authentic. Rather, despite claims to the contrary, such activists represent only one interpretation of a given tradition. Related to this is the tendency to view religion in monolithic terms, and to conflate diverse groups and ideas into an amorphous notion of religious politics. In doing so, one overlooks the *intra-communal* conflicts within religious communities over precisely such issues as scriptural literalism, the role of women, and the limits of individual freedom. Ironically, on these issues conservative Muslims often have more in common with Haredi Jews and Evangelical Christians than they do with liberal or secular Muslims.[16] Similarly, the assumption that Western civilization and modernity are defined by Enlightenment values is itself problematic. Rather, Western societies throughout the modern period have had their own debates between open and closed visions of social life. The recent efforts by the Bush administration to limit individual freedom in the interests of security reflect the precariousness of the West's own commitment to Enlightenment norms. An essentialist approach to religious politics, in short, overlooks the ambiguity within all traditions—secular and religious—over precisely such issues as tolerance, dissent, freedom, and equality.

Another problematic feature of the essentialist view of religious politics is that it deemphasizes other considerations, material considerations. This is particularly evident in the discourse of Islamofascism. By characterizing the war on terror as a conflict over religion or values, the salience of political and economic considerations is greatly minimized. The language of terrorism consequently obscures the strategic significance of the oil-rich Persian Gulf and the material interests that have shaped American policy in the region since World War II. Similarly, the discourse of Islamofascism shifts the focus of public debate away from government policies—as well as the history of Western intervention in the Middle East and South Asia—and focuses instead on the people and the religion of the Islamic world. The root cause of Islamist terrorism, according to this view, lies in religious tradition, that Islam did not undergo a reformation akin to that of European Christianity. This is an ironic reading of the contemporary record given the role of various intelligence services, including the Central Intelligence Agency (CIA), in helping to create an international Jihadist movement to combat the Soviet Union in the 1980s.[17] Authors such as Norman Podhoretz and Lawrence Wright wholly overlook the influence that the U.S.-backed war in Afghanistan had on the formation of al-Qaeda and other elements of the international Islamic militant network.[18] This ideological interpretation of the war on terror also fails to account for the ongoing Western support for autocratic states such as Saudi Arabia and Pakistan that continue to promote Islamist ideas and, frequently, militants.

## *The Materialist Perspective*

An alternative understanding of contemporary religious politics picks up on this last set of issues and offers a largely materialist perspective on the broader trend. Generally speaking, this approach sees the failure of economic development to improve people's lives as the basis of a popular discontent that has found expression in religious terms. Although such movements may articulate their grievances in a religious and cultural idiom, the underlying impetus is said to be economic and political.[19] The issue, in short, is not religion but politics. This is the basis of the arguments that the resurgence of religious politics reflects a failed development strategy, or that fundamentalisms are a reaction to a rapidly changing social, economic, and political environment.[20] The absence of political freedom, widespread corruption, and sharp inequities between rich and poor, it is argued, feed popular discontent. That the grievances associated with these trends are articulated in terms of religion or identity does not detract, however, from the political and economic roots of the problem.

There are several dimensions to this argument. On the one hand, there is the social and psychological explanation for the resurgence of religious politics. From this perspective, the anomie that derives from the economic dislocation of modernization fuels a return to religion. Saad Eddin Ibrahim, for example, has argued that the preexisting communal bonds characteristic of traditional societies were torn asunder as economic modernity transformed their social landscape.[21] This was manifest in the large-scale migrations of rural populations into urban centers over the last fifty years. Although secularization theory saw this trend as the beginning of a decline in religious belief, sociologists and political economists argued that it had the opposite effect.[22] In destroying traditional societies, this type of socioeconomic change bred alienation and spurred the return to religion on a large scale. By retreating into religion, individuals were able to find a home in their transformed world.

A second feature to this perspective is the argument that shifts in economic production and the crisis of unmet expectations have contributed to the appeal of religious politics. Economic dislocation has politicized those segments of society whose livelihoods are threatened or are otherwise missing out on the benefits of economic development. This argument is rooted in a quasi-Marxist view which holds that economic modernization has led to the dislocation of preindustrial or premodern workers and the "progressive immiseration of the proletariat."[23] In the first instance, economic modernity threatens to destroy a traditional source of livelihood, while in the second, workers are left with nothing to lose but their chains. Similarly, the inability of development strategies (whether socialist or liberal capitalist) to raise living standards—particularly for those holding advanced degrees—has generated a new pool of potential dissidents. In each case, there is a tendency toward radicalism (or at least the tacit support for radical ideologies) and support for movements that articulate a revolutionary critique of the status quo.[24]

The forces of economic globalization are consequently seen as contributing to the recent resurgence of religious politics. This claim is premised on the deleterious effects that economic liberalization—deregulation, structural adjustment, and privatization of economic resources—has had on both states and individuals. Such policies undermine the state's autonomy in economic matters by opening it up to international trade and investment flows. This limits the ability of political leaders to control economic resources and allocate them to favored constituencies. Neoliberal economic policies thus limit the state's ability to coopt or repress different groups within the national community. Second, economic liberalization generates displacement and insecurity, which in turn creates an opportunity for political entrepreneurs to rally affected citizens behind sectarian movements. By linking appeals to a shared identity with a common sense of suffering, such activists are able to mobilize their constituency in order "to obtain scarce resources through illiberal political ideologies and tactics."[25]

This emphasis on material factors helps to explain the context of contemporary religious politics and the emergence of a climate of protest. The arguments offered by political economists, however, do not necessarily explain why it is religion that has become the basis of such activism and not some other ideological resource.[26] This is significant because there are any number of radical critiques of the status quo, including many leftist ideologies, that were dominant in the 1950s and 1960s. The question remains, then, why is it a religious discourse that emerged at this time, and not a Marxist or other alternative? This is an especially difficult question because it raises the issue of why workers ally with communal or nationalist elites when their economic interests are antithetical to those whom they back. Why, in other words, did blue-collar voters support Ronald Reagan and George W. Bush and Hindus of lower caste back the Bharatia Janata Party in India? Why would such people place cultural considerations ahead of their economic interests?[27]

A second critique of the materialist perspective is that it reflects a particular predisposition of Western (and particularly American) scholars. In this critique, the assumption that economic factors are the defining features of human action reflects an "unwarranted exaggeration of the influence of materialism upon human affairs."[28] It also raises the concern that overemphasis on materialist factors reinforces the essentialist understanding of religion and religious tradition.[29] By positing a fundamental conflict between the modernization process and traditional ways of life, many political economists assume religion to be monolithic and reactionary by definition, while modernity, on the other hand, is perceived as liberal, democratic, and tolerant. A more accurate depiction of the modernity/tradition dichotomy, however, would be to recognize that religion is not necessarily averse to modernity—even if some interpretations are opposed to the influence of westernization and secularization—but is rather defined by a variety of responses to an altered sociopolitical environment.

## Religion, States, and the Construction of Order

Both the essentialist and the materialist approaches to the study of religious politics offer important insights into contemporary trends. The materialist perspective is helpful in explaining the socioeconomic context in which religious revival movements emerge, while the essentialist view sheds light on the concerns of religious activists. On its own, however, each approach has its limits. The theoretical alternative offered in this book charts a middle path between these two perspectives and seeks to integrate their respective contributions. This alternative, or integrative, approach emphasizes the interaction of religion and politics to explain particular outcomes. It also argues that religion remains central to modern politics because it shapes collective identities and provides a moral framework for political action (or calls to action). In other words, it is precisely the traditional qualities of religion that make it so useful to modern politics. This approach ascribes to religion a degree of causality and autonomy, even if particular expressions of religious politics are shaped by other, material factors. It follows, then, that religion is an essential part of the construction of modernity, even though it manifests in diverse ways: priestly and prophetic, liberal and illiberal.

This integrative approach to contemporary religious politics is premised on the notion that religion and politics are fundamentally similar endeavors.[30] Both deal with issues of normative content, collective identity, and legitimate authority. Consequently, religion has an important bearing on the realm of politics because it is uniquely able to sanctify a particular political agenda as culturally authentic or to stigmatize alternative ideas and policies as outside the bounds of acceptability. Religion is also important because it imbues political action with moral or spiritual meaning. It is consequently able to situate political authority, or claims to authority, within a transcendent moral framework. This provides an emotional (or irrational) basis to politics and a vehicle for mobilizing populist sentiment. Similarly, political actors who invoke religion influence internal religious debates. Whether this is intentional or not, the use of religion by political leaders has the effect of validating particular interpretations of religion at the expense of others. The result is that disputes over religious interpretation are easily replicated within the public realm, as diverse political actors appeal to differing elements of a shared tradition to support their competing ends. Political conflicts subsequently come to mirror religious divides.

Where this integrative understanding of modern religious politics differs most dramatically from the perspectives discussed above is in its view of religion. Unlike the essentialist approach, the emphasis here is on the complexity of religion, not its uniformity. All religious traditions are defined by competing elements that vie with one another for dominance. They have no fixed and permanent meanings but rather are defined by "trans-generational arguments" that recur over time.[31] Islam, for example, has multiple interpreters (and interpretations), and the struggle to define religious orthodoxy in public life is a continuing feature of contemporary Muslim politics. The same can be said of Hinduism, Christianity, Judaism, and any other faith. It is this *intra-communal* dimension of religious conflict that is of particular interest for this book. As each of the cases illustrates, the primary source of religious competition—and the corresponding debate over values—manifests in communities over the proper role (and interpretation) of religion in public life. The real "clash of civilizations," in short, occurs within traditions, not between them.[32]

This last point is crucial. The more familiar understanding of religious conflict is the *inter*-communal dimension, which is characterized by the political competition between communities whose ethnic or national identities are defined by different religions. As noted in the introduction, inter-communal religious conflict assumes that differing confessional groups hold divergent political interests, while members of a similar community have shared interests. This understanding of religious communalism can be seen in Huntington's "Clash of Civilizations" thesis and in the assumption that ethnic conflicts reflect ancient hatreds. This book, however, focuses on intra-communal conflict, which operates from a different set of assumptions, one that sees communities as divided by class and social background and by differences over values. Members of a common community, in other words, clash over a variety of issues and do not necessarily have shared interests or shared values. Although such differences are frequently over matters of religion (whether God's Will is best known via reason or revelation) or authority (who rightly interprets a common tradition), there are also political differences over the nature of social life. At the heart of each case, then, are two intertwined debates: the competition between political actors over how to interpret a shared religious tradition and the proper expression of that tradition in state policy.[33]

A final feature of the integrative approach to religious politics that differentiates it from the others is its recognition of the "modernity of tradition."[34] Modernization theory, and its corollary the secularization thesis, argued that religion would diminish in importance—both for the individual and the community—as economic and political development spread to the broad mass of people.[35] In other words, as the ideas and institutions of modernity became more pronounced, the centrality of religion in human affairs would diminish and, ultimately, disappear. The defining feature of this trend was the influence of modern states and market capitalism on social organization. As these central institutions of the modern world became more important, it was argued, they would displace the church and other formal religious organizations as a central feature of public life. It was also assumed that personal belief would decline. Just as markets and states marginalized the church, the rise of science and reason would displace religious belief as a basis for explaining the world. Insofar as religion remained, it would be a personal affair and limited to individual matters of conscience. Modernity then came to be defined by a differentiation of social life into a variety of spheres: secular and religious, public and private.[36]

The central premise of modernization theory was its dichotomous reading of religion and modernity. Modernity, in this view, was assumed to be invariably secular and progressive, while religion was seen as sectarian and traditional. The state, moreover, was the quintessential agent of modernity and, hence, of secularism. Despite the demise of modernization theory, this basic idea continues to inform the essentialist and some materialist interpretations of contemporary religious politics. This is particularly evident in the argument that the resurgence of religion represents a revolt of traditional populations against secular elites. It is also evident in the content ascribed to "modern" and "traditional" values by the World Values Survey and in this project's claim that societal value systems are linked to levels of economic development.[37] As the cases in this book illustrate, however, reality is more nuanced than that. Although the modern state may have displaced the church as the central institution in modern life, it has nonetheless retained a need for moral legitimacy. Religion has come to fill this void through the discourse of modern nationalism and communalism. Religion in this context, however, has manifested in a variety of forms. Hence, the approach of this study is not to assume a priori a particular relationship between religion and modernity or between religion and the state but rather to examine these relationships and how they have changed over time.

## *Religion, Nationalism, and the State*

The relevance of religion for modern states lies in its ability to sanctify an existing pattern of power relations. By informing nationalist or communal ideologies, religion provides a normative framework—and, hence, meaning—to modern politics, and modern political institutions. It also provides a mechanism for cultivating popular acceptance. Although this may reflect a traditional understanding of religion in political life, it is nonetheless relevant to the modern (and postmodern) context.[38] The "centralizing tendency" of modern states, it has been argued, relies on a homogenizing and monolithic "ideology of unity," and religion is able to provide such an ideational framework.[39] The normative content of religion endows political authority with moral legitimacy, while the link between religion and identity facilitates social solidarity and obedience. It also lends a universal and sacred quality to what is, in essence, a particular set of political arrangements. It is these religious properties of modern nationalism, moreover, that are its most important feature.[40] As Anthony Marx has argued, within the European context, "religious fanaticism was the basis for popular engagement with—for or against—centralizing state authority. . . . Nationalism emerged when the masses were invited onto the political stage or invited themselves in. But that invitation did not come inclusively from books, enrichment, or schooling, but rather from sectarian conflicts, enraging sermons and callings. The passions of faith were the stuff of which the passions for the state were built."[41]

Theorists of the state tend to focus less on these normative issues than on the coercive basis of state power. This reflects the significance of warfare in the process of state formation and the Weberian emphasis on the control of legitimate violence as the defining feature of statehood.[42] It also reflects the continuing centrality of force to order and to the regulation of social life. Whether it was the development state and its emphasis on economic transformation or the less benign totalitarian version, modern state institutions have been defined by the effort to penetrate and restructure society through the use of coercion, education, media outlets, and bureaucratic governance. This is in contrast to traditional modes of political organization that had only a limited ability (and inclination) to regulate the minutiae of social life.

Despite the state's capacity to impose its will, generating popular support has always remained a challenge. The issue is not one of power per se but one of consent. The claim to exercise power in a legitimate way is premised on a belief that those in positions of authority have a right to rule, and the same logic generates a corresponding obligation to obey. The legitimacy of state power relies on some notion of popular acceptance to transform a given set of power relations into genuine authority. Ideology is important in this regard because it provides an ideational—and often emotive—basis to power or the claim to power.[43] Through the manipulation of ideas, rhetoric, and symbols, political actors and institutions situate themselves in a context of cultural meaning, and state authority (or the claims of those who seek to control it) is sanctified. In this way, ideology converts a relationship of power between ruler and ruled into a cosmos of accepted rights and duties. Without this type of support, "the state would be little more than a mechanism of coercion."[44]

These themes reflect what Weber called the problem of order. At issue is the effort of political leaders to identify their rule with a larger "frame[work] of meaning that commands the loyalty of its members, [and can] generate a willingness to obey." Political discourse and rhetoric are used by state (or economic) elites to link their privileged position in society to some conception of justice or morality. This means cultivating the perception that the core institutions of social life are somehow "in harmony with the ultimate structure of things, and, consequently [are] right" or just.[45] Similarly, opposition groups regularly critique existing patterns of social order in moral or cultural terms, arguing that their policy alternatives reflect the true values of society.

Religion is central to the issue of legitimacy because it provides a moral and cultural basis for the competing claims to political leadership. Religion is especially relevant for modern state elites, as their authority is premised on a close connection between the institutions that govern social life and the underlying values that sanction them.[46] Although this underlying moral order need not be explicitly theistic, it commonly is. Whatever the orientation—conservative, progressive, religious, secular—modern states have regularly employed a religious vernacular to build national solidarity and ideological legitimacy. By using religion to "order and interpret [a shared] historical experience," the state and other political elites provide the national community with an "aura of transcendence" and divine purpose.[47] More to the point, the invocation of religion provides the kind of legitimacy to which Weber was referring above. Religion places a particular set of political arrangements within a "cosmic frame of reference," thus tying an otherwise ephemeral set of power relations to a broader cosmological scheme.[48] This has the effect of sacralizing particular social constructs and situating them within an enduring natural order.

Although nations per se are not primordial, the ideologies from which they are constructed draw heavily from the cultural resources of religious tradition. This includes, first and foremost, the idea of a "chosen people" that share a common past and, ostensibly, a better future. This quintessential feature of modern nationalism derives from the covenant tradition of Biblical religion. It is also frequently intertwined with notions of providential mission, ethnic election, and other types of religious imagery such as the depiction of national territory as a promised land. These ideas are also reinforced by social narratives of cultural uniqueness. At the heart of these nationalist constructions is a belief that the community has a special role in human history and hence is blessed with divine favor and protection. Such divine favoritism, however, is frequently colored by a conditional salvation, where its unique standing in a larger cosmic drama is premised on the enactment of God's Will on Earth. The chosen community must live up to God's commandments in order to fulfill this covenantal relationship.[49]

This type of ethno-religious mythology has a number of implications. First, in constructing a group identity, religious ideologies "homogenize [the community] and differentiate" it from all others.[50] That is, it deemphasizes divisions within groups and exaggerates differences between them. The separation of communities along national (or ethnic) lines, moreover, reinforces the basic assumptions of communalism: that groups defined by a common religion have the same economic and political (that is, secular) interests, while those of differing groups have opposing, often antithetical, interests.[51] Hence, the "secular" interests of one religious (or cultural) community are perceived as antithetical to the interests of other communities defined along similar lines. In this regard, the *trans-national*—or, perhaps more accurately, *trans-border*—religious appeals of Islamic activists reflect the same type of religious communalism inherent in religious or ethnic nationalisms. In both cases—be it domestic communalism or trans-border religious appeal—the assumptions are that the community in question has a shared set of political interests that derive from their common cultural or religious heritage and that other groups defined along similar lines have often incompatible, and even hostile, interests.

A second feature of these types of ethno-religious mythology is that they assume that God's Will is knowable and properly understood by the political leadership of a particular group. It is this claim (whether implicit or explicit) that provides the normative justification for political and cultural self-assertion. By associating political action with nationalist or religious purpose, political actors find moral sanction for their endeavors. This facilitates the perception that particular leaders genuinely act in the national interest or that government policy reflects the broader commandments of religious or national purpose. Whether it is the state or opposition groups, the invocation of religion is meant to clothe their respective political agendas—and claims to power—in an aura of religious and moral legitimacy. In other words, the appeal to religion by political actors is intended to depict the particular interests of some group as reflecting the common good of the community and hence as consistent with God's Will. Those who oppose them, on the other hand, are typically characterized as either unpatriotic or irreligious, or both. In this way, religion allows political actors of all stripes to claim for themselves the mantle of cultural authenticity and the corresponding right to rule.

## Competing Visions of the Nation

To argue that modern nationalisms are the product of social construction—and that religion is a significant part of this process—says little about the nature of these phenomena. This is important because of the competing tendencies that exist in both religion and nationalism. Although "civic" forms of nationalism are defined by an inclusive (that is, liberal) conception of political community, "ethnic" variants are characterized by exclusive or illiberal conceptions. These two types of nationalism, in short, embody very different visions of social order. The first, civic or liberal nationalism, is typically defined by the tolerance of diversity and an inclusive cosmopolitanism. It recognizes the heterogeneity inherent in multiethnic, multireligious societies and consequently extends full membership in the political community to all who live within the territorial boundaries of a given state. Civil status, in short, is not tied to ethnic identity. Alternately, the ethnic or illiberal conception of nationalism perceives the nation as an organic entity in which membership is determined by birth. Its defining features are informed by the religious motifs of the dominant community and other elements of its culture, language, and history. Civil status is consequently linked to religious or ethnic identity, with preference given to those of the dominant group. Individual or minority rights are perceived as secondary to the demands of majority self-determination. Such illiberal forms of nationalism are also argued to be more prone to violence and are associated with varying degrees of intolerance toward minority populations and political dissent.[52]

This distinction between civic and ethnic—or liberal and illiberal—nationalism mirrors Karl Popper's understanding of "open" and "closed" societies. Popper's explanation of these two forms of social order was articulated in *The Open Society and Its Enemies*.[53] Popper argues that modernity is defined by a tension between two fundamentally different visions of social life. The first was the free or open society, which is characterized by an emphasis on the Enlightenment values of individual freedom and democratic self-governance. Respect for the individual, and particularly his or her capacity for critical reason, was at the core of the Enlightenment and hence of the open society. So, too, was the notion of accountable government, the rule of law, and political and legal equality. From Popper's perspective, the open society represented the peak of human civilization, which, at the time, was found only in Western democracies. The alternative or closed society was embodied in the various forms of totalitarianism (and ethnic nationalism) prevalent in the early twentieth century. Rooted in an exclusive vision of social life, these societies were defined by a tribal or hierarchical political structure that placed a disproportionate emphasis on social control and obedience. Priority was given to the community over the individual, and the notion of freedom that it embodied was that of collective self-expression, not individual autonomy. Whether it was right-wing fascism or left-wing communism, the defining feature of the closed society was its emphasis on fostering political unity through a coercive uniformity.

This distinction between liberal and illiberal conceptions of the nation—and between open and closed visions of society—is questioned by those who believe that any form of nationalism is inconsistent with the prerequisites of pluralism. From this perspective, *all* types of nationalism tend toward the communal or closed society, while the very idea of liberal nationalism is said to be a contradiction in terms. At issue is whether or not members of different cultural communities can genuinely be incorporated into a common political framework, or whether primordial identities will always trump a civic or cosmopolitan sense of citizenship. In other words, can a genuine political unity be forged from religious or ethnic diversity, or will the state necessarily "privilege certain cultural practices, and disadvantage others, in the interest of social unity"?[54] The answer, of course, is that it depends on both the popular understanding of the nation and the commitment on the part of political leaders to accommodate diverse communities. This debate is confused, however, by the fact of liberal and illiberal nationalisms being ideal types that are more accurately characterized as poles on a spectrum than distinct phenomena. Moreover, both liberal and illiberal conceptions of society are latent in all political communities and coexist uneasily with one another. This reflects "the profound dualism at the heart of every nationalism."[55] Although some examples may be explicitly chauvinistic—Serbian nationalism of the Milosevic variety, for example—and others more tolerant, they all contain competing elements that vie for dominance. Thus, while the vision of the nation advocated by Jawaharlal Nehru or President Bill Clinton may have been inclusive, these conceptions of the nation were always at odds with more exclusive forms promoted by members of their own community.

Religion is relevant to this discussion because differing interpretations of religious tradition inform each of these competing visions of the nation or society. Liberal or modernist interpretations of religion, for example, provide the basis for an inclusive or civic form of nationalism that typifies Popper's open society. This understanding of religion is premised on the uncertain nature of belief and the fallibility of humans to interpret either scripture or God's Will accurately. Liberal religious interpreters consequently read their tradition as metaphorical, not literal, truth and question all forms of dogmatism and monopolistic claims on religious truth. There is a corresponding emphasis on the use of reason to understand religious tradition and to reinterpret the meaning of scripture for a contemporary context. In the liberal or modernist tradition, greater priority is subsequently given to individual conscience. Those who recognize that none hold an exclusive claim on absolute truth are more willing to tolerate diversity and pluralism in matters of belief. Religion, from this perspective, is relegated to the realm of conscience and seen as a private, not a public, matter. This approach to religion is greatly influenced by the Enlightenment and is consistent with a willingness to accommodate the individual on matters of conscience and freedom of thought.

Illiberal or exclusive interpretations of religion, on the other hand, are more typically associated with the kind of ethnic nationalisms evident in Popper's closed society. This includes theologically conservative, fundamentalist, or other interpretations of religion that take a more literal reading of their various traditions. As such, these interpretations emphasize revelation, scriptural literalism, and a belief that religion is defined by an unchanging moral framework as applicable today as it was five hundred or two thousand years ago. Illiberal approaches to religion also tend to believe that their understanding of tradition (and *only* their understanding) is true and right and reflective of God's Will. Such religious certitude diminishes the proclivity for religious tolerance, since differing perspectives are seen as either heresy (incorrect belief) or apostasy (lack of belief).[56] Hence, the realm of individual conscience is greatly circumscribed by illiberal interpretations of religion, and there is greater emphasis on conformity in matters of belief. This intolerance of alternative views is similarly extended to political dissent, and those who oppose the will of the community (or its self-proclaimed spokesmen) are commonly characterized as unpatriotic, treasonous, or self-hating members of the group.

The struggle to define the nation, then, involves both a political conflict over the nature of social order and a religious dispute over the interpretation of a shared tradition. Whether it is the culture wars of American politics, the "secular-integralist" debate of Egypt, or the longstanding struggle to define the Indian nation, these ideological debates are informed by competing views of both religion and society. Although the broader dispute is commonly seen as a question of social order, it also involves debates over the proper relationship of religion to political authority, and the desirability of alternative understandings of religion or fundamental belief to be tolerated, let alone given equal treatment in the public sphere. Moreover, these ideological conflicts have a direct bearing on the balance between minority rights and majority preferences. They consequently raise basic questions about tolerance and equal treatment. Should the institutions of social life be nondiscriminatory in matters of religion and morality, or is there a legitimate reason for privileging particular beliefs (or groups) at the expense of others? In this context, those who support an inclusive vision of religion and the nation are invariably at odds with those who advocate a more central place for their particular religion or identity.

The competition between these differing visions of religion and order are a defining—and enduring—feature of modern political life. This was evident in the early post–World War II period, when leaders of the newly independent states such as Egypt and India found themselves governing societies whose national borders did not correspond with the ethnic or demographic realities on the ground. The central challenge of that time was to create *both* a national identity *and* a political order that was not premised on the exclusion of certain communities or the privileged status of others. This challenge, and the corresponding response, was what Clifford Geertz called the "integrative revolution."[57] The integrative revolution entailed, above all else, the creation of "over-arching [political] loyalties that [could] transcend the more primordial ones of ethnic affiliation, religious affiliation and linguistic identity."[58] Without some common basis for social life—including a minimal notion of shared identity—inter-communal rivalries would rip these nascent countries apart. Leaders such as Nehru, recognizing this fact, consciously sought to dampen communal conflict by building an inclusive nationalism that embodied "a civil politics of primordial compromise."[59] These same considerations were behind the adoption of a secular constitution at the founding of the United States almost two centuries earlier.

Institutionalizing such a compromise, however, still remains a challenge. At issue is the perennial debate over whether society (and, hence, the nation) ought to be defined along cosmopolitan lines—and inclusive of diversity—or whether the ethnic and religious identity of the majority should be given precedence in the institutions of nation and state. This question is commonly manifest in the form of whether the nation ought to be defined in religious or secular terms. Civic forms of nationalism argue for an inclusive political framework defined along secular—that is, religiously neutral—lines, where the state does not give preference to one religion or community above all others. Alternatively, an inclusive social order that recognized the historical culture of a dominant community could be possible, so long as its institutions were nondiscriminatory in nature, particularly with regard to religion. On the other hand, those who advocate an ethnic vision of nationalism argue that a closer relationship between religion and political authority is essential for the self-actualization of the majority population. Moreover, since, as some believe, there can be no morality without religion, only a more prominent role of religion in public life can remedy the ills of modern society. For these activists, the secular project is a betrayal of both faith and nation, as is the civic nationalism that it embodies.[60]

## Religion, Secularism, and Social Order

This struggle to define the nation remains a central feature of contemporary religious politics. Similar to the years after World War II, political elites today are confronted by the challenge of developing a national community that is inclusive of religious, ethnic, and racial diversity. However, finding a balance between majority demands for self-assertion and minority concerns of equal treatment remains a defining issue in today's nationalist and religious politics. Although inclusive conceptions of social order—that is, territorial or civic conceptions of nationalism—are intended to mitigate the tensions between the competing claims of majority and minority communities, the ethnic vision of contemporary nationalism (or communalism) tends to exacerbate them. Exclusive notions of religion and community, moreover, tend to promote a crude social Darwinism where one group's gains are perceived as coming at another's expense. Instead of providing a context for integrating diversity, this type of exclusive religious politics remains a source of division.

The debate between these differing conceptions of social order has been marred by several misunderstandings. Perhaps the most common problem has been the assumption that secular nationalism is *by definition* the antithesis of religion and is actively hostile to it as such. This interpretation of the secular tradition understands secularism as a moral doctrine that is rationalist in orientation and focused solely on worldly affairs. There is no reference to God in this understanding of the doctrine, and it consequently tends to be equated with atheism or is seen as hostile to religious belief of any kind. This interpretation of secularism differs, however, from the understanding discussed above. In the earlier sense, secularism as a political project was intended to be nondiscriminatory in matters of belief; it simply entailed the separation of religious authority from political authority. These differing interpretations of secularism reflect two competing impulses within the concept: one seeks to eliminate religion from the public sphere, while the other seeks to accommodate a diversity of perspectives on matters of fundamental belief.[61] In practice, both impulses have been evident, although it is the latter that has been historically more important. The religious diversity of society has demanded that no particular religion (or denomination) be given a preferential status in state institutions vis-à-vis all others. The teachings of a given religion could be referenced in the public realm—indeed, this would be welcomed—but not used to justify the exclusion of other religious communities or ideas.

Both religious activists and academic critics, however, have argued that it is the exclusive tendencies of the *secular* tradition that have been predominant in recent history. Whatever the intention, secular norms have been used to remove religion from the public sphere, not to accommodate it. Critics like Ashis Nandy and T. N. Madan, for example, argue that states (at least the Indian state) have fallen into the trap of "secular fundamentalism" and refused to recognize the manner in which religion legitimately informs human life and society. These arguments are echoed by religious activists across various traditions. Similarly, William Connolly has argued that secularism, in practice, has set itself up as the authoritative (and intolerant) arbiter of truth in the modern world. By attempting to remove religion altogether—and by transforming secularism into a totalizing worldview—state policies have inadvertently contributed to the kind of religious assertiveness and fanaticism that it was originally meant to avoid.[62]

A second misunderstanding in these debates lies in the assumption that religion is necessarily hostile to the inclusive nature of the open society. As noted earlier, differing interpretations of religious belief inform competing visions of the nation and national identity. Some are inclusive and some exclusive. Moreover, the interpretation of religion that one advocates tends to affect the corresponding political disposition toward the values associated with open and closed conceptions of society. Liberal or modernist views of religion, for example, are typically associated with pluralist notions of society (including inclusive secularism), while illiberal, communal, or fundamentalist interpretations of religion tend to embrace more exclusive notions of social order. There are, of course, exceptions. An example would be Roger Williams, the seventeenth-century Protestant leader, who, despite being theologically conservative, advocated a tolerance of alternative beliefs and eschewed a close link between religion and state.[63] This reflected his concern about the impact of politics on religion and illustrates the divisions within the Puritan tradition over conflating religious and political authority. In a manner similar to John Locke in *A Letter concerning Toleration*, Williams believed that the magistrate did not have the rightful authority to determine matters of conscience. As good Christians, then, both Locke and Williams were obligated to ensure freedom of conscience from the intrusion of political power. In this instance, conservative religion supported a liberal vision of social order that constrained political authority.

A more nuanced depiction of the religious-secular divide, then, would distinguish among four different interpretations of social order, each reflecting the different way in which religion and secularism inform competing visions of society. These include inclusive conceptions of both religion and secularism ("civil religion" and tolerant secularism, respectively) as well as exclusive conceptions of religion and secularism (religious nationalism and secular fundamentalism). A simple typology, then, would link inclusive interpretations of both religion and secularism with cosmopolitan norms of national identity. Conversely, exclusive (illiberal or communal) interpretations of religion and secularism tend to correlate more closely with closed conceptions of community.[64] (See figure 1.) Hence, the liberal interpretation of religion is more inclined toward a cosmopolitan interpretation of national identity, while those who claim a unique understanding of the sacred are more likely to institutionalize a privileged position for their religious or communal identity. The main point is that there is nothing antithetical between religion and the demands of the integrative revolution; rather, the issue is how a given religious tradition (or an official secularism) is interpreted, and whether or not this allows for a politics of primordial compromise.

| Conceptions of Social Order | | |
|---|---|---|
| | *Inclusive/Open* | *Exclusive/Closed* |
| Religious | Liberal or Civic Nationalism | Illiberal Nationalism or Communalism |
| Secular | Inclusive Secularism | Secular Fundamentalism |

*Figure 1.*

It is also important to reexamine the way in which political actors have either supported or opposed these differing interpretations of religion and the corresponding visions of social order. State actors can be secular in orientation and still appeal to religion in order to justify their rule. Again, this is commonly referred to as the priestly function of religion and is defined by the use of religion to support a given political order. Similarly, opposition groups (as well as reformers within state institutions) regularly use religion to critique existing political arrangements by challenging the normative basis of that order. Again, this is referred to as the prophetic function of religion. By "contesting the nation" in this way, opposition groups seek to challenge existing authorities and posit their own religious *and* political claims as preeminent. In each instance, political actors—whether state or opposition—use various interpretations of religion to clothe their claim to power in cultural and normative terms.

These diverse modes of religious discourse and their relationship to different political actors, however, are extremely varied. Just as states are not necessarily secular, neither is there a direct correlation between conservative religion and support for state authority. Similarly, there is no direct connection between liberal religion and opposition politics. Rather, liberal interpretations of religion tend to support inclusive conceptions of social order, while conservative religion is commonly tied to exclusive conceptions of order.[65] As a result, liberal religion has at times provided a priestly affirmation for a given political order (such as in the immediate post–World War II era), while at other times it has challenged existing political arrangements. Similarly, conservative interpretations of religion, while historically associated with status quo ideologies, have also been mobilized in opposition to government policies.

What is really at issue in each instance is the conception of social order that religion either supports or opposes. State elites, for example, relied on liberal religion and secular norms to support their modernist programs in the 1950s and 1960s. However, in later years, they embraced a more conservative religious discourse when their goals shifted from progressive reform to preservation of the status quo. Similarly, liberal religion has been a common means for opposition groups to advocate progressive social and political change. This was clearly evident in the civil rights movement in the United States and in the Indian independence movement in the early twentieth century. In both cases, liberal religion supported a vision of social life that was much more inclusive than the prevailing order.

On the other hand, conservative or illiberal interpretations of religion have been used by opposition groups toward a variety of ends, though they are most commonly employed in opposition to programs of progressive social change. It was religious fundamentalists and conservative political actors, for example, who were most opposed to the secular vision of state elites in the mid-twentieth century and who appealed to illiberal interpretations of religion to maintain traditional patterns of social order. Similarly, state actors have commonly used ideologies rooted in conservative religion to defend existing patterns of social and political authority (such as those discussed above). Finally, an illiberal (or conservative) variant of religion, at least in the Middle East, has also provided a radical critique of social injustice, and has readily appropriated the revolutionary appeal of third-world nationalism even if its prescription for social life remains exclusive and hierarchical. This type of Islamic fundamentalism reflects an anti-Western bias that links liberal and secular visions of social order with westernization and continued Western dominance. As such, it remains largely communal in orientation, despite its prophetic orientation.

The essential theme of this typology, then, is that illiberal interpretations of religion tend to support hierarchical and exclusive patterns of political order— in other words, closed visions of society—while liberal interpretations of religion tend to support the requirements of an open society. This tends to be the case whether it is the state or the opposition that is promoting these particular interpretations of religion and nation. It follows, then, that states are not necessarily secular or supportive of inclusive patterns of society despite commitments that may have held in the past. Similarly, religious actors are just as likely to be advocates of progressive change as they are to be defenders of a punitive status quo. Although different interpretations of religion inform competing visions of order, neither state nor opposition is unalterably tied to one sort or another. A more accurate rendering of contemporary religious politics, then, can be seen in figure 2.

| Attitudes toward Social Order | | |
| --- | --- | --- |
| *Interpretation of Religion* | *Political Actors* | |
| | *State* | *Opposition* |
| Liberal | Progressive[66] (and largely inclusive) | Nonviolent and Progressive Social Movements[67] (largely inclusive) |
| Illiberal or Communal | Hierarchical[68] (and largely exclusive) | "Fundamentalist Movements"[69] (largely exclusive) |

*Figure 2.*

## Constructing Modernity

The conclusion one draws from this analysis is that the manifestation of religion in modern politics is highly variable. Although religion can support existing power structures, it also provides a basis for social reform. In neither instance is religion necessarily liberal or illiberal. Rather, different renderings of religious tradition underwrite differing visions of social life and hence differing politics. A second, and related, conclusion is that neither modernity nor states are necessarily secular or liberal. On the contrary, states are just as able to promote an exclusive vision of religion and society as not. Even in the ostensibly secular West, states commonly invoke religion and patriotism in order to cultivate the unquestioning allegiance typical of the closed society. This is where the essentialist view of modern religious politics goes awry. It assumes a priori that modernity—and particularly Western modernity—is defined by the Enlightenment norms of individual freedom and accountable governance instead of treating this as a claim to be investigated. Moreover, by assuming that modernity is secular, the essentialist view also accepts at face value the claim that religious fundamentalism is either a rejection of modernity or, in its less extreme form, an anomaly in the modern world. None of these assumptions hold, because they fail to recognize the variable nature of both modernity and the nation-state.

Similarly, religion is not, by definition, exclusive or antimodern. On the contrary, as discussed above, certain interpretations of religion are consistent with the Enlightenment values of individualism, reason, and dissent, even if other interpretations are not. Either rendering, though, is by definition "modern" insofar as it represents an effort to reinterpret religious tradition for the contemporary period. The debates over how to define the nation, then, are informed by differing readings of religious tradition and represent competing aspects of modernity. The cosmopolitan understanding of nationalism and identity, for example, has roots both in a liberal understanding of religious belief *and* in European Enlightenment thought. Liberal religion, in other words, is consistent with Popper's open society and the nondiscriminatory understanding of secularism. Similarly, ethnic and religious nationalisms may be chauvinistic and antithetical to Enlightenment norms, but they do not necessarily represent a retreat into tradition. Rather, these communal ideologies embody a particular understanding of modernity, even if they draw heavily (and selectively) from religious tradition.

This last point is particularly important, especially with respect to the modern roots of contemporary religious fundamentalisms. As this book illustrates, the ideologies and organizations associated with modern fundamentalisms only emerged in the early decades of the twentieth century. During this period, Islamic activists such as Hasan al-Banna and Mawlawna Maududi and Hindu communalists such as V. D. Savarkar sought to codify their diverse and contradictory religious traditions into a more uniform set of ideas and principles. This was done intentionally to adapt religious tradition to a modern context. The driving force, moreover, was political. By reinterpreting religious tradition, these early activists sought to develop a model of social organization that could challenge the European dominance of their respective societies. Hence, they saw in religious revivalism both the redemption of their political community and an effective means of challenging Western power. However, while these activists called for a "return to religion" and a greater role of religion in public life, their understanding of religion was highly selective and very much imbued with nationalist ideas. In other words, they were consciously reconstructing their tradition within a nationalist framework. The resulting ideologies included references to a "golden era," mythologies of chosen-ness, and claims to self-determination. By creating a religious identity that was more explicitly nationalist and cohesive, they also hoped to make it more uniform, more assertive, and hence, more influential. Their vision of political community, moreover, was distinctly communal: it privileged the religious majorities—or at least the self-proclaimed representatives of the majority community—and contained an overt hostility to minorities, liberals, and other so-called enemies of tradition.[70]

These early fundamentalists were also shaped by the ideological competition that defined interwar Europe. Al-Banna, Savarkar, and other activists in the colonized world were attracted to fascism's organic conceptions of the nation and the primacy it gave to the collective over the individual. They modeled their political parties on the organizational structure of the fascists of Italy and Germany and rewrote their national histories in a manner that reified notions of communal identity. The perceived enemy of these early religious activists, however, was not modernity per se but the cosmopolitanism espoused by Western liberalism and the moderate religious leaders within their own communities. These early religious fundamentalists, in short, embraced the communalism of ethnic nationalism and its corresponding opposition to the Enlightenment norms of the open society.

These fundamentalist interpretations of both religion and society were at odds with those who sought to build a liberal or inclusive vision of modernity. Hence, the debates that defined the mid-twentieth century in Egypt and India (as well as in the United States) pitted the communalism of religious fundamentalism against the secular and liberal alternative. Although the arguments commonly involved the relative merits of creating a religious state and the proper role of religion in public life, what was really at issue was how to define the nation. Religious nationalists advocated a more central, and explicit, role for their interpretation of religion in public life, one that also entailed a preferential status for members of the dominant religious community. Religious renewal, in this context, was seen as a first step toward the empowerment of the majority community. Liberal religious activists and secular intellectuals, on the other hand, worked together to oppose religious communalism and its inherent intolerance. In their view, the creation of an explicitly religious state would marginalize minorities and sow the seeds of social and religious conflict. These societies subsequently replicated the divisions that existed in Europe between corporatist modes of social organization and the liberal alternative.

The limited success of communalism in the mid-twentieth century was due largely to the opposition of state leaders and their effort to promote a secular vision of modernity. Particularly in the 1950s and 1960s, state actors were the articulators of a progressive vision of national development and saw in secular nationalism a means of integrating diverse communities into a common political life. These key political elites appealed to liberal religion to support a civic interpretation of nationalism and were not above using the coercive mechanisms of the state against religious communalists. Although an inclusive political framework can be seen as a practical response to the challenge of diversity, it was also central to the modernist program of national development. Especially in Egypt and India, religion was associated with a reactionary past that carried with it a continuing danger of sectarian division. India's Nehru, for example, feared the religious communalism that claimed a half a million lives during the 1947 Partition and that continued to threaten the country's fragile democracy. Similarly, in Egypt, conservative religion was perceived as an obstacle to the kind of economic and political reform that Nasser wished to implement. The Islam of the Muslim Brotherhood and the establishment *ulema* (religious scholars) was tainted, in Nasser's view, by its association with reactionary elites. For these modernizing state actors, secularism was a prerequisite for both freedom and development.

It was this trend that informed the assumptions of modernization theory as well as the idea that modernizing states were secular by definition. This hypothesis is readily understandable because it reflected the spirit of the time. During the mid-twentieth century, political leaders around the world worked assiduously to embed secular norms in state institutions and actively promoted a vision of national development that transcended ethnic and religious difference. They also appealed to liberal religion and secular norms in order to sanction a more inclusive national identity. Modernization, during this period, was perceived to be invariably secular and was typically associated with a program of progressive social change. This was evident in the modernist programs of India and Egypt as well as the New Deal and Great Society policies in the United States. In each instance, state policy was, at least theoretically, committed to social justice, nondiscrimination, and the elevation of living standards for the poor. Commentators at the time saw in this trend the "passing of traditional society" and the emergence of a new, secular modernity that was economically progressive and politically left of center.[71]

Debates over religion in public life and the corresponding struggle to define the nation, however, did not go away. On the contrary, they reemerged during the late twentieth century, periodically resurrecting longstanding debates over the proper role of religion in public life and the proper orientation—secular or religious—of the state. At one level, these debates involved questions about the compatibility of religion and secular norms; however, at a deeper level they involved disputes over religious interpretation (modernist versus orthodox) as well as over competing visions of social order (inclusive versus exclusive). They also involved questions of economics and state policy. The resurgence of religious politics in the post–Cold War era and the reemergence of religious fundamentalisms reflect, then, another iteration of these intergenerational debates.

Although the context may have changed, the nature of the argument had not. Religious activists continued to ascribe the ills of modern society to the loss of religion and consequently called for a more central role for *their* interpretation of religion in government. Implicit in this argument is a belief that cultural uniformity is a key to political unity and hence communal empowerment.

Although the substance of these debates may not have changed much from previous years, the position of state elites certainly had. By the 1970s and 1980s, state elites had largely abandoned earlier commitments to a secular vision of social order and, with it, the commitment to progressive social change. Although the 1950s and 1960s had been characterized by an effort to cultivate cosmopolitan notions of civil order—and a prophetic call for social and political reform—this was abandoned in favor of a more priestly use of religion that supported existing patterns of social hierarchy. The interpretation of religion that the state leaders embraced, moreover, was largely exclusive and illiberal. The rhetoric of religious communalism, in short, was coopted by state actors who sought to enlist the passions of faith in support of a reconceived notion of state authority. The premise behind this strategy, particularly for leaders like Anwar Sadat or Indira Gandhi, was that conservative or illiberal interpretations of religion could be channeled into an unquestioning support for state authority. Religion would help provide stability by cultivating popular quiescence and by sanctifying a particular configuration of political power. It was also assumed that the passions of faith could be readily controlled. Both of these assumptions were mistaken. In both Egypt and India, state actors failed to recognize that conservative (or illiberal) religion could be radically prophetic and could just as readily be used to challenge their grip on power as support it. In short, they failed to see that the use of an illiberal religious ideology could backfire disastrously. They also failed to appreciate the long-term costs of the strategy. By appealing to sectarian identities and consciously manipulating religious sentiment, state actors fanned the flames of communal division. This not only led to the demise of the secular order, it also bred communal antagonism, a deeply divisive national politics, and a less tolerant public life.

## Conclusion

The religious politics of the 1990s is informed by this legacy. On the one hand, the fundamentalist movements that emerged in the post–Cold War era were not new but, rather, found their origins in the early part of the twentieth century.

As such, they embodied the exclusive ideologies developed in that earlier period and expressed the type of religious communalism inherent in ethnic conceptions of the nation. On the other hand, the political viability of these groups greatly improved in the 1970s and 1980s, when state actors sought to coopt illiberal religion rather than repress it. Unlike earlier decades, fundamentalists found a more permissive political environment once state leaders abandoned the earlier commitments to secular norms and sought to promote illiberal visions of religion and nation for their own purposes. In doing so, these ostensibly secular state actors sanctioned the ideas and activists associated with religious fundamentalisms and greatly influenced the intra-communal debates over both religion and nation. They also undermined liberal visions of society. By stigmatizing dissent and minorities as hostile to the nation—and clothing this rhetoric in religious terms—state elites helped to normalize the kind of chauvinism associated with the closed society. Whether this entailed the denigration of Muslims in India, Coptic Christians in Egypt, or homosexuals and African Americans in the United States, the state-led discourse of religious nationalism helped make intolerance acceptable in the political mainstream.

This alternative understanding of the relationship between religion and the modern state sheds light on modernization theory and its corollary, the secularization thesis. In many respects, modernization theory was right. The authority of organized religion was greatly diminished vis-à-vis the state and the market, and this trend had enormous implications for social life. This transformation also had a significant impact on popular perceptions of religious tradition, particularly as state elites worked assiduously in the mid-twentieth century to diminish the influence of reactionary and illiberal elements of religious belief. In other respects, however, modernization theory missed the mark. Science and reason never displaced religious belief, nor was the distinction between the secular and the religious ever as sharp as many assumed.[72] More to the point, religion never left the public sphere. On the contrary, the debates over social order in the mid-twentieth century—ostensibly the height of the secular era—were commonly infused with religious ideas, which underscored the fact that religion remained a potent vernacular of political discourse. However, the nature of this religious language varied greatly. On the one hand, liberal (and modernist) religion was used to promote an inclusive vision of social life and found favor among secular elites and progressive reformers. On the other hand, theologically and politically conservative religion remained influential, if often marginal, because of its continuing appeal to the communal sentiments of dominant communities.

The resurgence of religious politics in recent years, then, is not simply the product of a failed modernity project or of a renewed religiosity among traditional populations. Rather, it represents another round of the longstanding debate over the nature and basis of social order. What makes this latest round of ideological struggle so significant, though, is the outcome. Unlike earlier periods, liberal interpretations of modernity were displaced throughout the 1980s and 1990s by modes of political discourse infused with exclusive religious sentiments. Although many attribute this transformation solely to the strength of religious opposition groups, the changing orientation of state elites played a critical role in reshaping the context in which these debates played out. Instead of opposing communalist ideologies, as had happened in the earlier period, state actors actively sought to coopt these ideas, and that decision transformed the ideological milieu in a manner that privileged exclusive notions of religion, nationalism, and society.

The resurgence of religious politics in the late Cold War era and the corresponding demise of cosmopolitan or secular norms consequently reflects an ideological shift to the right. The modernist program of the 1950s and 1960s was closely associated with economic and social policies aimed at mitigating inequalities in wealth and opportunity. It also included state-led efforts to limit the discrimination of minority populations and to integrate a diverse population into a common political community. Modernity in the mid-twentieth century, in short, was distinctly left of center. The shift toward a more overt religious politics—and the role of state elites in this process—was thus part of a broader assault on the policies of social reform. Conservative or illiberal interpretations of religious tradition were used to reify existing patterns of social hierarchy and to stigmatize the ideas associated with the political left. It also coincided with the end of previous commitments to eradicate poverty and the demise of the use of the state to promote economic development and mitigate inequality. The abandonment of secular norms was merely part of a broader shift away from the liberal vision of national development and toward a new era of conservative politics.

This more nuanced interpretation of the contemporary resurgence of religious politics sheds light on many of the debates over the broader phenomenon. Perhaps the most important insight is the recognition that the dichotomous view of religious politics is largely unhelpful. To view such trends as either religious or political in orientation fails to capture the interaction of the two factors and their influence on one another. It also overlooks the ideological context in which modern religious politics has occurred and the materialist influences that have shaped competing visions of religion and religious politics. Similarly, the dichotomous understanding of tradition and modernity "obscures more than it reveals."[73] Neither states nor modernity are as secular as most believe, nor is religion antithetical to a progressive vision of modernity. Rather, the discourse of modern politics and modern nationalisms is imbued with a religious imagery that can be interpreted in many different ways. Similarly, secular modernity can be either inclusive or exclusive in orientation. The point is that nationalist ideologies are by definition modern phenomena, and the ambiguity that they demonstrate reflects the differing conceptions of religion and society that inform each of these modern constructs.

The resurgence of religious politics of the 1990s, then, should not have been terribly surprising. It occurred in the context of unresolved debates over religion and public life. The complicity of state elites, however, is another matter. Because of their earlier commitments to an inclusive social order, it is surprising that state actors would be so intimately involved in the politicization of ethnic and religious identities. The idea of India, the social contract basis of the American tradition, and even the Arab nationalist tradition all represented attempts by leading national figures to develop a basis of citizenship that deemphasized the sectarian nature of religious nationalisms. The promotion of illiberal religious ideas by state actors—and the corresponding demise of the integrative revolution in each of these cases—represents, then, an inability or unwillingness of subsequent political figures to carry on the project of building a nonsectarian political community. It also reflects the continuing reliance of state actors on religion as a source of legitimate authority and the enduring lure of religious sectarianism. In either case, the contemporary resurgence of religious politics does not represent a more authentic understanding of community—much less a "return" to some traditional past. Rather, it is simply a byproduct of the modern nature of contemporary mass politics.

# CHAPTER TWO

# The Rise and Decline of Egyptian Secularism

In the early 1990s, the Egyptian security services were engaged in a violent struggle with Islamist militant groups. Over the course of several years, thousands of Islamic activists—moderates as well as militants—were imprisoned, killed, or driven underground. Although some of these activists escaped into exile, the organizations that challenged the state were crushed, and by 1997 they had ceased to be a viable threat. The government's tactics, however, were controversial. Egypt's security services used torture, arbitrary detention, and extrajudicial killings to eradicate the Islamists who threatened the Mubarak regime's hold on power. The government also relied on a system of military and security courts that bypassed the ordinary judiciary in order to ensure the conviction of those charged. Such extreme measures demonstrated the regime's belief that the Islamists were an existential threat to its rule and that any means necessary to eliminate them were justified. Western governments similarly feared a "fundamentalist" takeover of the country, and turned a blind eye to the human rights abuses and emergency tactics that the government was using to win its war against Islamist militancy.

Although the government succeeded in removing the militant threat, the conflict did little to lessen the significance of Islam in Egyptian politics. On the contrary, during this period, an illiberal interpretation of Islam became thoroughly entrenched in public life. This was evident in a series of high-profile assaults on intellectual and artistic freedom and in the continuing persecution of Egypt's Coptic Christians. Apostasy cases were brought against secular intellectuals, and books were banned even as the militant threat receded. The government's inaction, and often complicity, in these cases—and in the violence against the Christian minority—raised questions about the Mubarak regime's commitment to a pluralist conception of social order. It also generated concern about Egypt's future. Although one would assume that the political victors would be able to define the new "rules of the game," in this instance the Islamist challenge—even in defeat—was able to reshape the vernacular of political discourse.[1] Why was this occurring? Why was the Egyptian government winning the battles but losing the war?

The explanation for this paradox can be found in the efforts of successive governments to promote Islam as a source of ideological legitimacy. Despite the assumed secularism of the Egyptian state, it never, in fact, broke free of its religious moorings. Instead, state leaders preferred the time-honored use of an official Islam to sanction political authority. Even during Gamal Abdel Nasser's tenure, the modernizing state never sought to eradicate religious belief but, rather, worked to coopt it. There was, however, a key difference between Nasser and his successors. Nasser appealed to a liberal or "modernist" interpretation of Islam as a means of challenging traditional elites and sanctifying his political vision. Islam was an essential part of the nationalist discourse, but it was an interpretation that was consistent with both secularism and socialism. This emphasis changed, however, during the tenure of Anwar Sadat and, later, Hosni Mubarak. Beginning in the Sadat era, the Egyptian government promoted a more literal or Salafist interpretation of Islam as part of a broader effort to redefine the direction of Egyptian politics. The Sadat regime used this theologically conservative rendering of religious tradition to eradicate the continuing influence of the political left and to construct a new basis of political authority rooted in Islam. These policies helped to validate the Islamist vision of society and greatly affected longstanding debates over whether Egypt should have a religious or a secular state.

The question of religion in public life—that is, how to define the nation—was the subject of much contention throughout the twentieth century. Nasser sought to resolve this debate in the 1950s by embedding secular norms within state institutions. To be clear, Nasser was no liberal. His anti-Western sentiments and autocratic policies were responsible for driving large numbers of Greeks, Jews, Italians, and other members of foreign communities from Egypt. This type of exclusive nationalism had an enormous impact upon the traditional cosmopolitanism of Egyptian society and changed the face of the country. However, the Nasserist regime did promote a *religiously* inclusive vision of Egyptian national identity as a means of integrating Egypt's diverse population. The inclusion of the Coptic Christian minority and the promotion of a liberal or modernist interpretation of Islam were subsequently key features of Nasser's secular Arab nationalism. So, too, was the persecution of the Muslim Brotherhood and other elements of society associated with Egypt's traditional leadership.

The debate over Islam in public life was resurrected in the wake of the 1967 war with Israel and again in the early 1990s. In each instance, the central issues were whether Islam was compatible with secular principles and whether Islam ought to be given greater prominence among the modern institutions of nation and state. These debates also involved religious questions such as whether Islam is open to interpretation (*ijtihad*) or if its origins in divine revelation preclude analysis by any apart from the recognized custodians of the faith. Although these debates were largely theoretical in nature, they had practical implications that were far-reaching. What was ultimately at issue in these debates was whether the nation ought to be defined in an inclusive manner consistent with Enlightenment norms, or whether it should be explicitly religious, and Islamic, in orientation. In other words, should Egyptian national identity include religious minorities, or ought it reflect the religious communalism of a closed society?

The following two chapters chart the evolution of these debates and the manner in which they unfolded over time. This first chapter describes the way in which secular norms were institutionalized in the Egyptian state during the early and mid-twentieth century—culminating in the Nasser period—and how they were subsequently disembedded (or deinstitutionalized) during the Sadat era. An essential part of this narrative is an examination of the differing interpretations of Islam and how they reflect competing visions of social order. In Egypt, as in the other cases in this book, religion is intertwined with the construction of nationalist identities, albeit in different forms. Nasser used Islam to sanction his secular vision of modernity and to offset the ideological challenge of the Muslim Brotherhood, Saudi Arabia, and other traditional elites. Nasser's opponents, on the other hand, similarly invoked religion but appealed to a Salafist or illiberal rendering of Islamic tradition to challenge the socialist and secular policies of the new state.

During the tenure of Sadat, this dynamic changed in a fundamental way. Sadat abandoned the secular program of his successor and promoted an illiberal vision of both religion and nation in its place. This reflected a distinct shift in state policy and a new ruling coalition. Sadat opted for an alliance with those who had been marginalized by Nasser's reforms in opposition to the unreconstructed left, who now challenged the new president. This changing orientation toward religion and secularism, then, provides the context for understanding the rise of the Islamist movement. The Sadat regime rehabilitated the Muslim Brotherhood, reached out to Saudi Arabia, and helped to institutionalize a Salafist Islam within the institutions of the Egyptian state. The policies associated with this shift dramatically changed the political fortunes of Islamic fundamentalism and illustrate how the debates over religious orthodoxy were affected by state policy. Sadat's assassination by Islamist militants also demonstrates the limits of this strategy and the regime's inability to control the forces it set in motion. These trends provide the context for understanding the religious politics of the Mubarak era, which is the focus of chapter 3.

## Religion and State Formation in the Early Modern Era

The relationship between Islam and politics in Egypt is neither as unified nor as unproblematic as many argue. The centers of religious and political power developed quite distinctly from one another in Sunni Islam, and this generated a system of dual authority that was replicated throughout the Islamic world. This pattern was clearly evident in seventeenth- and eighteenth-century Egypt, where religious authorities and political authorities were largely separate. These different community leaders nonetheless tended to cooperate because they remained dependent on one another: political rulers required moral legitimacy, while religious leaders needed the temporal authorities to uphold Islamic law. The relationship between these two groups, however, was often tense. Political elites sought to dominate religious figures—as well as the doctrine of Sunni Islam—to pursue their temporal ends more ably. They were also not above using force to attain compliance. The *ulema* (religious scholars), on the other hand, struggled to maintain their independence—and integrity—with many recognizing the corrupting influence of political power both on themselves and on Islamic doctrine.[2]

If the premodern era was characterized by a system of dual authority—with each side trying to gain the upper hand—the early modern era was defined by the emerging dominance of the political. With the French occupation in 1798, Egypt was opened to the modernizing influences of European political, economic, and ideological thought. The subsequent transformation of Egypt's social and political life began in earnest during the nineteenth century by Muhammad Ali (1805–1863) and, later, by his successor Ismail Pasha (1863–79). Two key elements of their common agenda was the elimination of the previously dominant Mamluk leadership and the curtailment of the traditional religious elite. Reining in the *ulema* entailed, above all, separating them from their source of economic livelihood: tax farms and religiously endowed properties (*awqaf*). It also meant minimizing their control over education and the law. This was intended to make the *ulema* dependent on the state, and the move paved the way for the introduction of Western-style education and legal codes.[3] The corresponding social revolution of the mid- to late nineteenth century helped to establish the dominance of a political elite in areas traditionally controlled by religious scholars and left to the latter only a very limited, and re-conceived, realm of religion.

This era had a lasting impact on the modernization of Egyptian public life. The construction of an intrusive state by Muhammad Ali and Ismail was very much intertwined with a program of secular modernization, indicating a desire among Egypt's political elite to emulate the European model of development. This period was also characterized by the diminished influence of the ecclesiastical caste and saw the emergence of a distinctly secular political leadership. These social and political changes set the stage for the early nationalist period. Egypt had long been a province of the Ottoman Empire, though had been largely autonomous during the nineteenth century. However, British financial and strategic interests in the region—including control of the Suez Canal—led to British intervention in Egypt and, ultimately, to direct colonial rule in 1882.[4] The nationalist revolt of 1919, led by the liberal nationalist Wafd Party, was a reaction to British rule. The events of that year forced a negotiated withdrawal and at least nominal independence in 1922. Even though British armed forces remained in the country, the uprising laid the foundations for Egypt's liberal experiment of the 1922–52 period. The 1923 constitution enshrined a secular vision of society and provided for a shared basis of citizenship premised on national, not religious, loyalties. This civic conception of national identity remained influential throughout the first half of the twentieth century.

It was also under British rule that an Islamic reform movement first emerged. The movement was largely a reaction to colonialism and had strong national-ist overtones. It sought to challenge the West by reinvigorating the political community through religious reform. Leaders of the early movement included Jamal al-Din al-Afghani (1838–1897), Muhammad Abduh (1849–1905), and, later, Rashid Rida (1865–1935). Abduh in particular was enormously influential. He served as mufti of Egypt (chief judge of the *sharia* courts) and was a leading reformer in Al-Azhar University, the preeminent university and mosque in the country. Abduh sought to reinterpret Islam in a modern context and to dem-onstrate that Islam could viably challenge Western modes of modernization. He and his supporters advocated a decidedly liberal interpretation of Islamic tradition and saw the reformation of Islam as an important means of revital-izing the national community. A central part of this project was a conscious effort to break the hold on society of an interpretation of religious tradition defined by "unquestioning imitation" (*taqlid*). Instead, the liberal reformers ad-vocated *ijtihad* (interpretation) as a means of changing Islamic thought and in-stitutions. Abduh also recognized that science and reason were essential for ma-terial progress and argued that enlightenment norms were entirely compatible with Islamic tradition.

The movement's emphasis on religious reform *and* political change became a model for conservative (or illiberal) activists as well. Rashid Rida, one of Abduh's disciples, embodied the conservative aspect of Islamic reform. Rida led what was known as the Salafiyya Movement, which advocated a strict interpretation of Islam based on the example of the early community (*salaf* means predeces-sor or ancestor). The Salafis represented an alternative to the secularism of the 1920s and 1930s as well as to Abduh's liberal or "modernist" Islam. The reform movement also influenced Hasan al-Banna, the Islamic teacher who founded the Muslim Brotherhood in 1928 and codified many of the basic precepts of early Islamic fundamentalism. Although Rida and al-Banna differed with Abduh on a variety of theological issues, they shared with the liberal reform movement a belief that a reinterpreted and reinvigorated Islam could provide the basis for political activism. They also shared a common animosity to Western dominance of Egypt. To this end, the early Islamists believed, as did the liberal secular parties, that Egypt was a unique nation-state and deserved independence from British colonial rule.

Although all of these individuals and groups were committed to an amorphous Egyptian nationalism, they differed greatly over what this entailed. The liberal Wafd Party, for example, advocated a more secular and cosmopolitan conception of the nation. By breaking from traditional views on Islam in public life, they hoped to develop their country along more European lines. Similarly, the Islamic reformers advocated an inclusive vision of social life, consistent with secular principles, that was premised on a reconceived notion of Islamic tradition. Abduh and others viewed Europe as a model of progress, despite its role as oppressor.[5] The Muslim Brotherhood, on the other hand, interpreted Egyptian nationalism in terms of an exclusive and communal vision of Islam. They believed that Egypt's weakness was rooted in its effort to emulate the West, particularly the country's adoption of a secular political framework. By mimicking its colonial rulers, al-Banna and others argued, Muslims were internalizing the values of imperial subjugation and betraying their cultural heritage.[6] In other words, they were straying from the true path of Islam. It was this loss of religion, al-Banna believed, that was the source of Egypt's corruption and decay. It followed, then, that only by "returning to Islam"—that is, creating an "Islamic order" (*al-nizam al-Islami*)—could the nation regain its strength and challenge the West. These competing views marked the contemporary origins of the debate over Egypt's social order and the beginnings of the re-traditionalization of Islam.

The liberal nationalism of Egypt's Wafd Party was politically dominant in the aftermath of the 1919 revolt and enjoyed a limited degree of success during the country's liberal era directly afterward. The Wafd Party benefited from the animosity of the Egyptian public to British rule and the fear that the Western powers were undermining Islam. However, their ideas of liberal secularism remained somewhat alien to the deeply religious population. Moreover, the inability of the constitutional government to deal with such core issues as socioeconomic development, corruption, and the continuing dominance of Britain in Egypt's politics discredited what little faith there was in the idea of democratic constitutionalism. Not surprisingly, other political parties expanded to fill the ideological vacuum. These included the right-wing nationalist Misr al-Fatat (Young Egypt)—modeled on the fascist parties of Italy and Germany—as well as the Muslim Brotherhood and several left-wing parties, including the Communists and the Socialists. The communalist orientation of all these groups demonstrated the dominance of such tendencies in Europe during the same time period (1930s and 1940s). Although the left-wing communalism of the Communists and the right-wing revivalism of the Muslim Brotherhood differed over the basis of society, they shared a common rejection of the individualism inherent in liberal democratic constitutionalism.

## Egypt after 1952: Embedding and Disembedding the Secular Order

*Nasser and the Secular Vision*

In July 1952, a handful of young military officers, led by Gamal Abdel Nasser, overthrew the ruling government and sent Egypt's monarch, King Farouk, into exile. The military intervention ended months of political crisis and inaugurated a new period in Egyptian history. The established order that Nasser and the "Free Officers" sought to transform was dominated by a landed aristocracy, an ineffectual monarch, and continuing British influence. Economic inequality and class divisions were a defining feature of Egypt in the early twentieth century, as was a large degree of ideological pluralism. The nationalist movement that had grown up in the interwar period—and that opposed both the British and the Monarchy—illustrated the diversity of Egyptian society at the time: the Muslim Brotherhood on the right, the Communists on the left, and the liberal Wafd Party in the center. These groups all agreed on the twin goals of economic development and independence from foreign rule but on little else. They differed over how to achieve these goals, what would follow a British withdrawal, and, most important, who should rule. Many in the military—which was the most stable institution in Egyptian society—saw the politicians as unable to accomplish either of the two overarching goals. The intervention of these young military officers into the country's politics in 1952, then, was their response to Egypt's political crisis.

The July 23 Revolution of 1952 started off as little more than a coup. Nasser and his allies did not lead a mass movement, nor did they espouse a clear ideology. What separated the Free Officers from their political rivals was the support of the armed forces. This provided them with the ability to take power and to institute some degree of order. The failings of the ancien regime, moreover, and its inability to improve life for ordinary Egyptians disposed the population favorably toward these young officers of modest origins. Although there remained skepticism that the new rulers would be significantly different from the old ones, there was some reason for hope. The dissolution of the monarchy and the departure of British troops in 1954 marked the end of Ottoman and European control of Egyptian politics. As such, it was "the first time in over two thousand years . . . [that] Egypt was ruled by Egyptians."[7]

It was only after the military takeover, however, that the struggle to define the revolution—and the nation—began. Although the 1952 revolution would ultimately be characterized by economic and social transformation on a large scale, the initial priority was to consolidate political power. The Free Officers also had to build a populist—and nationalist—basis of support. It was these latter two features of the Nasser period that would come to define the post-1952 era: the development of a strong centralized state and the continuing struggle to cultivate popular acceptance for military rule.[8]

Nasser and the Free Officers saw the state as the vehicle for modernizing and transforming Egyptian society. Based on the Soviet model, the regime created a one-party state whose influence spread into all areas of Egyptian life. Although there was a split within the ruling elite over whether or not to return to constitutional rule, this ended with the marginalization of the advocates of democratic constitutionalism. Egypt's first president, General Muhammad Naguib, was a leading advocate of the return to parliamentary rule but was deposed in 1954 by Nasser, who became the new president. The dominant institutions of the new state, then, included the armed forces, the newly expanded security services (the *mukhabarat*), and the single party. These institutions were initially directed by the Revolutionary Command Council (RCC), a ruling body set up in 1952, but it later came under direct control of the Office of the President. The Nasser regime also sought to eliminate potential rivals by banning the political parties that were controlled by the landed elite and that had dominated Egyptian politics in the interwar years. The Muslim Brotherhood was allowed to continue its activities in return for its support of the revolution, but this policy was reversed in 1954.

Economically, the regime promoted major initiatives on land reform and state-led industrialization. This reflected its commitment to socioeconomic reform and a more equitable distribution of wealth. Such policies were also a central feature of Nasser's political strategy. The land reform was intended to disempower traditional elites, who opposed the regime's policies, specifically the landowners and traditional religious leaders. It was also designed to generate support among the peasantry, who benefited from the redistribution of land. A program of state-led industrialization was also an important mechanism for providing jobs to urban workers, another major constituency of the new regime. Nasser looked to such policies as a means of building support for the government and of mobilizing Egypt's "subordinate classes against landed elites and private business [interests]."[9] By emphasizing the class divisions of society, Nasser was able to cultivate popular support for his program of socioeconomic reform and to stigmatize the "feudal elements" and "reactionaries" who opposed the regime. The rapid expansion of the public sector and the nationalization of various industries also created a new class whose interests were closely tied to the state.

These efforts to centralize political and economic control of the country went hand in hand with the effort to construct a new basis of state authority. In order to generate popular support, the Free Officers went on public speaking tours and used the mass media to bypass traditional political channels and communicate directly to the masses. The dissolution of alternate political parties and the development of a single mass party was central to this strategy. By removing the mechanisms by which opposing political interests could be organized, the regime was better able to control opposition groups.[10] It also sought to exclude supportive groups, such as students and unions, from real power. A series of political organizations were created, including the Liberation Rally (1953), the National Union (1956), and, finally, the Arab Socialist Union (1962).

What Nasser wanted from these mass parties was not a vehicle for participation but rather a mechanism for building consent. The goal was to organize support for the regime and provide a link between the government and the people. In developing these new political organizations, Nasser was able to expand the social base of the regime to the lower classes that had previously been excluded from political life. This marked a new era of politics, defined by populist appeals and mass mobilization. It also ushered in a new social contract. The peasantry and the working classes accepted the authoritarianism of the military-bureaucratic elite in exchange for the promise of higher living standards and economic opportunity.[11] Thus, "by destroying the party system and replacing parliamentary democracy with the referendum, [Nasser] brought the Egyptian (and Arab) masses into play," which led to a new era of Egyptian politics.[12]

Ideologically, the twin themes of Arab nationalism and Arab Socialism defined the Nasserist period. The latter of these was evident in the program of state-led development and modernization and in Nasser's program of social reform. Arab socialism, however, was *not* intended to replicate the Soviet system, with its hostility to religion but rather to adapt it to an Arab context. Nasser participated in the nonaligned movement because he wanted to develop a model of development similar to, but independent of, the Soviet Union. The truly defining feature of the Nasser era, however, was Arab nationalism. This was a belief that the Arab peoples—defined by language, history, and culture—were a "nation" and ought to be politically unified. This was an important element in developing an inclusive Arab identity not based on religious affiliation. Rather, it was a secular ideology that consciously sought to include Arab Christians as well as Muslims.[13] There was also a strong anti-imperialist sentiment to this, one that saw the European powers as a primary obstacle to Arab development. Hence, Arab nationalism can be seen as *politically* illiberal in orientation—at least in terms of the regime's autocratic tendencies and its anti-European bias—even if the ideology is premised upon a *religiously* inclusive notion of identity. Despite a failed political union with Syria (1958–61) and animosity from the Gulf monarchies, the ideology of Arab nationalism reinforced the international focus of the regime and made Nasser a hero among the Arab masses.

The Nasser regime was greatly aided in its effort to promote the ideas of Arab nationalism—and to construct a new basis of state authority—by a series of events in the mid-1950s. The failed attempt on Nassser's life in 1954, the Suez crisis of 1956, and the growing appeal of third-world nationalism all heightened the charismatic quality of the new leader and strengthened the legitimacy of the regime. With the expansion of the state security forces, the capacity of the state to monitor and control its perceived enemies in these early years also grew. The adoption of a series of constitutions between 1956 and 1964 similarly strengthened the hand of the state. These concentrated power within the Office of the Presidency and, at least in the 1964 constitution, created a new system of security courts to try political cases. What ultimately emerged was a strong centralized state that was able to mobilize popular sentiment behind the ideology of Arab nationalism. As one commentator phrased it, "Identification with the people in a ritualized cult of symbolic relationships went hand in hand with the development of the control function of the nation-state, the formation of an elite of army officers, and the use of rubber stamp organizations and assemblies."[14] This was Nasser's new secular order.

## Challenging Conservative Islam

The primary challenge to the Nasser regime remained three residual elements of the old order: (1) the loyalties of the establishment *ulema* (religious scholars) to the landowning class; (2) the popularity of the Muslim Brotherhood; and (3) the grip of traditional Islam on the population. To deal with these issues, Nasser undertook a series of steps to counter the influence of conservative Islam. First, leaders of the RCC sought to mobilize popular religious senti- ment for their own purposes. This entailed working with local religious leaders (*imams,* or prayer leaders), preaching in various mosques at Friday prayers, and otherwise using religious actors to emphasize the compatibility of Islam with the socialist policies of the state. This strategy included a concerted effort to depict the leadership as devout men. Nasser, for example, undertook a well-publicized pilgrimage to Mecca (*Hajj*) in 1954, fulfilling one of the primary command- ments of Islam. Similarly, the government sought to gain greater control over the mosques throughout the country (both public and private) by placing them under the direct supervision of the Ministry of Religious Endowments. The regime also made significant contributions to the construction of new mosques and had local preachers endorse state policies from the pulpit.[15] The interpreta- tion of Islam that was promoted throughout this period, however, was theologi- cally liberal and modernist.

Starting in 1954, the regime also took a confrontational stance toward the Muslim Brotherhood and its brand of conservative Islam.[16] Although the Broth- erhood was initially supportive of the 1952 revolution, their relationship with Nasser was a complicated one. The Brotherhood had longstanding ties with many of the Free Officers, including relations with both Nasser and Sadat, who some believe had previously been members.[17] Moreover, the Brotherhood's ini- tial support of the revolution was important for the Free Officers in both chal- lenging the secular Wafd Party and in providing a religious sanction for the military takeover (what the Brotherhood originally referred to as the "Blessed Movement"). The Muslim Brotherhood had been a major force in Egyptian politics throughout the 1930s and 1940s and, despite repression under the old regime, it retained extensive grassroots network as well as a militant wing. Its longstanding opposition to the monarchy and the British also gave the orga- nization a great deal of legitimacy, which the Free Officers initially sought to coopt.

Relations between the two groups, however, broke down fairly quickly. The Muslim Brotherhood had hoped that their support for the new government would translate into some form of power-sharing arrangement. The Free Offi- cers, however, were reluctant to forge a genuine partnership. Members of the two groups subsequently clashed over the Muslim Brotherhood's membership on the RCC and over a request by its members for a formal role in developing legislation. Neither concession was granted. This tension was due, in part, to the inherent rivalry between the Brotherhood and the Free Officers and the ongoing competition for the loyalties of the same constituencies (urban laborers, rural peasants, and the lower middle classes). More problematic, however, were the ideological divisions and the fundamentally different visions that each had for the nation. Although the Free Officers, and Nasser in particular, sought to modernize Egypt along secular and socialist lines, the Brotherhood advocated a more central role of religion in public life. The ideological division hinged, in short, upon whether to create a religious or a secular state.

The debate over these competing visions of the nation was embodied in two books published during this period. The first was Khalid Muhammad Khalid's *Min Huna Nabda* (*From Here We Start*, published in 1950), which argued the secular position. This text echoed an earlier and controversial argument by Ali Abd al-Raziq, who wrote that true Islam has little to say about the nature of political or social order. On the contrary, the type of state structure adopted by the country was, for the most part, religiously immaterial. Accordingly, there was nothing inconsistent between Islam and a secular state as long as certain minimal prohibitions were upheld. Khalid further argued that secularism would be preferable given the danger of too close a linkage between religious and political power. As he argued in the book, a religious state would hinder Egypt's development since the unification of religious and political authority would be corrupting to both sides and would more likely undermine the development of liberty and justice than create it. What was truly needed, Khalid argued, was a social revolution. Such an alternative, however, would be hindered by a "priesthood" that "colluded with tyrants" and—in their pursuit of power—used religion to "keep the people poor and ignorant."[18]

Sheikh Muhammad al-Ghazzali represented the Muslim Brotherhood's position in this debate. Al-Ghazzali's book, entitled *Min Huna Na'lam* (*Our Beginning in Wisdom*, or more literally *From Here We Learn*) was also published in 1950, and it argued that Islam is a "comprehensive program" meant to regulate all facets of human existence. This necessarily includes the political and social realms of human life. To preclude Islam from a central role in governing the state would therefore be a violation of God's revelation. What this meant in practice, however, remained vague. In other words, it was not clear what an Islamic state would look like, nor what specific policies it would pursue. Al-Ghazzali simply argued that "the duties of the state are clearly and precisely outlined in the

*Qur'an* and the *Sunna* (tradition)."[19] The *need* for an Islamic state, he argued, was nonetheless clear. The return to Islam was a necessary requirement for a revived Islamic community, and this was all the more important given the imminent threat to Islam posed by a hostile, Christian West. In making this argument, al-Ghazzali appealed to the communal sentiments of a religious population and called on them to defend their tradition. Not only was Islam "threatened with extermination"[20] from outside, but those within the community, such as Khalid, who argued for a secular political authority were betraying their faith and were, in al-Ghazzali's words, "puppets of the enemies of Islam."[21]

The conflict between the Brotherhood and the Free Officers came to a head in 1954. The Brotherhood had been deeply divided over how to deal with Nasser's intransigence on the core issues of creating an Islamic state and of sharing power. One faction, which included Hasan al-Banna's successor, Hasan al-Hodeiby, sought to work with Nasser and persuade him to "turn toward Islam."[22] Another faction, led by Ahmad Sanadi (and which included Sayyid Qutb) pressed for a more forceful confrontation that would entail Nasser's overthrow. Al-Hodeiby was arrested in the autumn of 1954, and shortly afterwards an assassination attempt was made on Nasser's life, reputedly by a member of the Muslim Brotherhood.[23] Nasser used this event as an opportunity to confront the organization. Several thousand members of the Brotherhood (including Qutb and most of the Brotherhood's leadership) were arrested, and its influence within the military, the police, and other areas of Egyptian society was shattered.[24] A military tribunal subsequently convicted eight hundred members of the Brotherhood on charges of conspiring to overthrow the state, and six of its leaders were executed. With these actions, Nasser temporarily ended the Brotherhood's influence in Egyptian politics. He also put an end to the debate over whether Egypt would have a religious or secular state.

## Nationalizing Islam

The third and final step taken by Nasser to challenge conservative Islam was the regime's effort to take control of the Al-Azhar mosque and university complex and other institutions of the religious establishment. This was undertaken with the goal of undermining and coopting the religious elite and occurred in three phases. Initially, there was the 1952 land reform, which placed all "*waqf*" properties (land associated with religious endowment, literally holy lands) under the control of a new government ministry. Since the religious institutions of the country, particularly Al-Azhar, depended on income from such land to operate, this move curtailed their autonomy and made them reliant on the state for financial support. It also allowed the government to distribute *waqf* resources in such a way as to "reward those who followed [its] lead . . . and punish those who did not."[25] Second, Nasser abolished the *sharia* courts, which had operated as a parallel court system since the nineteenth century, and merged them into the national judiciary.[26] Although the stated goal was to unify a fragmented judicial system, it had the effect of bringing this alternate court system under the direct control of the state.

Finally, in 1961, Nasser passed a law that radically reorganized Al-Azhar University, one of the leading centers of Islamic teaching in the Arab world. Nasser saw the control of this institution and its curriculum as important both for Egypt's domestic and regional politics. The reorganization subsequently placed the entire institution under the jurisdiction of the Ministry of Religious Endowments and gave to the president of Egypt the power to appoint its director, the sheikh of Al-Azhar. The reorganization also introduced into the university's curriculum modern courses of learning and entirely new faculties, including medicine and engineering. By implementing these changes and bringing the institution under the rubric of a state bureaucracy, Nasser was able to exert control over the *ulema* without having to eliminate them as a social force.[27] Those within Al-Azhar who opposed the reforms were subsequently replaced with those who were more supportive of the regime.

The reformation of Al-Azhar and the effort to control the country's mosques were intended to tame Islam and employ it in the service of the state. Domestically, this was driven by the need to deny other groups, such as the remnants of the Muslim Brotherhood, the resources of religion with which to oppose the government. In particular, the regime sought to limit the ability of Islamists to charge Nasser with advocating a "godless secularism." The new policies also gave the state a monopoly on religious interpretation. Thus, while the Nasserist regime was defined by a program of socialist modernization—and derived much of its authority from the idea of Arab nationalism—it found ample justification for its mission in the *fatwas* (religious rulings) issued by the official religious establishment. The regime also established the Supreme Council on Islamic Affairs for this purpose; it was an organization whose raison d'être was to demonstrate the compatibility between socialism and Islam.[28]

Nasser believed that creating a state-controlled monopoly on religion would be useful in supporting his regime against both internal and external enemies. As such, it was important that the *ulema* not be eliminated but rather subordinated.

Moreover, the strength and popularity of Islam throughout Egypt precluded the Nasserists from attempting to eradicate religion in the way that Kemal Atatürk had done in Turkey thirty years earlier. Particularly in the absence of a clear alternative, the Free Officers found it more useful to combine a modernist vision of development with a vague appeal to tradition. Cultivating a modernist Islam—one consistent with secular norms and social transformation—while suppressing the more radical interpretations was an essential element of Nasser's mass politics. Far from being hostile to religion, Islam became integrated into the state apparatus to provide the Nasser regime with a moral basis. In essence, Islam was nationalized.

The effort to mobilize Islam on behalf of the regime was also important in the international arena. The Nasser government was concerned with the conservative monarchs of the Gulf region, who greatly feared Nasser's socialist and republican ideas. This rivalry became more significant in the late 1950s and early 1960s when the Cold War dynamic was replicated in the Middle East.[29] Saudi Arabia was deeply troubled by the populist rhetoric and revolutionary policies of the Egyptian regime. Nasser's Arab nationalism directly challenged the legitimacy of Saudi Arabia's ruling family and their control of the region's oil wealth. On the other hand, Nasser perceived Saudi Arabia as a bastion of conservative reaction actively working against his interests. The Gulf monarchies' alliance with the West was, in Nasser's view, a perpetuation of the colonial relationship and kept the Arabs divided and weak. Both the Saudis and the Egyptians subsequently worked to limit the influence of the other in the region and set up competing Islamic institutions to promote their respective political agendas. These organizations each appealed to differing interpretations of Sunni Islam to promote the interests of the competing states. The war of words between Nasser and the Gulf monarchies culminated in more direct conflict during the civil war in Yemen, which broke out in 1962 and in which Egypt and Saudi Arabia backed opposing sides. The intra-communal conflicts within Egypt—and within Islam—were subsequently replicated in the region as a whole as the conservative Gulf monarchies promoted a Salafist Islam in opposition to Egypt's secular and socialist vision of the Arab nation.

Although the Nasser regime used Islam for ideological purposes, it was never defined by a commitment to religion. Nasser encouraged the reformists within Al-Azhar to reformulate Islamic thinking and to provide a new religious modernism to both state and society. This was important in the mid-1960s with the renewed activities of the Brotherhood, the emergence of Sayyid Qutb's extremist critique, and the continued call by Islamists for the implementation of *sharia*. However, much of the Nasserist leadership continued to associate Islam with the forces of reaction, and the Islamic reformism that Nasser had hoped to inspire remained less influential in ruling circles than a strident secularism. The Nasserist elite, in short, remained wary of Islam, seeing it as an obstacle "to the full realization of the nation-state, unless rigorously channeled and controlled."[30] And yet, the use of religion within a nationalist discourse remained a key link between the modernizing state and its traditional population. Nasser could reconcile this contradictory position as long as he retained his charismatic authority and as long as people believed in the progress and destiny that he embodied. This tenuous balance came to an abrupt end with the traumatic events of June 1967.

It is difficult to overestimate the impact on Middle Eastern politics of the Six-Day War in June 1967. The heights of optimism of the early Nasser era were matched only by the depths of despair that followed Egypt's stunning defeat by the Israeli military in those six days. The war was brief and decisive. Part of Egypt's army was bogged down in Yemen fighting an inconclusive proxy war, while corruption and ineptitude undermined the nation's preparedness for a war with Israel. Ideologically, the defeat had enormous implications. The complete rout of Egyptian military forces took the sheen off of the charismatic Nasser and his vision of Arab nationalism. In attempting to make sense of the defeat, different groups and classes struggled to comprehend what had happened, and why. According to one analyst, "The whole logic and symbolism of the nation-state, which had been developed as the only authentic language, was undercut and revealed as without substance in exactly those dimensions where it had most claimed to be powerful."[31]

The defeat also reopened longstanding debates over the proper basis of Egyptian public life. On its face, the debate was over the sources of the Arab defeat, yet the conflict, once again, pitted a secular vision of society against the Islamist alternative. On the one hand, the leftist critique argued that the Nasser revolution had not gone far enough in transforming Egyptian society. From this perspective, it was religion and the traditional mindset—embodied by the fatalism of Islam—that held society back, and this was the basis of the military defeat. The revolution, in short, had failed because it had not modernized Egypt's traditional society and had not been able to change popular attitudes. As Fouad Ajami has noted, "Among those [of the radical left] who wanted to get to the deep structure behind the defeat there was a consensus that the heroes of yesterday had made too many compromises with the past, that they had given in to that frustrating, hopeless body of attitudes and habits, that immutable thing called tradition."[32] Opposing this perspective was the religious critique posited by the Muslim Brotherhood and others of an Islamist orientation. From their perspective, it was precisely the loss of tradition and the straying from Islam that was behind the 1967 fiasco. The military officers' embrace of foreign ideologies—Marx was a German even if he was anticapitalist—and their attempt to refashion Egyptian society on foreign models was their downfall. Despite its efforts to justify socialism along Islamic lines, the regime was nonetheless seen as un-Islamic and the establishment *ulema* as without credibility. In short, the Islamists argued, the political leadership had lost touch with its own traditions, and the military defeat was the result. As one writer noted, "The Arabs had turned away from God, and God had turned away from them."[33]

### Sadat's Islamist Politics

Nasser died in September 1970, and he was succeeded by his vice president Muhammad Anwar Sadat. In his first speech as president, Sadat affirmed his commitment to Nasser's legacy and pledged to rule in cooperation with the collective leadership of the Arab Socialist Union (ASU). This was well received by the other members of the Egyptian ruling party. The facade of unity among the ruling elite, however, cloaked deep divisions over the future of the country. On the one hand, there were the Marxists, the Nasserists, and pro-Soviet "centrists" who remained in positions of influence within the state bureaucracy.[34] They were committed to the Nasserist project and to their privileged position within the existing political order. They were content with Sadat's presidency as long as he continued with the policies in place and agreed to rule in a collective manner. They were also under the assumption that Sadat could be readily controlled. On the other hand, Sadat (among others) had become disaffected with Egypt's socialist experiment and sought to chart a new course for Egyptian politics. Sadat's subsequent effort to consolidate political authority and to change the country's direction thrust him into the heart of Egypt's religious debates.

The tension between the unreconstructed left, led by Vice President Ali Sabri, the former secretary general of the ASU, and Sadat was immediately apparent. Sabri's faction sought to gain control of government policymaking by claiming to be the rightful interpreter of Nasser's legacy. Sadat responded by going outside the party structure to build political support among the traditional elites and landowners who had been marginalized under Nasser's rule. He also cultivated ties to the military, the security services, and influential people within the state ministries, all of whom shared a common distrust and antipathy for Sabri and his allies. The pursuit of an alternate base of support marked the beginning of Sadat's break with the left and the corresponding realignment of Egyptian politics. The conflict came to a head in May 1971, when Sabri's supporters were accused of conspiring to overthrow the government. This led to the arrest of ninety members of the Sabri faction and their removal from top positions in the government, the ruling party, and the military. Sadat also eliminated the "alternate power centers" within the state that had served as institutional bases of support for Sabri and his allies. These events came to be known as the Corrective Revolution.

The Corrective Revolution marked a significant reorientation of both Egypt's domestic and foreign policy. Rhetorically, Sadat committed his regime to abolishing the police-state tactics that had characterized the Nasser era and that were associated with Sadat's rivals. He also pledged greater liberalization of the political system and a respect for individual rights. The basic contours of the system, nonetheless, remained largely unchanged, at least in terms of the centrality of the state and the promotion of a populist nationalism. What did change, however, was the previous commitment to a socialist and secular vision of national development. This shift was evident in the adoption of more liberal economic polices (the *infitah*, or opening) which greatly benefited the business class, as well as a program of de-sequestration (reversal of land reform) to rectify the perceived ill treatment of landowners under the Nasser regime.[35] Sadat's new direction also entailed a new set of alliances with economic and religious elites as a bulwark against the left. This included a rapprochement with Saudi Arabia (which Nasser had initiated after the 1967 war), a decreased reliance on the Soviet Union, and an abandonment of Nasser's class politics.

Perhaps the most significant feature of this new orientation, however, was Sadat's promotion of conservative Islam. Although Nasser had used religion to provide legitimacy to his rule, Sadat embraced Islam with much greater fervor. More important, the interpretation of religion that would come to define Sadat's tenure differed dramatically from that of the Nasser era. Sadat's main concern was to provide a counterweight to the socialist ideas that continued to dominate Egyptian politics. To this end, he sought to construct a new political philosophy that linked Islam and Arab "civilizational values" to the government's program of economic liberalism.[36] He was also seeking to develop a basis of nationalist legitimacy that was more explicitly Islamic. Sadat consequently emphasized (and often conflated) the ideas of religious morality and Egyptian nationalism in his speeches and used these themes to reinforce traditional patterns of authority and social order.[37] The construction of an image of personal piety was a part of this strategy. Sadat was depicted as *"al-Rais al-Mumen"* (the believing president) and regularly had his participation in Friday prayers aired on state-run television. The regime's policies were also designed to cultivate a greater sense of religiosity among the population, reflecting the belief that a more religious population was a more obedient population. The government provided millions of dollars for Islamic education and promoted Islam through state-run television and radio. It also provided funding for the construction of thousands of mosques and granted favors (land, funds, television airtime) to popular sheikhs in return for their support.[38]

A key feature of this new direction was Sadat's active support for Islamic (and Islamist) groups at the expense of the political left. Although the expansion of Al-Azhar was an important part of this effort (about which more will be said below), so too was the rapprochement between Sadat and the Muslim Brotherhood. The Corrective Revolution had purged many of the leading leftists from positions of influence but did little to address the support for Nasser's socialist policies at the local level. Sadat's alliance with the Brotherhood was intended to provide a grassroots basis to his rule and to blunt opposition to the reversal of policies that helped the poor. The rapprochement between Sadat and the Brotherhood was mediated in 1971 by King Faisal of Saudi Arabia, Fouad Allam (the head of Egypt's State Security), and an Egyptian businessman and Sadat confidant named Osman Ahmed Osman. As part of a negotiated agreement, the Brotherhood agreed to renounce the use of violence and promised not to engage in anti-regime activities in exchange for its freedom and the right to continue its peaceful advocacy of Islam.[39] Many were also allowed to return from exile in Saudi Arabia and elsewhere. The Sadat regime also released thousands of political prisoners between 1971 and 1975. It used each release as an opportunity to highlight the torture and abuse of these individuals in order to expose the excesses of the Nasserist era.

The support of Islamic student groups (*jamaat*) on university campuses was another important feature of this effort to reshape Egyptian politics. The universities had been a primary arena of political activism and remained dominated by the Marxist groups that had developed under Nasser. Egypt's campuses were also the site of a series of protests during the 1968–73 period. As Rosefsky Wickham notes, this population had been "the most thoroughly socialized in the goals of Nasser's revolution and . . . were therefore the most disillusioned when its leaders appeared unable or unwilling to achieve them."[40] Consequently, leftist student groups took a lead role in the protests against the Sadat regime, arguing for more political freedom, greater social justice, and a more confrontational stance toward Israel. Sadat was concerned about the opposition of these groups and assumed that they were backed by pro-Soviet factions. The regime subsequently sought to undermine the influence of the leftist student groups in Egypt's universities and facilitated the growth of Islamist student organizations as part of this effort.

Prior to 1970, Islamists students were a minority on Egypt's campuses and had little if any influence in student politics. This changed after May 1971, when the regime decided to support the development of Islamist student organizations as an ideological counterweight to the left. Two important groups that emerged at this time were the Gama'at al-Shabab al-Islam (GSI, Youth of Islam Group) and al-Gama'a al-Islammiyya (GI, the Islamic Grouping; this is not the militant group of the same name), but there were others. The state-sponsored Youth Organization—an institution from the Nasser era—was also revived and given a new religious focus.[41] All of these groups were distinctly political in orientation and were defined by an anti-Marxist orientation. This was a sharp contrast to earlier Islamic student groups that had emphasized social and cultural activities. In the early 1970s, the government also turned a blind eye to the training camps run by Islamists, which served as schools for Islamic militancy. At the time, the Egyptian government saw the camps as little "more than an effective antidote to the Marxist ideology upheld by Communists and Nasserists."[42] The regime also increased its surveillance of leftist students and provided funds, and, some have argued, weapons to various Islamist organizations (see below). The government also spent a significant amount of money to promote religion on Egyptian campuses, and there are well-founded claims that the regime manipulated student union elections in the Islamists' favor.

The regime's support for Islamist student groups paid off. By the late 1970s, these organizations came to control a majority of the student unions throughout the university system, and in 1978 their candidates won the top positions in the national student union association. This represented a "sea change" in the culture and climate of the universities. As Muhammad Heikal described it, "Knowing they had the support of higher [government] authority, the Islamic students began to behave as if it was they who were running the universities. They decided what subjects were suitable to be taught, forcibly preventing, for example, lectures to be given on Darwinism. . . . [It] was clear that the religious students were not simply tolerated by the authorities but actively encouraged by them."[43]

The nature and extent of the government's support for the Islamic groups, however, remains a disputed point. Members of the Muslim Brotherhood, also called Muslim Brothers, who were involved in campus activism in the 1970s deny any overt assistance from the government but do concede a more open environment under Sadat, which allowed them to flourish.[44] Leftist activists, on the other hand, recall that the security services actively supported the election of Islamic candidates to student union offices. They did this, according to one former activist, by detaining leftist candidates in the midst of elections or by otherwise barring them from participation, both of which facilitated Islamist victories. There were also claims that security forces "used to arm Islamists," and that the number of Islamist groups "mushroomed" under the umbrella of state security.[45] Other independent reports note that the former governor of Asyut, Muhammad Osman Ismail, served as an intermediary between the Sadat government and the Islamist students on campuses in Upper Egypt, often providing them with both financing and instructions.[46]

The liberalization policies of the Sadat period also facilitated the dominance of a conservative Islam in Egyptian politics. By lifting some of the constraints on political expression, both official and unofficial Islamic groups were provided a greater voice in public affairs, ostensibly to support the government's new direction. This allowed groups such as the Muslim Brotherhood to engage in formerly prohibited activities, such as publishing newspapers and preaching, even if it did not confer upon them official status. It also afforded the establishment *ulema* new opportunities for promoting Islam in the public realm, something that Nasser would never have allowed. The liberalization of economic policies also allowed for a greater flow of funds from the Gulf countries, which financed Islamic companies and social service agencies run by the Muslim Brotherhood. Islamic investment companies with strong ties to the Brotherhood also emerged, all of which benefited from the oil boom of the early 1970s.

Sadat's strengthened ties with Saudi Arabia during this period were another important factor in reshaping the ideological context of Egyptian politics. Sadat effected the rapprochement between Egypt and its former rival in the early 1970s. The tilt toward Saudi Arabia and other conservative monarchies was an initial step in its broader alignment with the West. Sadat perceived the financial support that the Saudis could provide to Egypt as an essential means of developing the country economically. For their part, the Saudis were keen to eliminate the influence of Arab socialism in Egypt and to avoid the kind of conflict that defined the Nasser era, because "for them, Nasser was worse than Israel."[47] Thus began a period where the leadership of the Gulf countries began pouring money into the promotion of a conservative or Salafist Islam throughout the region and specifically in Egypt. The goal was to marginalize the left, to protect their economic interests, and to use religion to reify the existing economic and political order. This included financing Islamic groups and institutions, all of which had a lasting impact on Egyptian politics. As one journalist noted, "In 1971, when King Faisal of Saudi Arabia, at the behest of Sadat, offered the rector of al-Azhar, Dr. Abdel-Halim Mahmoud, $100 million for the campaign against Communism and atheism, and for the triumph of Islam, the political face of Egypt was transformed."[48]

The Sadat regime also involved the official religious establishment in the effort to redefine the ideological basis of the Egyptian state. Al-Azhar was ex-panded, with a new campus constructed with funds from the Saudi govern-ment. State funding for religious education through the Al-Azhar system was also increased, as was funding for religious publications produced by Al-Azhar and other religious institutions. These latter institutions included a reformed Supreme Council of Islamic Affairs, which defined and articulated the official interpretation of Islam for both state and society. The regime also initiated an antileftist campaign, which involved the *ulema* issuing a series of *fatwas* that equated communism with impiety and charged communists with having "no faith."[49] These efforts were all designed to stigmatize the socialist holdovers from the Nasser era and to use the population's intrinsic support of Islam as a means of strengthening their allegiance to state authority. The accusation of impiety inherent in such *fatwas* served as a dangerous precedent in the stig-matization of alternative ideas, a trend that would take an ominous turn in the Mubarak era when Islamists targeted secular thinkers on similar grounds.

Finally, the adoption of a new constitution in 1971 provided a greater role for Islam in Egyptian politics. Article 2 of the Constitution designated Islam as the official state religion, and *sharia* as "*a* principal source of legislation." Although the provision was vague, that *sharia* was mentioned so prominently in the consti-tution was itself significant, and it represented a victory of sorts for the Islamists. This provision was further amended in 1980 to make Islamic law "*the* princi-pal (or primary) source of legislation" (*al-masdar al-ra'isi*). The reintegration of Islam into Egypt's legal codes was further promoted by the National Assembly in the late 1970s. This was done in order to "bring Egyptian statutory law into total agreement with *Sharia* provisions," and was adopted largely under pressure from the Muslim Brotherhood.[50] In conceding these issues, Sadat completed the project of disembedding secular norms in Egyptian public life. Islam was now the official state religion, and both the political institutions of the country and the legal codes provided a means for the continued Islamization of the public sphere.

The October War of 1973 appeared to vindicate Sadat's turn toward conservative Islam and provided new legitimacy to the leader and his policies. Egypt's capture of Israeli positions across the Suez Canal helped shatter the myth of Israeli invincibility. It also allowed Egypt to claim victory despite significant losses and an indecisive end to the war. More to the point, the apparent victory was seen as a triumph of Islam. Although the war ended with a UN-brokered ceasefire, Egypt's initial success in crossing the Suez canal and the near-defeat of Israel was widely credited to Sadat's return to religion, a notion that the religious imagery surrounding the war did nothing to abate. The fighting was initiated during the holy month of Ramadan and was code-named "Operation Badr," an Islamic reference to war against infidels. It was even reported on national radio that angels had been fighting on behalf of the Arab armies.[51] The Saudi's embargo of oil to the West, which had a significant impact on the conflict, was further proof of the Arab world's newfound strength.

Sadat used this victory to press the policy initiatives that defined his presidency. These included the continued liberalization of economic policy associated with the *infitah*. These policies relaxed restrictions on foreign investment within Egypt, eased banking controls, and opened Egypt to the forces of the global economy. Sadat also pursued a limited program of political liberalization, which eased press censorship, freed political prisoners (mostly Muslim Brothers), and, in 1976, allowed for the creation of three political parties (left, right, and center). Although all were largely controlled by the state, competitive parliamentary elections did occur in 1976. The third policy initiative was the strategic realignment with the West and Sadat's famous overture to Israel. The signing of the Camp David Peace Accords in 1979 and the return of the Sinai Peninsula to Egyptian control were historic accomplishments. The peace agreement also marked a final break with the Nasserist legacy and the end of Egypt's leadership of the Arab nationalist movement. It was also very controversial. Not all viewed these events with favor—particularly Sadat's unilateral peace with Israel—and the contradictions inherent within these diverse policies would ultimately bring an end to Sadat's presidency.

## The Islamist Backlash

The regime's encouragement of Islamic groups proved to be a two-edged sword. Although the Muslim Brotherhood and the Islamic student groups were initially supportive of Sadat, they proved to be unreliable allies. The Islamists generally refrained from overt criticism of the regime until at least 1976. This was particularly true for the Brotherhood, which relied on the goodwill of the regime to continue rebuilding its grassroots network. The Brotherhood's deference to the government ended, however, with Sadat's trip to Israel in 1977 and with the advent of Sadat's close relations with the United States. The failure of Sadat's economic policies to raise living standards among the poor, despite the growth of a new commercial class, also generated significant discontent among the Islamists (as well as the population at large). The regime's reluctance to implement Islamic law fully was another point of contention with the Islamists. The subsequent reemergence of Islamic violence was a sign that the state had set in motion something that it was not able to control.

Signs of Islamist unrest were evident as early as 1974, when a number of cadets affiliated with a small Islamist group tried to take over the Technical Military Academy in Assyut. Although the action failed, it was undertaken in the hope of sparking a coup d'état, which the young militants perceived as necessary for the establishment of a truly Islamic state. A more significant incident was the 1977 abduction and assassination of Sheikh Hussein al-Dahabi, the minister of religious endowments. This was carried out by an organization known as Takfir wa Hijra (Repentance and Holy Flight). Both of these groups were led by former Muslim Brothers who endorsed the militancy by Sayyid Qutb and who had dissociated themselves from the Brotherhood's accommodationist mainstream.[52]

Sayyid Qutb, who was hanged by Nasser in 1967, was a leading ideologist of the radical wing of the Brotherhood. He produced much of his work while in Nasser's prisons in the late 1950s and early 1960s. Jailed in the 1954 crackdown, he (and other Muslim Brothers) were held in appalling conditions and savagely tortured. This experience radicalized Qutb and shaped his beliefs about the regime and the proper way to oppose it. At the core of Qutb's philosophy was the idea that both the government and society reflected a state of *jahilliya* (pre-Islamic ignorance) and that the use of violence in this context was not only legitimate but necessary. Qutb further argued that the government's actions—particularly its torture of fellow Muslims—demonstrated that these leaders were Muslim in name only. Similarly, the idolization of Nasser, the state, and the party meant that society as well as its leaders were worshiping something other than God. This was perceived as justifying the use of violence against the regime, since the prohibition on killing fellow Muslims did not apply to those who were *kafir* (unbelievers). Qutb's untimely death in 1967 meant that many of these ideas were never fully clarified. This left his philosophy open to interpretation, allowing a new generation of militants to conclude that *jihad* could be legitimately declared against anyone with differing beliefs.

The emergence of a new wave of Islamic militancy in the late 1970s was due in large measure to a generational split within the Muslim Brotherhood and the influence of Qutb's ideas on the younger generation. What Sadat had not realized during his negotiations with the Brotherhood in 1970 was that the organization was deeply divided between those who shared the accommodationist perspective of the older members, led by Hasan al-Hodeiby, and who had come to question the merits and efficacy of violence, and the younger members who were enamored of Qutb's writings and the advocacy of violent *jihad*.[53] Many of these younger supporters opposed accommodation with the Sadat regime and felt that the Brotherhood's newfound emphasis on *da'wa* (Islamic advocacy) was an ineffectual means of creating the Islamic society that they all desired.[54] As such, many of these younger cadres abandoned the Brotherhood in favor of the more radical groups that emerged during this time (see below). Moreover, Nasser's repression had created a radical core group that continued to believe that militant action was the only viable means of creating an Islamic state. Although the message of accommodation and peaceful change appealed to a majority of Brotherhood members—many of whom were aging and had spent many years in jail—it was less appealing to an alienated youth that was growing up in the urban landscape of 1970s Egypt.

The Islamic student groups that Sadat and his close associates had supported also turned against the regime as their disillusionment with the state turned into outright opposition. Some of these activists would later form the militant organizations of the 1980s and 1990s, which included al-Gama'a al-Islamiyya (The Islamic Group; this is the militant one) and al-Jihad (Holy War).[55] Other student activists would find alternative avenues of opposition, including the professional syndicates discussed in the next chapter. What radicalized the students were the same issues that turned the Brotherhood and others against the regime. On the one hand, there was discontent over the regime's failing economic policies and the lack of progress on such fundamental issues as education, housing, and transportation. The tensions created by the policies of economic liberalization—and the widening gap between rich and poor—boiled over in January 1977. Thousands rioted in the streets in response to the Egyptian government's cuts in subsidies for a range of consumer goods, which, in turn, were a response to demands by the IMF and World Bank. Although Sadat tried to characterize the unrest as a socialist plot, the uprising came to be known within Egypt as the "Revolution of the Hungry." On the other hand, Sadat's policies toward the West, particularly his overtures to Israel, similarly antagonized the Islamic students. Sadat's historic trip to Jerusalem in 1977 may have brought accolades from abroad but at home it opened him up to criticism from both right and left. The left felt he was betraying Nasser's legacy, while the Islamists felt he was betraying Islam. The end result was that the Islamist groups that had long benefited from the government's protection now "rebelled against the role [which] the regime had assigned them—that of counterbalancing the various forces of the left—and political Islam changed from being a functional supporter of the regime to posing the main threat to it."[56]

Sadat's policies had other unintended consequences, particularly for the official religious establishment and for Egypt's Coptic Christians. The state's use of Islam to sanction unpopular initiatives—the peace agreements with Israel and the elimination of the food subsidies—brought the credibility of establishment Islam into question. Although rank-and-file members of the official *ulema* were critical of these policies, the leadership went along with Sadat and provided the requisite *fatwas* needed to sanction both policies. Moreover, the tentative opening of political discourse had the unintended effect of breaking Al-Azhar's monopoly on religious interpretation. Islamic groups such as the Muslim Brotherhood and its more extreme counterparts emerged as alternative voices in the interpretation of Islam.[57] The criticisms leveled by these different groups against the state were thus extended to the *ulema* of Al-Azhar, in effect challenging the authority and legitimacy of both state and *ulema*.

The increasing assertiveness of the Islamists during the Sadat era also exacerbated tensions between Christians and Muslims. Many regarded this sectarian hostility as a direct result of the politicization of religion undertaken by the regime.[58] Nasser had promoted a conception of national identity that emphasized a common Arab origin, even if it was anti-Western and communalist in that regard. However, Sadat's embrace of Islam had reinforced the religious divisions of Egyptian society and undermined Nasser's secular conception of national identity. Moreover, specific policies intended to appease Islamic conservatives—such as the application of Islamic law to all Egyptians—created anxiety among Coptic Christians. Although debates over the nature of Egypt's communal life—should it be religious or secular?—were conducted in largely theoretical terms, it had very real implications for the Coptic minority, who became targets of discrimination and abuse.

The persecution of the Coptic minority was particularly evident in upper (that is, southern) Egypt, where the majority of Copts live. This took the form of a series of violent attacks on Orthodox churches and Coptic-owned properties in the mid-1970s and other instances of violence between sectarian (or religious) groups both in Upper Egypt and Cairo.[59] The persecution of the Christian minority also involved employment discrimination, which stoked a fear among this population of being relegated to the status of second-class citizens. The Orthodox Coptic Church was concerned that the government was doing little to protect the Christian community and was troubled by the government's overt support of Islam.[60] The constitutional amendments adopted in the early 1970s exacerbated Christian fears of persecution and of the many other implications associated with living in a state where Islamic law was a primary source of legislation.[61] The church consequently argued on several occasions that *sharia* should not apply to non-Muslims, particularly a proposed apostasy law that mandated execution for those convicted of unbelief. The Coptic Church also made regular complaints about constraints on the freedom of belief and laws from the Ottoman era that prohibited the construction (and renovation) of Christian churches without first obtaining presidential approval. Tensions between the Church and the Sadat regime became so frayed that Sadat arrested a number of priests and bishops in his infamous crackdown in September 1981 and even placed Pope Shenouda, head of the Orthodox Coptic Church, under house arrest.

The September 1981 crackdown targeted a wide array of groups and activists, religious and secular, leftist and Islamist. Although it was driven in large measure by the widespread opposition to the peace with Israel, of particular concern to the regime was the increased radicalism of the Islamic networks and the proliferation of militant groups. This created a situation to which the government had to respond. Sadat subsequently sought to reverse his earlier policies and tried both to depoliticize religion and to reign in the groups that his regime had earlier supported. The government took steps to ban the national student union and cut off their access to state funds. The regime also used the state-controlled media outlets and other means to discredit the Islamist students. In 1979, for example, Sadat gave a speech in which he denounced the student groups by name and argued that "those who wish to practice Islam can go to the mosques, and those who wish to engage in politics may do so through legal institutions."[62] He similarly sought to constrain the Muslim Brotherhood by shutting down its newspaper and by creating a new institution headed by the sheikh of Al-Azhar that had the authority to monitor and regulate all Muslim organizations outside the state apparatus.[63]

The regime also took a number of steps to gain greater control of the nation's mosques. This was a reaction to the concerns on the part of the security services that the Islamic militants were using the mosques as a basis for antigovernment activities. The regime nationalized a large number of private mosques and created regional offices of the Ministry of Religious Endowments in each of Egypt's twenty-six governates to monitor and control the sermons and personnel in all government mosques. These regional offices were also in charge of selecting *imams* and sermon topics, both of which were undertaken by local committees of official *ulema* and representatives of the ministry. Later legislation required preachers in private mosques to be "approved and licensed through the Ministry of Endowments."[64] Finally, Sadat reversed his earlier steps toward political liberalization in order to reign in the Islamic movement that he had helped to create. The end result was mayhem. As one analyst described it:

> When the influence of [Islamist] groups increased and the balance was tipped in their favor, Sadat retreated and tried to repress them. The magic of the believing President gave way to a policy of separating religion from the state. In the eyes of the masses and many intellectuals, his policies were depicted as a jumbled confusion: socialism, liberalism, religious faith, economic laissez-faire which benefited a few while the masses sank into a morass of inflation and poverty, oppression of liberals charged with left-wing views, subsequent repression of religious elements after exploiting them against liberals and scorn for the clergy.[65]

This was the context in which Sadat was assassinated. A month after the mass arrests, at the nadir of Sadat's popularity, the president was killed by four gunmen as he watched the annual military parade commemorate the 1973 war. The lead assassin, Lieutenant Khalid Islambouli, was a military officer from a family in the city of Mallawi in Upper Egypt. He was motivated in part by the fact that his brother, Muhammad, a student activist from the University of Asyut, was one of those detained (and mistreated) by Sadat's security services in the September crackdown. While conspiracy theories abound—for example, how did the militants infiltrate the army, obtain prohibited ammunition, and fulfill its deadly mission without inside help?—what is clear is that the men who carried out the attack were members of a cell within the Islamist militant organization al-Jihad. They were greatly influenced by the teachings of Sayyid Qutb and Abd al-Salam al-Farag, another Islamist thinker who echoed Qutb's radicalism and spoke of militant action as Islam's "neglected duty" (*al-farida al-gha'iba*). It was incumbent upon true Muslims, according to al-Farag, to take up arms against their misguided ruler and to establish a truly Islamic state by force.[66] Hence the irony of Sadat's demise. Those whom he had once supported had now turned on the believing president. On the day that was to mark the high point of his presidency, Sadat's presidency instead came to a sudden and shocking end.

## Conclusion

By the end of the Sadat era, religious politics in Egypt had taken on a life of its own. Islamist groups had emerged as the dominant opposition to the state, a movement ironically facilitated by the regime's own policies. Although Sadat had successfully marginalized the political left, he "had let the genie out of the bottle."[67] And with his assassination by members of al-Jihad, "the genie had struck him down."[68] Moreover, the orientations of both establishment Islam and the Islamist opposition were increasingly converging on a common message. Although there remained divisions over the question of violence—both within the Islamist movement and between the religious establishment and the militants—the interpretation of Islam advocated by the Brotherhood, the official *ulema*, and other Islamists were all influenced by Saudi Wahhabism, a byproduct of their common source of funding. As a result, these groups all sought a common goal of bringing "Egyptian society back to Islam" even if they differed over the question of who should ultimately rule.[69]

The end result was that Sadat's embrace of Islam had essentially resolved the debates over whether tradition was the problem or the solution to Egypt's ills, and whether the Egyptian state ought to be secular or religious. Unlike Atatürk's Turkey, Sadat's Egypt had abandoned the secular vision of national development, instead embracing a narrow interpretation of Islam as a means of sanctifying its military rule. The consequences were significant. Sadat's emphasis on religion as a basis of ideological support undermined the secular norms of the Nasser era and redefined the nation in explicitly Islamic terms. Sadat's policies also bred deep communal divisions within Egyptian society and relegated the Coptic community to second-class status. Moreover, the type of Islam that the state promoted was not liberal or modernist but rather represented a more illiberal (and ideological) interpretation of Islam that was more akin to al-Banna than to Abduh. Sadat's policies, moreover, helped to create a new generation of Islamic activists, many of whom were influenced by the radicalism of Sayyid Qutb and Abd al-Salam al-Farag. As such, the stage was set for the Mubarak era and a significant conflict with religious forces that were unleashed during the Sadat era. Illiberal Islam would be a fixture in Egyptian politics in the coming decades, though it would come to be used by both state and opposition for competing ends.

# CHAPTER THREE

# The Islamization of Egyptian Politics

The assassination of Anwar Sadat in 1981 and a simultaneous uprising in the city of Assyut demonstrated how dramatically Egypt's Islamic politics had spun out of control. The assassination was meant to spark a nationwide rebellion by other members of the militant group al-Jihad. A breakdown in communication, however, prevented the group's network from being activated and allowed the government to regain the initiative.[1] Government forces rounded up thousands of suspected militants and supporters, three hundred of whom were charged with murder and conspiracy to overthrow the government. The cases were tried in a military court that bordered on the surreal. Caged Islamists discussed their torture at the hands of the authorities and defiantly called for a return to Islam. The five immediate conspirators were sentenced to death and executed. Eighty-nine others were given prison sentences ranging from three years to life. Those who were acquitted left the courthouse chanting "the Islamic Revolution is coming," an ominous indication of things to come.[2]

Egyptian politics for the next thirty years was defined by the challenge of Islamic activism and the corresponding effort of the state to coopt the Islamist agenda. The government's strategy produced a confused, indeed often contradictory, set of policies. Although Hosni Mubarak, Sadat's successor, characterized his government as a bulwark against Islamic fundamentalism—and a defender of the secular vision of modernity—the government nonetheless promoted an illiberal vision of Islam in public life. The close association of religion and the state remained a hallmark of the Mubarak era, as the government sought to extend its hegemony into the realm of religious thought. It was the state, from the government's perspective, that was the authentic defender of Islamic tradition, not the Islamist opposition. The policies of the Mubarak regime subsequently emulated those of the Sadat era. The regime tolerated but constrained the Muslim Brotherhood and responded harshly to those who challenged the authority of the state. The Mubarak regime also used the religious establishment—including the *ulema* of Al-Azhar and the Dar al-Ifta (House of Fatwas) headed by the Grand Mufti—to sanction government policy. It similarly used the media, the educational system, and other institutions of the state to promote a more obedient Islam, one that was supportive of state authority and the continuation of military rule.

The regime's efforts to coopt Islam, however, greatly facilitated the Islamization of the public sphere. The government's struggle with the Islamist opposition was not defined by competing visions of society but rather by a competitive religious populism. Each group claimed to be the legitimate defender of faith and nation, and each used a Salafist interpretation of Islam to sanction its claims to power. Both state and opposition, in sum, promoted an exclusive vision of the nation—one that privileged an illiberal interpretation of Islamic tradition—even if they differed over who ought to govern. In pursuing this strategy, the Mubarak regime effectively ceded the ideological debate over religion and culture to the Islamists. Thus, even though the state was able to defeat the threat of Islamist militancy in the mid-1990s, the ideas that had animated the movement became increasingly institutionalized in Egyptian public schools, the media, and the official religious establishment. The state also took on the role of enforcing religious orthodoxy in Egyptian society. What subsequently emerged was an intolerant public sphere, where the persecution of Christians and dissenting religious opinions occurred without opposition from the state and often with its complicity. The regime, in short, finished what Anwar Sadat had started: it undermined the traditionally cosmopolitan basis of Egyptian society and the corresponding "rights . . . [to] participation and equal citizenship" that are the hallmark of an open society.[3]

## Mubarak and the Challenge of Islamic Politics

The Islamic politics of the Mubarak era did not occur in a vacuum. The support for the Islamist message was facilitated by widespread corruption in the government ministries and severe structural problems in Egyptian society. Rapid population growth coupled with an underperforming economy produced significant unemployment and underemployment. This, in turn, meant low living standards for the vast majority of Egyptians. The government's policies of economic liberalization, which continued under the Mubarak regime, benefited only a small segment of the population, while doing little to alleviate the country's endemic poverty. State policy, in short, perpetuated a socioeconomic environment conducive to political extremism and Islamic militancy.[4] The absence of state services in poor communities, moreover, was often filled by Islamist groups—funded predominantly by sources in the Gulf countries—which worked in neighborhoods abandoned by the state. The Muslim Brotherhood and other Islamic organizations subsequently came to run and manage an expansive network of schools, health clinics, and mosques throughout the country. Finally, the lack of political participation in Egypt—in many cases, its active suppression—forced political activity into alternate venues, particularly the professional syndicates and mosques, both of which became strongholds of Islamist sentiment.

The 1980s also witnessed an intense period of Islamic resurgence worldwide. Influenced by both the Iranian Revolution in 1979 and the Afghan war against the Soviets, political Islam emerged as an ideology capable of challenging existing patterns of political order. Political tracts by writers such as al-Banna, Qutb, and Mawlawna Mawdudi found a new generation receptive to their message. The subsequent resurgence of a politicized Islam combined the rejectionist ideas of these early Islamists with the anti-Western sentiment that had informed Nasser's Arab nationalism. Along with their political and economic critique of the status quo, the Islamists offered a positive (if nebulous) message that drew from the cultural and religious traditions of the population. This alternative was informed by fears that Islam was under attack from the West and that the *umma* (the Islamic community) was vulnerable because its leaders had strayed from the true path of Islam. The alternative that the Islamists advocated, then, was to restructure social and political life in accordance with the teachings of the Prophet, the Qur'an, and the Sunnah. Although the specifics of this "return to Islam" remained vague, the Islamists believed that it promised a more authentic alternative to Western models of development. It also resonated strongly with a dispossessed population. As such, Islam became a "potent ideology of popular dissent."[5]

## The Moderates

The Mubarak regime's initial approach to the Islamic resurgence was one of selective accommodation and repression. The state tolerated a limited amount of political activity while using the security services to respond to violence in kind. The goal was to temper the extremists and coopt the moderates, at least long enough for economic reforms to improve living standards. There was, however, never any intention of allowing the Islamist groups into the political arena or of otherwise sharing power with them. Like the early Nasserists, the Mubarak regime would not allow the Muslim Brotherhood a genuine role in governing. Rather, the state tolerated the organization's existence as long as it did not challenge the regime's right to rule. Although Mubarak created space in the religious and cultural spheres for those willing to cooperate with the state—and allowed groups like the Muslim Brotherhood to provide social services—the regime retained full control over what it perceived to be the core issues of economic and foreign policy.

The Muslim Brotherhood cooperated with the Mubarak government in the early 1980s and served as an intermediary between the state and the Islamic militants. The credibility of Al-Azhar had been diminished by its close association with the regime, and the state perceived a need for "a major force within political Islam" to communicate with the militants.[6] By accepting state authority, the Brotherhood was allowed to operate in a limited capacity. It published a newspaper, *al-Da'wa* (The Call), for a short period and continued to provide social services throughout the country. It was also allowed to run candidates in the 1984 parliamentary elections (in conjunction with the New Wafd Party) and again in the 1987 elections with the Socialist Labor and the Liberal parties. Despite the government's tampering with the election results, the Brotherhood was able to secure 17 seats in the 1984 elections and 36 seats in the 1987 elections.

The truly significant gains of the Brotherhood, however, were seen in Egypt's professional syndicates (professional guilds or associations). Many of the organization's younger leaders, such as Abdel Monem Abdul Fatooh and Esam al-Erian, had been active in Egypt's student politics during the 1970s. Unlike their more radical compatriots, however, they chose *not* to pursue a path of violence and opted instead to work within the system. In the 1980s, these young activists were able to bring their experience in university politics to the realm of the professional syndicates.[7] Capitalizing on the influx of university-educated Islamists entering the various professional fields, the former student leaders organized their potential supporters and ran candidates in the various syndicate elections. They made early gains in the Engineering Syndicate in the mid-1980s and by 1987 had won a majority of seats on that board.[8] They made similar inroads into the doctor's and pharmacist's associations and in 1992 they gained control of the board of the lawyer's syndicate. The Islamist victory in the lawyer's syndicate was of particular significance, since this association had historically been a bastion of liberal politics and a longtime symbol of secular modernity. It also demonstrated the strength of the Brotherhood and set the stage for "the confrontation [that] had to happen."[9]

This policy of "mutual accommodation" benefited the Brotherhood in its effort to reestablish itself as the leading Islamic organization in Egyptian society. Since it was unable to work openly in the political realm, it took its activism into the institutions of civil society. The organization's penetration in the professional syndicates and greatly expanded social service network significantly strengthened the group by offering it a new base of support. On the other hand, the state was able to use the Brotherhood as a moderating force in its struggle with Islamic militancy, which remained limited to a few groups in Upper Egypt. Accommodation, however, had its limits. The price of this arrangement was mutual infringement on the respective goals of both state and opposition: the state tolerated an Islamist actor in its midst, while the Brotherhood yielded to the state's demand for stability.[10] Members of the Mubarak regime, especially in the security services, were uncomfortable with this tacit alliance. Moreover, the government was never willing to recognize the Brotherhood as a legal political party or as a competitor in an open political environment. The regime was also concerned by the Brotherhood's gains in the syndicates. The Muslim Brotherhood, for its part, was disgruntled with the treatment it received from the regime. Its members remained under surveillance and were subject to arrest or detention by the security forces. Moreover, many former supporters of the Brotherhood split with the organization over this policy of accommodation; they either created their own political organizations or joined more militant opposition groups.

The Cairo earthquake of 1992 brought many of these tensions to the surface. In the aftermath of the quake—which occurred after government offices had closed for the weekend—the doctor's syndicate and the engineering syndicate quickly mobilized to respond to the crisis. They provided medical treatment, food, and temporary shelters for thousands of displaced people in the hardest-hit neighborhoods. The engineers also began inspecting damaged buildings to determine whether it was safe for their inhabitants to return. Both groups also provided money to those displaced by the catastrophe and to the families of those who had died. The government's response, on the other hand, was slow and ineffective. Unable to match the efforts of the Islamists and concerned about its poor showing, the government ordered the syndicates to cease their activities. It later sent troops into one neighborhood to tear down the shelters that had been constructed and took control of all private donations provided for relief efforts. It also passed a law that prohibited independent groups from receiving funds from abroad without prior government authorization.[11]

These events demonstrated the limits of accommodation and the government's ultimate refusal to tolerate a genuine alternative to its authority. The Mubarak regime's willingness to allow the Brotherhood to operate was premised on the organization's acquiescence and deference to the state on all matters of policy, in exchange for which the state allowed the organization to promote its vision of Islam. The Brotherhood's success in the syndicates and the parliamentary elections, however, represented a nascent threat to the state's monopoly on political control. It also highlighted a basic conflict between the state and the Brotherhood; the latter wanted greater political participation, while the former sought to maintain its monopoly on political power. This divergence of interests also contributed to a growing split within Al-Azhar and other elements of the official religious establishment. Although the leadership of these institutions tended to support the state, the Brotherhood had many sympathizers among the rank-and-file *ulema*. These basic contradictions became more apparent as the political violence increased in the late 1980s and early 1990s and the government's accommodation of the Brotherhood completely unraveled.

## The Extremists

The early 1980s were relatively quiet in Egypt, but violence returned with a vengeance in the late 1980s and early 1990s. This began with a series of attacks on Coptic Christians in Upper Egypt but escalated when militant groups began targeting government officials, particularly those involved in the security services. The violence increased dramatically in the early 1990s as militants attacked tourists, public officials, and secular intellectuals. The government's difficulty in responding to this violence was due both to the profusion of groups and to their informal organization. In all, there were thirty or forty different militant groups, most of which grew out of the campus activism of the 1970s.[12] After Sadat banned Islamists from campus activities, the student activists, having been forced out of the universities, took their message of Islamic reform to the population at large. Some engaged in proselytism or joined the Muslim Brotherhood, but others embraced violent extremism. Most Egyptians did not agree with the Islamists' puritanical views on morality, but their critique of government corruption, the lack of democracy, and the authoritarian tendencies of the state all resonated with a disaffected population. As one Egyptian phrased it, "People don't sympathize with the Islamic Group because they love it, but because they hate the government."[13]

These different militant factions were loosely organized under the leadership of al-Jihad and al-Gama'a al-Islamiyya. Al-Gama'a had its roots in the student movement in Upper Egypt during the 1970s, while the leadership of al-Jihad was drawn primarily from Cairo and Alexandria. Although these were distinct organizations, they did coordinate in areas of propaganda, operations, and finance. This somewhat wary cooperation began when the leaders of the two groups were imprisoned after Sadat's assassination. Although the militants differed on tactics—al-Jihad targeted political elites, while al-Gama'a attacked lower level state officials, police, and tourists—they shared a similar philosophy. This derived from Sayyid Qutb's argument that the government, despite being under the control of Muslims, was un-Islamic in its very nature. This was evident by the regime's continued repression of fellow Muslims, its alliances with the West, and its refusal to fully implement *sharia*, among other things. Despite the Mubarak regime's claims to religious piety, the Islamists viewed the government as an obstacle to the Islamic revolution they were advocating. From the militant's perspective, violence against the state was not only permissible, it was also a duty.[14] These ideas were a warrant for violence and a call to action.

The Soviet invasion of Afghanistan in 1979 and the subsequent war had an enormous impact on the capability and direction of these groups. The United States and Saudi Arabia provided significant funding and training for the *mujahedin* who were fighting the Soviet occupation. Working with the Inter-Service Intelligence (ISI) agency of Pakistan, the U.S. Central Intelligence Agency provided upwards of $6 billion in arms, equipment, and training over the course of ten years. This financial commitment was matched by the Saudi government, which viewed the threat of communism in similarly dire terms.[15] Additional contributions came from wealthy Gulf Arabs and others through an international fundraising network established during the war. These resources created the training camps, support systems, and operations for the largest covert war in history. It also created a truly international military network.

For its part, the Egyptian government—like other Arab governments—actively encouraged young men to join the *jihad* in Afghanistan. The regime's motives were mixed. On the one hand, the war in Afghanistan was part of the Cold War rivalry and an important front in containing Soviet expansionism in the region. On the other hand, Egyptian officials hoped to redirect the focus of their Islamists to an outside enemy. Hence, the regime was willing to release some militants who were then in prison if they would agree to leave for Afghanistan. The government assumed that many of these young radicals would not return. The Muslim Brotherhood also supported the *jihad* by recruiting volunteers and arranging their passage to Pakistan.[16] Several training camps were set up by the Brotherhood in the region to train the "Afghan Arabs" in fighting techniques and the use of modern weaponry. An integral part of this training was a process of indoctrination, where the basic tenets of militant (and Wahhabist) Islam were promoted by Islamic preachers associated with the war effort.

Estimates regarding the number of Egyptians who joined the fight range from several hundred to several thousand.[17] All agree, however, that they were coordinated largely by Islamist organizations. A number of the militant groups, particularly al-Jihad, saw this as an opportunity to rebuild their organizations after the repression stemming from the Sadat assassination. Consequently, many who had been jailed for their role in the events of 1981 left for Afghanistan immediately upon their release. This included among others, Ayman al-Zawahiri, leader of al-Jihad and future advisor to Osama bin Laden. Omar Abdel Rahman, the spiritual head of al-Gama'a who was commonly known as the "Blind Sheikh," was another participant in the broader effort. The Afghan war also provided the impetus for the creation of an international financial network for *jihadi* groups. Fundraising organizations were created with branches in Western capitals and the Middle East to funnel money into Islamic militancy. When the war ended, however, these networks and activists continued to operate and began redirecting their focus to other venues. As one former government official noted, when the war ended, "the movement [began] looking for a cause, [and] the militants for something to do."[18]

The fallout from the Afghan war thus contributed to a new level of conflict between the Egyptian militants and the state. As the Afghan war wound down and many of those who fought returned to their native countries, the capacity of both al-Jihad and al-Gama'a increased dramatically. So, too, did the level of violence. Many of these returning combatants had been trained in explosives and guerrilla tactics in Afghanistan. Their expertise was now being turned on the regime, just as happened in Algeria, Kashmir, and Chechnya. Moreover, the Egyptian military was largely unprepared to deal with this new level of expertise and commitment. Unlike those radicals who had never left Egypt, these men knew what they were doing. The attempted assassination of Interior Minister Zaki Badr in 1989 was the first vivid example of what the security services now faced. Although the attack failed, the use of explosives detonated by remote control demonstrated a level of sophistication that had not existed earlier in the decade. Of equal concern was the international network that gave these groups financial and logistical support, a situation created, somewhat ironically, by the U.S., Saudi, and Pakistani intelligence agencies.

The escalation of the conflict between the state and the militants began in early 1990 with a series of provocations by Islamic activists. Although some actions were nonviolent—a peaceful march by al-Gama'a through a Cairo slum, for example—others were more aggressive, including a number of anti-Christian riots and attacks on churches in Upper Egypt. The government responded by going on the offensive: it assassinated the spokesman of al-Gama'a on the streets of Cairo and sent its spiritual leader, Sheikh Omar Abdel Rahman, into exile.[19] Al-Gama'a retaliated by assassinating Rifaat Mahgoub, the speaker of the National Assembly. After a year and a half of relative quiet—during which time the Gulf War occurred and the Algerian military intervened in its parliamentary elections—Islamic violence escalated once again. In the spring of 1992, thirteen Christians in Upper Egypt were slaughtered by a small faction; just a few months later, Farag Foda, a leading secular intellectual, was assassinated. Although these events did little to provoke the government, it was the attack on foreign tourists in the autumn (and the announcement by al-Gama'a to undertake a concerted campaign against Western tourism) that prompted the government to strike back.[20]

The government offensive began in earnest in December 1992—two months after the earthquake in Cairo—when the Mubarak regime went after a stronghold of al-Gama'a in the heart of Cairo. Al-Gama'a had taken over the residential district of Imbaba, a neglected slum area along the Nile with more than a million inhabitants. Al-Gama'a was providing basic social services to the residents of Imbaba and had, for all practical purposes, become the governing authority in the district. Essentially, it had created a "state within a state." The urban district had also served as a basis for the group's operations, which at this point predominantly entailed proselytism and protests, although the organization did have a military wing committed to violent action. From the regime's perspective, this situation was intolerable. It represented a direct challenge the government's authority and highlighted the inability of the state to govern the entire country. Government troops sealed off the area for five weeks and sent fifteen thousand soldiers into the district to search for Islamic militants and their supporters house by house.

The regime's internal security services continued to raid villages and "popular" (that is, poor) neighborhoods throughout 1993 in an effort to destroy the militant networks. Thousands of people were arrested or detained without charge, and many were tortured and killed in police custody. Despite government gains, however, both al-Gama'a and al-Jihad continued to operate. The groups made several assassination attempts on government officials, local police officers, and security officers and engaged in violent attacks on Coptic Christians. Militants targeted Coptic businesses to steal their money and to strike at the cosmopolitan fabric of Egyptian society. Some of the more high-profile attacks included a failed assassination attempts on Interior Minister Hassan al Alfi and Prime Minster Atef Sedky. The attack on Sedky proved disastrous, as it claimed the life of a local schoolgirl, which the state media outlets covered extensively. There could be no doubt: violence was escalating, and the government didn't seem to have much in the way of an answer.[21]

The government response to the conflict was to use increasingly brutal tactics to eradicate the extremists and their supporters. Relying on the emergency laws enacted in the aftermath of Sadat's assassination that suspended constitutionally protected individual rights, the government arrested and detained without charge "tens if not hundreds of thousands of Egyptians."[22] Many were held without trial for several years, while those who did face charges were tried in military courts. The use of the military court system gave the government greater control over the process. They could ensure convictions, limit the rights of appeal, and, in some instances, hasten executions. The military court system also had more lenient rules of evidence and allowed confessions induced by torture. The arrest and torture of family members of suspected militants—"hostage taking," it was called—was also a common practice used to force suspected militants to turn themselves in. This use of torture as a tool of regular police work was extremely widespread.[23]

The government also targeted civil society actors and used the threat of terrorism to place tighter controls on moderate opposition groups, religious and secular alike. The government harassed journalists, human rights monitors, and lawyers associated with Islamist causes.[24] The Mubarak regime passed a law designed to undermine the control of the professional syndicates by the Muslim Brotherhood. It provided the government with the power to appoint board members for the professional syndicates in instances where the electoral turnout did not reach certain levels (50 percent in an initial round of voting, 33 percent in a subsequent round). Since virtually all syndicate elections fell far short of these levels, the law in effect gave the government the ability to overturn the results of such elections.[25] The government also passed a law barring the political activities of groups that had not been registered as political parties and cracked down on the activities of the Muslim Brotherhood. In a further step to contain Islamist groups, the regime announced that it would "nationalize" the country's 140,000 private mosques and place them under the direct control of the Ministry of Religious Endowments.[26] This step was taken in an effort to eliminate the institutional basis of the radical Islamists and deprive them of a forum from which they could criticize the government. As one government sheikh noted, "Exercising control over all mosques is meant to guarantee that the sermons delivered therein are in strict compliance with true Islamic teachings."[27]

By late 1994 the government's heavy-handed tactics had begun to pay off. Several key leaders of the militant movement were either captured or assassinated, and the security sweeps of the previous two years had removed many activists from operation, diminishing the militant network's effectiveness.[28] By 1995, the fighting had been effectively isolated to the remote areas of Upper Egypt, where the conflict "degenerated into the timeless politics of vengeance and vendettas, an endless cycle of killings and reprisals."[29] Within a year, the situation had largely stabilized, and the government was able to declare victory and announce that it had gained "full control" over its territory.[30] Militant activity continued, though, with two attacks in September and November 1997, the latter of which was a gruesome attack on tourists in Luxor that left sixty-three dead. In this instance, six men associated with a splinter faction of al-Gama'a slaughtered European and Japanese tourists as they arrived at the Temple of Hatshepsut, a famous destination in Luxor near the famed Valley of the Kings.

Far from marking a resurgence of the conflict, however, the 1997 Luxor attack marked the end of the war. The use of violence in such an indiscriminate and barbaric manner undermined popular support for the Islamist movement. As long as the militants limited their attacks to government officials and the security services, the population was to varying degrees supportive. When the Islamists shifted tactics, though, and targeted foreign tourists and Egyptian civilians, popular support rapidly plummeted. This was due in part to the detrimental impact that the decline in tourism revenues had on the livelihood of ordinary Egyptians, particularly in Upper Egypt. However, it was also that most Egyptians simply did not see such killing as legitimate, regardless of the theoretical arguments. The targeting of unarmed tourists, in particular, was morally repugnant to most Egyptians, as it did not strike them as consistent with the teachings of Islam. It was largely in response to these issues that imprisoned members of al-Gama'a distanced themselves from the 1997 Luxor attack, reiterated their calls for a ceasefire, and ultimately rejected the use of violence as a legitimate means of pursuing their agenda.[31] This rejection of violence was subsequently elaborated in a series of books written by members of al-Gama'a and published in the late 1990s. Over thirteen hundred people had been killed in the fighting between 1990 and 1997, and more than seventeen thousand remained in custody.[32]

## The Official Ulema

Although the state was able to deal with the security threat posed by the militants, the ideological challenge proved more difficult. Particularly as the violence escalated, the regime's tactics greatly undermined its own credibility. Moreover, the ability of the official *ulema* to blunt the Islamist critique was limited by its earlier support of unpopular policies during the Sadat era. By the early 1990s, however, the religious establishment was increasingly able to offer a successful critique of Islamist militancy.[33] This had much to do with the Islamists' willingness to use violence against civilians. Although the Islamist message largely resonated with the population—particularly its critique of the government— the philosophical basis of the militant violence decidedly did not. Second, the militant groups were not a guerrilla movement per se, and they never had broad popular support. It was not difficult, therefore, to characterize these militant young men as a threat not simply to the state but also to the nation. Third, and most important, the religious establishment used the conflict between the state and the militants to distance themselves from the regime and attend to its own credibility issue. By asserting a degree of independence, members of the official *ulema*, led by Gad al-Haq, the sheikh of Al-Azhar in the early 1990s, appeared to be more reliable commentators on religious and political matters.[34]

How this transformation occurred is significant. When the *ulema* defended government policies in the 1960s and 1970s, they were perceived as puppets of the regime. This willingness of the religious leadership to go along with the government created a split within Al-Azhar between those who supported the government and the rank and file, who largely did not. Although this division carried forward into the 1980s and 1990s, the balance shifted toward those who were sympathetic to the Islamist opposition. Islamist sympathizers infiltrated the institution and took it over from within.[35] This trend was also evident in other institutions such as the judiciary and the Ministry of Education, which meant that Islamist ideas were increasingly present in the public school curriculum.[36] Although the religious scholars within the official establishment may have opposed the militants' use of violence, they generally agreed with the Islamist vision of social order and had strong ties to the Muslim Brotherhood. Their theological conservatism, moreover, was increasingly represented in the religious leadership, who pursued a more assertive relationship with the regime. Consequently, when the Mubarak government enlisted the *ulema* in its battle with the militants, it had the unintended consequence of empowering (and emboldening) an official religious establishment whose views on the role of religion in public life did not differ greatly from those of the Islamists who were challenging the regime.

Despite differences between the government and the religious leadership—and divisions between the mufti of Egypt and the sheikh of Al-Azhar—these groups found common cause in their shared opposition to the militants. The Mubarak regime needed the official *ulema* to counter the religious critique of the militants, while the leadership of Al-Azhar needed to address the militants' challenge to its authority. The religious leadership was thus willing to work with the regime in order to reassert its role as the ultimate arbiter of Islam.[37] A tacit agreement was eventually struck between the regime and Gad al-Haq in 1992: the sheikh of Al-Azhar would support the government in opposition to the militants, and in exchange the conservative *ulema* would be granted greater opportunity to express their beliefs.[38] The official *ulema* offered a theological critique of the militants, in particular their use of violence against fellow Muslims. They argued that the radicals' ideas were based on a fundamental misreading of the Qur'an and the Sunnah. In return for its cooperation, the Mubarak government provided significant resources and a degree of independence to Al-Azhar and the Ministry of Religious Endowments. As a result, a wide spectrum of conservative *ulema* were able to promote a depoliticized Islamist worldview through state-controlled radio and television, in government mosques and pub-lic schools, and through other means. This also validated Al-Azhar's position as the ultimate arbiter and interpreter of Islamic tradition.[39]

The forum that was provided to these religious leaders, however, was not always used to benefit the regime. In April 1993, for example, a group of *ulema* issued a report criticizing *both* the militant violence *and* the repression of the security services. It also called on the Mubarak government to release activists then in detention and to negotiate with the Islamist opposition. Similarly, in 1994, Gad al-Haq attributed the rise of Islamic extremism to the state's manipu-lation and control of religious affairs, implicitly arguing for a freer hand in reli-gious interpretation. He also became less willing to issue blanket condemnations of attacks on tourists and Copts, focusing instead on issues of public morality. In taking these steps, the *ulema* were presenting themselves as an alternative to both Islamic extremists and the state.[40] This allowed the *ulema* to develop an agenda of their own, albeit one that expressed the Islamist call for a reform of society and a "return to religion." The religious authorities had come a long way from their defense of Arab nationalism and socialism.

The result of Egypt's conflict between the state security forces and the Islamic militants, then, was highly ambivalent. Although Islamic militants were removed as a threat to the government—the Mubarak regime remained in power—the Islamist vision of social life became further entrenched in Egypt's religious es-tablishment, the media, and education. Moreover, the conflict led to a greater Islamization of political discourse and, subsequently, to greater Islamization of the public sphere. The regime's alliance with the religious establishment pro-vided a greater degree of autonomy to the conservative *ulema* and reinforced their position as the ultimate arbiter of orthodox Islam. Large numbers of Is-lamist sympathizers had also assumed influential positions within Al-Azhar's dif-ferent institutions, the judiciary, and other government institutions. In short, militant Islam had been dealt a blow, but the conflict "precipitated a revival in society,"[41] because members of the official religious establishment were working to create a more explicitly Islamic nation. As Ajami aptly phrased it,

> Tough police work was one side of the response to the terror of the Islamists; the other was a discernible retreat on the part of the regime from secular politics and culture. Historically the agent of social change, the one great instrument for transforming this old land and pushing it along, the state now seemed to slip into a cynical bargain with some devoted enemies of the secular idea. It granted these

preachers and activists cultural space as long as the more strictly political domain (the police power of the regime, its hegemony over defense and foreign affairs) was left to it.[42]

## State and Society: The Islamization of Egyptian Politics

The policies of the Sadat and Mubarak regime had an enormous impact upon Egypt's ideological politics. Although ostensibly opposed to the Islamist vision of society, the efforts by both Sadat and Mubarak to coopt the discourse of conservative Islam helped to normalize the exclusive vision of religion and society that the Islamists advocated. This trend represented a sharp break with both the secular-oriented Nasser period and the reformist Islam of the liberal era. It also greatly affected the role of women in society, as the misogynistic elements of Saudi culture became equated with Islamic tradition. Of equal concern was the tendency of government support for an exclusive vision of social life to undermine the traditional tolerance and cosmopolitanism of Egyptian society. Although Egypt was a leading political and intellectual force in the early twentieth century—it had produced much of the Arab world's literature, film, and modernist thought—this was no longer the case. Rather, Saudia Arabia now set the cultural agenda of the region, a "catastrophe" for Arab thought and culture, according to one commentator.[43]

The fallout from these policies was evident in three key areas. The first was the resurrection of longstanding debates over the role of religion in public life. Although the "secular/integralist" debate was not new, it had a very different outcome in the post-oil boom years of the Mubarak era than in the Nasser period. Related to this was the intellectual persecution and infringements on artistic freedom that characterized the 1990s. The state's support for an illiberal rendering of religious tradition created a climate in which those with dissenting opinions—religious or political—became targets of attack. Moreover, those carrying out such attacks were commonly associated with or had some degree of support from state institutions. Finally, the persecution of the Christian minority and the communalization of Egyptian politics were other important consequences of the government's religious politics. Religious minorities found themselves to be increasingly persecuted in their own country and suffered systematic harassment from government officials. Instead of providing a common basis of citizenship, the Mubarak regime's cynical bargain with Salafist Islam led to the political fragmentation of Egyptian society. The state's compromise with conservative religion, in short, made the country's historic commitments to an inclusive national identity and religious tolerance the first victim of the struggle to maintain power.

### Constructing Modernity: The Secular/Integralist Debate

At the heart of the Islamist challenge is the question of how to define the Egyptian nation. At issue is the conflict between those who advocate a society based upon a Salafiyya (or Islamist) vision of social order—defined by the establishment of an Islamic state and the full application of *sharia*—and those who embrace a secular or liberal vision of modernity. The premises of this debate are identical to that of discourse about the open and closed societies. The secular position is premised on a commitment to liberal norms of tolerance, inclusion, and individual freedom. The integralist (or Islamist) position, on the other hand, promotes an exclusive vision of society defined by a high degree of cultural uniformity. Although this may understandably be interpreted as a communitarian approach to social order, it nonetheless calls on the state to enforce religious belief and practice.[44] The religious motifs of the dominant community, moreover, inform the integralist vision of the community and in practice have provided a basis for discriminating against dissenting opinions, whether religious or political. These competing visions of social order—and of modernity—have been at odds in Egyptian politics for much of the last century.

As discussed in the previous chapter, the liberal and secular reformers dominated this debate throughout much of the early and mid-twentieth century. These early religious reformers sought to bring the light of reason to the Islamic tradition and reinterpret it for a modern context. The goal was to purge the unquestioning obedience to religious authority—and the lack of critical thinking associated with it—that these reformers felt had severely hindered Arab development. They also argued that religion ought to be relegated to the private sphere and that science and critical thinking ought to be a central feature of public education. The premise behind this argument was that only by reforming religion and society along secular lines could Arab societies revitalize society and challenge Western colonial dominance. The more culturally conservative elements in Egyptian society rejected this reasoning, seeing the European influence as an intrusion in traditional Egyptian life. Arabs were not held back by the presence of Islamic tradition but rather by their effort to emulate the West.

These debates were resurrected in the 1990s in the midst of the militant violence.[45] The first and last public forum on this debate occurred during the

Cairo Book Fair in 1992 and hosted panelists from the Muslim Brotherhood, Al-Azhar, and secular organizations. At issue in this debate were the relative merits of an Islamic state as opposed to a secular state. The basic split between Egypt's Islamists and secular intellectuals had changed little since the debates in the 1950s between Nasser and the Muslim Brotherhood. As in those earlier years, the secular argument generally took one of two approaches. The first was to argue that nowhere in the Qur'an does it specify a particular form of government, meaning that a secular form is consistent with Islamic tradition. This is reminiscent of Khalid Muhammad Khalid's argument from the 1950s. Secularists also claimed that the independence of social life from the dominance of any institutionalized religion is important, if for no other reason than that the diversity of the national community requires it. The Wafd Party's slogan in the early part of the twentieth century, "Religion belongs to God, the homeland belongs to all" (*"al-din li-Lah, wa al-watan li al-jami"*) reflects the premise that social harmony is best ensured when religion is relegated to the private sphere.[46] It was not that the early Wafdists were necessarily hostile to religion. Rather, they were concerned about the politicization of ecclesiastic authorities, and the manipulation of religion by political actors, particularly the monarchy.

If this first issue raises concerns about the influence of religion on politics, a second addresses the effect of politics on religion. Contemporary authors such as Muhammad Said al-Ashmawy are deeply disturbed over the politicization of Islam. Although he eschews the label of secular, Ashmawy's position is premised on the belief that religion, and specifically Islam, deals fundamentally with human spirituality, not with politics.[47] During the 1990s, he argued that the proper realm of religion is that of conscience and that the transformative quality of faith comes from within. Moreover, the fundamental nature of religion is universal and inclusive, while the essence of politics is "particular, tribal and limited in space and time."[48] Faith, from this perspective, can never be imposed or coerced, so defining the proper approach to God is not the legitimate purview of any government. Like John Locke and Roger Williams, Ashmawy believes that political authority and religious authority are best kept apart.

Problems arise when either political or ecclesiastical authorities attempt to use the religious impulse for political ends. According to Ashmawy, the politicization of religion, just like the sacralization of politics, tends to transform religion into ideology and hence into a means of control. It also detracts from religion's ability to provide the spiritual path that it is intended to be and must be. He goes on to argue that Islam in its original form was a largely apolitical religion, and he is critical of the oft-repeated argument that Islam governs all facets of life. Ashmawy sees in this argument an ideology, not the "real" Islam whose concern is with spiritual and ethical issues.[49] Although the tradition may have a long history of politicization, this reflects the dominance of politics, not the essence of the religion. Individuals such as Ashmawy also fear the abuse of power that is inherent in any state that claims to be the "custodian of the faith."[50] Human rights abuses and infringements on freedom of belief are characteristic of states that do just this. Once *sharia* is established, the secularists argue, any opposition to the government could be equated with heresy, and dissent would "become an insolence in the face of God's law . . . that has to be punished by applying the appropriate *hadd* [Qur'anic punishment]."[51] As Farag Foda asked during the 1992 panel discussion at the Cairo Book Fair, "Which of the contemporary Islamic states, Iran or the Sudan, would you want us to take as a model?"[52]

The contemporary proponents of an Islamic state—the Islamists or "integralists"—reject these arguments. Like their predecessors in earlier decades, these activists believe that a close affiliation between religion and politics is not just preferable but also essential. The core of their argument lies in the claims that Islam has never known a distinction between public and private realms and that all aspects of human existence are meant to be regulated by God's Will as defined in the Qur'an, the Sunnah (example of the Prophet), and *sharia*. Their basic assumption is that without religion, there can be no normative basis to political life and, hence, no morality. The integralist position also argues that secularism is a Western phenomenon that emerged from the European experience of a dominant Roman Catholic Church. Within Islam, the argument goes, the situation is completely different. There is no formal church, no conflict between religion and science, and no distinction made between the spiritual and material realms. Hence, secularism is simply not applicable to Islamic society.[53]

It is important to note, however, that secularism from this perspective is understood as either a matter of unbelief (*kufr*) or active hostility to religion. The alternative to an Islamic state from this view is not a "civil state" but rather an *irreligious* one. The separation of religion and state—even the advocacy of such a separation—is consequently seen as apostasy and not a simple matter of disagreement.[54] Moreover, the Islamists take issue with the claims that an Islamic state would be discriminatory or that a secular state would be more effective in providing an inclusive basis for public life. On the contrary, they argue that Islam, unlike other religions, has a history of tolerance, so that the fears that an

Islamic state would infringe on the rights of minority populations are simply unfounded. As Mamoun al-Hodeiby, the former head of the Muslim Brotherhood, has remarked, Islam is inherently respectful of the rights and liberties of religious minorities; therefore, the Coptic Christians in Egypt "are the happiest minority in the world."[55]

These debates, moreover, are much influenced by the historical legacy of colonialism. Consequently, Islamists tend to view such matters as human rights, secularism, and even democracy as foreign values imported from a culturally dominant and intrusive West. These ideals not only displace indigenous values but, from the Islamist (or integralist) perspective, also represent "a violation of their right to community."[56] Alternative interpretations of Islam, moreover, are commonly stigmatized as either heresy or *bida* (innovation). Hence, that secularism is perceived as either an import from the West or a sign of unbelief has meant that secular intellectuals are open to the charge of being either *"kafir"* (unbelievers) or enemies of Islam. Consequently, they are seen as being culturally inauthentic at best and deserving of death at worst.

### The Struggle to Define Orthodoxy in Public Life: The Assault on Intellectual Freedom

The events of the 1990s greatly affected the debate over the role of religion in public life, though not in a way that most observers assume. Although the government may have opposed the Islamist militants—and their claim to rule—it similarly worked against the secular vision of society. As we have seen, the state sought to coopt, not confront, the Islamist worldview, and it defined its version of Egyptian nationalism in distinctly religious terms. This was not an aberration, moreover, but went to the heart of the modern state project in Egypt: media, education, and the production of an official Islam by state institutions all contributed to the close association of Islam and the Egyptian national identity.[57] By promoting an overtly Islamic vision of public life—and tying state authority to religious tradition—the Sadat and Mubarak regimes sought to situate their rule in a moral framework that linked ruler and ruled in a web of religious obligation. In doing so, however, it essentially validated the Islamist arguments about religion and public life at the expense of the secular alternative. This was not, however, a retreat into tradition but rather a vision of modernity that drew heavily, if selectively, from the cultural resources of the country's religious heritage.

Although the state sought to define "normal religion," it was able to do so with only "varying degrees of success."[58] The promotion of Islam by both the

Mubarak and Sadat regimes—and the state's ability to make binding determinations on religious authenticity—was limited by the regimes' dependence on the official *ulema*. This created an opening for conservative Islamists to influence the debate over the nature of Egyptian society. It also confirmed the most dire warnings issued by Ashmawy and others. By setting the state up as the custodian of the faith—and allowing state institutions to become the arbiters of religious belief—dissent of all sorts became subject to persecution. This was most clearly evident in a series of court cases brought against secular intellectuals in the 1990s that redefined the limits of free thought in the public sphere. These legal cases (and corresponding public relations campaigns) were initiated by Islamist lawyers and journalists who targeted intellectual work that the Islamists deemed to be violations of public morality. These Islamic activists relied, though, on conservative *ulema* within state institutions to either ban or censor such work and sympathetic judges to rule in their favor. In effect, the state machinery was forced to uphold the religious ideas that the government was promoting as a basis of its legitimacy.

The attacks on intellectual and artistic freedom took place largely through the court system, though they were associated with *ulema* within Al-Azhar who had the authority to ban books, films, music, and other forms of creative expression. This power was exercised through the Academy for Islamic Research (*Majma al-Buhuth al-Islamiyya*),[59] an institution within Al-Azhar that has historically reviewed books and films with religious content. The Mubarak regime expanded Al-Azhar's jurisdiction in this area in a 1994 *fatwa* issued by the Department of Fatwa and Legislation in the State Council.[60] The ruling was made in response to a request for clarification by the sheikh of Al-Azhar of both the scope and nature of its authority in censoring artistic works. In making this clarification, the regime extended Al-Azhar's review authority to all matters of public order and morality and made these determinations binding. In effect, the ruling gave Al-Azhar the authority to censor film and television.

A key basis of the State Council *fatwa* was the argument that "the unity of the nation can only be cemented by ensuring unity of thought."[61] The *fatwa* also noted the centrality of Islam as both the religion of the state and the religion of the majority. Consequently, it is "regarded that Islam and Islamic principles and values permeate public order and morality and are therefore contained within the higher interests of the state."[62] Not only is Islam a basis of social order, the *fatwa* argued, but its proper interpretation is important in "building modern Egyptian society." The ruling went on to argue that the sheikh of Al-Azhar is the "final arbiter in all religious matters" and that it is within the purview of the Islamic Research Academy (which the sheikh chairs) to "review all research and studies published on Islam and the *Turath* (tradition), at home and abroad, whether it contains sound opinion or, if not, to reply to it and rectify it."[63]

The ruling thus affirmed the centrality of Islam for ordering Egyptian public life and identified Al-Azhar as the leading authority and interpreter of Islamic tradition. This move sparked controversy, particularly among members of the human rights community, who viewed the government's actions as subordinating the civil rights of the population to the official *ulema*. Many of these fears were justified. The state's capitulation to the conservatives in Al-Azhar helped to validate the integralist position discussed above. It also sanctioned the attack on intellectual freedom by allowing the support for secularism to be viewed legally as a sign of disbelief. This was the basis of various lawsuits brought by Islamist lawyers against outspoken critics, lawsuits that forced the Mubarak regime to condemn or defend them. The targets tended to be secular intellectuals, liberal Islamic scholars, and other critics of the Salafist (fundamentalist) movements. These scholars were characterized by their Islamist opponents as either apostates or agents of the West. Artists and novelists were similarly attacked and their works banned. The regime was unwilling to defend these individuals because it wanted to portray itself as the protector of religious orthodoxy.

Although the infringements on intellectual freedom were numerous, a few warrant particular attention. One of the first instances was the 1990 case of an author who was sentenced to eight years in prison for a novel that was deemed blasphemous by an organization within Al-Azhar known as the Al-Azhar Scholars Front (Jabhat Ulama al-Azhar). Alaa Hamed, who worked as a tax inspector by day and wrote fiction by night, had his book *A Distance in a Man's Mind* banned for including imaginary conversations with Islamic prophets. The case was significant in that it was the first to be tried in the state security court system on charges associated with the anti-subversion laws, a practice typically reserved for Islamic militants. Although the Islamic Research Academy had recommended other cases for prosecution, this was the first to be taken to trial. The timing of the case and the complicity of the state security services in it led many to conclude that the government was trying "to prove to the public that it is as religious as" the Islamist opposition groups that it was then fighting.[64]

More shocking was the 1992 assassination of Farag Foda, a leading secular writer and founder of the liberal group al-Tanwir (The Enlightenment).

Foda was assassinated by Islamic militants two weeks after a senior sheikh from Al-Azhar, Muhammad al-Ghazali, declared him to be an apostate. Foda had participated in the 1992 Cairo Book Fair forum, during which he had insulted the sheikh.[65] Foda's writings were also declared blasphemous by the Al-Azhar Scholars Front, which issued a *fatwa* designating him a *kafir*, for which the punishment is death. The Islamic militants who killed Foda claimed in a press release to be carrying out Al-Azhar's sentence. Moreover, during the murder trial, al-Ghazali testified that those who opposed the implementation of *sharia* were guilty of apostasy and thus could be killed legitimately. The attempt on Egyptian Nobel Laureate Naguib Mahfouz's life two years later was similarly galvanizing. In both cases, the efforts by establishment clerics to ban the books of secular thinkers or otherwise identify them as apostates provided a warrant for subsequent attacks by religious militants. Despite the outrage among secular intellectuals, the government's response was one of ambivalence. Although willing to support secular thinkers in their criticisms of Islamist militancy, the regime was less willing to aid them when challenged by members of the religious establishment.

The 1993 trial of Nasr Hamid Abu Zeid, a former professor at the University of Cairo, represented another high-profile case of intellectual freedom. Abu Zeid was a scholar of Islamic studies and Arabic literature and promoted the application of hermeneutics to the interpretation of the Qur'an. In essence, he sought to reinterpret the Qur'an in light of its contextual basis. He also read scripture as metaphoric, not literal, truth. Several colleagues with whom he had long differed considered this heresy and worked with Islamist lawyers to have formal charges brought against him. The apostasy case filed against Abu Zeid was initially dismissed because the lawyers who brought the case had no standing (that is, they had no personal interest). However, on appeal, the Islamists found a more receptive judge. Abu Zeid argued his case on the grounds of freedom of thought and expression, which was a constitutional matter. Those bringing the case invoked the rules of *sharia*, arguing that Abu Zeid's writings were a threat to the community of Muslims. The basis of this charge was the Islamic rule of *hisba*, which places an obligation on all Muslims to promote good and oppose evil. To the shock of many, the court sided with Abu Zeid's accusers and declared him a heretic (*murtadd*). It also ordered him to be divorced from his wife, since "being married to an apostate from Islam was a violation of the rights of God."[66] Although the divorce decree was overturned in 1996 by an administrative ruling, the conviction of apostasy remained. Abu Zeid and his wife were forced to leave Egypt for reasons of personal safety and have lived in exile in Holland ever since.

Muhammad Said al-Ashmawy, the former Chief Justice of the Cairo High Court, found himself in a similar predicament. Although formally trained in the law, al-Ashmawy has written extensively on Islam and was a leading critic of the Salafist tendency. An advocate of "humanistic Islam," al-Ashmawy argues that the politicization of religion by both state and opposition is contrary to its essence. Moreover, he has been critical of the literal—and selective—interpretation of Islam advocated by official Ulema and Islamist alike. Al-Ashmawy argues that Islamists tend to base their arguments on "temporary verses" as opposed to "permanent verses" in the Quranic tradition and ignore the difference between the two. According to al-Ashmawy, only the latter is the product of divine revelation and is not meant to be superseded by the former.[67] His positions on these and other issues led to several attacks by both members of Al-Azhar and the Muslim Brotherhood. In 1992, the Islamic Research Academy recommended that a number of his books be banned and ordered the confiscation of five specific texts. A leading member of the Muslim Brotherhood also called for him to be put on trial because "he has attacked the Islamic creed and maligned several Islamic values."[68] Other members of Al-Azhar supported this position, charging that al-Ashmawi's works "spread distorted information about Islam."[69] President Mubarak, a former friend of al-Ashmawy's, intervened in this instance and reversed the confiscation order. However, in 1996 a similar order was issued for his book *The Truth on the Veil*. In it, he argued that there is nothing in the Qur'an or the Sunnah that requires woman to wear a veil and that this is solely a matter of custom. The Islamic Research Academy ordered confiscation of the book. Al-Ashmawy noted at the time that "this confiscation is like a religious order to instigate my assassination."[70]

Other leading scholars in Egypt were similarly targeted, including author Sayed Mahmoud al-Quimni, whose book *The God of Time* was banned by the Al-Azhar Scholars Front in 1997. The basis for the group's action and for al-Quimni's subsequent trial was a report published on his work by the Islamic Research Academy. The report was critical of al-Quimni's depiction of the Third Caliph, Uthman, as well as his use of the Old Testament in characterizing the Prophet Abraham's life (which, it was argued, was contradicted by Quranic sources). The attack on *The God of Time* was part of a broader campaign against 196 books that Al-Azhar deemed blasphemous. The case was submitted to a

State Security court on the request of Al-Azhar; al-Quimni was subsequently charged with "propagating ideas that denigrate Islam" under Article 198 of the Criminal Code.[71] The Islamic newspapers seized on the case, immediately labeling him a *kafir*. Although he was ultimately acquitted on all charges (the judge's ruling specifically referred to provisions in the constitution ensuring freedom of expression), he, like Ashmawy, had to live with the threat of assassination.

Hasan Hanafi, a professor of philosophy at Cairo University and a leading advocate of "Leftist Islam," faced a similar attack by the Al-Azhar Scholars Front. Influenced by Martin Heidegger and other Western philosophers, Hanafi has promoted an interpretation of Islam that emphasizes social justice. He also advocates free thought. The Al-Azhar group accused him in 1997 of "harming Islam and denying established religious facts." They were particularly critical of two books entitled *Heritage and Renewal* and *From Conviction to Revolution*. The Al-Azhar Scholars Front argued that these books "scorned, mocked and derided every feature of the nation's religion" and that Hanafi "uses his lectures to spoil the minds of the nation's youth."[72] The books were written five years earlier, which supports speculation that the organization was prodded into action by comments Hanafi made in a lecture in front of four thousand students and faculty members at Al-Azhar in March 1997.

Finally, a dispute surfaced over the reissue of a book written in 1983 by Syrian author Haidar Haidar entitled *A Banquet for Seaweed*. In the spring of 2000, the Islamist newspaper *al-Shaab* (The People) printed a scathing review of the book and argued that the text was an affront to Islam. It also criticized the Ministry of Culture for reissuing the book as part of its Modern Arab Classics series. The author of the article noted how shocked he was that the Egyptian government was promoting "rank atheism and blasphemy."[73] Soon after the review was published, it became the topic of fiery sermons and sparked a riot at Al-Azhar University in Cairo.[74] *Al-Shaab* ran with the story, published denouncements of a number of secular literary figures, including Tayeb Salih.[75] Despite a review committee's report that the book was a "valuable literary work that actually exalted the role of Islam," the Egyptian Parliament's Religious Affairs Committee demanded that the book be burned.[76] The government's response was to arrest several junior officials of the Ministry of Culture on charges of "assaulting revealed religion" and shutting down the newspaper that printed the review. It also banned the book after a committee at Al-Azhar pronounced it to be "a dangerous departure from accepted religious understanding and an assault on what is sacred in religion . . . and likely . . . to shake the solidarity of the nation."[77]

The underlying debate in all of these cases—the limits of free expression and the ability to question revealed religion—was not new. As noted above, there has long been a debate over the interpretation of Islam. Historically, the debate has been between by those who adopt a narrow interpretation of Islamic tradition and those who "perceive Arab-Islamic culture as a [more] complex phenomenon."[78] What is new—relatively new, that is—is that members of the state-supported *ulema* have joined forces with non-Azharite Islamists in attacking the opinions of secular and liberal writers. The Azharites have opposed what they perceive as unorthodox interpretations of Islam and have used their positions within state institutions to mobilize popular sentiment against such heterodoxy. More disconcerting, though, is the Mubarak regime's complicity in such attacks. The intolerance of alternative opinions on religious matters has been normalized by state policies designed to encourage religious piety and political quiescence.[79] In promoting such policies, the state has helped to redefine religious orthodoxy in Egyptian public life and has provided the basis for stigmatizing religious and political dissent alike.[80]

## Coptic Christians and the Problem of Minority Rights

The dominance of Islamist ideas in Egyptian public life has also had a profound impact on Egypt's Christian minority. Despite official commitments to equal treatment of religious minorities, the effort to appease Islamic conservatives has led state actors to tolerate abusive and discriminatory practices against Coptic Christians, the largest minority in the country.[81] This discrimination is evident in a variety of issues ranging from the official population count to the systematic exclusion of Christians from positions of authority.[82] There are no Christian governors or mayors in Egypt, for example, or cabinet-level officials. Members of the Coptic community are also unrepresented in the upper ranks of the security services and are largely absent in the realm of academia. Of Egypt's fifteen state universities, none have a Coptic Christian in a key administrative post—dean or president—and only a very few Christians hold teaching positions. Similarly, Christian students are not allowed to attend Al-Azhar University despite its public funding. As one of Egypt's preeminent universities, this discrimination has long-term implications for future job prospects in medicine, law, and engineering.

Other forms of discrimination are evident in matters of religious freedom and marriage. Although a Christian may convert to Islam, Muslims who convert to Christianity have been subject to harassment by local law enforcement officials. For example, converts are frequently arrested for tampering with official documents after they alter identity cards to reflect a new religious status. Although such conversions are not specifically prohibited, neither are they recognized by the state. Similarly, a Muslim woman is legally prohibited from marrying a Christian man, though a Muslim man may marry a Christian woman. There have been reports of Coptic girls being abducted and forcibly converted to Islam by Muslim men. Although there are no reports of government involvement in such abductions, the local police and government officials have harassed Christian families seeking redress, and the government has clearly failed "to uphold the law" in such instances in which the daughter is under the age of 21.[83] Finally, an Ottoman-era law prohibiting church construction and repair without government approval has been eased but nonetheless remains in force. As one Coptic activist noted, "It is easier to get a license to open a nightclub than to fix a church."[84]

The communalization of the Egyptian polity, moreover, has deeply affected local government and security forces. Local police harass members of the Christian community and have consistently been slow to respond to inter-communal violence. In many instances, the government has done little to hold members of the majority community accountable for violent assaults on the Coptic minority. During the Islamist attacks on Christian communities in the late 1980s and early 1990s, for example, state actors did little to protect the Coptic community and routinely depicted the assaults as the byproduct of local disputes. This was the case even in the early 1990s, when such violence was commonly carried out by Islamic militants. Moreover, the state-regulated press did little during the 1990s to counter allegations made by Islamists that Copts were either converting or sexually abusing young Muslims. As such, Egypt's mass media contributed greatly to antiminority prejudice and to an environment that "provided a fertile staging ground for anti-Christian violence."[85]

Religious discrimination remains a major source of tension in Egypt, as the 1999 incident at Al-Kosheh indicates. On New Year's Eve of 1999, violence in the southern city of Al-Kosheh led to two days of rioting. During this period, Muslims burned and looted Coptic stores and killed twenty Christians. Two Muslims were also killed. The violence was an expression of long-simmering tensions between wealthy Christians and less affluent Muslims. When two Christians were killed the previous year, the government rounded up one thousand Copts—torturing many—convinced that Christians were behind the killings. An official organ of the Orthodox Church described this as "blaming the victim."[86] The government's response to the 1999–2000 violence indicated a similar unwillingness to address the issues raised by the violence. The initial trial indicted 96 defendants—58 Muslims and 38 Copts—of which 92 were acquitted. The remaining four were convicted of only minor crimes. According to one analyst, "The verdicts were intentionally light in order to avoid fanning the flames of sectarian strife."[87] The verdicts nonetheless outraged many in the Coptic community who felt that "the investigation and court deliberations were biased."[88] A subsequent retrial similarly freed all but two.

Behind the anger over the Al-Kosheh affair was the continued sense of persecution derived from the exclusive conception of national identity and the continued rejection of a minority "other." As Fahmi Howeidy, a prominent intellectual and journalist, described the situation, "What happened is not a crisis of a village or sect, but a crisis of a nation."[89] Although the Egyptian government refuses to recognize the Coptic community as a minority—and argues that the Egyptian nation is entirely of one ethnic fabric—the government has nonetheless refused to allow for equal treatment of the Christian population. The Coptic community soon comes to believe that they are considered second-class citizens and thus not fully Egyptian.[90] Moreover, the large proportion of Islamic programming on state-run television and radio has in the past either demeaned Christianity or emphasized the benefits of conversion to Islam.[91] Similarly, Islamist newspapers commonly denigrate Christianity and the Coptic community, as do the sermons at Friday prayers in mosques around the country. Each of these trends contributes to the further communalization of public life and has increased Coptic alienation. As one analyst noted, "You have to feel affiliation and respect in society, and this [the Copts] don't have."[92]

These issues were again resurrected in 2001 when an Arabic-language weekly, *al-Nabaa*, published a lengthy story—with pictures—of a defrocked priest having sex with women at a revered monastery. A major protest erupted among the Coptic community that included several days of demonstrations in Cairo. Although the immediate cause of the protest was the publication of the article, these unprecedented street protests were driven by the community's sense of continued persecution. The protestors were expressing longstanding frustration with the Mubarak regime's unwillingness to protect minority rights and included a variety of criticisms of both the government and the church leadership. One protester described the newspaper article as "part of an ongoing campaign to defame the church" and the community, tying it to broader themes relating back to the El-Kosheh affair and the Christian communities' inability to receive justice in that case.[93] According to another protester, it is precisely these types of actions that "weaken our sense of belonging to this country."[94]

Although the Mubarak regime has sought to promote interfaith dialogue and other means to ease tensions between the communities, the state's own communalism has had a lasting impact on Coptic as well as Muslim identity. This has not been helped by the tendency of the regime to take community issues up with the Coptic Church but not with representatives of the Christian community who are unaffiliated with the church. Moreover, while there remain plenty of Muslims and Christians willing to reach out to one another, they frequently face opposition within their own communities over such issues as inter-communal dialogue and the advocacy of reform. This is especially evident in the internal divisions that exist within the Coptic community over how to respond to both the state and the sectarian tensions. Expatriate Coptic groups often differ with local groups over how to approach many of the issues raised by their minority status. Similarly, the communalism fostered by the state has constrained those in both groups who try to promote religious tolerance and mutual understanding. As one Coptic activist who works with Muslim groups noted, "Sometimes what is needed is *intra-faith* dialogue; it is not the Muslim-Christian dialogue that is the problem, but rather getting each side to speak with one voice."[95]

## Consolidating the Illiberal Order

The response of the Mubarak regime to Christian persecution and to the assault on intellectual freedom—as well as the broader effort to redefine public morality—was muted. Reluctant to be perceived as a defender of apostasy, the regime let the courts determine the outcome of cases brought against liberal and secular writers, only intervening in extreme circumstances. In many instances, the regime was also a proactive participant, as evident in the *Banquet of Seaweed* debacle. Similarly, the regime has done little or nothing to address the core concerns of the Coptic community. Although theoretically committed to an inclusive (and secular) vision of modernity, the Mubarak regime has readily ceded the basic debate over religion and public life to conservative clerics. Since the majority of the population is Muslim, neither the regime nor the state-controlled media outlets wish to be perceived as un-Islamic. Moreover, promoting a conservative, albeit depoliticized, Islam among the population is seen as conducive to an unquestioning acceptance of the government's right to rule. Conservative religion—and a mutually supportive relationship between religious and political authority—ostensibly supports a politics of the status quo.

That this adversely affects communal relations and free debate is clear, but the complaints of Christians and secular intellectuals were peripheral to the core economic and political concerns of the regime. As one commentator noted, the state does not care about these issues as long as the people "don't start asking questions about unemployment and power."[96]

Ironically, the state's efforts to contain the Islamist opposition in the 1990s were extremely effective. On the one hand, the state-controlled media outlets discredited the militants in the eyes of the population and created an image of Islamic militancy as intolerant and boorish, little better than thugs. Popular television serials and films also depicted the young militants as uneducated and manipulated by cynical leaders. The intent of this media strategy was to contrast the "proper official understandings of Islam against the misreadings and misinterpretations of uneducated Islamic extremists."[97] On the other hand, the security forces largely eradicated the militant organizations. By 1997, al-Gama'a and al-Jihad were a fraction of their former size, and most of their members were dead, in prison, or in exile. It was also clear that the Islamists' resort to violence undermined their credibility and, ultimately, their cause.

The government's victory over the Islamist militants provided a moment of opportunity for the regime to address the underlying sources of extremism. At the time, there was something of a consensus in Western policy circles that argued for limited economic and political reform as a means of breaking the cycle of repression and extremism that had defined the previous two decades. This type of incremental reform, or "liberalization" (as opposed to "democratization"), included the cultivation of the institutions of civil society and a renewed commitment to economic development and the rule of law.[98] Improving the material conditions of the population was seen as a necessary condition for establishing a greater stability in Egyptian political life. The endemic poverty and unemployment in the country may not have created religious extremism, but these material conditions certainly provided an environment in which it could flourish. As U.S. National Security Advisor Anthony Lake noted at the time,

> In the Middle East as throughout the world, there is indeed a fundamental divide. But the fault line runs not between "civilizations" . . . [but] between oppression and responsive government, between isolation and openness, between moderation and extremism. . . . Our foe is oppression and extremism, whether in religious or secular guise, . . . [and extremism flows] from common sources: disillusionment,

a failure to secure basic needs, dashed hopes for political participation and social justice. Widespread disenchantment breeds an extremism of hatred and violence—and extremism by no means unique to the Middle East or the Muslim World.[99]

Instead of moving toward greater political openness, however, the Mubarak regime used this opportunity to reassert its hegemony over all aspects of the public sphere: ideological, political, and economic. One of the initial steps involved a crackdown of the Muslim Brotherhood and a concerted effort to rein in the Brotherhood's influence within the professional syndicates. This entailed the passage of several laws providing the government with legal authority to intervene in syndicate elections. It also included the periodic arrest and detention of various members of the Brotherhood. The government also reformed the *hisba* laws, which had allowed Islamist lawyers to bring cases of Islamic morality to court. In 1997, the state passed a law that precludes all but the state's district attorney from initiating such cases. This was done largely as a response to the Abu Zeid case and had the goal of disempowering the Islamist lawyers by denying them a mechanism to bring such cases in the future. The detention of members of the Muslim Brotherhood has continued in recent years, particularly after their success in the 2005 parliamentary elections.

The regime also sought to rein in the more reactionary elements of Al-Azhar in the late 1990s, such as the Al-Azhar Scholars Front and the Islamic Research Academy. Their opening was the 1996 death of Gad al-Haq, the longtime sheikh of Al-Azhar. In his place, President Mubarak appointed the former mufti of Egypt, Sheikh Muhammad Sayyid Tantawi, who was seen as more liberal in his views. Tantawi, for example, was supportive of the regime on a number of controversial matters, such as Egypt's participation in the 1995 International Conference on Population and Development (ICPD), the issue of bank interest, female circumcision, and the wearing of the *hijab* (veil or head covering). Gad al-Haq opposed the government on many of these issues and had even joined with the Muslim Brotherhood in opposing the 1995 population conference.[100] The dispute sparked an institutional conflict over whose rulings were in fact binding, the *Dar al-Ifta* (House of Fatwas, headed by the Grand Mufti) or the Institute of Islamic Research, headed by the sheikh of Al-Azhar. With Gad al-Haq's death and the appointment of Tantawi as sheikh of Al-Azhar, many assumed that these debates were settled now that the moderates were in charge of both institutions.

Tantawi may have been more compliant, but this did not significantly change

Al-Azhar. To be fair, Tantawi did work to restrain the more extreme elements of the *ulema*, and he held more progressive views on many issues than his predecessor. Tantawi condemned the attacks of 9/11, for example, and opposed female circumcision. He also supported the government position on bank interest and on the status of Palestinian suicide bombers (which Tantawi condemned and which the Front of the Scholars of Al-Azhar deemed "martyrdom operations"). He was also able to win many battles with the more extreme members of the *ulema* and was instrumental in dissolving the Al-Azhar Scholars Front in 1998. However, little in the institution actually changed.[101] This was partly because Tantawi had trouble gaining control of what is, in fact, several institutions. As one analyst noted, "There are any number of Al-Azhars,"[102] including the Mosque, the different colleges, the president's office, the independent institutes, among other parts of the larger institution. Moreover, the rank-and-file members of Al-Azhar remain sympathetic to the Islamist vision of society, and the educational program of Al-Azhar continues to be influenced by the Salafist interpretation of Islam.

The continuing predominance of the Islamist vision within Al-Azhar, however, is also due to Tantawi's own policies and actions. Like his predecessor, Tantawi guarded Al-Azhar's institutional role as the authoritative interpreter of Islam and remained loyal to a vision of society that is premised on a close association of religion and political authority. These positions, consistent with an Islamist approach to political rule, were evident in Tantawi's response to a 2004 conference on religious and political reform in Egypt. The conference participants called for greater freedom in both the political and spiritual realms, and specifically argued for the right to *ijtihad* (religious interpretation). In an interview with a Kuwaiti newspaper, Tantawi observed that those who participated in the conference "have a destructive influence on Egyptian society and they must be stopped and brought to trial."[103] Similarly, on the question of *ijtihad*, Tantawi articulated an orthodox position that allows interpretation *only* so long as it is consistent with accepted scholarship—a curious, if not outright contradictory, position on theological dissent. Tantawi was also one of the critics of *The Banquet of Seawood*, labeling it blasphemous. Like other elements of Al-Azhar, in short, the sheikh remained a pillar of an exclusive political order that sees its role as "defend[ing] rights and virtues, and [answering] whoever deprecates Islam."[104]

These positions illustrate the Mubarak regime's approach to religion since 2000. The inability (or unwillingness) of the regime to take a consistent position on religion and secularism has allowed for the continued entrenchment of a Saudi-influenced vision of Islam in Egyptian public life. Moreover, the government has increasingly taken upon itself the role of enforcing Islamic orthodoxy. As such, the regime has used the myriad institutions under state control—mosque, university, media outlets, and security services—to promote a depoliticized, though deeply illiberal, version of Islam. It has also continued to ignore the complaints of Coptic Christians, secular intellectuals, women, and other minorities. The government, moreover, has persecuted individuals and groups who are accused of insulting religion or otherwise professing heterodox views of Islam.[105] To this end, the security courts have been used to try cases involving religious freedom, and government prosecutors have actively gone after liberal Muslim and secular thinkers alike. One liberal group, the "Quranists," base their reading of Islam solely on the Qu'ran—not on the Sunnah. Their members have been declared apostates (by Sheikh Tantawi, among others) and arrested. Similarly, the regime has prosecuted cases involving unorthodox social behavior, such as homosexuality. Similarly, the regime has refused to acknowledge the Bahá'í faith and has denied members of this religion legal standing. Zealous police officers have even arrested or fined individuals who were seen eating or drinking in public during the fasting period of Ramadan.[106]

The persecution of religious dissent and the promotion of religious uniformity reflect the Islamist position that the state has an obligation to enforce religious belief and practice. This reflects the arguments of moderate Islamists, or "Islamic constitutionalists," who see the state's enforcement of *sharia* as essential for the maintenance of the *umma*.[107] Even though the state has disallowed Islamist lawyers from bringing *hisba* cases, for example, the regime has, ironically, taken on this role for itself. Under the rubric of "doing good and forbidding evil," the government has intruded into the realm of religious practice—and conscience—and actively used the coercive mechanisms of the state to create a more uniform and illiberal Islam. In short, the state has secured for itself monopolistic control over matters of religion and belief. In doing so, it has "repeatedly sent a clear message that religion is not a private matter and that any 'deviation from the true religion' will not be tolerated."[108]

Very much related to the state's promotion of an exclusive Islamic orthodoxy is a second feature of the postmilitant era: the political de-liberalization of the public sphere. In the aftermath of Sadat's assassination, a state of emergency was declared. This emergency law provided for the suspension of individual rights, detention without charge, the suspension of press freedoms, and other restrictions of political freedom. It also created a separate court system: civil courts for the disposition of ordinary cases and a security court system for politically sensitive cases. Even after the militant violence ended, the state of emergency remained in effect. Moreover, in 2007, the Mubarak regime codified many of these provisions in the Egyptian constitution, obviating the need to renew the state of emergency every three years. Although the restrictions on individual freedom were ostensibly a response to the challenge of militant extremism, these emergency measures have been used against all forms of opposition, religious and secular alike. Once the militants were under control, for example, the Egyptian government extended its repression to other groups, including secular intellectuals, democracy activists, and other members of the moderate center. The arrest and imprisonment of Saad Eddin Ibrahim, one of Egypt's preeminent democracy activists in 2000 and again in 2002 was indicative of this trend. By calling for clean and fair elections and a genuinely representative government, Ibrahim offered an alternative vision for Egyptian society that was neither Islamist nor authoritarian. The state-run media outlets subsequently sought to destroy his reputation by portraying him as a tool of the West. Moreover, by arresting Ibrahim—and charging him with accepting money from abroad without prior government approval—the regime was sending a clear message to Egypt's human rights and NGO community. If an individual with connections to both the regime and the West could be removed, then no one was safe.

The point of such attacks is to eradicate any alternative to the state's dominance of the public sphere. By discrediting secular intellectuals and marginalizing religious centrists such as members of the Wasat Party, a moderate offshoot of the Muslim Brotherhood, or the Quranists, the Mubarak regime has been able to portray itself as the *only* alternative to Islamic extremism. In this way, the Egyptian government has created a false impression in the West (particularly among Western governments) that there are only two choices in Egypt: the religious totalitarianism of the Islamists or the continued rule of the Egyptian security state. The fear of Islamic fundamentalism, in short, has been and continues to be used by the state to stifle democratic development, to fend off calls for genuine reform, and to eradicate the liberal center. The state has also used the chaos of post-2003 Iraq as a warning to domestic constituencies of the danger inherent in a weak state. Playing on such fears at home and abroad has allowed the Mubarak regime a free hand in consolidating an illiberal political order. The irony, of course, is that it is the danger of an illiberal Islam taking over the public sphere that justifies the state's continued exclusion of the Egyptian people from the political process and legitimate forms of dissent.

## Conclusion

Like the Sadat regime before it, the Mubarak government continues to use religion and nationalism to cultivate an unquestioning acceptance of state power. This has contributed to the Islamization of the public sphere and the communalization of Egyptian politics. It has also created a political environment in which the persecution of Coptic Christians, secular intellectuals, and those with dissenting religious opinions has occurred with regularity, and often with state complicity. It has also shaped popular perceptions about the role of women in society. This situation violates the Mubarak government's claims to support a vision of modernity defined by tolerance, pluralism, and economic development. The successful promotion of an inclusive and open society requires at least some autonomy for social actors and a greater emphasis on the rule of law and accountable government. It also requires an embrace of critical reason instead of passive obedience to authority. Yet, the state remains committed to a set of policies that largely precludes each of these goals. It retains its preeminence in political affairs and actively promotes an interpretation of religious tradition that discourages independent thinking and creativity. Moreover, the state's communalist vision of society—and its depiction of illiberal religious belief as culturally more authentic—has greatly affected Egyptian society. By promoting conservative religion in public life, the modern state has helped to create an increasingly devout—and communally divided—society over the last thirty years.[109]

By using Islam to eradicate the left—and, later, to counter the militants—both the Sadat and Mubarak regimes undermined the intellectual basis for a liberal modernist Islam. They also discredited the idea that religion was open to interpretation. The most significant victim of the ideological battles of the last thirty years, then, has been the conception of Egypt as a plural society. The right to differ, either intellectually or politically, has been stigmatized and often equated with heresy or treason. Moreover, the failure to cultivate an inclusive basis of national identity—and a political culture of tolerance and compromise—has contributed to divisions in society and continuing social tensions. It has also undermined the requirements of economic and social development. These issues were highlighted in the 2002 UNDP Arab Human Development Reports that spoke of the three primary deficits in Arab society: political freedom, women's rights, and the creation of a knowledge society.[110] The state's promotion of a conservative Islam and its efforts to monopolize the public sphere have been a key factor in undermining the country's development in each of these areas. The close relationship between state and religion, in short, has undermined the prerequisites of an open society and excluded large segments of the population from public life. This has also led at least one commentator to conclude that in Egypt, "conservative Islam is wrapped up in political authoritarianism; it is an unholy alliance to keep people down."[111]

# CHAPTER FOUR

# The Rise and Decline of Indian Secularism

The resurgence of Hindu nationalism was a defining feature of Indian politics in the 1990s. Although the ideas and organizations associated with the trend have roots in the early twentieth century, they were politically marginalized for much of the post-Independence period. Even in the 1980s, the political party that represented Hindu communalism, the Bharatiya Janata Party (BJP), was peripheral, capable of winning only two seats in the 1984 parliamentary elections. Yet, by 1991, the BJP was the second-largest party in the country, and by 1998 it was leading the ruling coalition. Perhaps more important, the ideology of Hindu nationalism, or *Hindutva* (literally "Hinduness"), had become part of the ideological mainstream. Such a dramatic reversal of fortune was puzzling. What had happened in the intervening years that allowed for the reemergence of a set of ideas and organizations that had not held much sway among the Indian population for many years? How, in short, does one explain the dramatic resurgence of religious politics in India?

The precipitous rise of Hindu nationalism and the communalization of Indian politics can be explained in large measure by the changing attitude of state leaders toward the secular ideals of the Nehru period.[1] In the years immediately following independence, the Indian government, led by its first prime minister, Jawaharlal Nehru, promoted a secular vision of modernity. The government's support for secular norms and identities was premised on a belief that an inclusive understanding of the nation was necessary for integrating India's diverse ethnic and religious groups into a common political framework. A secular vision of nationalism was thus institutionalized in India's first constitution. This commitment to a nonsectarian social order, however, was not universally shared. Even within the ruling Congress Party, there were those who believed that national identity was more properly defined in religious terms. This reflected the desire among Hindu nationalists to create a *Hindu Rashtra* (a Hindu-dominated political order or Hindu state) and to place control of state power exclusively in the hands of the Hindu majority.

The struggle to define the nation has remained a central feature of Indian politics over the past six decades. At issue is whether the national community ought to be defined inclusively—with membership extended to all members of the population—or whether full membership should be reserved for those of the dominant community. In other words, should the nation be defined along religious or secular lines? Nehru and his supporters were concerned about the conflict and division that would result from marginalizing minority populations. Particularly in the aftermath of Partition, which separated Pakistan from India in 1947, the politicization of religion was discouraged, particularly any form that might fan the flames of sectarian violence. The early Congress Party leadership subsequently campaigned against efforts to institutionalize preferential status for the majority population or otherwise to link civil status to religious identity. This commitment to an inclusive social order faded, however, with Nehru's death in 1964, especially after the Emergency period (1975–77). During this latter era, Congress Party leaders abandoned Nehru's secular vision and sought to coopt the rhetoric and symbols of Hindu nationalism for their own purposes. Unlike Nehru, Indira Gandhi and her son, Rajiv—Nehru's daughter and grandson—appealed to the religious sentiments of the majority population and portrayed the Congress Party as the one true and able defender of the Hindu nation.

Although the Congress Party leadership's embrace of an exclusive religious politics was driven by electoral considerations, it also reflected a more fundamental transformation. Along with the abandonment of a secular vision of Indian nationalism, Congress Party leaders also relinquished earlier commitments to social justice, minorities, and the poor. The religious politics of the Indira and

Rajiv Gandhi era, in short, was part of a new strategy to mobilize support along communal, instead of class, lines. Although this majoritarian strategy worked for the Congress Party in the short term—most spectacularly in the party's 1984 electoral landslide—it had dire consequences in later years. By overturning the Nehruvian consensus, the Congress leaders helped to disembed the secular norms that had governed Indian public life for most of the post-Independence era. This contributed greatly to the communalization of local governments and police forces and to an increase in communal violence. It also cost Indira her life and the Congress Party its dominance. By invoking the themes of Hindu communalism, the Congress Party leaders gave the organizations associated with this ideology a credibility that they had historically lacked. Congress thus helped to normalize what was previously seen as a sectarian and discredited ideology and paved the way for the rise of the BJP.[2]

## Historical Context

The roots of India's religious politics go back to the religious reform movements of the late nineteenth century. As in the Middle East, there was a conscious effort among colonized populations to reevaluate their religious traditions as part of a broader effort to understand and respond to British colonial rule. This reevaluation entailed a variety of responses. For some, the central issues were the cultural stagnation of the region and the need to adapt religious tradition— whether Islamic or Hindu—to the challenge of modernity. For these liberal and "modernist" reformers, religion was dominated by superstition and legitimized a dysfunctional social order characterized by caste and gender discrimination. What was required, then, was to retain the positive elements of religion while shedding the accretions that had come to distort it. Others, however, were less concerned about reconciling religion with Enlightenment norms than they were with preserving the centrality of religion in social life. From this perspective, religion was central to cultural identity and was worth preserving in whatever form. Ironically, both groups perceived religious reform (and revival) as a neces- sary means of revitalizing the political community and confronting the West.[3] Religious reform movements subsequently proliferated in late nineteenth-cen- tury and early twentieth-century India as they had in Egypt and elsewhere.

The advocates of liberal or modernist reform were evident in both Muslim and Hindu communities. Influenced by the ideals of the European Enlighten- ment, these early religious activists tended to be humanist in orientation, rationalist, and, at times, supportive of religious universalism. They also commonly echoed the ideas of Abduh and al-Afghani. For many of the Indian activists, religious reformation was part of a broader social reform; they believed that improving the material conditions of society outweighed blind adherence to tradition. This was particularly relevant when dealing with issues such as child marriage, the treatment of women, and low-caste oppression. Many Hindu reformers, for example, placed great emphasis on the liberation of both the individual and the community from the influence of superstition, unscrupulous "holy" men, and the unreflective acceptance of tradition. The Indian National Congress, a political organization established in 1885 that would ultimately lead the independence movement, was influenced by these trends. Its early leadership was made up of individuals—both Muslim and Hindu—who were sympathetic to the goals of liberal reform. Even if the national leadership embraced a degree of religious universalism, however, the rank and file still tended to speak the language of Hindu communalism.

The tensions within the Indian National Congress (or, simply, the Congress or Congress Party) mirrored deeper divisions within Indian society. Many traditional leaders, both Hindu and Muslim, rejected the liberal positions on religious reform and were actively hostile to the vision of modernization associated with British influence. Their version of religious revivalism was meant to preserve—not overthrow—existing patterns of social life. They also looked to religion to strengthen communal solidarity and rejected the universalism of the liberal reformers. In the Hindu context, such groups wanted to resurrect a golden era of Hindu dominance by returning to what they perceived as traditional religious values. This interpretation of reform sought to standardize Hindu thought and practice, a difficult task given the absence of any religious establishment or agreement on doctrinal issues. Similarly, within the Muslim community, there was significant opposition to British influence in the areas of education and cultural reform. Illiberal (or conservative) Islamic revivalists, like their counterparts in the Middle East, perceived the loss of political power to the British as a reflection of the community's failure to live in accordance with proper Islamic teachings.[4] The reform that they advocated entailed ridding Islamic practices of its local Hindu influences and rejecting many of the accommodations made by Islamic modernists with Western ideas.

Although these groups ostensibly represented a return to or a defense of tradition, what was in fact occurring was the construction of new ideologies that drew quite selectively from older religious traditions.[5] This was due in large measure to the nature of the political environment. Under British colonial rule, political recognition and power was conferred on organized interests who could credibly represent (or at least claim to represent) a given community. This contributed to the competition *within* communities between liberal "modernists" and illiberal "revivalists" over which group ought rightfully to represent the community. Associated with this political struggle was a religious debate over how to interpret their shared tradition. That this competition occurred in the context of the colonial public space helps to explain the ideological—and modern—character of religious activism. It also explains the tendency to articulate these debates in nationalist terms. Regardless of whether they advocated liberal reform or sought to maintain traditional patterns of social order, the language and organization of these various activists were strikingly similar. Recognition from government officials, moreover, was important for establishing the legitimacy of one group or another and, hence, one interpretation of tradition over another. Unfortunately, British policymakers at the time tended to regard each religious group as a separate nation and assumed that these communities had interests that "were different from and conflicted with the rest of the population."[6]

## The Emergence of Religious Nationalism

The efforts to organize and reform the various communities began in the late nineteenth century, but it was only in the 1920s that extreme forms of religious communalism became entrenched in Indian politics. Again, by communalism I am referring to the belief that members of a given cultural or religious community have common economic and political interests and that the satisfaction of those interests necessarily comes at the expense of other, similarly defined communities.[7] What defined the intervening period was an oscillation between cooperation and competition among (and within) the different communities. There was also an enormous amount of diversity. Differences of caste, class, region, and language divided followers of both Islam and Hinduism and made it difficult to regard these groups as genuine communities with shared interests. Moreover, while many Muslims and Hindus opposed British rule in India, others supported it. The colonial rulers played on these differences and frequently allied with landowning elites, tax collectors (the *zamindars*), princes, and minority leaders to undermine the Indian National Congress. The British government also encouraged the communalization of Indian society as a means of maintaining its rule. Through such "divide and rule" policies, the British empowered communalist organizations at the expense of liberal reformers.

The British partition of Bengal in 1905 represented one such effort to foster religious differences. This action divided the province of Bengal—then the most populous region in India and a stronghold of the nationalist movement—into two regional governments. The intention was to dilute the influence of the Congress Party by cutting the Bengali population in half. It was also intended to encourage Muslim communalism by providing a Muslim majority in eastern Bengal and thereby give them a vested interest in British rule. Similarly, the Government of India Act of 1909, known as the Morley-Minto Reforms, introduced the concept of separate electorates. This gave Indians an opportunity to participate in the colonial government but did so through communal representation. It provided separate seats for Muslim constituencies (for which only Muslims could vote), thus giving legal standing to a separate Islamic identity. It also empowered Muslim groups with only a limited following within their own community to make claims on behalf of Muslims writ large.[8]

The Montagu-Chelmsford Reforms of 1919 expanded this system of sectarian representation. The legislation increased the electorate, expanded the scope of regional councils, and provided self-government at the local level. However, it also extended the notion of separate electorates to Sikhs, Christians, and low-caste Hindus. Despite official statements, these reforms were put forward in order to emphasize the divisions within India and to reaffirm the idea that different religious and cultural groups had separate political interests from those of other communities. It was also designed to cultivate vested interests in the status quo and to strengthen British arguments that India's diversity was not well represented by the nationalist Congress. The implementation of a regular census furthered the emergence of communalism by formalizing a set of group identities that had hitherto been amorphous.[9] These different categories provided the basis of government employment, education, and, ultimately, representation.

Although British policy encouraged and politicized such divisions, religious communalism had a domestic constituency as well. This was rooted in the landed elites' opposition to the kind of changes advocated by secular and liberal nationalists. Such traditional elites appealed to ethnic interpretations of nationalism in order to generate support for a vision of a social order defined by hierarchy and communal preference. Although this was articulated in terms of shared communal interests, implicit was a social conservatism that protected the economic position of large landowners. Consequently, reactionary leaders invoked religion—and ethnic conceptions of nationalism—in order to depict their own interests as representing those of the larger community. The emergence of a popular press contributed to this trend by bringing the ideas of ethnic preference to a wider audience. It was also a shift away from traditional elite-based politics to a new politics defined by the "creation and mobilization of [mass] public opinion."[10]

## Prelude to Independence

The political discourse that emerged in the early decades of the twentieth century was informed by a variety of competing visions for India's future. At one end of the spectrum were the competing communalisms of Hindu nationalism, Muslim nationalism, and Sikh nationalism. These trends emphasized the corporate or ethnic conception of group identity, and these groups increasingly came to see their communal interests as opposed to those of all others. They tended to endorse traditional patterns of social hierarchy and found their principal support among the landowning elites, wealthy merchants, and rulers of India's "Princely States." At the other end of the spectrum was the emergence of a composite Indian nationalism. This drew from a variety of liberal tendencies, both secular and religious, and found its most potent expression within the Indian National Congress.

The defining debates within Indian politics, however, were not between communities but within them. The Hindu community, for example, was divided among three distinct trends in the early 1920s: secular nationalism, Hindu traditionalism, and Hindu communalism.[11] These groups tended to have different bases of political support and sharp differences over their interpretations of both religious tradition and national identity. The secular nationalists, for example, tended to eschew the exclusive tendencies of the other two groups and supported a cosmopolitan view of Indian nationalism. They advocated inter-communal cooperation and believed that national identity in a future India should not be based on religious affiliation. Although many of the liberal nationalists were actively hostile to religion, individuals such as Mohandas (Mahatma) Gandhi came to this position from a distinctly religious perspective.[12] Gandhi's interpretation of Hinduism emphasized its historical tolerance of diversity, and the tactics of *satyagraha* (literally, "truth force," of which nonviolence was an integral part) were rooted in Hindu notions of resisting injustice. The image of him as a Hindu ascetic was also an important element of his moral authority.[13]

A more significant schism, however, was between the liberal and the traditionalist wings within the Congress. Composed of individuals such as Lajpat Rai, Madan Mohan Malayviya, and Sardar Patel (the future home minister), the Hindu traditionalists were socially and religiously conservative and had strong ties to landed elites. They tended to be less westernized than many of their liberal counterparts and promoted Hindi as a national language and laws banning the slaughter of cows along with their advocacy of independence. Many also disagreed with Gandhi's emphasis on nonviolence. They advocated a more confrontational and militant approach to *both* the Muslims and the British.[14] The traditionalists also disagreed with the liberals' entreaties to the Muslim community—an approach many saw as appeasement—emphasizing instead Hindu solidarity as a basis of political activism. Many of the traditionalists within the Congress were also members of more explicitly communal organizations such as the Hindu Mahasabha.[15]

The Mahasabha was a Hindu nationalist group created in 1915, and it re-emerged in a more assertive manner in the aftermath of communal riots of 1922–23. Vinayak Damodar Savarkar, president of the Mahasabha between 1937 and 1942, was a central figure in developing the ideas associated with modern Hindu fundamentalism. Under his leadership, the group organized politically, participated in elections, and offered itself as an alternative to both the Congress and the Muslim League (the leading Muslim political party). Savarkar also articulated the ideological basis for Hindu nationalism in his book *Hindutva: Who Is a Hindu?* The vision Savarkar articulated in *Hindutva* was based on a conception of Hindu identity that drew heavily from the ethnic nationalisms of Europe.[16] His central argument was that the Hindus constitute a distinct nation and race (*jati*). Savarkar also spoke of a Vedic "Golden Age," where Hindu society flourished and where God had revealed to his "chosen people" the perfect knowledge of the Vedas (ancient Hindu scripture). Although the indigenous population, the Aryans, intermarried with non-Aryans, their culture and blood nonetheless produced the Hindu nation. A Hindu, from this perspective, is one who feels united with other Hindus through these ancient bloodlines and who regards India as both fatherland (*pitribhu*) and holy land (*punyabhu*).[17]

A second communal organization that emerged during this period was the Rashtriya Swayamsevak Sangh (RSS), which was founded in 1925. Under its first leader, K. B. Hedgewar, the RSS spread throughout northern India, though only later, under his successor M. S. Golwalkar, did it systematically articulate its vision and doctrines. Influenced by Savarkar's *Hindutva*, the RSS's primary focus was the transformation of Indian society through the spread of a reinter-preted Hindu culture. The defining features of the early RSS were its military organization, its anti-Muslim sentiments, and the asceticism of its followers. It also sought to inculcate a martial Hindu spirit among its youth cadres. Although the RSS was more of a social movement than a political party, it shared with the leaders of the Mahasabha a communalist vision of national identity. This was evident in Golwalkar's 1939 book, *We, or Our Nationhood Defined*. Although both the RSS and the Mahasabha ostensibly appealed to tradition, their ideas were consistent with the right-wing politics of the 1930s.[18] The conservative elite (both Muslim and Hindu) had historically been reluctant to engage in mass-based politics, since such movements were typically associated with left-wing radicalism. In the 1930s, however, the nationalist movements in Germany, Italy, and Spain provided a model of right-wing populism that both Hindu and Muslim communalists emulated. This led Nehru to conclude that the Hindu nationalists represented "an Indian version of fascism."[19]

Muslim activists were similarly divided between liberal and communal ten-dencies during the 1930s. Despite the inter-religious tensions of the mid-1920s, a large number of Muslims supported the Indian National Congress and advo-cated a secular vision for India's future. Very few advocated the creation of a separate state. The *ulema* of the Jamiyat al-Ulama, for example, a religious orga-nization founded in the early 1920s, allied with the liberal and secular Mus-lims associated with the Congress Party. So, too, did the students of Aligarh University and the Jamia Millia Islamia (National Muslim University) based in Delhi. These different Muslim groups supported a composite Indian nation-alism and worked with Congress activists in opposition to a British initiative on constitutional reform (the Simon Commission of 1928–29).[20] Many of them also participated in the Congress-led civil disobedience campaigns of 1930–31. An explicitly nonsectarian Islam was promoted within the Jamia Millia Islamia. Influenced by Gandhi and Rabindranath Tagore, the school dedicated itself to greater crosscultural understanding and a liberal, or "modernist," interpretation of Islam. It is for this reason that Muhammad Ali Jinnah and other members of the Muslim League criticized the school's leaders for turning it into a "Hindu stronghold" and for threatening the very existence of Islam in India.[21]

The Muslim League embodied the spirit of communalism within the Islamic community, though it, too, vacillated over the merits of Hindu-Muslim cooper-ation. The group periodically collaborated with Indian National Congress, yet its leadership remained independent from the nationalist movement. The Muslim League also emphasized the distinct nature of the Muslim community and its separate interests as a minority population. The Muslim League's activities, moreover, were premised on the ideas that Muslims need to be better organized to defend their interests and that the Muslim League alone was the authentic representative of the Muslim community.[22] Although this did not preclude the party from working with the Congress in the 1920s, such cooperation became untenable as the more reactionary elements of the organization gained positions of influence. A growing antagonism between the Muslim League and the Congress Party was evident on a variety of issues throughout the 1930s.

One of the primary issues of concern for the Muslim community was the unwillingness of the Congress leadership to confront Hindu communalism head on. That prominent Congress members led the Mahasabha did not help the situation, nor did the anti-Muslim activities of regional Congress leaders. Events surrounding the 1937 elections further contributed to this animosity. In these elections, the Muslim League failed to win even a quarter of the seats reserved for Muslim candidates.[23] Moreover, a failed effort to form a coalition government in the United Provinces (UP) confirmed for many Muslim leaders that the Congress was determined to subjugate the Islamic community to Hindu interests. Taken together, these two trends led the Muslim League to embrace a more confrontational and communal attitude. Assailing what it argued were anti-Muslim policies in Congress-governed provinces, Jinnah and other League members sought to instill the fear of Hindu domination in a future India governed by the Congress. They claimed that Islam was in danger and that Muslims faced religious persecution under Hindu rule. League members depicted the Congress as a religious organization and argued that "it is useless in the light of past experience for Muslims to expect from the Congress anything like fair and equitable treatment."[24]

The policies of Congress at the regional level also helped to reenergize support for the Muslim League. Muslim landowners and urban professionals were concerned about their elite status, and how this would be affected after independence. Like their Hindu counterparts, these Muslim landlords were deeply troubled by the peasant movements and the support that social reform was finding in the Congress. Particularly after legislation protecting peasant rights was passed by a Congress government in the UP, many of the landlords "rushed to the League to thwart [the] 'Bolshevik menace'" represented by Congress.[25] By allying with the moneyed elite, the Muslim League found new sources of support and influential allies. It also helped support the league's emergent right-

wing populism. Learning from its previous mistakes, the league shed its elitist image and constitutionalist strategies and reformed itself as a party of the
masses. Drawing heavily on Islamic symbols and references to Islam's former
dominance in the Subcontinent—and playing on the fears of the Muslim community—the Muslim League promised the creation of a new Islamic state.

This surge in Islamic communalism came to fruition in the early 1940s as
Jinnah and the Muslim League emerged as the sole spokesman of the Muslim community. The idea of Muslims as a separate nation soon gained greater
salience, and the demand for a separate state became a key part of the league's
platform.[26] The conflict with the Congress, moreover, was depicted as a struggle
between faith and infidelity (*kufr*). Similarly, there was a concerted effort to
undermine the pro-Congress *ulema* and other liberal Muslims who supported a
secular Indian nationalism. Well-respected Islamic scholars who differed with
the Muslim League were publicly vilified for their views and depicted as traitors
to Islam. This was the context in which Independence and Partition transpired.
As World War II came to an end, England had neither the will nor the power
to retain its control over India. As debates over the future of the Subcontinent
commenced, major riots were instigated in Calcutta and Bihar by both Muslim
and Hindu communalists, leaving upwards of twelve thousand dead. The violence had the intended effect of undermining a constitutional arrangement that
would preserve the territorial integrity of the nation and closing off all options
apart from partition. In August 1947, the English withdrew from the Subcontinent, and India and Pakistan were created as separate states.

## The Nehru Era: Defining a Secular Order

### The Nehruvian Consensus

In the aftermath of World War II, India, like Egypt, faced the task of bringing
social and political cohesion to a newly independent country. This was made
more difficult by the growing divisions within the Congress, which was formally
reestablished as a political party in independent India.[27] India had gained its
independence, but there was little consensus—either within Congress or outside of it—regarding the nature and basis of this new polity. Although many of
the early debates focused on issues of socioeconomic reform, one of the most
pressing concerns was the question of religion and public life. Should the new
social order reflect the secular ideals of Indian nationalism, or, having conceded
the issue of Pakistan, should the new Indian state (and nation) be defined along

religious lines? Why, in other words, should Hindus be denied a preeminent position in the new political order now that the Muslims had their own state? The answer that emerged in the early years of Independence was a pragmatic one. Nehru, now prime minister, and other Congress leaders felt that the most pressing need of the new republic was to overcome the communal and linguistic divisions that were dividing the nascent political community. Since unity could not be taken for granted, the cultivation of a shared national identity became a top priority. The secular alternative was thus seen as a more viable basis of national unity.

The primary obstacle to Nehru's secular vision, however, was the continuing support for communal preference associated with organizations such as the RSS and the Mahasabha. For these groups, constructing an organic Hindu nationalism and establishing a Hindu state were seen as prerequisites for the self-actualization of the community. Defining the nation consequently entailed a pitched struggle between these competing forces in Indian society. These basic issues were debated in the Constituent Assembly that drafted India's constitution between 1946 and 1949. Although the assembly was dominated by members of the Indian National Congress, the movement (now a party) contained a broad diversity of perspectives. As a result, the debates within the assembly mirrored the intra-party conflicts discussed above. Although Nehru led a wing of the Congress Party that advocated an explicitly secular and socialist developmental state, he faced resistance from other members of the party's elite, which held to the upper-caste views of the Hindu traditionalists who opposed both socioeconomic reform and Nehru's emphasis on secularism. But Nehru's supporters dominated the assembly, and they were able to shape the new constitution.

The "Nehruvian consensus" that emerged from this debate was defined by several interconnected elements. The first was the constitution's emphasis on democratic governance, universal suffrage, and basic human rights. A second feature was the commitment to socioeconomic reform and the eradication of poverty. Although there were early divisions between Gandhi and Nehru over the nature of India's future economy, a consensus emerged that supported Nehru's vision of modern industrial development.[28] This included a program of state-led economic development modeled on the socialist paradigm typical of the time. This pillar of the new order involved government intervention in the economy and a program to restructure the agrarian sector. The development state also directed investment into heavy industry (mining, energy, metal working, and machine building), provided extensive public services (education, transportation, health care), and implemented a progressive taxation scheme.

Although the priority given to economic development reflected Nehru's desire to create a more egalitarian society, it was also seen as a key component to the resolution of India's many social issues. Rapid economic growth would help eradicate poverty, while the development of a welfare state would address the considerable needs of the population. A key premise of these policies was the belief that caste discrimination, gender inequality, illiteracy, and communal division were associated with economic deprivation and poverty. By raising living standards, it was assumed, many of these problems—particularly the communal problem—would become less pressing. In short, creating a more egalitarian society would also mean building a less divided one. Thus, the early efforts to restructure landlord/tenant relations, provide workers' rights, and reform the landownership structure were all meant to have social as well as economic effects. National integration and nation building was, as a result, very much intertwined with issues of social justice and economic reform.[29]

A third feature of the Nehruvian consensus was its secular orientation. For Nehru, the new order had to be nondiscriminatory in its treatment of minority populations. The key to such tolerance, from his view, was state neutrality in matters of religion and belief. The government was not intended to be irreligious or otherwise hostile to religion but rather *equidistant* to all religious traditions. Civil status would not be linked, either positively or negatively, to membership in one religious community or another. In this sense, secularism meant nondiscrimination. As Nehru described it, "We call our State a secular one. The word 'secular' perhaps is not a very happy one and yet for want of a better, we have used it. What exactly does it mean? It does not obviously mean a society where religion itself is discouraged. It means freedom of religion and conscience, including freedom for those who may have no religion. It means free play for all religions, subject only to their not interfering with each other or with the basic conceptions of our state."[30]

Implicit in Nehru's secularism, however, was a suspicion of religion and an underlying belief that many of the social ills—the caste system, denigration of women, and poverty—were associated with the religious outlook so prevalent in India. Thus, despite the overt support for an idea of secularism as neutrality, lurking within Nehruvian secularism was the belief that religion as a social force ought to be diminished. According to this view, the economic and social development of society—that is, its modernization—depended on relegating religion to the private sphere and actively constraining those organizations that promoted communalist ideas.[31]

The urgency of this issue was due, in part, to the continuing strength of communal tendencies in the late 1940s. Five hundred thousand people were killed during Partition and more than twelve million displaced (six million of them Hindus from Pakistan). The violence had put the entire society on edge, not least the twenty-four million Muslims who had decided to stay in India. Hindu nationalists, moreover, actively campaigned against the secular project and opposed efforts to ensure minority rights, pass a "Hindu Code Bill," and institutionalize other elements of the secular order.[32] This opposition, however, did not succeed, in large measure thanks to Nehru's efforts to counter both the discourse and activities of communalist organizations. Nehru and his supporters made extensive use of radio and public forums to promote religious tolerance and consistently portrayed inter-communal harmony as a core value of the Congress Party. Nehru also did not hesitate to use state power to constrain Hindu communalists. For example, he blunted an effort in 1949 to politicize a dispute over the Babri Mosque in Ayodhya—which some claimed was built on the birthplace of the Hindu god Rama—by preemptively arresting members of the Mahasabha and others involved in the agitation.

Nehru also faced opposition from the Hindu traditionalists in his own party. The traditionalist faction was sympathetic to the Hindu communalists and their call for a more explicit link between religion and national identity. The traditionalists also differed with Nehru on the issues of Pakistan, Kashmir, and the treatment of the Muslims who had remained in India.[33] Although Nehru was intent on creating a society that protected minority rights, the traditionalists argued that the new government ought to be more concerned about the wishes of the Hindu majority. Sardar Patel, the home minister, noted that if Congress were to adopt a more "Hindu" approach to these questions, it would be able to gain the support of activists in both the Mahasabha and the RSS. In a 1948 speech, Patel laid out these views, arguing that the Hindu nationalists were an important constituency that could (and should) be absorbed into the Congress Party.[34]

The ability of Nehru and his allies to fend off such challenges—and dominate the Constituent Assembly—was greatly facilitated by several factors. The first was the independence movement and the legitimacy that it carried. The commitment of the Congress to a secular constitutional framework during British rule continued to shape much of the debate after Independence. A second factor was the violence and trauma associated with Partition. Although the riots and large-scale killing exacerbated communal tensions, it also illustrated the dangers of religious extremism. Third, the assassination of Gandhi in 1948 by a Hindu nationalist greatly delegitimized their cause. Gandhi was shot by Nathuram Godse, a former member of the RSS who had ties to Savarkar, the Mahasabha leader.[35] Godse claimed that Gandhi had betrayed the Hindus by accommodating Muslim concerns and, further, that he had been responsible for the Partition of India. For these actions, so the logic ran, the killing of Gandhi was legitimate.[36] The response by the Hindu community was one of shock and horror. In areas such as Maharashtra, it sparked anti-Brahman violence because of the close association of the Hindu Nationalists with the Brahman upper caste. The assassination also strengthened the hand of the secularists. Nehru—long wary of the RSS and its sectarian beliefs—immediately banned the organization and had many of its leaders arrested.[37] Arguing that Hindu militancy represented a threat to the new republic, the government prohibited any organization that openly advocated communal hatred and violence. The Mahasabha was temporarily forced out of party politics, and the RSS's standing was greatly diminished.

The tensions between the secular leadership and the various communal forces, however, continued. One area of contention involved repealing the ban on the RSS. Golwalkar, the RSS leader, had written to both Nehru and Patel, urging an end to the ban, arguing that there was no direct evidence linking the organization to Gandhi's murder. Moreover, in one letter he implored Patel to recognize their common interests and urged an alliance between Congress and the RSS in opposition to the left.[38] Although Patel was sympathetic to Golwalkar's position, Nehru remained adamantly opposed. Nehru was deeply concerned about the militant character of the RSS, seeing it as a threat to the government. Nonetheless, secret negotiations between Patel and the RSS leadership continued, and a Congress working committee voted in 1949 to lift the ban and allow RSS members to join the Congress Party. The vote, undertaken while Nehru was out of the country, sparked a dispute between supporters of Patel, who endorsed the vote and those of Nehru, who opposed it. The vote was ultimately reversed.

Debate over rebuilding the Somnath Temple in Gujarat was another point of conflict. Ostensibly attacked by Muslims during the Mughal era, both Patel and K. M. Munshi, a former member of the Mahasabha who was serving as a Congress Party minister, championed the restoration of this temple.[39] Munshi's support of the project was extremely popular with those who saw the temple's reconstruction as an affirmation of Hindu rule. This was especially significant since the region where the temple was situated was a former Princely State (Junagadh) whose Muslim leader had tried, without success, to affiliate with Pakistan. The proposed reconstruction, however, remained controversial. Although Patel had argued that the restoration of the temple "would be a point of honour and sentiment with the Hindu public," the liberal nationalists felt that it undermined the secular basis of the new republic.[40] The secularists felt that public funds should not be used for such explicitly communal purposes, and many, including Nehru, thought that the president of India, Rajendra Prasad, should not perform the installation ceremony. A compromise was reached whereby Prasad performed the ceremony, but as a private citizen and not in his official capacity as president.[41]

The election of Purushottam Das Tandon to the presidency of the Congress Party represented another flashpoint in the debate. In August 1950, Tandon, with Patel's backing, was elected president of the party in a tightly fought race. Nehru had opposed Tandon because of his communalist sympathies.[42] The election itself became a symbol of the struggle between the secular liberals and the Hindu nationalists. Members who supported the Mahasabha and the RSS backed Tandon's presidency, while Nehru and his allies opposed it.[43] Realizing the importance of retaining control over the party structure, Nehru, then prime minister, intervened in the affair. During the party conference in August 1951, Nehru pitted his popularity against that of Tandon and forced the latter's ouster. At the same meeting, Nehru got the Congress Party to pass a series of resolutions explicitly endorsing his policies on social and economic reform. Nehru was elected president of the party, reflecting his dominance of the Congress as well as of India. The outcome of this struggle was facilitated by the death of Patel in December 1950, which left the Hindu traditionalists without a leader of Nehru's stature in either the party or the government.

### Consolidating the New Order

The defeat of Tandon marked a turning point for the secular nationalists. The willingness of Nehru to put his prestige on the line greatly facilitated the institutionalization of secularism in public life. He continued in this vein over the next several years, consistently working to pass legislation that would further consolidate the secular order. One such measure was a law adopted in 1951 that specifically forbade the use of religious symbols "or the invocation of the 'threat of divine displeasure' during an election campaign."[44] Other laws were passed during the first session of the Indian Parliament (1952–57), that were motivated by similar intentions. These latter measures amended, and attempted to standardize, Hindu personal law. Although not a uniform civil code, it did address some of the more egregious issues of female inheritance, polygamy, intercaste marriage, and the adoption of girls. However, the law only applied to the Hindu community; it did not affect Muslim personal law and hence did not apply to members of the Muslim community. Similarly, Nehru pushed through a piece of legislation in the mid-1950s, the Citizenship Act, that emphasized the inclusive nature of national identity by extending the right of citizenship to any immigrant from Pakistan, regardless of religious affiliation.

These bills sparked strong opposition among Hindu nationalists, who portrayed them as having an "anti-Hindu" bias. The legislation reforming Hindu personal law, for example, was described as a "threat to the stability and integrity of traditional forms of marriage and the family in Hindu society."[45] More damning, perhaps, was the criticism that the law exempted minorities and thus failed to create a genuinely uniform civil code. Similarly, communal groups opposed the Citizenship Act because it extended the rights of citizenship to Muslim refugees. Although the debate over these bills involved a variety of topics, at issue in each case was the Indian national identity. The communalist position on the Citizenship Act, for example, sought to limit the right of citizenship to Hindus. This reflected an ethnic conception of national identity, while the inclusive nature of the law yielded a more universal interpretation. Similarly, the opposition to Hindu personal law reform was led by orthodox Hindu leaders, who perceived such reforms as undermining the traditional moral order and, with it, their authority in Indian society.

What is remarkable about these debates, however, was the ineffectiveness of the Hindu nationalists. Even among the Congress traditionalists, there was little popular support for the communalist position on these bills. Nehru's legislative victories demonstrated the degree to which the secular consensus had come to define public discourse, at least at the national level. They also highlight the degree to which Nehru was able to define the frame of debate and to characterize his communal opponents as sectarian, divisive, and antinational. Moreover, the government's willingness to confront the Mahasabha, the Jana Sangh (a political party created in 1951 by Syama Prasad Mookerjee, former government minister and leader of the Mahasabha), and other communalist elements furthered the process of secularization. The government's willingness to arrest and detain Hindu nationalists seriously limited their ability to mobilize the Hindu population on such sensitive issues as the Ayodhya mosque, the treatment of Hindus in Pakistan, and cow protection.[46] By restricting the actions of these groups, the central government effectively curtailed their ability to promote Hindu communalism.

The electoral victories of the Congress Party in the early general elections also facilitated the consolidation of the Nehruvian consensus. In the first three general elections (1951, 1957, and 1962), the Congress Party won nearly 75 percent of the seats in the Lok Sobha (the lower house of the national Parliament), even though they only captured 45 percent of the popular vote.[47] The major opposition parties—the Socialists, the Communists, the Jana Sangh (Hindu nationalist), and the Kisan Mazdoor Praja Party (representing the landowners)—fared poorly. What emerged, then, was a one-party system, where outside groups worked with allied forces within the party to pursue their respective agendas. Although opposition parties were able to play a greater role in national politics than their numbers would indicate, they were nonetheless forced to operate within the "Congress system." Moreover, the support of the major leftist parties—the Socialists and the Communists—on such core issues of secularism and state-led development helped Nehru and his allies against more conservative forces in the party. Such a progressive agenda—which linked modernization to progressive social change—was a primary source of Nehru's popularity and empowered him to promote a secular vision of social order.

The Jana Sangh's inability to generate a mass following also showed the weakness of Hindu nationalism during the 1950s and early 1960s. The government's active opposition to communal agitation had effectively blunted the communalists and their call for a *Hindu Rashtra*. When rioting broke out in the early 1960s, for example, Nehru responded with force. Recognizing that these riots had been carefully planned and organized, Nehru ordered his state ministers to detain communalist organizers and prevent them from doing further harm.[48] He also sought to constrain religious appeals by sectarian parties. Just before the 1962 elections, for example, the government announced its intention to strengthen the 1951 law that prohibited the use of religion in electoral campaigns by extending the prohibition to any language that "promoted the disaffection among the people on the grounds of religion, race, caste or language."[49] These constraints severely curtailed the activities of the Jana Sangh and kept them from explicitly "playing the Hindu card." Although the party's supporters remained committed to the ideas of *Hindu Rashtra*, the communal discourse was downplayed at the national level, reflecting the parameters of what was perceived as permissible debate.

The weakness of the Jana Sangh was also due to the continuing strength of the Hindu traditionalists within the Congress Party at the local level. Particularly in Uttar Pradesh and Madya Pradesh—key elements of the "Hindi Heartland"—Congress officials within the local and regional governments had taken strong positions on a number of key "Hindu" issues. The Congress-ruled government of Uttar Pradesh, for example, had made Hindi its official language in 1951 and banned cow slaughter in 1955.[50] The state governments were also slow to implement various demands from the central government regarding the recognition of Urdu as well as a number of proposed social and economic reforms. Finally, local Congress governments took a strong stand on the issue of Christian missionaries, thus depriving the Jana Sangh of yet another campaign issue in one of its strongholds.[51]

Although the recalcitrance of the regional governments may have undercut the effectiveness of the Jana Sangh, it was also a major obstacle to Nehru's vision of social change. Nehru had complained about the lack of commitment to the secular idea among his colleagues in the Congress Party, especially at the state and local levels. Similarly, many of the socioeconomic reforms passed by the central government remained unimplemented by Congress-run governments at the local level. The departure of the Socialists within the Congress in the mid-1950s further undercut Nehru's position by removing potential supporters from the party structure. As a result, Nehru's ability to implement reforms was limited by the Congress Party's reliance on traditional landowners and other rural elites for political and financial support. Opposition to agrarian reform, India's alliance with the Soviets, and the growth of the public sector became major points of contention within the party. These trends, coupled with the disastrous 1962 border war with China, seriously undermined Nehru's position, setting the stage for a major renegotiation of the Nehruvian consensus in the years following his death in 1964.

## Indira Gandhi and the Decline of the Secular Order
### *State Crisis and Indira's New Populism*

Nehru's death presented a series of challenges to Congress Party rule. His passing deprived the Congress of a pillar from the independence movement and the progressives their strongest voice within the party. It also raised issues about

Congress's leadership and future direction. The first matter was resolved by the selection of Lal Bahadur Shastri to be prime minister. He was chosen by a group of party bosses, known collectively as the Syndicate. Shastri's death in early 1966, however, reopened the question of succession and thrust Indira Gandhi into the premiership. Indira was similarly chosen through the auspices of the Syndicate, who felt that Nehru's daughter would be an asset in the upcoming elections and also someone they could readily control. The direction of the country, however, was a more complicated matter. The communalist organizations outside the party were working with sympathetic Congress members to reassert themselves. During the year of Nehru's death, the Vishwa Hindu Parishad (VHP, World Hindu Council) was established toward this end. The VHP worked to promote the Hinduization of Indian public life because, like their allies in the RSS, the VHP leadership believed that the political weakness of Hindus was rooted in their religious division. The strength of the community, from this perspective, could only be achieved through greater unity and religious uniformity. This led the VHP to promote a standardized version of Hindu thought and practice, which it portrayed as a more authentic interpretation of Hindu tradition.[52]

Although the activities of the VHP and the RSS were portrayed as cultural, they had clear political motivations. This was evident in the VHP's effort to stigmatize various "threats," such as Christian proselytizing and Muslim separatism, in order build Hindu unity. One such effort was the cow protection mobilization of 1966–67. Although ostensibly aimed at eliminating the slaughter of cows—a symbol of Hindu identity—this issue was also used to denigrate Muslims, who were commonly involved in the leather trade, and to mobilize Hindu sentiments behind the Jana Sangh. The government's response, however, was forceful. After a large demonstration marched on Parliament in November 1966—sparking a confrontation that left eight people dead—Prime Minister Gandhi dismissed the home minister, arrested several activists, and threatened the RSS with administrative action. In doing so, she demonstrated her resolve in the face of a communalist challenge and reinforced her government's commitment to secularism. The swift action also ended the VHP agitation.

The controversy over cow protection, however, highlighted the deep divisions that continued to exist within the Congress Party. This polarization between the left-of-center secularists and the more conservative traditionalists had been exacerbated by the economic policies of the 1950s. Nehru's efforts to reform the agricultural sector—particularly his proposed caps on land ownership and a failed cooperativization program—had alienated large segments of the economic elite. Despite the limited nature of these reforms, they were none-theless perceived as an assault on private enterprise. This helped to coalesce right-wing opposition to the broader program of state-led development. Ironi-cally, the entrenchment of the one-party system at the same time undermined the impetus for reform. The emphasis on socioeconomic justice, which had characterized the early reformist period, had given way to the temptations of power. The Congress Party was now increasingly seen as dedicated to the pur-suit of patronage and the spoils of office, not poverty alleviation. In short, it was no longer an agent of social change but had become instead the "underwriter of a inequitable status."[53]

The 1967 elections were a disaster for the Congress Party. Although it re-tained power at the center, the Congress Party lost a large number of seats in the Lok Sabha, and also lost control of several state governments. It was a sign of popular disdain for the leadership and affected the balance of power within the party. The polarization along the left-right axis had been in the making for some time, becoming more pronounced as progressives moved to support Indira against the conservative leaders. The political right advocated greater reliance on private enterprise, while the left sought to reaffirm Nehru's empha-sis on socioeconomic reform. The struggle between these factions continued over the next two years, coming to a head after the death of President Zakir Hussain in May 1969. Although the presidency is a ceremonial position, it was felt that the struggle to nominate his successor would likely tip the balance of power to one faction or the other. A candidate supported by Mrs. Gandhi won the vote. At the same time, Indira stripped Morarji Desai, a conservative min-ister, of the finance portfolio and took control of the ministry herself. She then nationalized fourteen banks, eliminated preferential policies for former princes, and watched her popularity soar. These actions split the party, however, leading to the formation of rival organizations in November 1969: the Congress (R/Requisitionists), headed by Indira, and the Congress (O/Organization), which represented the conservative opposition.

Indira's politics and rhetoric during the 1971 elections were marked by an increasingly leftist populism. Since the split with the conservative faction, Indira had come to rule India with a coalition of minority and leftist parties.[54] Her main opposition was a coalition alliance composed of the Congress (O), the Jana Sangh, and other right-wing parties.[55] These groups mobilized around the motto *"Indira Hatao!"* (Remove Indira!), to which Indira's supporters responded with *"Garibi Hatao"* (Abolish Poverty). By emphasizing the issue of poverty,

Indira was able to refocus the 1971 campaign on the core themes of Congress legitimacy: socioeconomic reform, secularism, and socialism. A key issue in the campaign was the abolition of the payments to the former princes known as "privy purses," which Indira had previously tried to eliminate. Similarly, Indira spoke throughout the campaign of the need to defeat the opponents of her efforts to bring about social change. She also targeted the Jana Sangh for its support of communalism and promised the middle classes a strong, stable government.

The Congress (R)'s victory in the 1971 elections was a monumental event. The party won an outright majority, capturing 352 of 518 seats in the Lok Sabha, and Indira emerged as a dominant force, with both a mandate and a political base. Moreover, the forces of conservatism were decisively defeated, and the Nehruvian consensus was re-validated. Indira's standing was further bolstered by the war with Pakistan in 1971–72. Perhaps the most significant conflict between the two countries, the crisis led to the military defeat of Pakistan and the creation of Bangladesh. Mrs. Gandhi's determined leadership and the ultimate success of the conflict translated into tangible electoral benefits, as her party won control of all the regional governments in state assembly elections held the following year. The opposition was unable to portray itself as either more populist or more patriotic than Gandhi, so had difficulty putting together a coherent campaign platform. She was at the height of her power.

Mrs. Gandhi's tenure, however, was deeply problematic. The most challenging issue was a pervasive discontent among the population. Despite the electoral gains of 1971 and the war with Pakistan, Indira's leadership rapidly fell into crisis. Much of this derived from the poor economic performance of the state. Despite early economic gains in the 1950s and 1960s—and the passage of various antipoverty programs—industrial development remained stagnant, unemployment high, and poverty pervasive. In rural areas, land was still concentrated in the hands of a few, and the inability (or unwillingness) of the Congress Party (R) to implement genuine reform left the social structure of rural India largely unchanged. This led to the emergence of a militant peasant movement in Bengal, among other challenges.[56] The expectations among urban laborers and the middle classes went similarly unfulfilled. These trends were exacerbated by the 1973 economic crisis—sparked by the oil shock of the 1973 Middle East war—which led to higher food prices, inflation, and recession. The resulting dissatisfaction expressed itself in a series of industrial actions across the country, culminating in a bitter railway strike in 1974.

Another important trend that defined Indira's rule was the centralization of state power and party control. Indira's defeat of the former party bosses and the electoral gains of Congress (R) significantly shifted the balance of power. Under the new regime, the leadership of the central government appointed the chief ministers of the various states, who served only so long as they had the center's support. This gave Mrs. Gandhi a degree of control over the regional governments that had not existed during her father's tenure. Similarly, within the party, Mrs. Gandhi sought to undermine the state branches that had previously been the institutional base of the party bosses. Internal party elections were eliminated, and positions within the party structure at all levels were "filled by appointment from above rather than by election from below."[57] This strategy decisively weakened the party as an institution.

Related to this point was the emergence of a new form of populist or mass politics. The traditional party structure had long relied on the local party machinery to interact with regional elites and deliver the popular vote, a sign of the ability of local party bosses both to direct voter preferences and to mediate between national demands and local interests. Although this structure was not without its problems, Indira's new populism was premised on bypassing the traditional party structure entirely.[58] Through nationwide media campaigns, the Congress (R) developed a new style of politics to communicate directly with the population. Associated with this trend was the Congress Party's loss of ideological commitment. Although the debate in 1971 was a serious one—and represented a major challenge to the Nehruvian consensus—the policies that had prevailed in the election remained unimplemented; perhaps they were never intended to be implemented. Indira's populism was in part a product of a largely instrumental approach to ideology and a certain lack of substance in the political debate. As elections came to be fought through the mass media, serious policy issues were replaced with campaign slogans. Elections were transformed into populist referendums that hinged on simplified, emotional, and even misleading "questions, . . . like whether [people] wished to see poverty removed."[59] This style of politics—and the corresponding decline of the traditional party structure—reflected a new era of Indian politics.

## The JP Movement and Emergency Rule

In 1974, the volatility inherent in this new style of politics led to the emergence of the JP movement. This popular revolt was sparked by discontent over an increase in the price of food in Gujarat and Bihar. The result was widespread civil unrest, rioting, and anarchy. This, in turn, prompted a violent backlash by the government. Although initially led by students, opposition parties quickly joined the young activists. In the spring of 1974, Jayaprakash (JP) Narayan, a former socialist leader, came out of retirement to lead the agitation in Bihar, seeking to transform it into a nationwide movement against government corruption. Touring northern India, JP called for the removal of Congress, in particular Indira, whom he identified as the "fountainhead" of corruption. Opposition parties on both the right and the left rallied behind the JP Movement, as it became known, spreading it to other areas of the country. Despite its amorphous ideology, the movement was united in removing Mrs. Gandhi and found that socioeconomic grievances were an effective means of mobilizing popular sentiment behind their anti–Congress (R) attack.

The involvement of the Jana Sangh, the RSS, and the Congress (O) in the JP movement was significant. On the one hand, the participation of these communalist organizations provided the movement with a nationwide infrastructure. The RSS and Jana Sangh in particular were essential in organizing street protests and popular agitations around the country. RSS activists subsequently became a major force in the movement. On the other hand, these groups saw the JP movement as an opportunity to move into the mainstream of Indian politics. Narayan's respectability, his ties to Gandhian idealism, and his former association with the Socialist Party provided an aura of legitimacy to the other organizations. Similarly, while the Jana Sangh's base of support was upper-class and upper-caste notables, the JP movement provided an opportunity for them to work with grassroots voters on matters of popular concern. The influence of the Hindu right on the JP movement can also be seen in its program of reform. The JP movement depicted India as in a state of "total crisis," which was as much cultural as economic or political. The subsequent call for "total revolution"—that is, a "revolution in every sphere of social life and organization"—were appealing to the RSS and VHP, which had long argued for the cultural transformation of society.[60]

The violent response by the government to the strikes, demonstrations, and protests (*gheraos*) continued to fuel the tension between the state and opposition. When, in the summer of 1975, an Allahabad High Court ruling declared Mrs. Gandhi's 1971 election to the Lok Sabha to be fraudulent, the opposition called for the prime minister's resignation and announced a nationwide civil disobedience movement intent on removing her from power.[61] Two weeks later, on June 26, 1975, Indira declared a state of emergency, arrested the opposition leadership, and put an end to the JP movement.

The 1975 emergency was justified on the basis of preserving the nation. Mrs. Gandhi stressed this theme in several speeches and radio broadcasts, arguing, as she did in one speech, that "the stability, security, unity, the fabric and the very survival of the nation were in danger due to national and international threats."[62] Although emergency rule initially brought a degree of stability, it greatly diminished Mrs. Gandhi's popular support. It was also during this period that Congress (R)'s break with the traditional ideals of the Nehruvian consensus became clear. The harassment and corruption associated with this era, along with policies detrimental to the poor, damaged Mrs. Gandhi's credibility as a force of progressive change. Particularly egregious were the "family planning" and "urban beautification" programs overseen by Mrs. Gandhi's son, Sanjay. These government initiatives mandated coerced sterilization and forced relocation of the urban poor. Both the slum clearances and the compulsory sterilizations disproportionately affected Muslim and lower-caste communities, both traditional constituencies of the Congress Party. Sanjay's close ties with private enterprise and authoritarian tendencies also characterized a new trend in the governing elite.[63] When elections were finally held in March 1977, not only did Congress lose, but Mrs. Gandhi and Sanjay lost their seats in the Lok Sobha.

## Indira's Revival

The coalition government that took power in 1977 did not last long. Made up of many of the same groups associated with the JP movement, it had made the elections a referendum on the state of emergency. As such, they soundly defeated Indira and her Congress supporters. However, the so-called Janata Front coalition, as it was known, quickly fragmented. Apart from a shared opposition to Mrs. Gandhi, it had no unifying ideology, no agreement on state policy. This became particularly problematic when tensions in India's rural areas turned violent. Many of the rural elites, who had long backed the right-wing parties, used the 1977 electoral victory to roll back what few socioeconomic reforms had been implemented in the previous years. This led to caste violence and the confiscation of land distributed through earlier reforms in the rural areas. At the same time, communal violence and crime escalated as well. Unable to deal with these issues, the Janata Front leadership was barely able to keep its coalition together. Moreover, the effort to arrest and prosecute Mrs. Gandhi was badly mishandled, a situation that inadvertently helped her regain popular support. As the Janata

Front coalition crumbled, a number of former defectors returned to Indira's Congress, known as Congress (I). When elections were called in January 1980, Congress (I) swept into office. Mrs. Gandhi was back in power.[64]

The Emergency and its aftermath were emblematic of a deeper crisis in India's democracy. Mrs. Gandhi's rule prior to 1975 had been defined by the consolidation of political authority in the hands of a few.[65] This centralization of state power, however, and the demise of the Congress Party as an institution sapped the government's ability to address local needs and problems. It also forced dissent outside of normal political channels. The concentration of state power also coincided with increased criminality in Indian politics.[66] There was a heightened degree of corruption in the form of kickbacks and bribes and large numbers of people entering politics with criminal records. Many of the younger cadres recruited by Sanjay Gandhi fit this description. Perhaps more problematic was the emergence of a gangster element, which was employed by various political factions for the purpose of murder and intimidation. This was even evident in local police agencies, which had become increasingly "corrupt, criminalized and lawless."[67] These trends were also tied to an alliance between India's economic elites and its political leaders, who had found that they shared an interest in constraining the poor. New laws were passed banning the right to strike, and the state—working in conjunction with the landowning elite—targeted the rural peasantry for violence.

Associated with these authoritarian tendencies was Mrs. Gandhi's articulation of a nationalist discourse rooted in religious communalism and fear of minority separatism. The turbulence of the 1970s—particularly in regard to the radicalization of the poor and their disaffection from the party—created a crisis of legitimacy, to which the ruling party had to respond. It did so by emphasizing the Congress Party's historical role as the representative of the nation. Dissenting voices were stigmatized as threats to national unity, and the ruling Congress elite was portrayed as the only group capable of protecting the community.[68] The majoritarian nature of this discourse, with its connotations of security fears, ethnic conceptions of the nation, and demonization of minority populations, was troubling. By depicting the separatist tendencies and minority grievances that had emerged under her rule as anti-national, Indira was able to marshal the Hindu majority behind her rule.

There were several important features of this new discourse. First, it was intended to redirect populist mobilization along communal, not class, lines. The democratization of the 1950s and 1960s had politicized the population and built a strong base of support for the leftist program of social reform. These forces, however, became frustrated as the opportunities for advancement remained closed and state-led development failed to raise living standards on a large scale. The Emergency can be seen, then, in part as an effort to restrain the populist forces that were unleashed by the Congress Party, forces that would come to threaten its rule. Although the JP movement had been infiltrated by communal organizations—some would say hijacked—it nonetheless fed off the populist impulse associated with the disgruntlement of the lower classes. Despite Congress's traditional commitment to economic equality, little had changed in the thirty years of Congress Party rule. The state could not allow the continued mobilization along class lines, so it sought to shift public discourse away from socioeconomic issues to those of faith and nation.[69]

A second feature of this new discourse was its religious imagery and its clear appeal to the Hindu majority. The turn toward religion could be seen, superficially, in Mrs. Gandhi's public demonstrations of religious devotion, as she visited (and inaugurated) temples around the country and cultivated an image of devoutness.[70] She also began reaching out to activists within the Hindu nationalist community, relying on her nephew Arun Nehru as a conduit and increasingly surrounding herself with "godmen."[71] The communal nature of Congress (I)'s orientation was more explicitly evident, though, in Mrs. Gandhi's rhetoric of the early 1980s. Initially, this was articulated in terms of the "nation in danger"—threatened by both internal and external enemies—but it became increasingly religious in orientation as the challenges were defined as emanating from antinational minorities. In a 1983 speech, for example, Mrs. Gandhi noted that in "certain places"—code for Kashmir and the Punjab—minority populations have been guaranteed rights and privileges, while the "majority community was being suppressed."[72] In another speech in November 1983 to the Arya Samaj, a Hindu organization founded during the reform movement of the late nineteenth century, she explicitly stated that the country's religion and traditions were under attack.[73] This theme would be reiterated the following year, when, in the aftermath of the assault on the Golden Temple in Amitsar, she claimed that "the Hindu Dharma was under attack" and appealed to her audience for support in her efforts to save Hindu tradition "from the attack that was coming from the Sikhs, the Muslims and others."[74]

Implicit in Mrs. Gandhi's claims was a link between continued Congress rule and the two paramount goals of national unity and state security. By emphasizing the existence of amorphous security threats, the Gandhi regime played on the fears of the population, holding the Congress out as the one force that could make them safe. Criticisms of Mrs. Gandhi and Congress Party rule were then depicted as attacks on the nation. Similarly, all dissent was characterized as either antinational or treasonous and hence handled as a problem of law and order, not politics.[75] The result was that *political* conflicts, deriving fundamentally from a crisis in relations between the state and the regions, increasingly became articulated in *religious* and also nationalist terms. They were treated as threats to national security, not as matters for political compromise.

The Congress Party's discourse of religious nationalism was evident in the elections of the early 1980s. In the 1983 assembly elections in Jammu and Kashmir, for example, the Party played on Hindu fears of domination by the Muslim majority. The main opposition to Congress in this state was the National Conference, a predominantly Muslim political party, which Mrs. Gandhi depicted as "anti-national" and "pro-Pakistani."[76] Moreover, Indira's assault on incumbent chief minister and longtime supporter Sheikh Abdullah divided the electorate along religious lines and helped push a good many Hindu supporters of the BJP in the direction of Congress.[77] Similarly, in the 1983 local elections in Delhi, separatist movements in Punjab and Kashmir were made central campaign themes. In this context, it was argued, only Congress could defend the interests of the majority from the anti-national forces that were seeking to weaken the nation. As James Manor noted about the 1984 parliamentary elections, "Although it may seem difficult to believe that Hindu Chauvinism and anti-Sikh sentiments were important elements in the Congress-I election campaign, it was, in fact, the case."[78]

The Congress Party's communal strategy was quite opportunistic. On the one hand, it reflected the demise of the Congress Party's electoral base. The failures of Congress Party rule and the excesses of the Emergency had undermined the party's traditional coalition, which included the rural poor, Muslims, untouchables, and urban elites. Moreover, Mrs. Gandhi now perceived the dangers of relying on minorities and the poor. The proliferation of Muslim and low-caste parties also siphoned off support from the Congress, while majority complaints over reverse discrimination were becoming harder to ignore. Upper-caste Hindus, in particular, perceived themselves as suffering discrimination from the types of affirmative action programs that were designed to address historic inequities. The result was a "Hindu backlash" against policies that were perceived as "pampering minorities," a criticism that had become a staple of the Jana Sangh's successor, the BJP.

On the other hand, the shift toward an explicit Hindu majoritarianism her-
alded a much broader ideological transformation. Since the Congress Party's
historical commitment to a progressive agenda was no longer credible, it needed
a new basis of ideological legitimacy. The party was forced to develop a new
strategy that relied on popular support from the Hindu majority, particularly
the middle classes of the Hindi Heartland. This strategy was premised on out-
flanking the BJP by appropriating both its message and its base of support.[79]
The Congress Party's losses in the southern states of Karnataka and Andhra
Pradesh in January 1983 heightened the importance of developing a stronger
base of support in the northern states. There are claims that Mrs. Gandhi made
overtures to former opponents in the RSS as part of this new political realignment, but the degree of cooperation remains unclear. Nonetheless, there were
many reports of RSS activists working with Congress (I) in Kashmir, Delhi,
Andra Pradesh, and elsewhere in the early 1980s. The Congress (I) was also
reported to have allied with the Shiv Sena—one of the more militant communal organizations—in state and municipal elections in Maharashtra in 1983.[80]
Unlike her father Nehru, who vehemently opposed communalism, Mrs. Gandhi
opted to "ride it as far as it would take her."[81]

Ironically, the Congress (I)'s embrace of religious nationalism occurred at a
time when the BJP was moving away from the kind of chauvinism that had historically marginalized Hindu nationalists. In an effort to broaden their base, the
BJP had sought to attract Muslims and low-caste Hindus by emphasizing social
issues and "play[ing] down its Hindu character."[82] The BJP's strategy, however,
was not well received among members of the Sangh Parivar (literally, "family of
Hindu organizations," including the VHP, the RSS, and others), who perceived
the BJP's secular turn as backsliding on principle. This disfavor led to its poor
showing in the 1983 midterm elections, in which RSS cadres abandoned the
BJP in favor of the Congress (I) candidates in various local constituencies. The
BJP's electoral strategy failed, however, not because its message did not appeal
to a more mainstream audience but because the party had lost its core supporters to the Congress. By their defections, the RSS activists had demonstrated
that they were "not exactly delighted with the direction the party was taking."[83]
This criticism was expressed in an editorial from a journal sympathetic to Hindu
nationalism, which noted that "it is time for the BJP to make up its mind. It has
to decide, once and for all, whether it is going to play the part of a Secular party
or a Hindu National Party. . . . It should have found from experience that the
Congress (I) has decided to appropriate its Hindu Nationalist base, rendering

the party superfluous in the process if the BJP continues to be equivocal on the issue."[84]

The normalization of Hindu communalism, its movement into the mainstream of Indian politics, led to a sharp increase in communal violence. Instances of Hindu-Muslim rioting occurred in Moradabad (1980), Biharsharif (1981), Ahmedabad (1982), Meerut (1982 and 1987), Bombay (1984), and Delhi (1987). Although many of these riots targeted Muslims as a religious community, the impetus was generally linked to economic and political rivalry, not ancient hatreds. The compulsions of political competition, in short, "turned communal violence into another form of organized [mass] politics."[85] What is most striking about this violence, however, is not the number of incidents but rather the role of the government authorities in instigating and abetting it. Although many of the riots were associated with sustained campaigns by communalist organizations like the VHP or the Shiv Sena, the anti-Muslim bias among the police was an increasingly significant element. In a number of cases, local police worked with the RSS in targeting minority populations, stealing their belongings, and engaging in murder and arson. The central government, moreover, did little to rein in such atrocities or to hold those associated with them accountable. As a result, the state was increasingly seen as culpable for minority violence. It also showed how much the state machinery had itself become communalized.

## *The Communalization of Politics in the Punjab and Kashmir*

The manipulation of religious identities was not limited to the Congress Party's majoritarian strategies. It was also evident in Mrs. Gandhi's efforts to control regional governments, which was essential to the control of the central government. This led her, along with other Congress Party officials, to pursue increasingly confrontational policies with opponents in the various regions. The centralizing tendencies of the national government generated a number of grievances among individual states. These political disputes, however, were defined in religious and communal terms. This set the stage for bitter, indeed often violent, conflicts between the national leadership and regional actors, the most significant of which took place in Kashmir and the Punjab.

In the states of Jammu and Kashmir—where longstanding disputes over its rightful status had prompted several wars with Pakistan—Hindu-Muslim relations were considerably strained by Mrs. Gandhi's conscious manipulation of communal sentiments. This began in 1982, when she sought to undermine the existing ruler Sheikh Farouk Abdullah in an effort to consolidate her control over the region. Despite Farouk's commitment to keeping Kashmir in India, Mrs. Gandhi cast aspersions on his loyalty and worked assiduously to remove him from power. She accused him of trying to internationalize the problem and of taking money from Arab monarchies. Other charges against Farouk included claims that terrorist camps were operating in the state, and that the state government was tolerating anti-national activities.[86] Campaigning in the region in 1983, Mrs. Gandhi appealed to communal sentiments by emphasizing the discrimination of Hindus in the southern region. She offered herself as the only force able to protect them from the Muslim majority, on the one hand, and from the Pakistan-backed militants, on the other.[87] After losing the election, Mrs. Gandhi did not give up. The following year, in July 1984, she bribed members of the state assembly to defect from the coalition and then dismissed the democratically elected government. These "games" between Delhi and Srinigar, the capital of Kashmir, played out over the next five years, leading to the "disaster" of the 1989 uprising and fourteen years of troubling violence.[88]

Perhaps the most significant regional conflict, however, was in the Punjab, where tensions over economic and political considerations—particularly those involving the control of water and territory—came to be defined in religious terms. This was somewhat odd, given the longtime cooperation between Hindus and Sikhs in the region. In the 1950s and 1960s, for example, the Congress Party consistently relied on both Sikh and Hindu votes in state elections. Similarly, the Akali Dal, a Sikh political party and the main rival of the Congress, only came to power through alliances with other Hindu parties. It formed a coalition government with the Jana Sangh in 1969 and with the Janata Party in 1977. After the 1977 elections, however, the political dynamic changed. In an effort to undermine the Akali Dal, officials within the Congress (I) party engineered the rise of a young Sikh radical known as Sant Bhindranwale. The intention was to weaken the Akali Dal's support among the Sikh community by creating an alternative religious party associated with Bhindranwale.[89] This strategy was initiated by Sanjay Gandhi and the former Congress chief minister of the state (and later president) Zail Singh and was facilitated by both the Congress Party publicity machine and the appeal of Bhindranwale's "revolutionary Sikhism." It also represented a sharp departure from Congress's earlier confrontation of Sikh communalism in the 1950s and 1960s.[90]

Bhindranwale was a religious leader who mixed a fervent religious revivalism with an explicit political agenda. Although he supported the creation of a separate Sikh state (Khalistan), he worked with Congress (I) in the late 1970s and early 1980s in opposition to the more moderate Akali Dal. In 1980, he campaigned on behalf of Congress (I) candidates in the state assembly elections, although his contributions were minimal. It was Bhindranwale's militancy, however, and his willingness to use violence against the Nirankari and other dissident Sikh sects that raised his stature within the community. Even after the Congress (I) had captured the state government, the party activists continued to support Bhindranwale as a means of keeping the Akali Dal on the defensive. The Congress (I) operatives, however, soon lost control of their creation. In 1980–81, Bhindranwale was involved in a series of murders, including that of a high-profile journalist, and was only kept out of prison by the intercession of Zail Singh.[91] Meanwhile, the Akali Dal was forced to take more assertive steps (though not militant ones) to protect what they perceived as legitimate Sikh interests. This was done to establish their preeminence as the authentic representative of the Sikh community and to confront the Congress (I) over regional autonomy.

On both fronts, the Akali Dal was undercut by the national leadership of the Congress Party. On the one hand, the central government refused to concede many of the issues concerning state autonomy and, some have argued, actively blocked an accommodation on water issues and the status of disputed lands.[92] On the other hand, the Congress Party's encouragement of Bhindranwale greatly undermined the moderate leadership of the Akali Dal, forcing them to compete for Sikh populist sentiments in the same terms as that of the radical Bhindranwale. This contributed to both a hardening of Sikh communal identities and the emergence of a competitive populism among Sikh political leaders. The central government, in turn, characterized the Akali Dal as antinational and secessionist and hence outside of the political mainstream. Religion and politics became so intertwined in this context—and Bhindranwale's religious militarism so popular—that "secular Sikhs could stand aloof only at the risk of being called traitors to the Sikh cause."[93] In effect, what had occurred was that Congress had "ethnicised secular issues in order to marginalize its opponents [from the mainstream of national politics]. The fact that the demarcation of state boundaries is superimposed by linguistic and or religious markers provided the temptation for the regional political formations to lapse into the ethnic slot the Congress (I) was pushing them into. While Farooq Abdullah [of Kashmir] . . . came perilously close to it, the Akail Dal blundered straight into it."[94]

By 1983, the situation in the Punjab was so bad that murders of Hindus by Bhindranwale's activists as well as violent clashes between communities were both quite common. Whatever influence the Congress (I) leadership had once had over Bhindranwale was no longer evident. Although there remains some debate over Bhindranwale's role in the violence, matters had clearly spiraled out of control.[95] The political grievances of the Sikh community had turned into a full-fledged separatist movement, and the complicity of state actors in creating these events was clear. As a deputy police commissioner from Amritsar would later conclude, "The government not only sponsored terrorism but by its inaction helped it to grow and flourish."[96] Perhaps more problematic were the deep divisions now evident within the police forces, making them less than trustworthy in taking on the Sikh militants associated with Bhindranwale.

The conflict in the Punjab culminated in a confrontation between the government and the Sikh militants in June 1984. On June 5, the Indian army began a siege of the Golden Temple in Amristar, in which Bhindranwale and his supporters had barricaded themselves. In the ensuing assault (code-named "Operation Bluestar") close to five hundred militants were killed, including Bhindranwale. Several hundred Sikh pilgrims were also killed or wounded, and large sections of the temple complex—the most sacred site in the Sikh religion—were destroyed. The desecration of this important *gurudwara* (Sikh temple) shocked Sikhs throughout the country, leading to mutinies in the armed forces and the resignations of Sikh members of Parliament. Four months later, in October 1984, Indira Gandhi was assassinated by two of her Sikh bodyguards in revenge for the defilement of the Golden Temple.

## Conclusion

The assassination of Indira Gandhi and the communal riots that followed were a fitting end to the Nehruvian consensus. The assault on the Golden Temple, Indira Gandhi's assassination, and the subsequent violence epitomized the kind of communal antagonisms that Nehru and his associates had so feared. It also contributed to a hardening of communal identities in India. The depiction of Sikh claims as antinational and the systematic retaliation against the Sikh community for Mrs. Gandhi's death greatly sharpened their sense of persecution. Similarly, Muslims in India watched the attacks on a fellow minority group with great unease. Ironically, the violence in the Punjab reinforced Congress (I) Party claims that country was in danger of fragmentation and that a heavy-handed approach to regional issues was necessary. Minority leaders in Kashmir and Assam were subsequently depicted as a threat to the nation and linked to unnamed "external forces." Congress Party leaders, in short, used a thinly veiled religious nationalism to mobilize Hindu support behind their continued rule.

The disembedding of the secular consensus was thus well under way by the early 1980s. The effort to coopt Hindu nationalism may have been driven by electoral considerations, but it was also a choice by Congress Party leaders to abandon earlier commitments to secular norms and social reform. It is ironic, then, that it was under Indira's rule that the secular vision her father had struggled so arduously to institutionalize would come to an end and that a new era of communal politics would begin. Surprisingly, Mrs. Gandhi's majoritarian strategy served the Congress Party well throughout the remainder of the decade. Regardless of the government's complicity in Bhindranwale's rise, Mrs. Gandhi's assassination and the subsequent events helped to consolidate Hindu support for Congress throughout the 1980s. The turmoil also appeared to vindicate the fears of minority separatism that Mrs. Gandhi had enflamed. This political balancing act that Mrs. Gandhi had so artfully constructed—appealing to the sentiments of the Hindu majority while superficially claiming a secular grounding—would unravel, however, during the tenure of her son, Rajiv Gandhi, as prime minister.

# CHAPTER FIVE

# Embedding Communalism in Indian Politics

The instrumental use of religion by Indian state officials continued throughout the 1980s and 1990s. Although ostensibly opposed to the chauvinism associated with religious communalism, Congress Party leaders consistently sought to coopt the ideas and rhetoric of Hindu nationalism for their own ends. This was evident in the electoral strategy of the 1984 national elections, called shortly after Mrs. Gandhi's death, and in other campaigns throughout the decade. During this time, Rajiv Gandhi, who was elected prime minister in 1984, used the fear of minority separatism and the external threat of Islamic Pakistan as a means of consolidating support among the Hindu majority. Fear, religion, and nationalism were central elements of this majoritarian strategy. In abandoning its earlier commitments to secular nationalism, however, the Congress Party effectively ceded the ideological debate to the Sangh Parivar. It also increased tensions among India's different religious groups, which led to a fragmentation of the political community. This trend was manifest in the anti-Muslim agitations of the period, in the proliferation of violence, and, most dramatically, in the 1992 destruction of the Babri Masjid (the Mosque of Babur) in Ayodhya.

The debate over the Ayodhya mosque—and its ultimate destruction—was symbolic of the broader struggle to define the Indian nation. For Muslims and secular Hindus, the mosque reflected India's religious diversity and the nation's cosmopolitan character. For Hindu nationalists, though, it symbolized unwarranted deference to minority interests. By seeking the mosque's destruction, the groups associated with the Sangh Parivar struck at India's cosmopolitan identity, consciously using the issue to redefine the nation in explicitly Hindu terms. State complicity in the Ayodha affair and in the attendant violence was the defining feature of this tragic event and demonstrated the degree to which religious communalism had became embedded in the institutions of the Indian state.

The efforts by Congress Party leaders to coopt Hindu nationalism help to explain, then, the precipitous rise of the BJP. By appealing to the religious sentiments of the majority population, the Congress Party had normalized the discourse of Hindutva. Congress, in short, had created an ideological environment that ultimately served the interests of the BJP, not those of the Congress. Hindu communalists had rallied behind the leadership of Indira and Rajiv Gandhi in the 1980s, but this changed dramatically in the early 1990s, when these same constituencies switched their support en masse to the BJP. In doing so, they brought to a head an ideological transformation that had been under way for some time. Hence, the BJP gains in the 1990s should not have been altogether surprising. It was not that religion suddenly became more important, or that the BJP had a new message. Rather, the BJP's influence showed how much the ideological context had changed and how widely accepted Hindu chauvinism had become. It was the willingness of Hindu nationalists to back the Congress Party in the 1980s that masked the depth of this trend. When the Hindu nationalists switched back to the BJP—bringing with them large sections of the Hindu middle classes—the BJP's fortunes rose dramatically.

By 2004, this period of religious communalism, however, had come full circle. The BJP, which led the governing coalition in the Lok Sabha from 1998 to 2004, tried to use its control of the state to institutionalize its exclusive vision of social order. This included efforts to promote religious ideologues into positions of authority, to manipulate academic textbooks and, literally, to rewrite Indian history. The BJP and its allies in the Sangh Parivar also used violence against minority populations. Although the Congress Party may have pandered to Hindu sentiment, it was the BJP and other organizations associated with the Sangh Parivar that were responsible for the most egregious human rights violations of this period. Such extralegal activities included the violence of Gujarat in 2002, in which BJP Party activists systematically murdered large numbers of Muslims in their community. As in earlier periods, this was not an irrational response of a "mob" gone wild but rather a coordinated attack on a minority community designed to polarize Indian society and strengthen the Hindu nationalists' hold on power. It was precisely this type of excess, however, that discredited the ideology of Hindutva and brought an end to BJP rule. Although the 2002 riots made Narendra Modi, the BJP chief minister of Gujarat, an icon of the political right, the violence shocked mainstream Indians. The extremism of the ruling party, in short, coupled with the limited ability of Hindu nationalism to address very real economic concerns led to the collapse of the BJP's popular support in 2004.

## Rajiv Gandhi and the Politics of Competitive Populism

### *The Majoritarian Strategy*

The parliamentary elections of 1984 and the subsequent Congress (I) victory were a product of several trends that emerged during Mrs. Gandhi's rule. These included, first and foremost, the communalization of the Congress Party. Despite the rhetorical commitment to secular democracy, the Congress (I)'s policies were articulated in terms of a religious nationalism that linked Congress Party rule to national unity and Hindu solidarity. As one editorial at the time noted, the "communalism of the majority community . . . can without too much difficulty be decked out in secular trappings to look like nationalism and patriotism. . . . It can in that sense be said that the ruling party has well and truly stolen the BJP's . . . clothes."[1] Associated with the Congress Party's abandonment of secularism was a corresponding shift in economic policy. The party's historical commitment to state-led development and economic equality was replaced by a new emphasis on market liberalization and private sector investment. This era was also marked by increased authoritarianism, criminality in government, and intolerance for dissent. Political opposition—economic or regional, secular or religious—was depicted as "anti-national" or unpatriotic and was frequently met with violence.

These trends were evident in the communal violence that followed Mrs. Gandhi's assassination. The bloodshed was especially acute in Delhi, where Hindu mobs attacked members of the Sikh community and burned their shops and *gurudwaras* (temples). Men of particular ages were specifically targeted and were often burnt alive in public spaces. Women were raped, Sikh homes and businesses looted. More disturbing, was the fact that Sikh communities—many of which had once supported the Congress Party—remained unprotected by government authorities; and that members of the police actively participated in the violence. Estimates vary, but according to the government's own sources, more than 2,700 people were killed over the course of a few days, roughly 2,150 in Delhi alone.[2] Numerous others were wounded and raped; more than a hundred thousand were forced from their homes.

It is clear that these "riots" were not the product of spontaneous outrage. On the contrary, as several investigations later indicated, there was a coordinated effort by Congress Party officials, including very high-ranking ones, to "teach the Sikhs a lesson."[3] Eyewitness accounts implicated Congress Party activists and police officers for participating and even directing the attacks. In several instances, members of the "mob" were bused in from outside areas and "led by local Congress (I) politicians and hoodlums of that locality."[4] As one fact-finding team noted,

> [We have come] to the conclusion that the attacks on members of the Sikh Community in Delhi and its suburbs during the period, far from being a spontaneous expression of "madness" and of popular "grief and anger" at Mrs. Gandhi's assassination as made out to be by the authorities, were the outcome of a well-organized plan marked by acts of both deliberate commissions and omissions by important politicians of the Congress (I) at the top and by authorities in the administration. Although there was indeed popular shock, grief and anger, the violence that followed was the handiwork of a determined group which was inspired by different sentiments altogether.[5]

The Congress Party's strategy in the 1984 elections played up these communal tensions as a means of building political support among the Hindu majority. Rajiv Gandhi had called for national elections in the weeks after his mother's assassination, in part to take advantage of the attendant sympathy factor. Her death, however, was also used to underscore the dangers of minority separatism and to depict India as a nation in mortal danger. On the campaign trail, Rajiv raised the specter of Sikh and Muslim separatism as a significant threat to the national community. Moreover, he repeatedly linked the major opposition parties to separatist groups in a manner that was "sweeping, abrasive and less than accurate."[6] In a number of speeches around the country, he accused his opponents in the BJP of "instigating the agitationists in Punjab and Assam, and the secessionist forces in Jammu and Kashmir for their own political ends."[7] Other party activists linked the BJP to the Akali Dal, arguing that it was the BJP that had encouraged the Sikh militancy now threatening the unity of the country. The ruling party's attack on the patriotism of the opposition continued throughout the campaign, albeit with no evidence to back up their claims. In response, the opposition parties issued denials and counter-claims that the Congress was to blame for Sikh militancy.[8] The nature of this debate led one correspondent to conclude that it "appeared to be part of a well considered plan to narrow down the election debate to the Punjab issue . . . [with the aim of] winning over the support of the Hindus in the Hindi belt."[9]

The internal threat of separatism was also linked implicitly to Pakistan and other Muslim countries. This, in turn, prompted a call from the Congress Party for a strong centralized state to handle threats "from across the border."[10] In one speech, Rajiv claimed that "external forces were responsible for the murder of Indira Gandhi" and that these forces were continuing to provide financial and military support to the separatist groups inside of India.[11] Moreover, he accused opposition parties in Kashmir, the Punjab, and Assam of receiving foreign assistance and of working against the interests of the nation. The previous Janata government was similarly accused of sowing the seeds of conflict and of undermining the state's capacity for dealing with security threats. In contrast, the Congress (I) offered itself as the only party capable of providing the kind of leadership necessary to address the challenges threatening the nation. As one campaign advertisement noted, "There has never been a lack of enemies as far as India and her freedom are concerned. From within and from without. . . . Only the Congress (I) can give India a strong Centre. And only a strong Centre can ensure a strong India. Your vote will decide whether India stays strong or becomes weak."[12]

The Congress (I)'s strategy proved enormously successful. By depicting the election as a referendum on unity and stability—and casting the Congress Party as the only purveyor of that good—they were able to sweep the election, winning four-fifths of the Lok Sabha seats, even though they only garnered 50 percent of the vote. They did particularly well in the Hindi Belt, where separatist concerns were of greater salience and where "the 'Hindu backlash' . . . earned for Rajiv Gandhi rich dividends."[13] Although the sympathy factor was significant, the communal overtones of the Punjab crisis and Mrs. Gandhi's assassination were the defining issue of the campaign, particularly for the Hindu middle classes in the north. Even though many of these crises derived from the government's own mishandling of regional problems—and though the Congress (I) remained largely bereft of solutions—the party's majoritarian strategy proved an effective means of mobilizing popular sentiment behind their continued rule.

Ironically, the Congress Party maintained its rhetorical commitment to secularism and reiterated its respect for diversity even while promoting anti-Sikh sentiment. They accomplished this by depicting the various communal groups as those working against integration, linking them implicitly with Pakistan and other outside forces. In this way, the Congress (I) was able to portray the BJP as in league with Sikh and Muslim separatism even as the Congress (I) Party was stealing the BJP's traditional theme of Hindu unity. Moreover, in a rhetorical sleight of hand, the Congress Party simultaneously claimed that it was best able to protect minority communities, because "only the Congress (I) is free from regional interests and communal shades."[14] This was, of course, challenged by opposition leaders, who protested the party's blatant manipulation of anti-Sikh sentiments. Charan Sing, a leader of the Dalit Worker Peasant Party (the DMKP), for example, criticized Gandhi for making false accusations, noting that Rajiv Gandhi behaved as if a "big lie repeated often, can be made to appear as truth."[15]

The Congress (I)'s victory in the 1984 campaign also showed the party's internal contradictions. On the one hand, the appeal to communal sentiments had propelled Congress (I) to an unprecedented landslide victory, while marking a clear break with Nehruvian secularism. Congress (I) had effectively outflanked the BJP on the right, which at the time was trying to cultivate a more centrist position. The Congress (I) had also sought and gained the support of many RSS and VHP activists in the process, even while proclaiming its noncommunal orientation. This strategy was so effective that it thoroughly marginalized the BJP, which won only two parliamentary seats nationwide. On the other hand, the 1984 election demonstrated the weakness of the Congress (I) Party's structure. The party—and the political system—had been diminished to such an extent that there was little genuine debate over the issues facing the country. Moreover, instead of building a broad coalition of support across communities and interests, the campaign relied on a mix of fear, anxiety, and religious nationalism to mobilize the Hindu majority. As such, the 1984 elections represented the culmination of a trend away from a "retail" electoral strategy toward one based on mass politics. It also marked a sharp break with the party's traditional approach to the challenge of national integration. As Manor has noted, "Congress-I leaders after 1982 or so sometimes adopted the opposite of their former policy of arranging accommodations between social groups, subcultures, and regions and actually sought to set them against one another. This enabled the ruling party to absorb within itself discontented groups who saw it as the only party capable of providing stability amid chaos—which the Congress (I) had itself willfully helped to generate."[16]

## Ambivalence and Assertion

The party's position in regard to communalism remained characterized by inconsistency and ambivalence throughout the late 1980s. Rajiv Gandhi, recognizing that the confrontational style of the 1984 campaign was not an effective governing strategy, sought a more conciliatory approach once in power. He worked with a variety of regional groups to find an accommodation on many of the problems that had plagued his mother's tenure. In the Punjab, for example, Rajiv was able to reach an agreement with a longtime Akali Dal leader, Sant Langowal. The Gandhi-Langowal Accord represented a compromise on water issues, provided for the transfer of the city of Chandigarh to the Punjab in January 1986, and resolved other longstanding disputes between the region and the central government. Assembly elections in the state were subsequently held, and presidential rule of the Punjab ended.[17] Similarly, in Assam, an accord with dissidents was reached in August 1985, while in Kashmir a separate accommodation with Farouk Abdullah was worked out in 1986. These agreements marked a major improvement in center-state relations and something like a return to normalcy.

The forces that were unleashed in the previous years, however, were not readily contained. Gandhi's conciliatory approach to regional issues had alienated many who been attracted by his earlier confrontational style. Internal pressures also forced the government to back away from its accommodation of minority interests. Noting the displeasure with which the previous accords had been received, the Gandhi regime failed to follow through on many of its commitments. On the day before the transfer of Chandigarh from the state of Haryana to the Punjab, for example, the central government announced a postponement. Violence broke out, and Sikh militants initiated a new round of communal attacks. Similarly, in Kashmir, the prime minister's agreement with Farouk Abdullah failed to stem the rise of violence in the state. Much of this was directed at Farouk, who was now seen as "Delhi's man" in Kashmir. Pakistani support for Islamic militants and Delhi's heavy-handed response would make Kashmir a source of conflict for the next decade and a half.

The Congress Party's ambivalence toward communalism was further illustrated in a series of events leading up to the 1989 elections. The first of these was the Shah Bano affair. Shah Bano was a Muslim woman who had sued her husband of forty-five years for alimony under Indian civil law. The case was appealed to the Supreme Court because it raised a question as to which set of laws should take precedence: Indian civil law or Islamic customary law (*sharia*). When the court ruled in the wife's favor in 1985—thereby designating the primacy of civil law—Islamic conservatives protested. They argued that the court decision was an assault on a separate Islamic identity, thus representing "another attempt to destroy the autonomy of their religion."[18] Liberal Muslims supported the ruling, but the Islamic community quickly rallied behind the conservatives. This was due in part to a sense of insecurity among Muslims. The inter-communal violence of Indira's era, the increased activism of the VHP, and the anti-Sikh campaign of 1984 had all contributed to growing Muslim anxiety. Moreover, the perception that the Congress (I) had become a majoritarian party—and the defender of Hindu nationalism—had undermined the community's faith in the government. Thus, when the Supreme Court handed down its decision, conservative activists and clerics seized the opportunity to assert their authority and to portray themselves as the true defenders of Muslim interests.[19]

Rajiv Gandhi's response was similarly unhelpful. He conceded the issue to Islamic conservatives, validating their role as spokesmen for the community. The government also introduced a bill in Parliament, the Muslim Women (Protection of Rights on Divorce) Bill, which reversed the Court ruling and established the primacy of *sharia* in matters of family law. The significance of this legislation was far-reaching, as it demonstrated the government's ambivalence on communal issues and its continued willingness to cater to the demands of vocal members of a given community. There was also little sense among the governing elite of the implications of such a decision. By conceding the issue to Islamic conservatives, the government legitimized their claims at the expense of secular Muslims. The legislation was also a troubling sign of the continuing retreat from secular norms, illustrating the primacy of electoral considerations in government policymaking.[20] Perhaps the most important ramification, however, was that the government's actions sparked a backlash among Hindu communalists. They saw the policy as blatant appeasement and criticized the government for capitulating to Muslim demands. This opened the door to charges that the government was supporting a policy of "psuedo-secularism," whereby the majority was "persecuted" for demonstrating its faith and communal elements of the minority population were rewarded.

Although the initial ruling on the Shah Bano case outraged conservative Muslims, the subsequent response had a similar effect on Hindu sentiment. In one sense, the Shah Bano affair was symptomatic of the tendency to recognize group rights at the expense of individual rights. It was on this basis that members of the Sangh Parivar accused the government of pandering to minority sentiments. However, the Hindu nationalists also distorted the issue, using it as a means of furthering an ethnic interpretation of national identity. Leaders of the BJP, for example, argued that Hindus, though a majority, were systematically discriminated against, while minorities were accorded "special rights" as embodied in the Muslim Women's Bill. From this perspective, not only do Hindus have shared interests as a community but these interests were also threatened by the claims of an assertive minority. As a leader of the VHP described the situation in the late 1980s, "The fundamental issue today is whether minorities are going to enjoy the status of a privileged class or [should] they . . . be treated on a par with the Hindu counterparts. The fact is that they are enjoying the status of a privileged class and it is giving rise to communal tensions. . . . Thanks to the appeasement policy of the Congress towards minorities for the last four decades, today a Hindu in his own country is a second class citizen."[21]

The debate over the Shah Bano case also took place in an increasingly polarized ideological context. The VHP and the RSS were working at the time to politicize the status of several mosques, most notably the Babri Masjid in Ayodhya, and the Shah Bano case became intertwined with the mobilization of Hindu sentiment over the status of these mosques. The Babri Masjid was particularly significant because it was believed to have been built upon the birthplace of Rama, one the incarnations of the Hindu god Vishnu. It was on this site that an ancient temple dedicated to Rama was supposed to have stood. This earlier temple was said to have been destroyed in 1528 by a nobleman associated with the Mughal emperor Babar and replaced by the Babri Masjid. Although the status of the mosque had historically been a matter of dispute, this had not been a significant political issue for several decades. This was due in large measure to the Nehru government's firm stand on the matter. The position of the Indian government changed, however, in the 1980s. When the Ram Janmabhoomi ("Rama Birthplace") Action Committee was established in 1984, its stated goal was to "liberate" the Mosque—that is, tear it down—and rebuild the Rama Temple in its place. The intention of the VHP—which was behind the committee's creation—was to use this issue to promote a more explicitly communal understanding of Indian nationalism. The mosque was a useful political symbol because it linked a particular historical grievance with the folklore of Hindu mythology. In this way, the VHP used the controversy to promote both its vision of social order and a particular understanding of Hindu tradition. Ayodhya, one of the four sacred cities of Hinduism, was now depicted as the center of Hinduism, and the question of the mosque was quickly turned into one of national pride. It was, as Ashis Nandy argues, the culmination of a century-long "effort to convert the Hindus into a 'proper' modern nation and a conventional ethnic majority, and . . . [the] corresponding effort to turn the other faiths of the subcontinent into proper ethnic minorities."[22]

The Ram Janmabhoomi campaign was greatly aided in this effort by the Gandhi regime's own machinations. This was evident in a ruling in the Faizabad District Court in Uttar Pradesh in February 1986, the same month that the Muslim Women's Bill was introduced. The case in question concerned the status of the mosque. The judge in the case ruled that the mosque was, indeed, a temple and that the doors were to be unlocked and opened to Hindu worshippers. It was fairly clear, however, that the court ruling was an effort by the Congress Party government to cultivate favor with the VHP. As one eyewitness reported,

> The [Congress-I] Uttar Pradesh government . . . precipitated the confrontation. It deliberately stepped into the . . . controversy, and . . . actually took sides. . . . The [Congress-I] chief minister visited Ayodhya a few days before the . . . judgment [and met with VHP members]. . . . On 1 February, shortly before the order . . . was announced, a crowd of VHP supporters collected at the site. [T]his was seen as an indication by persons living there that they had advance knowledge of the verdict. A Doordarshan [government television] team too was present at the site, as if the government wished to publicize the entire event. The "victory" celebrations were filmed and telecast on the national network the same evening.[23]

The apparent strategy of the Congress (I) was to appease the communalists in both communities. As Arun Nehru, the prime minister's cousin, noted in an interview, "In early 1986, the Muslim Women's Bill was passed to play the Muslim card; and then came the decision on Ayodhya to play the Hindu card. It was supposed to be a package deal."[24] Although Arun Nehru sought to downplay his role in this matter, the essential strategy was apparent: the government leadership sought to use this politically divisive issue for its own benefit.[25] What troubled most observers, however, was that a compromise on the mosque issue was eminently achievable. Yet the Babri Masjid had become so important as a political symbol that both the ruling party and the various members of the Sangh Parivar sought to use it for political gain. The Congress (I), for example, was attempting to use the Ram Janmabhoomi issue to undercut Hindu support for its rivals in the BJP. Similarly, the VHP promoted this as a cause célèbre, seeking to take full advantage of the opening provided by the government. In response, leading members of the Muslim community formed the Babri Masjid Action Committee to mobilize their community on behalf of the issue.

The complicity of state leaders in opening the mosque and their unwillingness to broker a compromise demonstrated, again, the ruling party's abandonment of secularism as a foundational norm, a decision that was exacerbated by the communal violence that grew out of the issue. Riots took place in a number of states after the court announced its ruling, further dividing the population along religious lines. Moreover, the Congress leadership was in a position to confront the VHP and other elements of the Sangh Parivar but instead chose a policy of cooptation.[26] The degree of cooperation between the Congress leadership and the Hindu nationalist organizations, though, remains open to debate, because the RSS and the VHP were anything but reliable allies. Once the gates were open, for example, the RSS and the VHP continued to press the government for more concessions and persisted in their calls for the mosque's "liberation." The destruction of the mosque, however, was not something the government was prepared to allow, so the continued calls for its liberation put the government on the defensive. Moreover, by the late 1980s it was clear that the struggle over the mosque had gotten out of hand. It had become "the one issue which more than any other since independence [that] has poisoned the communal atmosphere, led to considerable loss of human life and property, and [which] threaten[ed] to get far worse."[27]

### *The 1989 Elections*

The dispute over the Babri Masjid was a significant feature of the 1989 national parliamentary elections. This was evident from the very start, when Rajiv Gandhi visited Faizabad, a town located a few miles from Ayodhya, to open his campaign on what he described as "the sacred soil of Ayodhya."[28] In his announcement speech, Gandhi also promised to work for the establishment of "*Ram Raja*" (literally, the rule or kingdom of Rama) if returned to power.[29] The prime minister was on the defensive after a series of corruption scandals had culminated in the Bofors affair, which involved allegations that a Swedish arms manufacturer had paid bribes to senior Indian officials in exchange for a defense contract worth US$1.25 billion. The charges, moreover, led all the way to the prime minister's office, resulting in the resignation of several close associates. The charges of corruption would become a defining feature of the campaign. It certainly seemed that Rajiv and his government were hoping to use the communal strategy as a means of deflecting attention from these other issues. The party denied the corruption charges and the claims that it supported communalism. On the contrary, the party's manifesto stressed its continuing commitment to secularism and its steadfast opposition to any sort of religious communalism.

The party's actions, however, told another story. In the states under Congress rule, violence against minorities—much of which was sparked by the Ram Janmabhoomi movement—continued unabated, frequently with the complicity of the local authorities. Similarly, the failure of the central government to confront either the VHP or the RSS contributed greatly to inter-communal tensions. The "Ram Shila" processions, for example, which were organized by the VHP and the RSS, provided a trigger for a great deal of violence.[30] These processions—whereby bricks intended for the future Rama temple were consecrated and carried through the streets of local cities and towns—were intended to be provocative, and yet they were tolerated by government authorities associated with the Congress Party. The processions were also a means of affirming Hindu solidarity and mobilizing popular sentiment along communal lines.

At the same time, the BJP sought to reaffirm its traditional position as a leading advocate of Hindu nationalism. Having learned in the 1984 elections that moderation in the current environment was a losing strategy, it embraced the Ram Janmabhoomi controversy in the 1989 electoral campaign. Rejecting any compromise on the issue, the BJP firmly committed itself to the Sangh Parivar position. As BJP President Lal Advani noted, "Let everyone understand, friends and foes alike, that the BJP's stand on this is categorical and unequivocal. The *Rama Janmabhoomi* must be handed over to Hindus and a temple must be reconstructed there."[31]

The dispute escalated further with the controversy over the *shilanyas*, the foundation ceremony for the Rama temple. The proposed ceremony became a flashpoint between Hindu communalists and the Muslim-led Babri Masjid Action Committee.[32] It also demonstrated, yet again, the government's inability (or unwillingness) to broker a compromise. There were two key issues in the dispute over the *shilanyas*. The first was of symbolic importance, because the temple had become equated with the reconstruction of the Indian state and nation along explicitly Hindu lines. As one VHP religious leader noted, the *shilanyas* "will not only be the foundation for the *Ram Janambhoomi* temple, but also for the *Hindu Rashtra* (Hindu State) which we will now establish."[33] The second concern derived from the way in which the debate had been defined: the construction of the new temple necessarily entailed the mosque's destruction. Several alternative sites and compromise solutions were repeatedly rejected by the VHP (and the ruling Congress Party) in favor of laying the foundation stone at the entrance of the existing mosque. Not only would this require the removal of the existing structure, an option wholly rejected by the Babri Masjid Action Committee, but an Allahabad court had also prohibited the use of this site for the foundation stone because it represented disputed property.

Despite these objections, the *shilanyas* ceremony went forward with the Congress (I) Party's approval. It was widely reported at the time that a deal had been struck between the ruling party and the VHP leadership, and the possibility of Rajiv Gandhi laying the stone himself was purportedly discussed.[34] The VHP agreed to throw their support behind the Congress (I) Party—at least in those areas where a BJP candidate was not running—in exchange for a free hand in Ayodhya. The government subsequently "found" that the plot of land on which the foundation was to be laid was not, in fact, part of the "disputed property," and allowed the ceremony to proceed. The repercussions were immediate. Hindu activists in the area threw their support behind the Congress, while others marched in the streets of Ayodhya to rejoice in their victory. Communal riots broke out in a number of cities, including some allegedly engineered by Congress activists to "mobilize Hindu votes, and frighten away Muslims from supporting Janata Dal [the primary opposition] candidates."[35]

The Muslim community, however, was deeply troubled by this turn of events. In a speech in front of the Jama Masjid, a central Mosque in Old Delhi, the imam's son, Ahmad Bukhari, accused both Rajiv Gandhi and his home minister, Buta Singh, of "being patrons of communal division, animosity" and of promoting a "rift between Hindus and Muslims." He also accused the Congress (I) of "pushing the country towards civil war" and promoting "confrontation between [the] two major communities."[36] Urging members of the Muslim community to vote against Gandhi, Bukhari went on to criticize the Congress government's handling of the Ayodhya issue, noting that, "desperate to remain in power, the ruling party has shelved all laws."[37]

The Congress Party's concession to communalist elements now appeared to be undermining its support. Its willingness to placate the VHP on the Ayodhya issue—both on the practical and symbolic aspects—had turned Muslim sentiment against the government. The persistent violence in various states also demonstrated that the Congress Party was no longer a "trustworthy friend."[38] More important, the Congress (I)'s willingness to compromise with the Hindu nationalists eliminated any pretense that it was still committed to the secular norms of the Nehruvian consensus. In order to capture Hindu votes, the party neglected its responsibilities to the minority communities. On the other hand, the party's support among the VHP and RSS activists was limited, since many of them remained loyal to the increasingly strident BJP, which they "regarded, in the long term, as a [better] alternative to the Congress (I)."[39] As such, the Congress (I) did not greatly benefit from its tactical collusion with the Hindu nationalists. The result was a disastrous defeat for Congress in the 1989 elections. Rajiv Gandhi was removed as prime minister, and the Congress Party was relegated to the opposition for only the second time since Independence. An opposition coalition came to power, led by the Janata Dal and joined by the BJP.

## The Rise of the BJP

The erosion of secularism under Congress rule and the corresponding rise of Hindu nationalism, came to fruition in the 1990s. Although the Janata Dal government lasted only two years, subsequent elections were marked by BJP gains.[40] The following decade was also defined by the increased prominence of the Sangh Parivar and the institutionalization of a "soft Hindutva" as a dominant idiom of Indian politics. Each of these trends was due in part to the Congress (I) government's actions in previous years. By appealing to the religious and nationalist sentiments of the majority population, the Congress (I) had hoped to mobilize a right-wing populism behind its rule. The chief beneficiary of this strategy, however, was the BJP. The party had dropped its centrist positions of 1984 and made explicit its clear support for the Hindu nationalist movement. The BJP's response to the Congress (I)'s strategy blunted the latter's gains in the Hindi-speaking heartland and helped the BJP emerge from virtual obscurity in 1984 to become the second-largest political party in 1991. The BJP's ascent culminated in the electoral victories in 1996 and 1998 and led to the formation of a ruling coalition in 1999, the National Democratic Alliance (NDA).

The BJP's rise was facilitated by a number of important factors. On the one hand, rapid economic transformation during the 1980s and 1990s laid the groundwork for an assertive Hindu communalism. The dislocation of some groups and increased affluence of others contributed to economic rivalries that were often articulated in religious and communal terms.[41] The growing affluence of many Muslims—due in part to family members working in Gulf countries—contributed to a greater prominence and political assertiveness of their community. Similarly, the Hindu middle class was rapidly expanding, though its members were less westernized and less committed to the secular ideal than were their counterparts in Nehru's generation. This new demographic also looked with suspicion on any group that enjoyed a "supposed special status— especially Muslims."[42] Rapid urbanization and the growth of Hindu and Muslim criminal organizations also fueled a sense of unease. The RSS, the VHP, and the other members of the Sangh Parivar worked assiduously in this context to make inroads into the new Hindu middle class. Their claims that Hindu society was under siege, both from within and without, and their call for a more assertive majoritarianism resonated with this group, even if their shock troops were drawn from the lower classes.

Another factor that contributed to this trend was the continuing problem of separatism, particularly in Kashmir and the Punjab. The emergence of an assertive Islamic fundamentalism in South Asia—driven largely by the Afghan war in the 1980s and Pakistan's own religious sectarianism—appeared to validate many of the VHP's claims. This was particularly relevant in Kashmir, where the popular uprising that began in 1989 continued throughout the 1990s. Although much of the conflict derived from longstanding grievances with, and human rights abuses by, the central government, the conflict took on communal symbolism as Islamic identities hardened in reaction to contemporary trends. These included the "Indira factor"—the Congress (I)'s aforementioned activities—as well as the Hindu agitations in Ayodhya.[43] The situation was made worse by the influx of arms and fighters from neighboring Pakistan. The involvement of the Pakistani intelligence services, the ISI, in both training and supplying troops significantly increased the cross-border tensions, turning this uprising into a veritable proxy war.

The conflict between India and Pakistan over Kashmir boiled over in the summer of 1999, when the two countries clashed in a region known as Kargil. Although the outcome was something of a victory for India, it raised grave concerns about a more serious conflict, given the nuclear capability of the two countries. Moreover, the clash greatly inflamed nationalist passions in India, creating a dynamic whereby the dominant political actors competed with one another to demonstrate their patriotism. The result was that political parties of all stripes were "sliding into a militarist pathology, [and] everyone was demanding more expenditure on defense . . . confrontation with Pakistan . . . and further expansion of the nuclear arms programme."[44] It was an indication of the continuing failure of the Indian government to deal constructively with longstanding regional grievances. The central government had defined these conflicts in terms of religion and minority separatism and had consistently taken a confrontational approach. This, in turn, encouraged the kind of militant nationalism "epitomized by the Hindutva movement."[45]

Finally, caste considerations also influenced the resurrection of Hindu nationalism. In 1991, V. P. Singh, prime minister and head of the Janata Dal government, announced that his government would accept the recommendations on caste issues from a 1980 government commission, what became known as the Mandel Commission. These recommendations provided affirmative action benefits for "schedule castes" (untouchables) and Other Backward Castes (OBCs). This program would reserve 27 percent of all government jobs for the OBCs, a large segment of the Hindu vote. This step, however, sparked major protests among upper-caste Hindus, who saw affirmative action as a threat to their dominance of Indian professional life. The RSS and the BJP (Singh's leading coalition partner) joined this "elite revolt," fearing that caste issues would divide the Hindu community. Moreover, the BJP was concerned that the increased salience of caste as a basis for voting would undermine its political fortunes by pitting upper- against lower-caste Hindus. The party could not directly oppose the reservation policy, moreover, for fear of alienating lower-caste Hindus. Consequently, the BJP sought to reinvigorate the Ram Janmabhoomi issue in an effort to change the debate and to focus national attention on communal divisions rather than caste issues.

## Ayodhya

In September 1990, Lal Advani, the BJP leader, sought to highlight the cause of the Rama temple by leading a "*Rath Yatra* (chariot procession) through the center of India. Advani's pilgrimage began at the Somnath Temple in Gujarat and wound its way through eight states, arriving in Ayodhya six weeks later. The event was coordinated with the VHP and was designed to emphasize Hindu unity while downplaying caste, sect, and socioeconomic differences. It also demonized Muslims as a means of dividing lower-caste (and lower-class) Hindus from their Muslim counterparts. Consequently, the procession focused attention on temples destroyed by Mughal rulers and the historical grievances associated with the desecration of Hindu holy sites. In this way, it sought to depict the Muslim as a "foreign invader" whose allegiance to India remained suspect while using the sense of Hindu persecution as a basis for communal mobilization.[46] As part of this campaign, the BJP published a series of newspaper advertisements that criticized the Congress Party's policy of "psuedo-secularism," arguing that it "pampered" minorities and disregarded the needs of the majority.[47]

Several features of Advani's tour are noteworthy. To begin with, it was the first time since Independence that a national politician traveled the country openly articulating a message of Hindu communalism. The very fact of the procession itself showed how much Hindu chauvinism had become mainstream, at least in the states visited by Advani. Second, the pilgrimage was covered extensively by the mass media, as it was intended to be. The procession was a spectacle, imbued with religious imagery and designed for a television audience. Advani, for example, rode a chariot built on an automobile chassis covered with Hindu swastikas and other religious symbols.[48] At one point, he also took up a bow and arrow, Lord Rama's weapons of choice. The intention was to cast Advani in the likeness of Lord Rama, making those who opposed him both anti-Hindu and antinational. The coverage of this event was extensive, and, frequently biased. This was particularly true at the local level, where the riots associated with the *Rath Yatra* were often depicted as the fault of Muslims.

The third, and most significant, issue concerns the militant character of the pilgrimage. Although Advani was careful *not* to call for violence in his speeches, the entire procession was imbued with an iconography of Hindu militancy. It thus sparked violent clashes wherever it went.[49] The violence, however, was not spontaneous, nor did it reflect some notion of ancient hatreds between communities. Rather, the violence for the most part "had been [well] planned . . . and enjoyed ample political backing," both from the local police as well as from some state governments.[50] The intention, as in the past, was to polarize the relevant communities and to reinforce the religious basis of national identity. Younger activists associated with the Sangh Parivar's more militant groups— including the Bajrang Dal, the VHP's youth wing—were responsible for much of the violence that left over 550 people dead.[51] Even in the state of Maharashtra, where the Congress (I) remained in power, the local authorities did nothing to stop the *Rath Yatra*, lest they be perceived as anti-Hindu. Similarly, Prime Minister Singh was reluctant to confront Advani, who had, during the tour, stated his willingness to withdraw from the ruling coalition if the Singh government blocked the Ram temple's reconstruction. After negotiations with the BJP broke down, the Singh government was forced to act, ordering the arrest of Advani before he reached Ayodhya. This sparked more violence and led to the BJP's withdrawal from the coalition government.

In the 1991 parliamentary elections that followed the fall of the Janata Dal coalition, the BJP mimicked the strategy of Congress (I)'s earlier campaigns. The BJP made the threat of minority separatism and terrorism a key feature of the elections and depicted itself as the party of assertive Hindu strength. The BJP, in short, portrayed itself as uniquely able to ensure the security of the nation. Added to this was an appeal to cultural identity—in the form of an upper-caste-dominated Hinduism—and an explicit antiminority sentiment. These themes played well in an increasingly communalized environment, and the BJP saw significant electoral gains as a result. It captured 120 seats in the Lok Sabha, emerging as the second largest party behind Congress (I).

The Congress Party's ultimate success in this election had a great deal to do with the assassination of Rajiv Gandhi by a Tamil separatist from Sri Lanka. Gandhi was killed by a suicide bomber affiliated with the Liberation Tigers of Tamil Eelam (LTTE), a Sri Lankan separatist group that opposed the Indian government's involvement in the Sri Lankan civil war. The Congress Party's electoral victory, however, was extremely limited in scope. The Congress failed to win a majority of seats and was forced to form a coalition government. The Congress Party that came to power in 1991, furthermore, was not the party it once was. Riven by factionalism and perceived as corrupt, it was rapidly losing its support—and its members—to the BJP. It also did not appear to have a clear ideological direction. The Congress Party had vacillated on the issue of caste reservations and promoted vague appeals to communal harmony despite its previous abandonment of state secularism. The BJP, on the other hand, was the leading advocate of assertive Hindu nationalism. It was also emerging as the one party with a coherent, albeit strident, vision for the future of India.

There remained tensions, however, within the Sangh Parivar over the most appropriate means of achieving their ultimate ends. At the center of this debate was the merit of continuing a strategy of ethno-religious mobilization. Although the violence associated with the *yatras* and ceremonial processions helped the BJP gain power at the state level, some feared that these tactics would ultimately damage the BJP's prospects at the national level.[52] Particularly after their performance in the 1991 elections, there was a push within the party to moderate its image and widen its appeal. This debate reflected the internal disputes that had characterized the BJP in the early 1980s. Although most members of the party embraced the idea of Hindu nationalism, some were more committed to an explicit *Hindu Rashtra* than others. This debate extended to the question of the Babri Masjid and its continuing usefulness as a means of mobilizing popular sentiment. Some felt that the issue had run its course and that there was little to be gained from continuing the movement.[53] More strident members of the BJP, however, as well as those in the VHP and the RSS, remained adamant about the need to rebuild the Ram temple. For them, the mosque remained "an invader's victory monument."[54]

It was in this context that the Babri Masjid was destroyed. On December 6, 1992, nearly two hundred thousand Hindu activists, taking matters into their own hands, descended on the temple town of Ayodhya. Coordinated by the various organizations associated with the Sangh Parivar and enjoying the apparent complicity of the BJP state government, the *"karsevak"* activists proceeded to demolish the sixteenth-century mosque. The state police forces, in the form of the Provincial Armed Constabulary, stood by as the demolition proceeded, refusing to intervene. The police even encouraged the participants, looking on as journalists were assaulted and other crimes were committed. The VHP propaganda, along with the complicity of local authorities, contributed to the belief among many activists that—by virtue of their extreme militancy—only they represented the "true Hindus; the rest were traitors."[55] Riots broke out in a number of cities across India, leaving more than one thousand dead in the course of a week. Some of the bloodiest violence occurred in Bombay, where local police were involved with Hindu militants in targeting members of the Muslim community. The riots in that city continued into late January and were associated with extensive criminal activity such as the confiscation of land, extortion, rape, and murder. Riots in other cities were sparked by the "victory processions" celebrating the destruction of the mosque. As in 1984, the activists behind these riots were usually aided by local authorities, who did little or nothing to protect minority communities.

In a manner also reminiscent of 1984, the destruction of the mosque and the subsequent riots were not spontaneous events. On the contrary, the BJP began its communal mobilization in July of that year, while the VHP initiated a publicity campaign several weeks before the December 6 event. This campaign, in which "anti-national" Muslims were targeted as enemies of the Hindu people, warned of a coming "war."[56] BJP activists similarly threatened Muslims in their speeches, warning that "dissent on the Ramjanmabhoomi–Babri Masjid dispute would be an act of treachery for which the Muslims would be banished from the country."[57] In Bombay, the Shiv Sena was involved in inter-communal violence and propaganda in the two months leading up to the attack and also during its aftermath. In the violence that followed the December 6 assault, Shiv Sena and BJP activists led and coordinated attacks on Muslim communities, often with the aid of voter registration lists and other municipal documents that identified Muslim homes and businesses.[58] The coordination of activities could also be seen in the use of local news outlets and party newspapers to incite inter-communal hatred. The complicity of the local police was another significant factor, reflecting a deep anti-Muslim bias in law enforcement. The Srikrishna Commission, set up to investigate the riots, also criticized the Congress (I)–led Maharashtra state government for failing to respond to the crisis, which the commission attributed to "politics-induced vacillation."[59]

Some argued that the destruction of the Ayodhya mosque hurt the BJP by demonstrating the dangers of unchecked communalism. This argument was borne out to some extent in the 1993 state assembly elections, where the party fared rather poorly. It is unclear whether these defeats were the result of incumbency and its inability to provide social services or whether it was due to the mosque issue. In any event, the BJP lost power in all but one of the five states in which it had previously ruled. Moreover, in the following year, the Congress Party was able to win an outright majority in the national parliamentary elections. However, neither of these events marked the end of Hindutva, nor were they indicative of a broader Congress comeback. Corruption scandals and continued infighting within the party continued to hamper the Congress (I)'s effectiveness. Of perhaps greater significance was the continued ideological drift of the Congress Party. Despite Prime Minister P. V. Narasimha Rao's initial response to the events of December 6, there was no concerted effort to oppose the BJP's communalism or to build a coalition of like-minded parties in support of secularism. On the contrary, Rao's initial ban on the RSS and the Bajrang Dal was left unimplemented—and was later withdrawn—while many of the activists arrested after December 6 were released within a week.[60] There was also little if any effort in the following year to investigate and prosecute those responsible for the destruction of the mosque. It quickly became apparent that "far from fighting the [*Sangh*] *Parivar*, Narasimha Rao sought to compete with it on the basis of the Parivar's agenda. Every step that was taken by the Government seemingly to fight the Parivar was all but sabotaged by the [Congress] Government itself."[61]

## Gujarat

The willingness of the Congress Party to concede the debate over secularism and national identity enhanced the BJP's credibility and contributed to its continued rise. State elections in 1994 and in 1995 saw major BJP gains, securing control of both Gujarat and Maharashtra with the Shiv Sena as a coalition partner. In 1996 the BJP won a plurality of seats in the Lok Sabha (161 seats), handing the Congress Party one of its worst electoral defeats in its history. The BJP also won the 1998 election (179 seats) and the 1999 elections as well. Although the BJP was unable to form a viable coalition in 1996, and in 1998 could only stay in power for one year, the 1999 coalition proved more enduring. The BJP subsequently emerged as a dominant force at the center, even though it relied on the other members of its coalition, the National Democratic Alliance (NDA).

Some argued during this time that the BJP's electoral success, especially the demands of coalition politics, moderated the party's ideology. In some respects, this was true. The desire to appeal to a wider audience diminished the party's ideological commitments, while the demands of alliance partners constrained the party's more extreme tendencies. A perhaps more accurate account might be that Prime Minister Atul Vajpayee of the BJP sought to balance the demands of his Sangh Parivar supporters with the needs of the NDA partners. This was evident in the 1996 elections, in which Hindu militancy was relegated to the background and a "soft Hindutva" was articulated in its stead. Although the more strident tones of the previous years had greatly influenced public discourse, some members of the BJP were concerned that more violence would ultimately hurt the party. The exigencies of politics, it was argued, was forcing the BJP to change its approach—if not its ultimate goals—because the party recognized that a mobilization based on religious militancy could only take it so far. This effort to normalize Hindutva illustrated the party's effort to distance itself from the violent militancy of previous years and to present a kinder, gentler face to the Indian public.

The degree to which the BJP abandoned its ideological commitments, however, is an open question. Although the leadership proved willing to tone down its rhetoric and to make accommodations to form a coalition government, the party nonetheless retained strong ties to the RSS and other members of the Sangh Parivar. These organizations, moreover, did not abandon their vision of creating a social order defined by Hindu preference and upper-caste dominance. On the contrary, they sought to use the BJP's control of the state to reorder society in a manner consistent with their vision of Hindu nationalism. This was evident in the effort by state officials to pressure the media to provide favorable coverage of Sangh Parivar activities and to normalize what, in one commentator's opinion, "was previously perceived as an extremist fringe."[62] Moreover, communal violence continued under BJP rule, as did VHP propaganda campaigns, both of which contributed to a "social environment of hatred and polarization."[63]

The BJP also used state ministries and institutions to embed its exclusive vision of the nation. This was evident in the transformation of education policy under the BJP as well as its effort to rewrite the textbooks, curricula, and Indian history taught in state-run schools. The BJP also sought to influence academic research by appointing individuals sympathetic to the ideals of Hindutva to institutions of higher education and removing those who opposed them. This included the replacement of a number of liberal historians and social scientists on the Indian Council of Historical Research and the Indian Council of Social Science Research.[64] Similarly, there were constraints on foreign scholars doing work on sensitive issues as well as on foreign donations to local academics and nonprofits. This "massive assault on the intelligentsia" was part of a concerted effort to legitimize and institutionalize the discourse of Hindu nationalism and to promote the idea that Indian nationalism implies some notion of Hindu dominance.[65] In doing so, these activists were using the institutions of the state to create a more uniform society for both electoral and ideological purposes.

The BJP's actions at the state level also belied the moderate rhetoric at the national level. In Maharashtra, for example, the BJP–Shiv Sena government worked to undermine the formal inquiry into the Bombay riots of 1992, abolished the commission established to hear minority grievances, and removed Muslims from their homes in Bombay in the name of slum clearance. Similarly, anti-Christian mobilization and violence occurred in a number of states, carried out largely by Bajrang Dal and VHP activists with the sanction of the local authorities. This type of endorsement emboldened local activists who "felt protected by the state machinery . . . [particularly] since the home minister, Lal Advani, by and large downplayed anti-Christian activities."[66] In addition to the attacks on individual Christians and churches, missionaries were also targeted. The most notable attack was the gruesome murder of an Australian missionary, Graham Staines, and his two sons, who were burnt alive as they slept in their jeep in 1998. The individual convicted of the murders, Dara Singh, was not a member of any Parivar group but was said to have been motivated by Christian efforts to "destroy Hindu religion." The popular press implicitly defended the attack, noting that while his actions may have been condemnable, his motivations were understandable. These attacks coincided with a Sangh Parivar campaign against Christian proselytizing.

More disturbing were the events in Gujarat in the spring of 2002. Earlier in the year, the VHP had resurrected the Ayodhya issue and set a date of March 15 for construction to begin on a new temple. Hindu activists made pilgrimages to the site as part of this mobilization. It was in this context that a train carrying Hindu activists on its way back from Ayodhya was attacked. The incident occurred in the town of Godhra, in the state of Gujarat, after a confrontation between Hindu activists and Muslim vendors on the train platform.[67] Two train cars were set on fire, and fifty-eight people perished, including Hindu women and children. Over the next three days, retaliatory violence erupted throughout the state of Gujarat, leaving over six hundred Muslims dead and two hundred thousand homeless; unofficial estimates place the number killed at two thousand. The local press and government authorities used the Godhra tragedy to incite violence against Muslims in other areas of the Gujarat. They depicted the incident as linked both to the Pakistan intelligences services and to a "'deadly conspiracy' against Hindus by Muslims in the state."[68] Pro-BJP newspapers further inflamed passions by fabricating stories about Hindu women being abducted and raped, while local television carried sensational depictions of the riots.

Although the BJP-led Gujarati government characterized the violence as a "spontaneous reaction" to the Godhra tragedy, it has since become clear that the attacks on the Muslim population were "planned well in advance."[69] Weapons were distributed, rioters were organized, and a process of mobilization was initiated weeks earlier. As in other riots, the attacks were carried out by Hindu militants from the Bajrang Dal, the VHP, the RSS, and others, though with "extensive police participation and in close cooperation with officials of the BJP state government."[70] There were also eyewitness accounts of BJP politicians directing attacks as well as reports that state officials had taken up positions in police headquarters. As in other riots, Muslim-owned businesses and homes were specifically targeted, indicating the use of voter registration or tax information to distinguish Muslim-owned property from that of Hindus. This combination of state complicity, hateful propaganda, and anti-Muslim violence led one commentator to note that what had occurred could not credibly described as a riot. Rather, it was "a fascist pogrom, conducted by organized death squads of the Hindu Right with the entire State apparatus at their disposal."[71]

There remain many unanswered questions as to why this occurred and why no charges were brought against any of the leaders involved in the violence. One explanation is that the riots were driven by electoral considerations, though not those discussed earlier. Rather, hardline elements within the Sangh Parivar had perceived the BJP's centrist positions as hurting the movement's electoral fortunes, particularly in Gujarat. Moreover, the party's ability to address many of the underlying social ills in a region severely harmed by deindustrialization was limited, which endangered its ability to retain control of the state government.[72] The violence in the spring of 2002 thus changed the political dynamics in the state by once again placing the dangers of Muslim separatism at the forefront of the political debate. This was reflected in the position of the state government, which argued that the Godhra incident was planned and the riots spontaneous. All this helped make Narendra Modi, the BJP chief minister and an RSS activist, a hero among many Hindus precisely because of his involvement in the violence.[73] The continuing viability of communalism as a basis of mobilization was borne out in the state assembly elections held six months later, in which the BJP won a landslide victory. Although the BJP had appeared vulnerable a year before, they were able to win the support of a broad cross-section of the Hindu community—including lower-caste *dalits* as well as middle- and upper-class Gujaratis. The Congress (I)'s unwillingness to condemn the violence and its effort to offer a "soft Hindutva to counter the BJP" contributed to its rout.[74]

The events of 2002 show how much Indian politics had changed since the Nehru era. The violence in Gujarat was facilitated by the antiminority sentiments that had become an increasingly common feature of Indian politics. These sentiments were evident in the remarks of Prime Minister Vajpayee after the Gujarat violence that "wherever Muslims live, they don't like to live in coexistence with others . . . and instead of propagating their ideas in a peaceful manner, they want to spread their faith by resorting to terror and threats."[75] The 2002 campaign in Gujarat was similarly defined by continuing references to the danger of terrorist attacks and the ever-present need for greater security.

Although the violence was, in part, a means of rallying the Hindu nationalist base, it also had the effect of diverting attention among lower-caste (and lower-class) Hindus from the more pressing concerns of economic dislocation associated with neoliberal economic policies. The VHP-directed violence once again helped emphasize the salience of communal divisions over those of class and caste. Moreover, the success of the BJP (and the forces of the Sangh Parivar) in pursuing this strategy was greatly facilitated by the Congress (I)'s own actions. One VHP leader characterized the 2002 state assembly election as a referendum on the ideology of Hindutva and predicted that the results would be a "decisive rejection of the ideology of Mahatma Gandhi and Jawaharlal Nehru."[76] This was only partially accurate, insofar as the Congress (I) had failed to defend its traditional ideological commitment to Gandhian tolerance and Nehruvian secularism. It even ran a candidate for the seat in Godhra who was himself involved in the anti-Muslim violence.[77] This led Chief Minister Narendra Modi to remark that "Congress was unable to place Nehru at the centre of its election. . . . [Instead] they had to campaign using the image of Sardar Patel [Nehru's longtime rival], a leader they had for long discarded."[78]

## *The Resurrection of Tolerance?*

Less than two years after the events in Gujarat, in May 2004, national elections saw the defeat of the BJP and the reemergence of a Congress-led coalition government at the national level. This election was clearly a repudiation of the BJP's tenure in office. The election result shocked many longtime observers of Indian politics and reflected a desire for greater moderation among the Indian electorate. Perhaps not surprisingly, the 2004 elections hinged more on economic considerations than cultural ones. The BJP government had done very little for the lower castes and the rural poor. Although many in these groups had supported the BJP when the party appeared to be defending them against communal antagonists, these same voters abandoned the BJP when its policies failed to provide tangible benefits. This demonstrated the shallowness inherent in the ideology of Hindutva. Once the communalist party was in power, no amount of processions, riots, or appeals to *Ram Raja* could distract the Hindu electorate from more pressing economic concerns. The promise of a Hindu Rashtra, in short, did nothing to create jobs or to solve the challenge of endemic poverty. Consequently, the BJP's 2004 campaign theme, "India Shining," did not resonate with the hundreds of millions of rural poor whose lives were scarcely affected (at least in a beneficial way) by the neoliberal economic policies of the BJP government.

The violence of Gujarat also tainted the BJP and gave the impression that the party was still dominated by extremists. It was clear, for example, that the party had strong ties to criminal organizations, particularly in Mumbai, which worked closely with local officials to carry out the 2002 violence. The excesses of Gujarat also undermined the BJP-led coalition and led the party's coalition partners to reevaluate their support for the Vajpayee government. The central government's inaction and the state government's complicity added up to a major liability for the BJP in 2004. The ideas of Hindu preference and exclusivity may have been a useful means of mobilizing populist support, but they did not provide a viable basis for a coalition government. Given the concern of national unity, a government guided by the principles of Hindu nationalism proved to be a recipe for disaster. In a multiethnic, multireligious society, the effort to promote unity through cultural uniformity—and privilege one community to the detriment of others—invariably bred its own demise. And this is what happened to the BJP. In trying to institutionalize an exclusive vision of Indian nationalism, the BJP overreached. Its ideological orientation fostered conflict and division, which ultimately cost it the support of the Indian middle classes.

It would be difficult, however, to argue that the 2004 elections reflected a genuine return to Nehruvian secularism. On the contrary, Congress Party candidates continued to invoke religious themes on the campaign trail in an effort to demonstrate their cultural authenticity. Moreover, the RSS, the BJP, and other elements of the Sangh Parivar remained unrepentant and retained a sizable degree of support among the electorate. Nonetheless, the 2004 elections—and the subsequent 2009 parliamentary elections—did reinforce a larger theme. Both the divisive nature of the BJP politics and its failures to address economic concerns proved to be liabilities. Although cultural concerns may have been a useful means of gaining power, they ultimately proved unworkable as a basis of governance. The purposeful division and polarization of the electorate that were the hallmark of the BJP electoral strategies simply proved unacceptable in a society as diverse as India. The legacy of Nehru's secular vision consequently remained relevant, as did the idea of India as an inclusive nation, particularly when contrasted with the violent extremism of the Sangh Parivar.

These themes—and the corresponding return to a more centrist, more moderate politics—were reinforced by the 2009 parliamentary elections. After five years under a Congress-led coalition known as the United Progressive Alliance, most commentators and analysts predicted an indeterminate outcome. Much to everyone's surprise—including Congress Party leaders—the election marked a clear vindication of Congress Party rule. Manmahan Singh, the Congress Party prime minister from 2004 onward, was reelected as prime minister, the Congress Party retained its majority in the Lok Sabha, and Sonia Gandhi, Rajiv's widow, emerged as an influential leader in her own right. An essential part of this victory was the rejection of the kind of divisive policies promoted by the BJP. Although individual Congress Party candidates continued to invoke religious themes, there was not the mimicry of the radical right seen in earlier years. In other words, the Congress Party had abandoned its own exclusive politics in favor of a more centrist vision of stability and competency. The Singh government had also sought to counter the institutionalization of Hindutva within school curriculum and in public life. The Muslim vote subsequently migrated back to the Congress, believing that only Congress could "provide a stable, secular government."[79] Despite the BJP's efforts to portray itself as a moderate party capable of fashioning a broad coalition, its traditional allies remained a liability, as did its legacy of violence. What became evident was that the extremism of the 1990s had only limited appeal. The politics of ethnic division, while successful in the short term, ultimately proved counterproductive in an open society such as India's. The Congress and the BJP were both surprised to discover this to be true in the elections of 2004 and 2009.

## Conclusion

The communalization of the Indian polity under Congress in the 1980s helps to explain the dramatic and rapid nature of the BJP's rise, a trend that few analysts had predicted. The BJP's gains in the 1990s came predominantly from the Hindu nationalists who had backed Indira and Rajiv's mobilizations in the 1980s but switched their support back to the BJP in the early to mid-1990s. To most observers, this represented a sudden overthrow of India's secular nationalism by the forces of Hindu communalism. However, the demise of secular norms was well under way in the early 1980s. The communalization of Indian politics, in short, did not occur overnight but transpired over the course of a decade. It was also very much the result of the Congress Party's willingness to coopt the themes of Hindu nationalism. This complicity was masked by a rhetorical commitment to secularism and official pronouncements of successive Congress governments claiming to defend minority interests. This secular veneer, however, belied a majoritarian strategy of right-wing populism. The Congress Party's efforts to coopt Hindu nationalist themes attracted, temporarily, members of the RSS and the VHP who had been willing to abandon the BJP in the early 1980s. When these Hindu activists flocked back to the BJP in the elections of the 1990s, its political fortunes rose precipitously.

The assumption that the BJP and the Congress, then, represented competing poles on an ideological spectrum—and that the former had overthrown the latter—is actually quite misleading. Rather, what emerged in the 1980s and

1990s was an interparty competition over cultural authenticity, with the BJP and Congress each appealing to the communal sentiments of the majority population. It was not a matter of secular versus religious but rather of competing claims to speak for the nation. Moreover, the willingness of the Congress Party to stay silent on such issues as Gujarat and to concede the ideological debate over the Babri Masjid to the BJP represented an abandonment of the secular vision of the nation. This is not to argue that the Congress Party was responsible for the extreme violence of the Hindu nationalists; the BJP and its related organizations bear that responsibility. However, it does implicate the Congress Party in the communalization of the public sphere. The normalization of the Hindu nationalist ideology placed a high degree of stress on civil society and led many to question the ability of India's traditional tolerance and pluralism to survive. Even as late as 2003, Indians tended to be divided between those who felt that the country's historical tolerance would constrain the "saffronization" of the public square (that is, the creation of a Hindu-dominated public sphere) and those who felt that the demise of pluralism was irrevocably under way.

The results of the elections in 2004 and 2009, then, represent a heartening historical turn for those who had feared the worst. Although the elections did not entail the end of communalism in South Asia—or a return to Nehruvian secularism per se—the results did represent a repudiation of extremism. There remains in India a tendency of all politicians to invoke religion as a means of demonstrating their morality, patriotism, or authenticity. However, this has been tempered by the tendency to eschew the more exclusive interpretations of religion that were associated with the violence of the Sangh Parivar. The more liberal rendering of Hindu tradition, as Mahatma Gandhi demonstrated, is entirely consistent with the cosmopolitan norms of an inclusive nationalism, and it is this vision of religion and society that has gained ground in the last two elections. The fragility of Indian democracy, however, and the enduring appeal of communalism in the region preclude sweeping judgments about the country's future. Nonetheless, recent trends indicate that the secular project remains a viable force in Indian society, as does the country's traditional commitment to an inclusive political order.

# CHAPTER SIX

# The Rise and Decline of American Secularism

Religion has always been a central feature of American politics. Despite an institutional separation of church and state, religion—particularly Protestant Christianity—remains firmly rooted in American nationalism and culture. So, too, is the belief that Americans are a chosen people with a unique destiny in the world. This messianic understanding of the American idea draws from the religious idealism of the country's Puritan origins and is evident in the tendency to associate democracy with Divine Providence. America's religious heritage is also a source of conflict, however, and has given rise to two competing visions of the nation. In its more benign moments, the transcendent elements of American nationalism have served as a "civil religion" that provides faith and meaning to public life.[1] This nonsectarian understanding of religion defined the liberal consensus of the post–World War II period and was largely consistent with a secular program of national development. At other times, however, Protestant Christianity has informed a more exclusive and aggressive religious nationalism. This variant of the American idea provides an explicitly Christian narrative to American history and links national purpose with the execution of God's Will on earth.

These divergent views of America's religious heritage reflect both different interpretations of the Judeo-Christian tradition and competing visions of the nation. They have also shaped the fault lines of political conflict for two centuries. On the one hand, the secular vision of American nationalism is premised on a liberal or modernist understanding of religion and an inclusive national identity. This reflects the Enlightenment ideas prevalent at the nation's founding and the inclusive elements of the Puritan tradition. It also reflected the diversity of American religious life. The U.S. Constitution consequently embodies a compromise on the question of religion: in order to protect religion (and conscience) from undue government interference, no particular denomination is given preference in the institutions of nation and state. This emphasis on religious freedom is central to the country's self-understanding as a free and open society. The alternative vision of American nationalism, however, rejects the secular tradition, seeing the United States as an explicitly Christian nation. This interpretation draws from the intolerant elements of the Puritan legacy and informs a more exclusive vision of national identity, one defined along ethnic, racial, or religious lines. Advocates of this view have historically been concerned about an excessive secularism that they believe is the source of contemporary social ills. A closer association between state and organized Christianity, then, is seen as a prerequisite for redeeming the political community and reinstilling a traditional sense of values in American public life.

These competing visions of the nation also involve very different conceptions about the nature and use of American power. Religion in the liberal context commonly served a prophetic function in American politics and has been invoked to constrain the exercise of temporal power (at least in such cases as the Vietnam War). As such, this worldview sees "the nation as under God and therefore responsible to God."[2] This mirrors Robert N. Bellah's original understanding of civil religion, in which the nation is subordinate "to the ethical principles that transcend it and in terms of which it should be judged."[3] Religious morality, from this view, ought to guide—and to constrain—government action, particularly given the potential for abuse by a fallible humanity. The more overtly Christian vision of religious nationalism, on the other hand, has tended to conflate religious purpose with that of the state or of a particular political party. As such, it has commonly provided a priestly affirmation for government policy and a license for action taken on behalf of the nation. American power—military, political, or economic—is consequently portrayed as benign precisely because it is associated with divine purpose. Patriotism and nationalist symbols (such as the flag) are subsequently elevated to religious status, making the nation itself an object of veneration. Instead of calling government to account, this approach makes goals like the protection of national interest (however defined) the basis for judging the morality of government policy.

Like the other two cases in this book, the political fortunes of these competing visions of religion and nation have fluctuated dramatically over time. Debates over the proper role of religion in public life defined the American experience at the outset, and they have recurred periodically over the past two centuries. The basic issues in these debates, moreover, are central to American politics and society: ought a particular interpretation of religion be institutionalized in American public life, or should America retain its secular character? Does religion provide a guide for government policy or a license for action? The following two chapters cover both the enduring nature of these debates and the ambiguity of the response. Although secular norms were embedded in the Constitution in the late eighteenth century, an overt religious nationalism has remained enormously influential. This tension was clearly evident in the mid-twentieth century, when liberal ideas about religion and nation were embedded in American institutions. Despite the dominance of the "liberal consensus," there were strong countercurrents prevalent at the time. The anticommunism of the "radical right" may have been seen as extreme in the early 1960s, but it remained a significant alternative to the liberal consensus, offering a competing vision of both religion and society.

As in the other cases, the secular nationalism of the mid-twentieth century was later displaced by a more illiberal vision of religious nationalism. The question, then, is why? Why did an exclusive vision of religious nationalism emerge so forcefully in the 1980s and 1990s, particularly given its earlier marginalization? Although a number of factors help to explain this trend, the variable that the following two chapters emphasize is the changing orientation of state elites toward conservative or illiberal Christianity. Beginning with Richard Nixon, Republican presidential candidates (and other party operatives) consistently appealed to exclusive visions of religion and nation to mobilize popular sentiment behind their claims for political power. In doing so, state elites sought to coopt theologically conservative religious leaders to support a new era of conservative politics. This was nowhere more evident than in the Republican Party's Southern Strategy. This strategy—used successfully by Nixon in the 1968 and 1972 presidential campaigns—invoked a mix of race, religion, and patriotism to appeal to the white Christian majority, particularly in the South. The intent was to politicize divisive social issues in order to polarize society along cultural, not class, lines. Republican Party strategists believed that this type of "positive polarization" could displace economic considerations as a primary basis of voting, thus splitting the Democratic coalition that had dominated the country since the 1930s.[4] An aggressive cultural politics, in short, could provide a party dominated by economic elites with a basis of mass populist support.

What makes Nixon's manipulation of religious politics so interesting—aside from its success—is that it reflected such a sharp break with previous practice. It also marked the beginning of the end of the secular order that followed World War II. Leaders like Roosevelt, Truman, Eisenhower, Kennedy, and Johnson had all viewed American purpose in religious terms but tended to embrace an ecumenical vision of religion and society. In doing so, they promoted a liberal or secular vision of American nationalism and worked to constrain the more exclusive interpretations of religious nationalism. During the mid-twentieth century, this vision of secular nationalism was not hostile to religion but rather reflected the liberal religious consensus of the era. The promotion of conservative religion by Nixon and his successors, on the other hand, undermined this consensus and allowed an exclusive vision of religion and nationalism to take its place. Evangelical Christianity, in the guise of "conservative values," was subsequently portrayed as culturally authentic, while liberal ideas and secular nationalism were denigrated as un-American. The results of this strategy would leave a lasting mark on American society. It contributed greatly to the polarization of American politics and brought the ideas associated with the radical right into the ideological mainstream. It also paved the way for the right-wing populism of the Reagan-Bush era, which is the focus of chapter 7.

## The Origins of American Secularism

The religious legacy of American history is a bifurcated one. Although secular norms were institutionalized in the founding Constitution, the early colonial period was defined by a close affiliation of religion and state. The original settlers of New England came to America in search of religious freedom. Facing persecution in England, they sought sanctuary in the New World. Reflecting the theological nationalism of England at the time, they saw themselves as the denizens of a "new Israel" in exodus from a country dominated by religious error. They also believed themselves to have a special "covenantal relationship" with God, and this inspired them to create a Christian nation in colonial

America. Their new society would be, in the words of John Winthrop, the first governor of Massachusetts Bay Colony, a "city upon a hill" that would provide a moral example to the world.[5] Neither the Pilgrims (who arrived at Plymouth Rock) nor the Puritans of Massachusetts Bay, however, sought to extend the principle of religious freedom to others. Nor did they see any reason to do so. The assumption, common at the time, was that religion provided the moral basis of society; hence, civil law was needed to promote religion and to persecute heresy. Moreover, since their interpretation of Christianity was seen as uniquely correct, tolerance of religious dissent entailed either the acquiescence of theological error or of unbelief. Because heterodox views were seen as a threat to social order, the early settlers saw it as entirely appropriate to use the coercive mechanisms of government to regulate religious thought. This close association of religious and political authority was similarly replicated in Virginia, which established the Church of England in its colony.

Religious freedom as it is understood today derived not from Virginia or New England but from the emerging pluralism of the mid-Atlantic region. In these colonies, the diversity of religious denominations demanded a greater degree of religious freedom than was tolerated elsewhere. This was facilitated by the pragmatism of local merchants—driven more by profit than religion—and by religious idealists like Roger Williams and William Penn. Both Williams and Penn established colonies that provided a haven for dissident sects. Williams, in particular, was driven by a conviction that freedom of conscience was required for religious purposes.[6] Williams had been exiled from the Massachusetts Bay Colony because of his view that civil powers had no right to coerce individuals in matters of belief. To do so was not just a violation of the individual's liberty of conscience but was also "against the testimony of Christ Jesus."[7] Moreover, Williams did not believe that civil magistrates ought to be in the business of promoting religion in the first place; rather, this "task belongs to God's scattered saints."[8] The subsequent separation of church and state in Williams's Rhode Island was intended to protect religion from political intrusion.[9]

There were other factors in Colonial America that contributed to the acceptance of religious freedom over time. One of these was the dearth of clergy in the early eighteenth century, which encouraged individuals to participate in the worship of other denominations. The first "Great Awakening," a religious movement that swept through the colonies in the 1740s, also informed the emphasis on free thought. The itinerant ministers associated with this movement traveled the colonies and spread their message with little regard for parish boundaries or church authority. It also led to a proliferation of new (dissenting) congregations and multiple denominations where only one had existed before. The influence of Enlightenment philosophy also had a significant impact on religious freedom in America. While recognizing the merit of religion as a basis of public morality, colonial elites were distrustful of both civil and religious authorities as arbiters of religious truth. This trend reflected the influence of deism—a religious perspective shaped by the Enlightenment—which gave priority to reason, as opposed to revelation, to interpret God's Will. Deism also rejected the inerrancy of scripture and questioned human authority in such matters. The philosophy of John Locke suited this temperament well; the role of the state, in Locke's view, was to protect individuals from external abuse and to enforce contracts, but little else. Like Roger Williams, these early deists believed that the state ought *not* to involve itself in the business of promoting particular interpretations of religion. Nor did they believe that government should ally with religious authorities "in the joint names of Caesar and God to impose their will on the people."[10] Religion, in other words, was a matter best left to the individual and to God.

In the aftermath of the American Revolution, these competing visions of the country's religious legacy were clearly in conflict. On the one hand, there were segments of early American society, influenced by their Puritan forebears, who advocated an explicit recognition of their Christian heritage in the Constitution. The basis of their argument was that church and state are inseparable within a Christian commonwealth, and that "power and law [together] serve God's moral design."[11] Moreover, the importance of religion to both morality and society required an active role for the civil authorities. Even if there was not to be an established church, many argued that there ought to be at least some reference to Christianity in the Constitution to acknowledge what they saw as America's unique destiny in the world.[12] On the other hand, many of the Founding Fathers, including Washington, Madison, Jefferson, and Franklin, opposed the various forms of establishment being offered and believed that religion was best left to the private sphere. These individuals saw established religion as one of the forms of tyranny that the Revolution had sought to throw off. Their support for an explicit separation of church and state was, thus, driven by a desire to limit the ability of religious and political authorities to intrude into the realm of conscience.

The relative merits of religious freedom and establishment were debated in the various state assemblies after 1776 and in the Constitutional Convention at the national level in 1789. At the state level, these debates were extremely rancorous, pitting dissenting sects against their Protestant brethren. At the national level, however, there was a surprising degree of unanimity for establishing a secular order. The Convention agreed to remove references to God from the Constitution, and the provisions affecting religion were negative. The defining feature of this was the First Amendment, which prohibits Congress from passing any laws that either proscribe religious freedom or establish a church.[13] Supporters of the secular alternative among the Founding Fathers included the deists as well as members of independent denominations who were *not* part of the established churches. Many Baptists, Quakers, and others, concerned about state interference in religious practice, were critical of earlier experiments in limited tolerance. Moreover, the "New Lights" (converts) of the Great Awakening agreed with deists like Jefferson that matters of conscience were an individual's concern. Consequently, they supported the institutional separation of church and state as the best means of ensuring religious freedom. The dangers of sectarian division and the growing number of dissenters also convinced many delegates to "put contending sectarians on an equal footing by giving special status to none."[14]

## The Nineteenth and Early Twentieth Centuries

If the institutions of the early American state were secular, the culture remained deeply religious. This was evident in early conceptions of American nationalism, which were deeply imbued with a Christian self-understanding. As in the previous century, the role of religion in public life was perceived as essential to public virtue and to a shared sense of citizenship, regardless of which type of Christianity one wished to practice. For some, these ideas represented a deist-Calvinist synthesis, which provided the basis for a common American culture.[15] This tendency was facilitated by the "Second Great Awakening," which followed the Revolutionary period. Beginning around 1800, a revivalist campaign reminiscent of the earlier movement of the 1740s swept through the country, infusing popular religious practice with an evangelical zeal. More important, it reinforced a common Protestant basis to the new Republic. Early American nationalism—which was very much promoted by the Second Great Awakening—linked Evangelical Christianity to the democratic ideals of the Revolution. Throughout the nineteenth century, Americans could wholeheartedly embrace both religion and nation, because the country was perceived as "God's chosen instrument to spread both Christianity and democracy."[16]

The religious basis of American nationalism was reinforced by the Civil War.

As Bellah describes it, the war was the second major event to shape America's self-understanding.[17] The significance of the war—aside from the issue of slavery and the sheer number of Americans involved—was that it tested the ideals of democratic republicanism. It also brought into question the viability of a society based on religious and democratic pluralism. For President Abraham Lincoln, this was a central challenge, "whether [this] nation, or any nation so conceived, and so dedicated, can long endure."[18] Moreover, that Lincoln framed the conflict and the blight of slavery in religious terms both drew from and reinforced the vision of America as both guided and judged by Divine Providence. His depiction of the conflict as "the wages of sin" reinforced the ideas that America had a covenant with God and that engaging in practices abhorrent to God (in this case, slavery) was what had brought "this terrible war" upon the country.[19] In this sense, religion provided a basis for judging the nation, not a warrant for action.

The influence of religion on American identity and politics carried over into the country's expansion, embodied in the idea of Manifest Destiny. The term, originally coined by a journalist in 1845, provided a religious justification for the settlement of the West. America was not only sanctioned in this endeavor but the country's westward expansion was also seen as a matter of Providential mission. This religious interpretation of American history extended to the imperialist undertakings in the Philippines and in Cuba and to the country's entry into World War I. In each instance, the belief that America was fulfilling a religious duty was omnipresent. It was also at this time that Protestant Christianity, corporate capitalism, and free market economic policies became closely intertwined. During the Gilded Age of the late nineteenth century, religion, nationalism, and capitalism were embodied in an amorphous vision of "the American Way of Life." Religion in this context provided a priestly affirmation for a pattern of social order defined by a high degree of social stratification and inequitable distribution of wealth. Christian mission also sanctioned the exercise of American power and imperial ambition in the hemisphere.

This vision of America—and the power structure that it represented—was challenged, however, by the social transformations of the era. Rapid industrialization and urbanization changed the face of America, as did the European migrations that increased the Catholic and Jewish populations in the country. Scientific development, Darwinism, and Marxist thought also brought into question the literalist religious beliefs of Evangelical Christianity. This social and intellectual ferment provided the context for a debate over both religion and social order in the early twentieth century. At issue was whether, and how, American religion ought to accommodate modernity, particularly its emphasis on reason over revelation and material progress over spiritual development. There was also a debate in America's churches over the proper focus of Christian work. At issue was whether to advocate social reform in the face of socioeconomic injustice (as in the Social Gospel movement) or to limit the efforts of organized religion to individual conversion. The radical social ills associated with early industrialization prompted many to place their emphasis on the former, while other religious leaders felt that this alternative ignored important elements of the faith. These debates—which divided Americans between "modernists" and "traditionalists"—prompted a group of Christian traditionalists to restate the "fundamentals" of their faith in a series of texts that emphasized biblical authority as the "inerrant and infallible world of God."[20] These books served as the basis of contemporary Christian fundamentalism.

The events of the 1920s had an enormous impact on this struggle. On the one hand, the Scopes Monkey trial of 1925 pitted the fundamentalists against secular modernists in a very public forum. The media coverage surrounding the trial, especially the depiction of Evangelicals as intolerant and backward, greatly affected popular understandings of Evangelical Christianity. It also hastened the modernist reformation of the mainline denominations.[21] Moreover, the stock market crash and the economic collapse that led to the Great Depression of the 1930s transformed popular perceptions of industrial capitalism and, by association, benign notions of the American way of life. The economic troubles of this period also entailed the political eclipse of the Republican Party, which had been closely allied with the business elite of the era. Tainted as it was by the corruption and economic excesses of the 1920s, the Republican Party lost control of both the presidency and the Congress in 1932.

The new consensus that emerged under President Franklin D. Roosevelt rejected the laissez-faire economic policies of his predecessor and provided for much greater government intervention in the economy. It also sought to address issues of poverty, promoting a vision of society that reflected the teachings of the social gospel. As Roosevelt argued in his campaign, the strength of the American nation was not found in levels of gross national product but in the "social and economic justice of the system."[22] The religious overtones of Roosevelt's rhetoric were also evident in the period leading up to World War II. Between 1939 and 1941, Roosevelt worked assiduously to turn popular opinion toward support of the coming conflict. In doing so, he invoked the religious narrative of

American nationalism and its democratic mission to the world. In his 1939 State of the Union address, Roosevelt argued that "there comes a time in the affairs of men when they must prepare to defend, not their homes alone, but the tenets of faith and humanity on which their churches, their governments and their very civilization are founded."[23] Roosevelt's religion, however, was distinctly ecumenical, reflecting the emergent liberal (and modernist) consensus in matters of faith. It was premised on a vision of social order defined by inclusion that portrayed America's pluralism as a virtue. The war had profound implications for American life—particularly in terms of race relations and the role of women in society—but none was more significant than the integration of different ethnic and religious groups into the American mainstream. In this way, World War II and the preceding New Deal policies contributed to a reinterpretation of civil religion that linked social justice and inclusion to American patriotism. Religion was a defining feature of this period, but it was promoted in the context of an ecumenical secularism.

### The Secular Idea in Postwar America

The postwar years in America were defined by rapid economic growth, social change, and an increasingly intense U.S.-Soviet rivalry. It was also marked by a resurgence of religion in both public and private life. In the private sphere, organized religion saw a dramatic increase in membership during the late 1940s and early 1950s.[24] The "baby boom" period was defined by an increasing number of people going to church and attending religious seminaries as well as a corresponding surge in church construction. This was driven by a variety of factors, including a newfound economic prosperity that provided for the expansion of the population into the new suburbs and, with that, the construction of new centers of worship. In one sense, America's religious renewal embodied an optimism that perceived the postwar period as a "time of new beginnings."[25] However, there was also a dark side to this trend. The religious revival of the nation reflected an era of increased anxiety. The postwar years were overshadowed by economic concerns—particularly for those who remembered the deprivations of the Depression—and by the specter of nuclear annihilation and the threat of Soviet Communism.

In public life, both Truman and Eisenhower consistently—and consciously—linked patriotism to Judeo-Christian beliefs. This connection between religion and American nationalism became more prominent as the Cold War began in earnest. Like the fight against fascism, American leaders appealed to the nation's religious tradition as a defining feature of its struggle with the Soviet Union. America's belief in God, it was argued, was a distinguishing factor between America and the godless communism of the East. Democracy and freedom, moreover, were said to be rooted in Christian principles and the right of free peoples to worship God in an unhindered manner. Communism, on the other hand, was depicted as a false philosophy, hostile to American values and the American way of life.[26] As in World War II, America saw itself as a moral leader in the world, and one which "believes that the Sermon on the Mount means what it says . . . that the law is the God-given law under which we live, that all our traditions have come from Moses to Sinai, and Jesus on the Mount."[27]

These themes were a central feature of Eisenhower's 1952 presidential campaign, which emphasized both government corruption—which was linked to the New Deal policies of the Roosevelt era—and godless communism. He also placed religious values at the center of his campaign. Eisenhower launched his candidacy from his hometown in Kansas, where he appealed to the traditional values of a simpler era. Using the language of religious revivalism, he urged America "to regain faith in the principles and religion of their fathers."[28] Even before declaring as a candidate, he had consistently stressed the link between open government and religious faith and deplored the tendency to remove religion from public life.[29] This link between God and country informed Eisenhower's depiction of the Cold War, which he characterized as a religious struggle between the forces of materialism and those of the spirit. It was his "unshakable belief that it is only through religion that we can lick this thing called communism."[30] The link between piety and patriotism was echoed in the 1956 campaign, in which Eisenhower's billboard ads read: "Faith in God and County: that's Eisenhower—how about you?"[31]

Eisenhower's understanding of religion, however, reflected the ecumenism of both Roosevelt and Truman. This is perhaps best captured in Eisenhower's famous remark that "America makes no sense without a deeply held faith in God—and I don't care what it is."[32] Religion during this period was promoted by both church and state, but it was done in a manner that deemphasized the divisions between denominations and that supported tolerance in matters of religious belief. Historical divisions between Catholic and Protestant and between Protestant and Jew significantly diminished during this period. Much of this was the result of the two world wars and the changing self-image of America as a multiethnic, multireligious society. That members of different ethnicities and religions could fight and die together was perceived as a testament to the idea of America as an inclusive, tolerant, and open society.

There was, however, a more aggressive and exclusive vision of American religious nationalism prevalent during this period as well. Preachers like Billy Graham, for example, articulated a worldview that characterized the Cold War as a religious struggle and associated conservative political policies with God's Will. In 1949, for example, Graham characterized the world as being divided between two camps, one of which was under the influence of Divine Providence, while the other was "inspired, directed and motivated by the Devil himself."[33] Moreover, Graham praised the work of the congressional investigations into domestic communism, which he felt was threatening the nation. Graham was not alone in these beliefs. A wide array of public figures echoed these sentiments, some even calling for a "holy war" against the scourge of communism.[34] General Douglas MacArthur, for example, tied religious fervor to patriotic duty, writing that it is "our Christian faith [that is the] mighty bulwark of all freedom."[35] Senator Joseph McCarthy also evoked an apocalyptic image of the Cold War, warning of a "final all-out battle between Communistic atheism and Christianity."[36]

The religious nationalism of the McCarthy era was also tied to the advocacy of conservative economic and social doctrines. Based on the three pillars of anti-communism, libertarian economics, and "traditional values," this ideological current provided the basis for what was then known as the radical right. It also laid the groundwork for the contemporary conservative movement.[37] Groups such as the John Birch Society blended Christian idealism, patriotism, and support for free market capitalism as a means of attacking Roosevelt's New Deal policies and bolstering traditional patterns of social hierarchy. The ideology of anticommunism, in particular, challenged the prevailing social order by stigmatizing liberalism and progressive government policies as un-American. Those sympathetic to the radical right were also opposed to organized labor and found support for these views in institutions such as the FBI, the U.S. Congress, and the American Chamber of Commerce. Labor unrest, in this view, was seen not as a byproduct of poor working conditions but rather the "creation of outside agitators, usually foreign-born, bomb-wielding Reds."[38]

Conservative Christian organizations, such as the American Council of Christian Churches (ACCC), the National Association of Evangelicals (NAE), and religious broadcasters such as Billy Hargis's Christian Crusade, similarly promoted a conservative political agenda along with their religious views. Leaders of these organizations accused liberal clergy of being communist sympathizers and were opposed to the modernist and ecumenical basis of the World Council of Churches, a coalition of mainline churches established in 1948. The ACCC and the NAE were especially critical of mainline clergy who questioned the inequities associated with unregulated capitalism. Evangelical publications like *Christian Economics* and *Christianity Today*, for example, promoted free-market sentiment and depicted social welfare policies as "nothing more than un-Christian covetousness and economic ignorance."[39] FBI Director J. Edgar Hoover used these publications to promote anticommunist themes and to warn about the dangers of communist manipulation of liberal ministers.

A dominant theme of the anticommunist sentiment of the 1950s was the threat to the nation posed by leftist radicals within the country. This strategy was distinctly populist, using ethnic, class, and regional rivalries as a potent vehicle for attacking the East Coast liberal establishment.[40] Political elites who supported New Deal policies were characterized as unpatriotic or of otherwise hostile to the interests of the nation. These themes came together in the Alger Hiss case, which symbolized the idea of a traitorous (and intellectual) liberal elite selling out the nation. Although Hiss may have been the immediate focus of investigation, the broader target was the Democratic administration. As one commentator described it, "The McCarthy period was an opportunity of revenge for all those who had opposed the New Deal."[41]

Despite the rapid decline of Senator McCarthy's career after 1954, Christian anticommunism remained a fixture of American politics throughout the decade. Weeklong anticommunist seminars were held around the country, particularly in the West and Southwest. These events were led by Evangelical ministers, who adapted old-style Christian revivalism to the modern discourse of American nationalism and anticommunism.[42] Groups such as the Christian Crusade and the Christian Anti-Communist Crusade reached millions of people through public meetings, radio, and television. They railed against communism and preached against such things as big government, the United Nations, racial integration, and the income tax.[43] These preachers were aided, moreover, by a National Security Council directive, signed in 1958, which directed government agencies "to arouse the public to the menace of the Cold War."[44] In practice, this meant that anticommunist seminars were organized by members of the armed forces in conjunction with the John Birch Society, the leaders of the Christian Anti-Communism Crusade, and others. The content of these seminars emphasized the threat of communist infiltration in the nation's "schools, churches, labor unions, [and] government offices."[45] The seminars did not limit their attacks to the Communist Party or to communism in general but criticized a range of groups and individuals, including "liberals, modernists, John Dewey, Harvard students, the *New York Times,* the American Friends Service Committee, pacifists, naïve ministers, and so on."[46]

This extreme variant of American religious nationalism both reflected and guided the Manichaean vision of the postwar years. However, its extremist overtones remained at odds with the mainstream liberal consensus that continued to endorse a more secular and tolerant conception of social order. Mainline religious leaders condemned the excessive quality of this religiously inspired anticommunism. In 1953, for example, the president of the Princeton Theological Seminary, the Reverend John McCay, warned that the hatred of communism was rapidly becoming a "new form of idolatry" that regards "passionate and unreflective opposition to the Communist demon as the one and only expression of Americanism and even of Christianity."[47] Communism was certainly an evil to be opposed, but the fanaticism associated with the right wing was creating "a substitute religion" that redirected devotion to something other than God. McCay argued, moreover, that the willingness of conservative actors to disparage those who disagreed with them threatened the very freedom for which the country stood. Noting that right-wing investigations were rapidly turning into "inquisitions," he warned that "every true American, especially every true Christian, should view [these trends] with concern."[48]

This critique of the radical right was also evident among leading theologians such as Reinhold Niebuhr. In Niebuhr's earlier work, he had highlighted the danger of subsuming individual morality to the collective, be it a tribe, a nation, or an ethnic group. Since nations and states act out of self-interest by their very nature, even the apparently altruistic sacrifice of the individual that is inherent within patriotic duty can be directed in an ultimately destructive and immoral end. Niebuhr's warning was especially relevant in the context of an assertive religious nationalism, where the self-interest of the community—its pursuit of power and wealth—was clothed in a more palatable rhetoric of justice, morality, and freedom. Similarly, the extension of these ideas to the economic sphere was problematic because of the tendency to portray the pursuit of self-interest in a moral and religious framework that it did not deserve. More to the point, Niebuhr saw in this broader tendency a fundamental misunderstanding of Christian tradition. He argued that the willingness to equate one's own goals with God's and to claim that one's beliefs uniquely reflected God's Will is simply "wrong religion."[49] True religion, he argued, "knows first of all its own partiality and so the falsity of its spiritual pride."[50]

Eisenhower's own religious pronouncements tended to reflect the liberal consensus of the era. He was staunchly anti-communist, but he eschewed the more radical elements of the far right, and he often found himself at odds with the conservative wing of his own party. Although Eisenhower frequently used religion in his public statements, the references remained inclusive, reflecting the more benign strain of civil religion advocated by his two predecessors. Eisenhower's stance on religious politics, moreover, reflected a deep philosophical split in the Republican Party. The liberal wing accepted many of Roosevelt's reforms, while the conservative wing sought to roll back the New Deal.[51] From a religious perspective, the position of the liberal Republicans reflected the support they received among mainline churches in the East and Northeast, while the conservatives were tied closely with the Evangelical churches in the West and Southwest. These divisions were evident in the 1960 campaign, in which Nixon's conservative supporters worked against the liberal Republicans who supported Nelson Rockefeller.

The Democratic Party was similarly divided along regional and philosophical lines. The socially conservative South coexisted uneasily with the more liberal North and Midwest. These factions differed to a limited extent on economic and foreign policy but were deeply divided on the issues of race and religion. Roosevelt had bridged this divide by refusing to press the race issue and by relying on the South's historic animosity to the Republican Party. Kennedy's strategy in the 1960 campaign reflected this pattern, and he was able to hold the Democratic coalition together. Despite Nixon's historical ties to the far right, he, like Kennedy, sought to portray himself as a centrist candidate who reflected the prevailing political consensus in America. This was possible in part because neither candidate in 1960 differed on such issues as the containment of communism, the support of free enterprise, and the acceptance of a limited social safety net. They also tended to believe that racial and religious equality were worthy goals and that continued economic growth would solve many of America's social ills. This consensus, for some, represented the end of ideology in American politics and the dominance of a liberal social order. The main issue in the 1960 campaign, then, was which candidate could most effectively achieve these ends.

## The Kennedy-Johnson Era

As Bellah has rightly noted, the Kennedy inaugural address was a quintessential statement of American civil religion. Infused with Christian symbolism and appeals to a nonspecific God, Kennedy tied the American project (and mission) closely to God's Will. In the speech, Kennedy highlighted the "obligation" of the nation and the president to a higher law that commanded both to action. In doing so, he set the stage for an activist role of government in addressing the social ills that faced humanity: "tyranny, poverty, disease and war itself."[52] By drawing on America's religious self-understanding, the inaugural speech provided a framework for government policies that embodied the values of the liberal consensus: social tolerance, opposition to political absolutism, and the reduction of domestic poverty—but not at the expense of the free enterprise system. However, the ecumenical character of Kennedy's address—particularly notable given his Catholic heritage—and its liberal orientation distinguished it from the more extreme religious nationalism of the period. In Kennedy's depiction, America is subordinate to the ethical principles of the Judeo-Christian tradition, and is called to uphold commitments to social justice, "knowing that here on earth God's work must truly be our own."[53]

In practice, Kennedy's brief tenure reflected a mix of political pragmatism and nationalist idealism. Domestically, the administration was torn over the race issue and slow to respond to the demands of the African American community. It did, however, back the Civil Rights Movement in the end and, in 1963, committed itself to promoting equal rights for all citizens. It was also slow to push for an expansion of the welfare state, opting initially to offer a tax cut as its centerpiece of economic policymaking. However, the administration was committed to addressing the very real problem of continued poverty in America, and had set in motion a concerted effort on this front. In terms of foreign policy, Kennedy was deeply enmeshed in the Cold War struggle, first with the Bay of Pigs, then with the Cuban Missile Crisis, and finally with Vietnam. Kennedy's assassination in 1963 placed the burden of seeing these initiatives through on his vice president, former Texas senator and Senate majority leader Lyndon Johnson. Despite the tensions between Johnson and the Kennedy brothers, the former embraced the administration's agenda and was enormously successful in enacting it into law. Johnson's accomplishments included, among other things, passage of the Civil Rights Act of 1964 and passage of the Voting Rights Act of 1965, which prohibited racial discrimination in matters of employment, access to public facilities, and voting. Johnson's tenure was also defined by the major expansions in the welfare system that would come to characterize the Great Society.[54] He also deepened American involvement in the war in Vietnam.

The 1964 presidential election was notable in part because it was defined by two sharply different visions of America's social order. Within the Republican Party, the liberal wing led by Nelson Rockefeller had been soundly defeated in the primary elections by Barry Goldwater and his conservative supporters. Goldwater espoused a conservative ideology that challenged many of the core assumptions of the Johnson administration and, hence, of the liberal consensus. A defining feature of Goldwater's critique was his ardent anticommunism that eschewed the policy of containment and argued for a more aggressive American posture vis-à-vis the Soviets. On domestic policy, Goldwater opposed the social programs of the Great Society and was extremely critical of government regulation of business. Goldwater also opposed, indirectly, racial integration by arguing that this was a matter for states to resolve, a position that reflected the views of Southern conservatives such as George Wallace. Johnson was able to turn many of these positions against Goldwater and depict him as an extremist who advocated positions outside of the political mainstream. Johnson's famous "Daisy" television commercial was perhaps the most succinct expression of this critique, juxtaposing a young girl and a nuclear explosion to demonstrate that extremism in defense of liberty was perhaps not as virtuous as Goldwater claimed.

Despite Johnson's easy reelection, the liberal consensus of the era unraveled over the course of the following decade. The Vietnam War, in particular, proved increasingly unpopular, especially among the college students subject to the draft. The Civil Rights Movement similarly challenged the liberal consensus and the evolutionary approach to change promoted by the Kennedy administration. Kennedy's reluctance to push a civil rights bill in the early 1960s reflected the deep opposition among Southern whites. Conservative Southern congressmen held key positions in both House and Senate, and they were intent upon blocking any reform that threatened traditional patterns of social order. The Civil Rights Movement, however—particularly the black churches—had found a powerful tool in the appeal to equal rights, freedom, and Christian ethics; by using the symbols and rhetoric of the Christian gospel, they were able to challenge the established order in the South. The television coverage of the protests aided their cause by depicting white Southern authorities as out of step with American values.

When Kennedy did step forward on the issue, he used the language of civil religion to define the conflict as a "moral issue . . . as old as the scriptures and . . . as clear as the American Constitution."[55] What Kennedy was advocating was the kind of integration with which other countries around the world were similarly grappling. At issue was the inclusion of groups into society that had historically faced severe marginalization and discrimination. Many of the Democratic leaders at the time recognized both the necessity of such a step and the steep price that would be paid. Johnson, for example, foresaw quite accurately that the passage of the Civil Rights Act by the Democratic Party would likely cede the South to the Republican Party for many years to come. Nonetheless, the basic values of American society were consistent with this change. The religious and moral overtones of the movement were reflected in Johnson's comments during the debate over the voting rights bill:

> Rarely are we met with the challenge, not to our growth or abundance, or our welfare or our security—but, rather to the values and the purposes and the meaning of our beloved nation. The issue of equal rights for American Negroes is such an issue. And should we defeat every enemy, and should we double our wealth and conquer the stars and still be unequal to this issue, then we will have failed as a people and as a nation. For with a country as with a person, "what is a man profited, if he shall gain the world, and lose his own soul?"[56]

The conflicts over Vietnam and civil rights were symptomatic of the ambiguity in American religion and society. The Civil Rights Movement grew out of the institutionalized inequality that had dominated American society, particularly in the South. The inconsistency between this reality and the American values of freedom and equality gave rise to the moral—and religious—impetus that propelled the Civil Rights Movement. Similarly, in Vietnam, those who opposed the war saw American power being used to support a repressive government with little commitment to freedom or democratic rule. In both instances, the critique of government policy was based on the country's failure to live up to its own moral values. If liberal religion provided the prophetic appeal for change on both issues, however, conservative religion offered a priestly affirmation of the status quo. Conservative political forces invoked religious elements of the American tradition—and the fear of anticommunist subversion—to support both the war in Vietnam and (euphemistically) states' rights in the South. The fault lines of American society, in short, involved differing visions of both religion and nation. These divisions not only split the country but ran through each political party as well. It was in this context that Richard Nixon was elected president.

## The Nixon Legacy

The 1968 presidential election was a turning point in American politics. Nixon's campaign tapped into the populist backlash to both the civil rights movement and the political unrest in the country. More to the point, Nixon sought to coopt conservative Christianity in order to destroy the political dominance of the Democratic Party. In doing so, he helped to redefine the frame of ideological debate for much of the next quarter-century. The Johnson administration's support for civil rights legislation had alienated Southern conservatives and fractured the New Deal coalition that had been the basis of Democratic Party rule since 1932. This, in turn, provided an opportunity for the Republican Party to attract working-class whites in the South and elsewhere.[57] This realignment also affected the Republican Party, whose center of gravity shifted away from the liberal, industrialized Northeast to the Sun Belt states of the Southwest. Although this political realignment would take some time to complete—delayed in large measure by the Watergate scandal—it continued throughout the 1980s and 1990s. The basic outlines of this realignment, though, were evident in the 1968 campaign, in the effort to transform the formerly Democratic South into a Republican stronghold.

A defining feature of the 1968 campaign—and the corresponding realignment of the two parties—was Nixon's Southern Strategy. The basic premise of this strategy was the assumption that there existed a natural majority in the country that was culturally conservative, as was evident in the congressional alliances between Republicans and conservative Democrats. It followed, then, that the Republican Party could be remade into a majority party with the support of conservatives throughout the South, the Midwest, and the West. Building this conservative coalition, however, would not be easy. It would entail bringing together regions of the country that had historically been divided by sectional concerns and interests. It could be accomplished, however, through a conservative populism that stressed cultural concerns at the expense of economic issues. In other words, it would entail a campaign strategy of "positive polarization" that would divide the American public along communal, not class, lines. This would involve running political campaigns that focused on "vertical" cleavages (race and ethnicity) while deemphasizing "horizontal" ones (class and economic disparity). Since "the new popular majority is white and conservative,"[58] race, religion, and nationalism were essential parts of this strategy. These themes needed to be articulated, however, in terms of culture or "social issues" in order to avoid the stigma of extremism or racism. There would be no overt appeals to segregationist sentiment, for example, but this could be achieved through coded references to "states' rights" and a "return to traditional values."

The 1968 campaign was defined by this new rhetoric of cultural politics. It was particularly evident in Nixon's criticism of the Johnson administration for catering to the special interests of minorities at the expense of the white majority. This helped Nixon gain the support of working-class whites who felt marginalized by the "negro-oriented social innovations" associated with Johnson's Great Society.[59] Although Wallace's third-party candidacy drew support away from the Republicans in the Deep South, Nixon was nonetheless able to build a winning coalition.[60] The Southern Strategy was greatly aided by political leaders such as Strom Thurmond, the former "Dixiecrat" presidential candidate who campaigned for Nixon throughout the South. Nixon also committed himself to withholding the federal funds that would be used to enforce integration, a position credited with helping Nixon "carry all but the deepest Southern states already lost to George Wallace."[61] These tactics, particularly the alliance with Thurmond, led *The New York Times* to argue that "this trucking to Southern racism is bad morality and bad politics."[62]

The 1968 campaign was also overshadowed by the year's traumatic events. The assassinations of Martin Luther King and Robert F. Kennedy contributed to a sense of crisis, as did antiwar protests on college campuses and riots in America's inner cities. The clash in Chicago between local police and student protestors during the Democratic national convention epitomized this trend. It also undercut the candidacy of Democratic nominee Hubert Humphrey, since the violence was linked in the public's mind with the antiwar wing of the Democratic Party. The Nixon campaign effectively used this sense of crisis against the Democrats. On foreign policy, the campaign charged Humphrey of being soft on Vietnam and, like Neville Chamberlain, of seeking "peace at any price."[63] The antiwar movement was also stigmatized as unpatriotic and un-American. On domestic policy, the Nixon campaign effectively linked the Democratic Party with the unrest in the nation and attributed the country's social problems to liberal permissiveness.

There were two related themes in Nixon's 1968 campaign that are of particular interest. The first was the issue of law and order, a centerpiece of the convention and the subsequent campaign.[64] The vagueness of this concept was a key to its appeal. A literal interpretation emphasized the Republican candidate's stand against crime and urban violence and portrayed the Republican Party as supportive of local law enforcement. Democrats, on the other hand, were depicted as "soft on crime" and "more sympathetic to perpetrators than victims."[65] Similarly, the emphasis on law and order linked antiwar protests and other types of political dissent with criminal activity and, hence, liberalism with deviance. More to the point, the campaign theme was widely interpreted as having racial overtones. Many African-American leaders saw the rhetoric of law and order as an explicit effort to "get the support of the white backlash people around the country."[66] Even Edward Brooke, a Republican senator from Massachusetts, was disturbed by the campaign rhetoric. Brooke met with Spiro Agnew to discuss the vice presidential candidate's many statements regarding the need for greater law and order, hoping that Agnew meant by this "equal justice, not keeping the negro in his place."[67]

The second issue of note was Nixon's continuing emphasis on the threat to American values. Implicit in the "values issue" was an effort to construct a discourse of political conservatism to counter both leftist activists and the liberal establishment. Although Nixon was in many ways a liberal pragmatist when in office—he was responsible for such policy innovations as the establishment of the Environmental Protection Agency, a national welfare program, and federal revenue sharing—he was thoroughly conservative on the campaign trail as well as ruthless in his strategizing. This reflected a conscious effort to campaign to the right while governing toward the center. Hence, in the context of a hard-fought campaign, Nixon emphasized his opposition to court-ordered busing, drug use, and abortion and sought to stigmatize liberal elements in American public life that were supportive of these issues. He also linked cultural politics to the Vietnam War and to the broader struggle against international communism. Nixon demonized those who opposed the war, particularly the "liberal elites," whom he characterized as willing to hand Vietnam to the communists.

Nixon's campaign themes reflected those of his earlier years as an anticommunist crusader in the 1950s.[68] The vision of social order that he advocated, for example, was premised on an unflinching faith in the inherent goodness of the American system and a belief that America's interests and values were coextensive. Vietnam was subsequently perceived as a moral issue emanating from the Cold War challenge of Soviet Russia, while the conflict over civil rights was assumed to be the result of radical activists outside of the American mainstream. Nixon was preoccupied with the beliefs that internal provocateurs were manipulating American college students and that the students had failed to see the real enemies associated with international communism. Similarly, the values issue addressed what Nixon saw as America's moral decay and the failure of will that was undermining American power in the world. The social disruption associated with civil rights and Vietnam, then, was not only illegitimate but also represented an internal threat to the greatness—and unity—of the nation.

Nixon's vision of America was imbued with an Evangelical interpretation of Christianity and an exclusive reading of the Puritan tradition. Whether this was due to his Quaker upbringing or whether his beliefs were even genuine is a matter of speculation. What is clear, however, is that his characterization of the country readily conflated religion and nationalism. From this perspective, faith in God and faith in the nation were not only compatible but mutually reinforcing. This blending of patriotism and piety reflected a conception of religion that was thoroughly priestly in orientation and that affirmed rather than challenged the hierarchical pattern of power and privilege in American society. For Nixon, the innate goodness of the American way of life was premised on its identity as a religious nation. Since he perceived the troubles of recent years as the work of a disgruntled few, his message was directed toward what he perceived as the conservative majority, what he referred to as the "silent majority."[69] By this he meant those who were not part of the political opposition, the counter-culture or the protests against the war. They were, in short, his target audience. He appealed to this demographic by invoking themes of patriotism and national destiny and by calling them to return to the faith of their forefathers. It was with this type of right-wing populism that Nixon hoped to cultivate a "renewed sense of national mission."[70]

Although Nixon eschewed explicit appeals to religion, his vision of the nation was infused with Christian rhetoric and symbolism. His common use of such theological terms as *spirit, faith, hope*, and *belief* contributed greatly to a religious—and Evangelical—sensibility. It was also very much in keeping with traditional conceptions of religious nationalism. In his inaugural address in 1969, for example, Nixon characterized the challenges facing the country as a "crisis of the spirit" to which were needed "an answer of the Spirit."[71] The language was revivalist in nature and, like a fundamentalist preacher, called the population back to its religious basis. Nixon also sought to portray himself as a man of faith, even if the image did not always square with reality.[72] This was part of the motivation behind the regular church services held in the East Wing of the White House. These services were intended to create an aura of traditional morality around the presidency, while also providing an opportunity to invite business elites and other Republican contributors to the presidential residence. The ministers who presided over these services were selected from variety of denominations, though all were politically conservative. Particularly on the issue of Vietnam War, Nixon wished to use conservative religious figures to counter the criticisms from religious leaders on the left.

Nixon's rhetoric also reflected the themes of his close friend, the Evangelist preacher Billy Graham. Graham, a leading Protestant minister, had not explicitly endorsed Nixon in his earlier campaigns but had, five days prior to the 1960 election, attended a Nixon rally in South Carolina to give the invocation. He had also made other public appearances with the candidate that had given the impression of an endorsement.[73] Nixon had also addressed Graham's revival meetings as vice president and did so again during the 1968 campaign. It was no surprise, then, that Graham presided over the first of the church services held in the White House. In his remarks at that service, Graham referred to the statement made by Nixon in his inaugural address concerning "the crisis of spirit" that faced America. Graham remarked, "I don't think I've ever read a passage that so pinpointed the problems of our generation in America and throughout the world." He went on to say that "only a personal relation[ship] with God" would be able to solve these problems.[74]

The two men also had similar views on the state of the nation. Graham was outspoken in his beliefs that activist government was undermining the country and that "something is wrong when the Supreme Court makes ruling after ruling that protects individual rights but opens up a Pandora's box of criminal activity."[75] He disagreed strongly with the Supreme Court's decision to ban state-led prayer in public schools and regularly emphasized the biblical injunction to submit to authority: "The Bible teaches that the policeman is an agent and servant of God, and the authority that he has is given to him not only by the city and the state, but is given to him by Almighty God."[76] For Graham, like Nixon, both religion and political authority were necessary to maintain a conservative vision of social order.

Nixon's religious politics was epitomized by an appearance he made at a revival meeting in May 1970. A month after he announced the bombing of Cambodia, Nixon flew to Knoxville, Tennessee, to participate in one of Billy Graham's crusades. At that meeting, he addressed a crowd of seventy thousand, directing many of his comments to the University of Tennessee students in the audience. The choice of venues was significant; it placed the president among a supportive crowd on a university campus at the height of the Vietnam War. This was a particular benefit when the speech was televised a few weeks later. In defending his presidency, Nixon appealed to the themes of God and country, linking—however subtly—his policies to the Evangelical beliefs of his host. Nixon argued in this speech that America could only solve her problems by turning to "those great spiritual sources that have made America the great country that it is."[77] The lines between religion and politics were further blurred by the attendance of Republican senatorial candidate William Brock, who was opposing the incumbent Democrat, Albert Gore Sr. As one commentator noted, "Observers could not help viewing the service as a GOP political rally."[78]

The Knoxville event highlights three key aspects of Nixon's cultural politics. The first was Nixon's use of religion to promote a particular vision of social order. By appealing to a theologically conservative interpretation of Christian tradition, Nixon sought to redefine popular conceptions of cultural authenticity and stigmatize liberal norms as un-American. In this context, conservative religion and politics were characterized as patriotic and culturally authentic, while liberal interpretations were portrayed as aberrant. Like Goldwater before him, Nixon used these themes to characterize the Democratic Party as being out of step with the American mainstream. As Goldwater had argued in 1964, the Democrats were the party of "anti-military, tax raisers, lobbyists for the welfare state and puppets of black and other minority special interest groups."[79] Republicans, on the other hand, were good Americans who supported the military, Christianity, and other pillars of traditional authority. This style of hard-hitting cultural politics, which characterized each of Nixon's bids for the presidency, had its roots in the conservative movement of the 1950s. It also contributed greatly to the polarization of American public life.

A second key aspect of Nixon's cultural politics was the content of his discourse. Nixon's vision of society tended to reflect that of Graham's, but the president was much more circumspect about appealing directly to religion in his speeches. Although Nixon frequently spoke of the spiritual sources of the nation, it was never clear whether he was referring to a specific tradition (for instance, Christianity) or the more ecumenical civil religion of Eisenhower and Kennedy. This deliberate imprecision indicates that Nixon did not need to say things explicitly that were understood implicitly. By appearing at a revivalist meeting with America's leading Evangelist, it was clear to those in attendance where Nixon stood. Moreover, the Nixon-Graham alliance drew from a long-standing connection between conservative religion and the right-wing anti-communism that had defined much of Nixon's career. Even though one can distinguish between the more extreme elements of the radical right and the Nixon-Graham vision of moral order, there were certain fundamental similarities that informed both groups.

Third, and finally, a key aspect of Nixon's cultural politics was the tendency to conflate religion, nation, and state. As Richard Pierard and Robert Linder have argued, the characteristics that Nixon attributed to the American spirit were "precisely those of the Christian deity—healing power, compassion for the helpless, forgiveness for the sinner, and the granting of freedom to all persons to choose their ultimate destiny."[80] Hence, the exercise of power in defense of the nation was, by definition, beneficial and consistent with the cause of human freedom. The religious basis of American nationalism that emerges from this discourse sees not just a charge and a destiny for America but a high degree of license as well. Here the ideology of American exceptionalism provides a moral justification for an assertive executive, either at home or abroad. That America stood in the past for such values as individual freedom and religious tolerance implies that it will continue to do so in the future. The rhetoric of the Cold War mirrored that of the struggle against fascism in the 1940s, even if American foreign policy had started supporting authoritarian regimes and was subverting the self-determination of peoples in postcolonial societies. It also informed an increasingly amoral approach to domestic politics, in which the ends justified the means.

These various themes were a key feature of Nixon's reelection campaign in 1972. The campaign was defined by a variety of dirty tricks orchestrated by the White House—including the Watergate break-in—but it was also characterized by an unrelenting use of cultural politics. The Nixon campaign, for example, played on anticommunist and nationalist sentiments by depicting McGovern as weak on defense and, hence, unpatriotic. Nixon, on the other hand, was held up as strong enough to protect the nation from its enemies—linking the themes of security, patriotism, and American military might—while downplaying the quagmire in Vietnam. As one campaign ad stated, "President Nixon doesn't believe we should play games with our national security. He believes in a strong America to negotiate for people from strength."[81]

The 1972 campaign was also characterized by a moralistic rhetoric that pitted

George McGovern's prophetic religion against Nixon's priestly affirmation of the status quo. McGovern's campaign theme—"Come Home America"— invoked the themes of repentance and return, implicitly arguing that the nation "had fallen from grace and stood in need of redemption."[82] His campaign on behalf of the poor and the disenfranchised embodied something of a religious crusade. It was, according to McGovern, a "coalition of conscience and decency" directed against the Vietnam War, the prevalence of poverty amidst plenty, and what McGovern defined as the "the most corrupt and immoral administration in history."[83] Nixon, on the other hand, didn't bother defending his administration—he defended the American system. Similar to 1968, the campaign relied on a cultural politics that charged the Democrats with putting minority interests ahead of those of the majority and with being the party of "acid, amnesty and abortion."[84] In short, the Nixon campaign pursued a strategy of positive polarization that sought to divide the American public between "a right wing majority . . . [and] a left wing minority."[85] By playing to the prejudices of the white majority, Nixon turned public attention away from the sources of dissent and redirected it toward the dissenters. In doing so, Nixon appealed to those who preferred the message of priestly affirmation to that of McGovern's prophetic condemnation and call to repentance.

The populist orientation of the Nixon campaign also reflected the Republican Party's continuing effort to build a conservative majority around cultural issues. Nixon sought to capitalize on the genuine sense of crisis in the country by portraying the ills of society as cultural in orientation, not economic or political. In this way, Republican strategists turned the class issue against the Democratic Party by making class differences hinge not on income levels but on cultural values. As such, Nixon depicted the Democratic opposition as a party of liberal affluence that was out of touch with mainstream America. Great Society programs, from this perspective, were portrayed not as helping the poor but rather as working against the interests of ordinary Americans by forcing unwanted changes on a traditional population. Social issues such as court-ordered busing, abortion, and funding for parochial schools became important campaign themes because they split traditional constituencies—Catholics, working class whites, Southerners—away from the Democratic Party. As one Nixon aide noted, "With the rise of George McGovern, the Democrats have donned the love-beads, prefaded denims and purple sunglasses of affluent liberalism . . . [and this is changing] lower-income perceptions of the two parties."[86]

## The Ford-Carter Interregnum

The events surrounding the Watergate scandal and the resignation of President Nixon were a defining moment in American public life. So, too, was the Vietnam War. The tragic quality of these events—coupled with the cynicism and duplicity of America's public officials—greatly undermined the voters' faith in the American system. It also stalled the electoral realignment that Nixon's conservative populism had initiated. The legacy of this era cast a long shadow over the presidencies of both Gerald Ford and Jimmy Carter. Ford had been appointed to the vice presidency after Spiro Agnew resigned amid allegations of financial irregularities and became president after Nixon's resignation in August 1974. Ford's most significant act as president was to pardon his predecessor, thereby avoiding the inevitable turmoil associated with criminal proceedings being brought against a former president. Whether or not this cost Ford his reelection is debatable, but it is clear that the Republican Party was largely in eclipse during the years right after Watergate.

The election of Jimmy Carter in 1976 was a reaction to the Nixon legacy. This was evident in the pervasive discussion of ethics and morality in government that defined the 1976 campaign and in the prominence of religion in the national debate. The religious overtones of the campaign were due in part to the assumption that morality flows from religious faith and in part to the centrality of religion in Jimmy Carter's life. What made Carter's candidacy unique was his status as a born-again Southern Baptist, which made him something of a novelty in national politics in the 1970s. He was theologically conservative—and a self-described Evangelical—although politically liberal. He was also concerned with issues of race, poverty, and international affairs, matters with which Southern Baptists did not traditionally preoccupy themselves. While his conservative and outspoken theological beliefs raised questions about his appeal to a largely secular society, it is also what made him uniquely viable. It was precisely Carter's religious beliefs—coupled with his commitment to a progressive political agenda—that allowed him to bridge the deep divisions in American society and to build a regionally and religiously diverse coalition.

Ford also appealed to religion on the campaign trail, but he was more circumspect about his personal beliefs than was Carter. Ford's campaign sought to diminish Carter's advantage on the issue by characterizing Carter as one who would "exploit the [religious] issue for political gain," while Ford, in contrast, was "a man of sturdy, though quiet faith."[87] The Ford campaign also made a point of reaching out to conservative Christians. He had been influenced by Michigan Evangelist Billy Zeoli in earlier years and had participated in a weekly prayer group as a member of Congress. As such, he discussed his "commitment to the Christian faith . . . [and] his relationship with Jesus Christ" when he met with Evangelical leaders, the National Association of Christian Broadcasters, and other conservative religious groups.[88] The Ford campaign's emphasis on Evangelical Christianity was intended to blunt Carter's appeal to this demographic. Ford, however, did not pursue the kind of divisive cultural politics that defined his predecessor. As E. J. Dionne has noted, "Ford utterly lacked Nixon's love for the social-issue jugular."[89]

Carter's victory in 1976 owed much to the Watergate scandal and reflected a deep desire for a politician whom the voters could trust. Perhaps more important, it was also due to Carter's ability to bring Southern voters back into the Democratic fold. Carter did extremely well with white Protestants, union workers, and conservative Southerners. His religious rhetoric and his willingness to talk openly about his conservative faith appealed to these groups and helped to refashion the Democrats' traditional coalition. Popular support for Carter, however, was short-lived, as was the "liberal renaissance" produced by the Watergate scandal.[90] The economic crisis of the late 1970s, double-digit inflation, and foreign policy crises like the Soviet invasion of Afghanistan and the Iranian hostage crisis all took their toll on Carter's popularity. The culture of Washington also bristled at Carter's efforts to inject a new morality into old-style politics. The traditional manner in which Congress conducted its business did not fit with the new president's moralism. Deep divisions within the Democratic Party, moreover, undermined the Carter presidency.

The critical nature of Carter's religion was also an issue. Like many others, he interpreted America's social ills as an indication of a deeper moral and spiritual crisis. Yet, unlike Nixon, Carter's response was largely prophetic, not priestly, in nature. Carter called into question the materialism and greed of America's consumer culture and the arrogance associated with its superpower status. During the 1977 National Prayer Breakfast, for example, the president stressed the need for greater humility in world affairs and called upon the country to live up to the ideals of its founders. At a similar event in 1979, Carter cited America's religious heritage to justify his social welfare policies. To the political and religious leaders gathered, Carter said: "We must avoid a distortion or rationalization because of materialistic inclinations in our own hearts, of our own religious faith and its beliefs. When any religion impacts adversely on those whom Christ described as the 'least of thee' it can have no firm foundation in God's sight."[91]

Many of Carter's actions also found little favor with the electorate. His reluctance to use military power to resolve the Iranian hostage crisis, however wise, was a liability. It was consistent with his Christian belief that such awesome power ought to be constrained and used only as a last resort, but it was enormously unpopular. Similarly, his refusal to support legislative or constitutional remedies for such key issues as prayer in school, abortion, or state-aid to religious schools proved a disappointment for the Evangelicals who had voted for him. The high price of oil and the inflationary policies of earlier administrations had also created a dire economic crisis, and Carter's response was not a popular one. In a defining moment of his administration, Carter gave a speech on energy policy, the "malaise speech," as it came to be known. In that 1979 address, Carter highlighted many of the themes of his presidency. He argued forcefully for the need to reform current habits of consumption, prefacing these remarks with a spiritual interpretation of the problems that America was facing. What he saw was a nation in crisis. This was evident in the "growing doubt about the meaning of our own lives and in the loss of a unity of purpose for our nation."[92] Moreover, he argued, the source of this crisis was the tendency "to worship self-indulgence and consumption," a trend that cannot ultimately "satisfy our longing for meaning."[93]

The defining feature of Carter's malaise speech was the choice that he offered the American people. One path was the status quo. This he believed embodied "a mistaken idea of freedom, the right to grasp for ourselves some advantage over others," the end result of which was "constant conflict between narrow interests ending in chaos and immobility." The other path was defined by "common purpose" and a return to the American values of freedom, independence, and unity. The initial challenge that Carter identified for the American public was on the issue of energy independence and whether or not the country would be willing to face the truth about its dependence on Middle Eastern oil. To achieve this, he advocated new production and development of alternative energy sources, but the emphasis was primarily on conservation and restraint. What Carter was spelling out, in short, was the need for Americans to change their profligate lifestyle.

The 1980 presidential campaign marked a stark choice for the American people. Although Carter had articulated a religious vision of America, it was one rooted in the prophetic tradition of McGovern and the Civil Rights Movement. During the campaign, Carter called America back to the idealism of its founding, emphasizing equality, social justice, and community responsibility. It reflected the themes of American civil religion, but, true to its prophetic orientation, it looked to the values of the Judeo-Christian tradition as a benchmark for judging the nation's actions, not as a sanction for the status quo. Carter's Republican opponent, Ronald Reagan, offered an alternative choice. He staunchly defended the American system in all its aspects. Like Nixon's 1972 campaign, Reagan embraced the inherent goodness of the American way of life, depicting himself as its authentic defender. Moreover, his support for unbridled capitalism and his vision of an America defined by unlimited resources were based upon a belief that unconstrained ambition served the interests of all. These themes were clothed, moreover, in the rhetoric of freedom, God, and country. The religious nationalism that Reagan articulated was distinctly priestly in orientation and marked a sharp departure from Carter's call to repentance and renunciation.

## Conclusion

The cultural politics of the 1960s and 1970s reflects the diverse interpretations of both religion and society that have long informed American politics. Liberal (or modernist) interpretations of Christian tradition were tied to the progressive politics of the American left, while a more literal, or Evangelical, interpretation was associated with the politics of the right. The liberal basis of the Kennedy-Johnson era thus reflected the modernist religion of the mainline denominations, while the Social Gospel tradition was evident in the Civil Rights Movement led by the African-American churches. Liberal religion consequently provided both a priestly endorsement of American power in the world and a prophetic call for social reform. This prophetic element of the Christian tradition was similarly evident in the politics of George McGovern and Jimmy Carter. Both were deeply influenced by religious teachings and the suspicion of worldly power inherent in the Christian tradition. The politics of both McGovern and Carter exemplify, then, the tendency of civil religion to use Christian principle to judge government action, not sanction it. President Nixon and the conservative wing of the Republican Party, on the other hand, invoked religion for more distinctly "priestly" ends. Their theologically more conservative religion was invoked to provide a blanket validation for the American system, even as it offered a prophetic challenge to the social welfare policies of the New Deal

and the Great Society. This tendency to conflate religion and political authority, then, reflected both the Puritan legacy of the country and the Christian
anticommunism of the years after World War II.

Nixon's religious politics thus marked a sharp break with those of his predecessors. Although virtually all American presidents have invoked religion of
some sort, the traditional understanding of civil religion that defined American
politics during the mid-twentieth century was ecumenical, inclusive, and consistent with secular norms. The exclusive religious politics of the Nixon era,
however, was different. It consciously sought to coopt the exclusive religious
nationalism that Nixon's predecessors had largely eschewed—and overturned
the liberal consensus in the process. In doing so, Nixon helped bring an end to
the postwar secular order and initiated a fundamental realignment of American
politics. The motivations for this strategy are significant. The invocation of
an illiberal rendering of religion and the conscious effort to coopt conservative religious leaders were part of a broader strategy to redefine the fault lines
of American politics. By mobilizing the majority community along cultural as
opposed to class lines, Republican Party operatives hoped to diminish economic
considerations as a basis of voting and provide the Republican Party with a populist base for its conservative politics. Although Nixon's right-wing populism
would not come to fruition for another two decades, the die had been cast. By
using the office of the White House and other institutions of the modern state
to promote an illiberal understanding of Christian tradition, Nixon effectively
intervened in America's religious debates and, in doing so, validated both conservative Christianity and the exclusive nationalism of the radical right. This set
the stage for the presidencies of Ronald Reagan and George W. Bush.

# CHAPTER SEVEN

# Religious Nationalism in the Reagan-Bush Era

The efforts of the Republican Party to build a conservative majority through appeals to race, religion, and culture came to fruition during the Reagan and Bush presidencies. The strategy that propelled Nixon to the White House in 1968 and 1972 became a staple of Republican Party politics in later decades. The party's emphasis on cultural politics defined the Reagan Revolution of the 1980s, the Republican takeover of Congress in 1994, and the presidential campaigns of George W. Bush in 2000 and 2004. It also figured prominently in John McCain's bid for the presidency in 2008, particularly his selection of vice presidential candidate Sarah Palin. In each instance, the Party's electoral strategy relied on a mix of patriotism, Evangelical Christianity, and divisive social issues to appeal to the populist sentiments of the white Christian majority. By consciously polarizing the American electorate along cultural lines, the Republican Party sought to minimize the salience of economic issues and draw working-class whites into a coalition that in actuality catered to the interests of the country's economic elites. It was this type of right-wing populism that informed the culture wars of the 1990s.

A central feature of the Republican strategy—and the corresponding culture wars—was the denigration of liberal norms as misguided and immoral. Liberal conceptions of religion and society were characterized as culturally inauthentic, as were such key features of the open society as dissent and tolerance of diversity. The strategy of positive polarization also relied on an obfuscation of such issues as poverty, the loss of American industry, and the costs of an expansive foreign policy. In the context of hard-fought electoral campaigns, these issues were subordinated to questions of abortion, patriotism, biography, and divisive wedge issues. The irony was that the Reagan era witnessed the demise of the manufacturing base in the industrial East and Midwest and, with it, middle-class standards of living for many Americans. The transformation of the U.S. economy and America's emergence as a debtor nation ought to have been central topics of debate, but they were surprisingly marginal. Rather, Republican Party operatives worked to coopt the discontent associated with socioeconomic dislocation and to redefine the ills of American society as a crisis of spirit, not a crisis of capitalism. To this end, they were greatly aided by conservative churches and groups such as the Moral Majority and the Christian Coalition.

The initial success of this strategy—facilitated in no small part by political operatives like Roger Ailes, Lee Atwater, and Karl Rove—held out the hope of a permanent majority for the Republican Party. This goal was apparently in reach after George W. Bush's controversial election to the presidency in 2000, which secured for the party control of the White House as well as both houses of Congress. It was this phenomenal success, however, that also produced the demise of the conservative revolution. The Republican Party's divisive politics injected a high degree of sectarianism into American public life and undercut the ability of government to function effectively. More to the point, the religious nationalism of the Reagan-Bush era was informed by an unreflective zeal that contributed to an intransigent patriotism and dangerous overreach. The result was the Bush administration's failed policies in Iraq and Afghanistan, damaged relations with longtime U.S. allies, and the alienation of key domestic constituencies. The willingness of the political leadership to embrace its own righteousness blinded them to the folly of their actions. The result was the collapse of the ruling coalition and the resurrection of the liberal vision of civil religion in the form of Barack Obama.

## The Reagan Revolution

The 1980 presidential election was informed by two conflicting visions of the nation. One vision was offered not just by Carter but by other interpreters of contemporary American secularism as well. In a series of rulings during the 1960s and 1970s, the Supreme Court banned organized prayer in public schools, legalized abortion, and reinterpreted the First Amendment to ensure nonbelievers equal treatment in the public sphere. Similarly, liberal activists promoted equal rights for women, African Americans, and homosexuals. It also supported various aspects of the Sexual Revolution. The vision of social order that informed these issues—often described as secular humanist—reflected an understanding of religion in public life that had evolved in earlier decades. Religion, in this view, was not the *sole* arbiter of morality but rather one of many moral bases for society and politics. The subsequent dominance and institutionalization of a moral order that recognized a plurality of value systems—and the fundamental diversity of the population—brought into question the enduring nature of any one particular set of values or religious beliefs. It also challenged "the very possibility of transcendent, authoritative standards of human behavior."[1]

This secular vision of social order was opposed by an increasingly well-organized network of conservative Christians, who felt that secularism was threatening the life of the nation. At issue was a belief that America's "traditional values" were being undermined by the activism of liberal judges and by the amorality of the secular state. For these conservative Christians, it was secularism that was the basis of country's drift toward moral relativism and the source of such contemporary problems as juvenile delinquency, crime, drug abuse, and violence. They argued, moreover, that the demise of traditional values was caused by the decline of religion and not the socioeconomic changes of the period. Hence, a more prominent role of religion in social life was necessary to revive the political fortunes of the country. Like religious fundamentalists in other countries, conservative Christian activists believed that religion was the *sole* basis of moral virtue and that the secular trend had institutionalized an anti-religious bias in society that was "trampl[ing] on the religious preferences of the majority."[2] As such, Christians were urged to fight back and to oppose the secular humanism that many believed had "declared war on Christianity in this country."[3]

Although the rise of the Evangelical right in American politics reflected a backlash to the secularism of the 1960s and 1970s, this was only part of the story. This "new" religious politics was in reality a continuation of the cultural politics of the Nixon era. Like Nixon before him, Reagan relied on a strategy of positive polarization to divide the American electorate along cultural lines rather than economic ones. This type of conservative populism was intended to redefine the dominant conception of legitimate authority in a manner that would privilege the resurgent conservative movement at the expense of other political actors. To this end, Reagan invoked the ideas and symbols of fundamentalist Christianity, American patriotism, and a staunch anticommunism, a combination that was reminiscent of the 1950s. Moreover, by depicting such issues as school busing and racial integration as "liberal" and "elitist," Republican campaign strategists were able to portray Democrats as out of touch with mainstream voters. It also allowed them to characterize their own policies as more sensitive to the interests of the white working class. In this way, the Republican Party used divisive social issues to split the New Deal coalition and capture the presidency. Reagan's 1980 campaign, then, was not so much a revolution as a restoration.

The conservative movement that emerged in the early 1980s, however, was divided among a variety of factions. These generally fell into three camps: economic conservatives, social conservatives, and neoconservatives. Among the first group were libertarians, business groups, and economists such as Milton Friedman, who advocated the elimination of government intervention in the economy, a rollback of the welfare state, and greater reliance on the market to solve society's problems. This provided the basis of Reagan's "supply-side" economics and a return to laissez-faire deregulation. The social conservatives, on the other hand, were deeply concerned about the kind of society that had emerged in the 1960s and 1970s and were distressed by the diminished role of religion in public life. Consequently, they supported a more activist government on moral issues and a closer relationship between government and organized Christianity. Finally, the neoconservatives were largely former Democrats who were interested in foreign policy issues and were concerned about what they perceived as a diminished commitment to America's struggle against the Soviet Union.

The Reagan campaign was able to unite these disparate wings of the conservative movement by linking right-wing political issues—strong defense, anticommunism, economic libertarianism—with conservative religion. The antigovernment message that appealed to libertarians also played well with cultural conservatives, who believed that government intervention in education and in the family was forcing secular values on a religious population. Reagan's assault on the welfare state—and his stigmatization of the poor—similarly appeased the various factions by promising lower taxes and emphasizing individual self-reliance. This theme resonated with conservative Christians who were more concerned with individual conversion than social justice, since they saw the welfare state as creating a "moral blight of dependency."[4] Moreover, these ideas were put forth in the context of an assertive—and redemptive—nationalism that echoed the Christian anticommunist themes of earlier years. Reagan's victory, in short, was a vindication of the Nixon electoral strategy, which succeeded in providing a populist basis of support that the Republican Party had historically lacked.

The increasing dominance of the far left within the Democratic Party played into the Republican strategy and in the corresponding political realignment of the country. Changes in party rules in 1972 weakened the hold of traditional party leaders and created an opportunity for a plurality of factions to assert themselves within the party's structure. These factions included racial and ethnic minorities, women, and others representing a variety of leftist causes. This trend, which continued throughout the 1980s, had a significant impact on the party. First, it hastened the departure of key Democratic constituencies, particularly working-class whites. This was evident in the large turnout of union voters who supported Reagan in 1980 and 1984—who became known as Reagan Democrats—and in the migration of white southerners to the Republican Party. Second, the changing dynamics in the party contributed to the perception that Democrats were intolerant of those with strong religious beliefs. The secularism of this period was seen not as a matter of studied neutrality but rather as active hostility to any form of religion in the public square. The party's position on such issues as abortion rights and school prayer seemed to reflect this assumption. The perception of an antireligious bias led to a trend throughout the 1980s wherein overtly religious Americans gravitated toward the Republican Party, while those who did not attend church on a regular basis found a home in the Democratic Party.[5]

Reagan's 1980 election owed much to the conservative organizations, think tanks, publications, and political action committees that had blossomed during the 1970s. Funded largely by corporations and conservative foundations, these entities—the Heritage Foundation, the American Enterprise Institute, the Cato Institute, The National Conservative Political Action Committee, *The National Interest*—provided a new means for promoting conservative policies in the Washington policy community and at the grassroots level. These organizations also served as the institutional base for the "New Right." Ideologically, the New Right was not significantly different from the radical right of the 1950s and 1960s. Both rallied around the "fusionist" ideals of laissez-faire economics, anticommunism and a return to "traditional values." The difference was that there were significantly more financial resources available from the business community and from private endowments, and these new groups were able to exploit advances in direct mail fundraising. Both of these trends enhanced the ability of the conservative movement to reach new constituencies.

What was also different about the Reagan era was the unqualified backing that the New Right received from mainstream political leaders within the Republican Party. It was in regard to this ideological commitment to the conservative movement that Reagan differed most dramatically from his predecessors. Reagan's strident opposition to the welfare state, his advocacy of unregulated market capitalism, and the rejection of deterrence as a means of dealing with the Soviet Union were all departures from the position of earlier presidents, including Nixon. Perhaps the most striking difference was the manner in which conservative Christianity became such a central feature of the party's identity. Although Nixon had readily politicized religion, he nonetheless spoke inclusively, leaving the more explicit articulation of religious themes to the likes of Billy Graham. Reagan, on the other hand, was much less circumspect about his identification with conservative Christianity and its various causes. On the campaign trail, for example, Reagan regularly condemned the "expulsion of God from the classroom," endorsed tuition tax credits for Christian schools, and urged that creationism be taught as an alternative to evolution in the public schools.[6] He also promised to "restore the nation to its God-ordained greatness."[7]

Despite these differences, however, the strategy and tactics of the Reagan campaign mirrored those of Nixon. Both used divisive social issues to court the Evangelical vote, ethnic Catholics, and southern whites.[8] Furthermore, both characterized contemporary social problems as a religious issue, one that only a return to conservative religion would solve. Reagan's 1980 speech before the Religious Roundtable in Dallas—an organization associated with the Christian Right—illustrated this point. In his speech to the fifteen thousand attendees, Reagan criticized the use of the Constitution "as a reason to keep traditional moral values away from policymaking" and argued that the Bible contains the answers to "all the complex and horrendous questions confronting us at home and worldwide."[9] Moreover, he applauded the group—and Evangelical Christians more generally—for reenergizing American politics. Recognizing that the group could not, by law, endorse a particular candidate, Reagan said, "I want you to know I endorse you and what you are doing."[10]

The meeting in Dallas was a defining moment for the newly emergent religious right. It reflected the entrance into the Republican Party of a constituency that had traditionally either voted Democrat or eschewed national politics altogether. The roots of this transition, however, lay in the efforts of conservative political activists and Republican Party operatives to recruit conservative religious leaders. In 1979, for example, leading members of the conservative movement, including Howard Phillips, Paul Weyrich, Ed McAteer, and Robert Billings, met with Jerry Falwell, urging the minister, who did not yet have a national profile, to become involved in partisan politics. This meeting led to the creation of the Moral Majority, an organization originally conceived as a vehicle for mobilizing religious conservatives for political ends.[11] The impetus for approaching Falwell was the influence of his radio and television programming, which was reaching fifteen million Americans weekly. Falwell and other religious broadcasters, such as Pat Roberson, Oral Roberts, and Jim Bakker, had developed television and radio ministries that reached vast audiences, raised significant amounts of money, and exploited extensive computerized mailing lists. The political operatives recognized the utility of these televangelists and the fact that these organizations provided "all the necessary parts for a political machine."[12]

## The Reagan Administration in Power

If Reagan campaigned on religious and cultural themes, his priorities once in office were tax cuts and military spending. The economic reforms of the early 1980s and the intensification of the Cold War were major shifts in policy from previous administrations. The transformation of fiscal policy, in particular, was informed by a new ideology that rejected not just the welfare state but also the Keynesian economics that had guided policymakers since the 1930s. Reagan's economic program also advocated a major rollback of environmental and regulatory policies, which were promoted under the guise of limiting big government. The policies of deregulation contributed to a period of economic expansion, albeit one defined by a widening gap between the rich and the poor. The accumulation of wealth during this period, moreover, was imbued with moral overtones, reflecting an underlying belief that earthly wealth is a sign of divine favor. As one commentator noted, "In the eighties, God and Mammon had merged and become inseparable."[13]

The Reagan administration's foreign policies, moreover, were articulated in the stark terms of a religious crusade. Reflecting the anticommunism of the 1950s, Reagan characterized the Soviet Union as the "focus of evil in the modern world."[14] Within his Manichaean view of world affairs, the United States and its allies were portrayed as the defenders of freedom and God and the broader conflict as a "struggle between right and wrong, good and evil."[15] In this context, the government's involvement in various proxy wars, for example, was cloaked in a rhetoric of moral certitude. This provided the basis for funding armed groups in Central America, Africa, and, later, Afghanistan. Reagan's fervent anticommunism also justified increased military spending, renewed support for certain authoritarian regimes, and a rejection of Carter's emphasis on human rights and diplomacy. It also entailed the denigration of international organizations and treaties, a sharp departure from the multilateralism of the postwar era.

The Reagan administration's religious nationalism was contentious and divisive. On the one hand, by arguing that its national security policies reflected America's moral destiny, the administration dismissed dissent as unpatriotic or, at best, naive. Reagan, for example, characterized the nuclear freeze movement to a convention of Christian Evangelicals as a "very dangerous fraud" and those advocating it as engaged in "simple-minded appeasement."[16] This sparked much consternation in religious circles among those who felt that the president's speech had "distorted Christianity to serve political goals."[17] The explicit link between Reagan's foreign policy and his religion also sanctioned the administration's support of unsavory regimes that supported U.S. economic and foreign policy goals. The religious overtones of this were evident in remarks by Secretary of State Alexander Haig, who noted that the resumption of arms sales to the right-wing government in Argentina despite its poor human rights record was based on their "shared values." Asked what those values might be, Haig responded, "A belief in God."[18]

There were tensions, though, between the Reagan administration and conservative Christian activists who felt that little was being done to promote their priorities. Banning abortion and restoring prayer in school had taken a back seat to economic and foreign policy. Even though Reagan frequently mentioned Christian social issues in his speeches, they were not a priority for his administration during the first term. Part of this inaction derived from divisions within the Republican Party over the Christian Right's agenda. It was also due in part to a distinct lack of support for such policies, both in Congress and among the American people. Whatever the reason, many conservatives began to wonder if "the religious right was being used by the Reagan forces" solely for electoral purposes.[19]

Although the Reagan administration was slow to act on the agenda of the Christian Right, it did cut off funding for family planning programs overseas, endorsed a constitutional amendment on school prayer, and blocked the Equal Rights Amendment, which eventually stalled in Congress.[20] Moreover, the administration nominated conservative judges to the federal bench who would help to reshape the judicial system in years to come. Perhaps the most significant contribution of the Reagan administration to the Christian Right, however, was its ability to bring illiberal interpretations of religion into the ideological mainstream. Although Reagan balanced his belief in moral absolutes with a rhetorical commitment to tolerance, he was committed to the political vision of his Evangelical supporters. More to the point, the administration conferred legitimacy on conservative issues and activists that were once seen as marginal and extreme. By promoting conservative religion in the public sphere, Reagan reinforced the message of the Christian Right and helped to normalize them in the eyes of the American electorate. As Hadden and Shupe have argued:

> One cannot possibly understand or account for the rapid movement of religious broadcasters into the political arena during the 1980s without examining the role of Ronald Reagan in legitimizing both their causes and their involvement in politics. Largely unnoticed by the media and, hence, the general public, Reagan's first term in office saw evangelicals enjoying unprecedented access to the presidency and the White House, with theological liberals and moderates virtually locked out. Reverend Jerry Falwell replaced the more establishment evangelical Billy Graham as the White House's unofficial chaplain. No president during this century has so completely snubbed the established religious leadership of this nation as has Ronald Reagan. His embrace of the New Christian Right has, in effect, rewritten the book on who is "The Establishment."[21]

## Reagan's Second Term

Reagan's 1984 reelection campaign reprised many of the themes that had proven so successful in 1980. The motto "Morning in America" emphasized a resurgent, if amorphous, national pride and a belief that the Reagan administration's policies were making America stronger both at home and abroad. Reagan's religious nationalism, moreover, was central. This was evident in his address to the National Religious Broadcasters that kicked off the campaign. In this speech, Reagan once again highlighted core social issues as abortion, school prayer, "family values," and the importance of the Bible to contemporary life. The speech tied these issues to the president's firm anticommunism and included an attack on the American Civil Liberties Union (ACLU). The ACLU was a particular object of scorn because of its support for secular norms. At the heart of Reagan's message was a belief that America's social ills reflected a deeper spiritual crisis that could only be solved by a greater role for organized Christianity in American public life. After deploring such issues as pornography and drug use, for example, Reagan argued that one could find in the Bible "all the answers to all the problems that face us today—if we'd only read and believe."[22]

A defining feature of this message was an explicit link between conservative religion and patriotism and the corresponding characterization of secularism as an aberrant feature of the national experience. Stating that America's "fundamental values have been under attack for far too long," Reagan argued that his administration was uniquely able to defend American values and, hence, the nation.[23] Reagan reiterated this theme in a prayer breakfast during the Republican National Convention in August 1984. In this speech, he highlighted the continuing struggle to define the nation—either in religious or secular terms—in which he sought to situate the campaign. Identifying his vision of society as one where "faith and religion play a critical role in the political life of our nation," he argued that this was the authentic creed of American nationalism. The centrality of religion in public life, he went on, had been the bedrock of the American founding and the source of America's strength for two centuries. It was only in the 1960s, he argued, that America took "steps toward secularizing our nation and removing religion from its honored place."[24] This, Reagan concluded, was the source of America's ills; for without religion, he argued, neither morality nor democracy would long survive.

The moral vision that Reagan promoted in these campaign speeches was one infused with religious idealism and an unquestioning faith in the righteousness of American power. God had not only chosen the American people for a unique destiny, according to this view, but had made America His instrument in fighting the godless communism of the East. In a Fourth of July speech delivered in Decatur, Alabama, for example, Reagan reprised John Winthrop's description of America as a "shining city upon the hill for all the world to see."[25] The context of this analogy was Reagan's discussion of Soviet totalitarianism and, opposed to it, America's commitment to freedom. Democracy, in this speech, was described as "just a political reading of the Bible," and the administration's support for militant groups around the globe—such as the *mujahedin* in Afghanistan and the Contra rebels in Central America—was linked to holy purpose. This vision of the United States was one defined by religious mission, a benign conception of American power, and the idea that America was enacting God's Will on earth.

The reference to America as a "shining city on the hill" is deeply imbued with the biblical idea of a covenantal relationship—and the ideology of American exceptionalism—but it overlooks the second half of John Winthrop's statement.[26] Winthrop, the first governor of Massachusetts Bay Colony, spoke to his fellow settlers of building a "city upon a hill" that would serve as a moral example for the world. However, he went on to argue that there is a corresponding burden placed on the community to live up to the ideals and commandments of God, lest "we shall shame the faces of many of God's worthy servants, and cause their prayers to be turned into curses upon us til we be consumed out of the good land whither we are a-going."[27] There is little in Reagan's speeches that recognize the second half of this covenantal injunction and the imperative of exercising power with moral restraint. Insofar as there is any recognition of a burden to abide by Christian teachings, it certainly did not apply to issues of foreign policy, economic equality, or social justice. Reagan's understanding of religion in the American tradition was distinctly priestly in orientation, not prophetic.

Reagan's campaign themes were reiterated by members of the Christian Right, who similarly argued that the nation was under threat: internally from the forces of secularism and externally from godless communism. The alternative, they argued, was a society defined by a more central role for conservative Christianity. In this way, the early constitutional debates over the proper role of religion in public life were once again resurrected. Jerry Falwell, for instance, argued that "our religious nation has been under attack from an amoral, antireligious segment of society involved in the destruction of life unparalleled in our history." Hence, the fate of the nation depended on opposing such forces and more clearly linking political authority to religious authority. According to Falwell, this could only be done by supporting Reagan, "who believes what we say here today."[28] Within this vision, secular humanists—and their allies in the Democratic Party—were perceived as the enemies of conventional morality and of a God-centered moral order. There was an obligation, then, for Christian activists to become more involved in national politics, because "the nation got in the shape it is in because Christians abdicated their responsibilities in public life."[29]

The argument against a de facto establishment of Christianity was made by those critical of the Reagan's politicization of religion. As one commentator noted, "The suggestion that God somehow is a 'value' of Republicans more than of their opponents makes mincemeat of any distinction between church and state . . . [and] cheapens the values it extols."[30] Similarly, many mainline religious actors were concerned about the manipulation of Biblical theology by Reagan and his clerical supporters, which they saw as artificially polarizing American society. Mainstream religious leaders, for example, argued that the debate over school prayer was "not between the godly and ungodly."[31] Rather, the debate over such issues as prayer in public schools raised genuine concerns among people of faith about government preference in matters of religion. To denigrate political opponents as ungodly, then, was good neither for politics nor for religion. The Democratic Party picked up on these concerns. In several speeches following the Republican Convention, Walter Mondale, the Democratic presidential candidate, critiqued Reagan's understanding of secularism, arguing that the Founding Fathers well understood the danger that politics posed to religion. He also warned of conservative groups that sought to use the Reagan administration to impose their beliefs on others. "In America," Mondale said, "our faith is personal and honest and uncorrupted by political interference. May it always be thus."[32]

Many American religious figures were similarly troubled by the administration's defense and budget policies, seeing in the campaign's emphasis on "social issues" a distraction from more pressing issues facing the country. Criticizing the impact of the Reagan administration's policies on the poor, for example, the United Methodist Conference canceled its plans to have Reagan address the church group, stating that it would be a "dereliction of Christian responsibility [to give] a prestigious election year forum to a public figure who represents so many positions contrary to those of our church."[33] Other religious figures, moreover, were disturbed that the administration had ignored the mainline churches and their emphasis on social justice and peace. Rather, the administration tended only to associate with conservative groups that supported its political agenda. As one Catholic official noted, the administration "wants to deal with church leaders, but they exclude all but the most dollar-wise and those who have no problem waving a flag in one hand and a crucifix in the other to attract followers, [and these tend to be] the side-show revivalist types."[34]

In the end, Reagan's victory in 1984 was a landslide. Like the 1968, 1972, and 1980 campaigns, the appeal to issues of cultural conservatism—abortion, school prayer, religion, and nationalism—allowed Republicans to make significant inroads into traditional Democratic bases of support. It also furthered the political realignment that was transpiring in the South and elsewhere.[35] This trend had two significant implications. First, the electoral strategy of positive polarization was poisoning the well of public discourse, with opponents of the conservative movement commonly being characterized as un-American or ungodly. It was artificially dividing American society. Second, the campaign demonstrated the degree to which cultural conservatives had come to dominate the Republican Party. Religious conservatives had increasingly taken over state and local party organizations, aided in this effort by the close ties between the New Right and the party's national leadership. After years of recruitment and cooptation by party leaders, the Religious Right was now a dominant force within the party. The nominating process and the platform consequently reflected the influence of Christian activists, indicating the extent to which "the far-right fringe of the Republican Party [had now become] its core."[36]

### George Herbert Walker Bush

Republican campaigns during the late 1980s and early 1990s reflected the same kind of right-wing populism and polarizing cultural politics of the previous two decades. This was an odd fit, however, for the presidential campaigns of George H. W. Bush. Bush was a pragmatic centrist, the product of a prominent and wealthy Republican family from the Northeast. Consequently, he was distrusted by movement conservatives, who saw him as a part of the East Coast establishment. The tensions within the party prompted a challenge in the 1988 Republican primaries from televangelist Pat Robertson, who had launched his own bid for the presidency. Robertson's strong showing in Michigan and Iowa stunned the Bush campaign, as it highlighted their weakness among cultural conservatives. Robertson also had strong support in the South and the Southwest, where state parties had become dominated by religious conservatives. To address this challenge, Bush reached out to those who dominated the nomination process, aided in the effort by his son, George W. Bush, who himself was a born-again Evangelical. The elder Bush also refashioned his image by taking strong stands on key social issues (reversing himself, for example, on abortion rights) and embracing Ronald Reagan's economic policies, which he had once derided as "voodoo economics."

It was in the Bush campaign's response to its Democratic challenger, Michael Dukakis, where the instrumental manipulation of religion and culture was most apparent. The Democratic primaries were very much imbued with religious and moral content. This was reflected in the Reverend Jesse Jackson's religious appeals to the social gospel and in Dukakis's ability to make a case for economic nationalism. Dukakis's Greek roots helped him in the ethnic communities, while Jackson's themes of racial and religious tolerance appeared to resonate with white Democratic voters. Together, these themes offered a progressive alternative to the Reagan-Bush legacy and reflected the liberal consensus of earlier years. By emphasizing government support for the middle class and a greater commitment to social justice, the Democrats appeared to have a genuine opportunity to refashion the Democratic coalition of earlier years. The response of the Bush campaign was to invoke the same kind of divisive cultural politics that had been central to earlier Republican campaigns. The goal was to use social (or wedge) issues to blunt the appeal of Dukakis's economic populism to caricature Dukakis as out of touch with the American mainstream. Although the Democrats tried to define the campaign in terms of economic justice and effective governance, the Bush campaign, led by Republican strategist Lee Atwater, sought to define it in terms of religion and culture.

At the heart of this strategy was an effort to portray Dukakis as culturally inauthentic. The Bush campaign attacked Dukakis's stance on such issues as abortion, gun control, and state-led prayer in school. The most damaging assault, however, involved the prison furlough of an African-American convict named Willie Horton. The television advertisement that highlighted the Horton case castigated Dukakis for allowing a convicted murderer out of jail to commit further crimes (in this instance rape) and characterized Dukakis as impervious to the concerns of crime victims. It also used race and fear to replicate the positive polarization that had defined Republican campaigns since 1964. Similarly, the Bush campaign seized upon Dukakis's veto of legislation that required public school children to recite the Pledge of Allegiance. Although the attorney general of Massachusetts described the legislation as unconstitutional and unenforceable, the Bush team nonetheless used the issue to portray Dukakis as unpatriotic and culturally out of step with ordinary Americans. As Bush stated, "I don't understand the type of thinking that lets first-degree murderers who haven't even served enough time to be eligible for parole out on parole so they can rape and plunder again, and then isn't willing to let the teachers lead the kids in the Pledge of Allegiance."[37]

A key feature of the 1988 Bush campaign was the demonization of liberalism and tolerance as un-American. Although loyalty oaths contravene the basic requirements of an open society, the Bush campaign team portrayed the debate over the Pledge of Allegiance as a matter of patriotism and cultural authenticity. The implication was that true Americans embraced an unquestioning loyalty to the structures of American power, while Dukakis's commitment to constitutional restraint was clearly aberrant. Similarly, the attack on Dukakis as "soft" on crime brought into question Dukakis's ability to defend the nation. The Willie Horton ad, for example, was a metaphor for the drug-afflicted poor that inhabited America's inner cities and that represented a hostile "other" in the midst of white America.[38] Such representatives of minority populations—especially African Americans—were a potent symbol of the internal threat to the majority community. Dukakis's prison furlough program and his membership in the ACLU thus fit into a broader narrative of liberalism giving priority to minority interests over the white Christian majority. Bush, on the other hand, characterized himself as a "good" American, arguing that "I am not a card-carrying member of the ACLU. I am for the people."[39]

The 1992 presidential election reprised many of the same issues that informed the 1988 campaign. President Bush, for example, facing a significant challenge from the conservative wing of his own party, once again sought to coopt, not confront, the more reactionary elements of the Republican Party. The Bush team consequently returned to the type of cultural politics that had defined the earlier campaign. The point man on cultural issues in this instance, though, was Vice President Dan Quayle. Despite his low profile in the administration, Quayle became a central figure in the effort to reach out to religious conservatives in 1992. In a series of high-profile speeches, Quayle linked the social ills of society to a "poverty of values" that derived from liberal social policies and a tolerance of deviant lifestyles. The first speech was given at the Commonwealth Club of California, where he spoke about the riots that had occurred in Los Angeles just three weeks earlier. Although the riots were sparked by the acquittal of white policemen in the beating of a black motorist, Rodney King, Quayle argued that what was really at issue was a crisis of values: "I believe that the lawless social anarchy which we saw is directly related to the breakdown of family structure, personal responsibility and social order. . . . For the poor the situation is compounded by a welfare ethos that impedes individual efforts to move ahead in society, and hampers their ability to take advantage of the opportunities America offers."[40]

Quayle argued in this speech that the poverty of values that characterized American society—and particularly America's inner cities—was caused by the disintegration of the traditional family and not by the dislocation associated with the economic transformation of postindustrial America. From this perspective, the problem was a lack of religion and morality, not poverty or capitalism. Quayle went on to link this trend to the deviant values (and lifestyles) that were embodied in, among other things, the television character Murphy Brown, who chose to have a child out of wedlock in an episode that aired during the campaign. It was in this context that he characterized the 1992 campaign as a "culture war" between those who espouse traditional family values and a cultural elite that denigrates family, God, and country. In a speech to the Southern Baptist Convention, Quayle took this argument a step further, stating that "the changes in our culture in recent decades [have] created a cultural divide in our country. . . . [And this divide is so great] that it sometimes seems we have two cultures, the cultural elite and the rest of us."[41] On one side of this divide were the intellectual elites associated with the "liberal media," academia, and Hollywood, while on the other side were "the homes and workplaces and churches" of America.

This theme was repeated throughout the campaign in a variety of settings.[42] President Bush, for example, gave a speech in New York in which he held himself out as the nation's "moral compass" in a period when "our whole Judeo-Christian tradition" was under siege.[43] Reiterating his opposition to abortion and his support for school prayer, Bush described an America in a state of moral disarray; his opponent, Bill Clinton, was portrayed as a supporter of the forces of liberal permissiveness that had contributed to such ills. Bush also spoke of "promoting religion as a force for good in our society" and allowing the "faith of our fathers back into [our] schools." He went on to argue that " a central issue of this election year should be, who do you trust to renew America's moral purpose? Who do you trust to fight for the ideas that will help rebuild our families and restore our fundamental values?"[44]

All of this rhetoric came to a head at the Republican National Convention in Houston, Texas. The party platform explicitly acknowledged a belief in God—Bush made sure to excoriate the Democrats' platform for failing to do likewise—and gave primacy to issues such as abortion, school prayer, and opposition to gay rights. The prevalence of Evangelicals and the conservative nature of the religious rhetoric, moreover, led Jerry Falwell to liken the convention to a "Baptist revival meeting."[45] The most poignant moment, however, was the speech given by former Nixon aide Patrick Buchanan. In his remarks, Buchanan attacked Clinton for supporting "unrestricted abortion on demand," homosexual rights, "environmental extremism," and the "radical feminism" embodied by his wife, Hillary. He contrasted this with President Bush's support for traditional values, freedom, and moral certitude. Echoing Quayle's earlier remarks, Buchanan argued that this was war:

> My friends, this election is about much more than who gets what. It is about who we are. It is about what we believe. It is about what we stand for as Americans. There is a religious war going on in our country for the soul of America. It is a cultural war, as critical to the kind of nation we will one day be as was the Cold War itself. And in that struggle for the soul of America, Clinton and Clinton are on the other side, and George Bush is on our side. And so, we have to come home, and stand beside him.[46]

## The Culture Wars Come of Age

The defense of cultural values, and the so-called culture wars, that defined the 1988 and 1992 electoral campaigns was driven in large measure by tactical considerations on how best to win an election. As such, it reflected a conscious effort to polarize the American public along cultural lines in order to minimize the salience of class or economic considerations as a basis for voting. In this regard, the Bush campaigns, taking a page from Nixon and Reagan, continued to invoke divisive social issues as a basis of populist mobilization. The conflation of conservative Christianity and patriotism were central to this strategy. Like the Indian elections of the same period, however, American campaigns had come to reflect the same instrumental use of ideology—and mass politics—that typified political discourse in that country. Campaign themes eschewed genuine matters of substance in favor of hot-button issues that mobilized niche constituencies. Elections were informed by simplified and emotional issues such as whether homosexuals can marry, or whether a fictional television character ought to bear a child out of wedlock. Serious questions about the country's industrial policy (or lack thereof) were marginal. Moreover, that even George H. W. Bush—a centrist politician originally of the party's liberal wing—could use this strategy effectively attested to both the strength of its message as well as its instrumental nature.

There was, of course, a reality to the culture wars that resonated with large segments of the population. Underlying these debates were fundamental questions about how to define the nation, and whether a particular (and exclusive) set of religious values ought to be embedded in the institutions of nation and state. For many devout Christians, these issues went to the heart of the American idea and the kind of country they wished to create. Nonetheless, these divisive social issues—passionate as many were about them—represented a distracting discourse that obfuscated the very real economic, political, and social challenges facing the country. Twelve years of Republican governance had overseen a dramatic expansion in the size of government and an explosion in federal spending. The national debt grew under Reagan and Bush from $900 billion in 1980 to $4.3 trillion in 1993. America had also gone from being the world's largest creditor nation to the largest debtor nation. The emphasis on economic deregulation, moreover, spawned a virtual collapse of the savings and loan industry and facilitated the decline of America's manufacturing base. It was the task of Republican Party operatives, then, to redirect the populist anger of the country away from these economic concerns and toward cultural issues. Insofar as they were able to define the frame of political debate in terms of culture or religion, Republicans would retain control of political power. If the campaigns were about economics, then the Democrats would win.

## The Clinton Era

Bill Clinton won the Democratic primary and the presidency in 1992. Despite allegations about marital infidelity and attacks on his morality, Clinton was able to articulate a vision of economic populism that appealed to centrist voters. Particularly in tough economic times, jobs, health care, and education became greater priorities for the American electorate than the social issues promoted by Quayle and Bush. The economic concerns raised by other candidates, notably Buchanan and third-party candidate Ross Perot, similarly heightened the salience of economic considerations in the campaign at the expense of cultural issues. Moreover, the religious message of the Bush-Quayle campaign was blunted by Clinton's own invocation of religion. Clinton's religious rhetoric, though, drew heavily from the social gospel and the progressive side of American religion. His populist message, which mixed religious and economic concerns, helped to redefine the terms of debate and demonstrated that liberal (and secular) norms had their own Christian basis. Clinton also criticized his opponents' illiberal religious politics, arguing that it sowed the seeds of intolerance and division. In a speech at Notre Dame University, Clinton said, "America doesn't need a religious war. America needs a reaffirmation of the values that for most of us, are rooted in our religious faiths."[47]

The Clinton campaign drew heavily from the civil religion of earlier eras and used religious rhetoric to promote a more inclusive vision of American society. The campaign was aided, moreover, by the National Council of Churches (NCC), which reinforced Clinton's critique of the Bush administration's religious politics. Buchanan's speech at the convention, among others, had struck a discordant note with mainstream religious leaders. Although Buchanan's comments were a familiar refrain among conservative Christians, the image of a culture war appeared extreme to most Americans. These concerns were articulated in a letter circulated by religious leaders from America's mainline churches. The letter expressed apprehension over the Bush campaign's politicization of religion and its tendency to promote one interpretation of religion to the exclusion of all others. It also called for a more tolerant civil discourse. The NCC letter stated: "Any partisan use of God's name tends to breed intolerance and to divide." Moreover, the statement argued that it is "blasphemy . . . to invoke the infinite and holy God to assert the moral superiority of one people over another or one political party over another."[48] Faith and God should be a basis of unity, the letter argued, not of division.

If Clinton's electoral success demonstrated a new "centrism," the trend was short-lived.[49] The Democratic Party lost control of both the House of Representatives and the U.S. Senate in the 1994 midterm elections. The result was electrifying. It not only overturned Democratic dominance in Congress but also represented the first time a Republican majority had controlled the House in forty years. The elections were extraordinary, but the basic dynamic was not. The Republican electoral strategy in 1994 relied on the same right-wing populism that had defined presidential politics for the previous three decades. Newt Gingrich, the leader of the conservative wing of the House Republicans, sought to stigmatize the Democratic majority as corrupt tax-and-spend liberals who were out of step with the concerns of America's working families. An essential part of this strategy was a continuing reliance on divisive social issues—abortion, school prayer, and "family values"—to obscure the more pressing concerns of soaring health care costs and the impact of neoliberal trade policies on society. The effectiveness of this strategy meant that the Republicans were once again able to mobilize lower-income religious voters, who voted "their beliefs, not their pocketbooks."[50]

The Gingrich revolution was aided by other factors, such as the advent of talk radio. The prominence of right-wing commentators on America's airwaves gave new meaning to the "permanent campaign" promoted by Republican strategists such as Roger Ailes, who had managed media relations for Nixon, Reagan, and Bush and who would become the founding CEO of the Fox News Channel in 1996. By providing an alternative venue for political discourse, conservative commentators were able provide an interpretation of events in Washington that differed from that in the mainstream media. Republicans were also effective in promoting—and benefiting from—popular disdain for Congress as an institution. Although there were several high-profile scandals that exacerbated this trend—the Keating Five scandal, the Savings and Loan debacle, the House banking scandal—the Gingrich faction helped to turn these issues into *Democratic* scandals. Finally, the Republican takeover was greatly facilitated by the Party's efforts to make local contests hinge on national issues, thus nationalizing local campaigns. In this way, the 1994 election represented the culmination of party's southern strategy, and the electoral realignment that Nixon had begun in 1968. 1994 witnessed the wholesale shift of the South as a region toward the Republican Party as longtime Democrats lost their seats in Congress and were replaced by conservative Republicans. Lyndon Johnson's prediction that the Democrats would lose the South for a generation due to civil rights was finally coming true.

The policies of the early Clinton administration also played into this new round of cultural politics. Clinton's support for nondiscriminatory treatment of homosexuals in the military, his support for gun control and abortion rights, and Hillary Clinton's prominent role in the early years of the administration all rankled white, conservative voters. His opposition to the Vietnam War as a young man and his efforts to create a diverse cabinet and reform health care reinforced his image as a Dukakis-style liberal. Conservative groups, energized in their opposition to Clinton, used direct mail appeals, talk radio, and think tanks to castigate the sitting president. The establishment of a special prosecutor to look into Clinton's financial past also provided a mechanism for investigating a much wider array of allegations, the most important of which proved to be sexual in nature. Even after a fairly easy reelection in 1996, the politics of cultural division continued to define the Republican base, and Clinton remained the primary target of the conservative animus.

Clinton's second term, however, was severely constrained by the Monica Lewinsky scandal. News of his sexual liaison with a White House intern broke in the major media outlets in January 1998, eventually to engulf his presidency. The sex scandal—and the effort to cover it up—fit the image of the immoral politician of conservative rhetoric.[51] Although the impeachment proceedings—based on his denial of the affair under oath—reflected genuine outrage among religious conservatives, most Americans were not convinced that the misdeed rose to the level of impeachment. Rather, they saw it as unfortunate and unseemly but certainly not rising to the level of "high crimes and misdemeanors," the constitutional requirement for the removal of a president from office. On the other hand, the vindictiveness of the impeachment prosecutors undermined their case in the court of public opinion. Many religious leaders, moreover, were critical of the conservatives' preoccupation with sexual misconduct, particularly while they were doing so little to help the poor. As one religious leader noted, "There's tremendous indignation about what Clinton did. I accept that. [But] where's the indignation about 12 million children without health care?"[52]

If the Lewinsky scandal failed to bring the Clinton presidency to an untimely end, it certainly cast a shadow over the 2000 presidential race. This could be seen in the influence of the "character issue" and the "moral values" issue in the campaign. In an unmistakable reference to the Clinton scandals, George W. Bush, then governor of Texas, insisted that he would "return honor and dignity to the White House."[53] Implying that the Clinton administration had sullied the office of the president, Bush sought to tie the Democratic candidate, Vice President Albert Gore, to the administration's tarnished reputation. Bush also made an issue of the vice president's character, arguing that he readily changed positions, a habit that reflected a preference for moral relativism over core convictions.

Bush's Christian faith was also a central part of the campaign strategy. By emphasizing his strong religious beliefs, Bush sought to distinguish himself from Gore, claiming that he did not waver in his convictions because he believed in moral absolutes. This was a key feature of Bush's appeal to Christian conservatives. Bush also began reaching out to Evangelical ministers in 1998, hiring Ralph Reed, former director of the Christian Coalition, to help his campaign. Bush spoke to several ministry leaders—including televangelist James Robison—of his "call" to run for president and his belief that "God wants me to run for President."[54] Bush's rhetoric on the campaign trail also regularly blurred the themes of God and country. He characterized Jesus as his favorite philosopher, "because he changed my heart."[55] Such overt appeals to religion led many conservative Christians to conclude that Bush was "one of us."[56]

The selection of Senator Joseph Lieberman to be Gore's running mate was very much a reaction to the religious (and moral) emphasis of the campaign. By selecting a conservative Jewish senator, Gore sought to distance himself from the Clinton scandals. Lieberman had been an outspoken critic of Clinton when news of his affair with Lewinsky first broke, and his selection reflected the Gore campaign's effort to blunt Bush's advantage on the morality issue. Lieberman's most significant contribution, moreover, was his outspoken support for a more explicit role of religion in American public life. He noted on several occasions that "the constitution guarantees freedom of religion, not freedom from religion."[57] He also argued that America had "lost its moral bearings"[58] and that "as a people, we need to reaffirm our faith."[59] Similarly, Lieberman was outspoken in his criticisms of the "toxic entertainment" that characterized the contemporary mass media landscape and promised a "new burst of moral and cultural renewal" as a means of reversing America's decline.[60]

This motivation behind Lieberman's selection and the attempt to coopt the moral values issue was controversial. Although Democrats had long used religion in their campaigns, it tended to be of a socially liberal stripe, not the kind of conservative religion to which Republicans traditionally appealed. As such, Lieberman's statements and positions appeared to validate, not oppose, the Bush campaign's core claims about an overly secular society breeding immorality. Although implicitly ecumenical, Lieberman's religious message was a distinctly conservative one, with little of the social gospel that had characterized earlier Democratic campaigns. As such, Lieberman's religious conservatism tended to reinforce the cultural war discourse instead of offering a genuine alternative. Lieberman's enthusiasm for religion on the campaign trail consequently did not always play well with the Democratic faithful. It was somewhat ironic, then, when the Anti-Defamation League called on Lieberman to refrain from such explicit appeals to religion, which they felt had "crossed [the line]."[61]

### George W. Bush and the War on Terror

The close and contested nature of the 2000 campaign accurately captured an electorate that was deeply divided along party lines. The American voters differed over a variety of issues, ranging from economic policy to America's role in the world. They were also divided over competing visions of the nation. In this regard, forty years of cultural politics had helped to create a deeply polarized society. On one side were cultural conservatives, who had been the bedrock of Republican electoral victories since 1968. They tended to be overtly patriotic, concerned with "traditional values," and supportive of a strong and assertive military. They also advocated a central role for Christianity in American public life. Bush's religious nationalism—a legacy of his three Republican predecessors—reinforced these ideas and empowered this community. It also provided a distinctly priestly affirmation for the American system (at least under Republican rule). Like the radical right of the 1950s, the Bush campaign, and later his administration, readily conflated conservative Christianity with patriotism and support for free market capitalism. If America was in a state of decline, this was not due to the economic policies of the previous thirty years but rather to the deviance of certain segments of the American population and a liberal permissiveness that tolerated immorality. Like Nixon and Reagan before him, then, George W. Bush called the country back to its evangelical roots in an effort to redeem American politics and society.

On the other side of the ideological spectrum were the more socially liberal elements of American society. They, too, were troubled by contemporary trends and by the coarsening of American public life. However, they were less concerned about sexual ethics than with government policies that worked against social justice and the interests of the poor. They were particularly disturbed by widening disparities in income, the lack of affordable health care, and the intolerance of the Christian Right. American liberals were also skeptical of an unregulated market's ability to provide public goods. They saw in contemporary capitalism the source of many of the social ills that conservatives decried. The crisis of American society, according to this view, was rooted in socioeconomic disparity, not an absence of religious belief. This group also viewed with skepticism efforts to embed conservative Christian doctrine in public institutions. George Bush's "faith-based" initiative was seen less as a vehicle for serving the poor than for spreading Evangelical religion. The concerns of the religious left—as well as of its secular counterparts—focused on the discrepancy between the overt declarations of Christian values that characterized the Bush campaign and the promotion of policies that catered to the rich and powerful at the expense of the poor.

Having won the 2000 election despite losing the popular vote, President Bush found little consensus, and no mandate, in this deeply divided political environment. His early policy initiatives stalled, and the effort to push a conservative agenda through Congress did not get far. Bush's program included the aforementioned faith-based initiative that directed federal dollars to America's churches and tax cuts that disproportionately benefited the wealthiest Americans. Concerned about the direction of the new administration, James Jeffords, a centrist Vermont senator of the president's own party declared his independence and shifted control of the Senate to the Democrats. Such early opposition, however, faded with the terrorist attacks of September 11, 2001. The horror and shock of this national tragedy helped to unify the country behind President Bush's leadership. It was clearly a defining moment for the new president, as well as a unique opportunity to broaden his support at home and abroad.[62] The administration used this moment, however, to strengthen its authority, setting in motion an open-ended "war on terror."[63]

The Bush administration's response to the 9/11 terrorist attacks reflected the cultural milieu in which Bush had come to power. The attacks and the subsequent response were described in a religious vernacular that drew heavily from the Christian narrative of American history. It also reflected the cultural conservatives' vision of the nation. In a carefully scripted memorial service held at the National Cathedral in Washington, President Bush spoke of a sacred cause to which a new generation of Americans was called. It was the country's "responsibility to history," he argued, "to answer these attacks and rid the world of evil."[64] The message was a clear example of American religious nationalism, one that conflated an amorphous notion of freedom with Christianity and the American way of life. By issuing his call to arms from a church pulpit, moreover, Bush used this potent mix of religion, nationalism, and militarism to justify a set of initiatives that would mark a significant shift in American foreign policy. It also helped to confer legitimacy on what had been until then a contested presidency.

Explicit in Bush's statement, and in others to follow, was the idea that America was under assault for its values, not its policies. President Bush argued that terrorism was defined by its hostility to freedom and the very idea an open society. Moreover, those that had launched the September 11 attacks were depicted as antimodern Islamic zealots. What was at stake was nothing less than a "war to save civilization itself."[65] Like the Cold War and the struggle against fascism in the mid-twentieth century, this new conflict was defined in ideological and religious terms. At issue was a competition between two different visions of social order. The West, by definition, was said to stand for the idea of an open society informed by Enlightenment norms, individual freedom, and tolerance of diversity. The Islamist alternative, on the other hand, was said to embody the exclusive vision of ethnic and religious communalism typical of a closed society. Although the administration eschewed the idea of a clash of civilizations, this depiction of the conflict clearly fit Huntington's religious framework.

This administration's characterization of the war on terror—what would later be referred to as the struggle against Islamofascism—reinforced the religious and inter-communal nature of the conflict.[66] America, it was argued, was fighting for human freedom, and in the struggle for liberty, it was argued, "God is not neutral."[67] The Christian overtones of this could be seen in President Bush's statement that freedom is not an American contribution to the world but "the Almighty's gift to every man and woman." This blending of Christian idealism, democracy, and freedom reflected the moral absolutism of the Christian anticommunist movement and informed the rationale for the invasions of Afghanistan and Iraq. It was also rooted in an assumption that the Bush administration was "carrying out God's own wishes."[68] As one neoconservative commentator noted at the time, 9/11 "transfigured" the Bush presidency. Out of the fire and ash of the World Trade Center towers, a "kind of revelation, blazing with a very different fire of its own, lit up the recesses of Bush's mind and heart and soul. . . . George W. Bush now knew that the God to whom, as a born-again Christian, he had earlier committed himself had put him in the Oval Office for a purpose. He had put him there to lead a war against the evil of terrorism."[69]

This characterization of events, however, was quite misleading. On the one hand, it did not take into account bin Laden's own explanation for his actions and the 1998 *fatwa* that provided the basis for his war on America. According to this statement, bin Laden and al-Qaeda were motivated by American policies in the Middle East, not American values.[70] These policies include such issues as American support for authoritarian governments in the region, the presence of the U.S. military in Arab countries (particularly Saudi Arabia), and an unqualified support for Israel and its occupation of Palestinian territories. These were the policies that fueled anti-American sentiment in the region and that bin Laden used to justify his actions to the Arab and Islamic world. The characterization of Islamist militancy offered by the Bush administration also did not account for the historical context of the international jihadist network. There was little discussion during the debates of 2001 and 2002 of the origins of al-Qaeda, its emergence from the Afghan war of the 1980s, or the longstanding ties between Islamist militant groups (including al-Qaeda) and the intelligence services of Saudi Arabia and Pakistan, two of America's key allies in the Middle East and South Asia. On the contrary, those who raised any of these issues—and who saw 9/11 as the unintended consequences, or blowback, of American policies from the Reagan era—were attacked as unpatriotic and blind to the "moral clarity" of 9/11.

The moral absolutism of the war on terror—and the notion that U.S. policy reflected Divine Will—may have been a useful means of marketing administration policy, but it ultimately proved counterproductive.[71] Bush's description of the attacks and his characterization of Islamists as "evildoers" seemed to ensure that a military solution was the only "realistic and reasonable response."[72] This troubled many religious leaders, who argued that additional violence would not bring an end to terrorism but rather perpetuate "fear, desperation, hopelessness and instability."[73] Moreover, Bush's choice of language and his extension of the conflict to an "Axis of Evil" (Iraq, Iran, and North Korea) reinforced a messianic vision of America's role in the world. This was not the civil religion of Bellah's formulation but rather a conflation of faith and nation that allowed for a policy free of constraint. When Bush spoke of ridding the world of evil, one commentator noted, "he's moving into crusade mentality, a holy war mentality."[74]

The Bush administration's approach to the war on terror also reinforced a view that America was promoting a clash of civilizations. Despite early efforts to differentiate between extremist and moderate Islam, the image of a clash between good and evil—and between Christianity and Islam—remained. This was a dominant perspective throughout the Middle East and South Asia. The war in Iraq, for example, was seen in the region as entirely dissociated from the September 11 attacks, driven more by oil and power than Enlightenment values. The indefinite detention of enemy combatants at Guantánamo Bay, Cuba, and the abuses at the Abu Ghraib prison in Iraq reinforced a view that America was operating outside international norms. As such, it fit easily into a narrative offered by Islamists who argued that the war on terror was really a war on the Islamic people. Similarly, some commentators in the United States reinforced this vision of the conflict. Jerry Falwell, for example, provided a biblical justification for the invasion of Iraq, arguing that the war was meant "to defend innocent people. . . . If we do not stop the spread of evil, many innocent lives will be lost and the kingdom of God suffers."[75] Evangelical ministers throughout the country made similar comments from the pulpit in the runup to the invasion.[76] The most controversial comments, however, came from Lieutenant General William Boykin, who argued in a series of speeches that the war against Islamic militancy (and, hence, the endeavor in Iraq) represented a "spiritual battle" against the forces of evil. That Boykin made his speeches in Pentacostal and Baptist churches—and in uniform—reinforced a vision of militant religious nationalism reminiscent of the anticommunist seminars of the 1950s. The substance was also similar. Boykin's message was that this was a religious war and that, as a Christian nation where "God reigns supreme," victory depends on the nation's coming together "in the name of Jesus."[77]

The irony is that, despite the rhetoric, the means used to carry out the war were antithetical to the Enlightenment norms of an open society. The Bush administration's policies did little to promote freedom; on the contrary, they were designed to strengthen foreign security services and regional dictators in order to fight Islamist militancy. The administration also expanded government power within the United States at the expense of the individual, particularly in regard to the treatment of noncitizens. These efforts entailed a high degree of government secrecy and a willingness to operate outside the bounds of either U.S. or international law. Policies such as rendition, coercive interrogation, and the operation of secret prisons were all justified by the claim that moral restraints did not apply to the pursuit of national security in a time of war.[78] The notion of freedom that was extolled by the administration, in short, amounted to little more than the collective self-assertion of American power, not a defense of individual liberty or respect for human rights. Although rhetorically infused with the ideals of human freedom and Christian mission, the nationalist discourse of the Bush administration appealed to the same kind of communalism typical of a closed society. By conflating Christian purpose with American interests, the administration was using religion "to provide moral justification for what is, in effect, a strategy of empire."[79]

The presidential election of 2004 was overshadowed by these issues and, more specifically, by the war in Iraq. The Democratic contender, John Kerry, argued that Iraq had diverted attention from al-Qaeda and that the continuing war there was undermining America's position in the region and the world. The Bush campaign responded by conflating Iraq and 9/11. It reiterated its claim that the invasion of Iraq was central to the broader war on terror and to the continuing struggle for human freedom. Those who disagreed were alternately denigrated as unpatriotic or weak-willed appeasers. Fear, terrorism, and national security were the dominant themes in the Bush campaign, a trend that marked a striking similarity to the Indian elections of the 1980s and early 1990s. So, too, was the claim that only the Republican Party could keep the nation safe.[80] Photographic images of the destroyed World Trade Center, New York firefighters, and other symbols of 9/11 were used in the Bush campaign's media strategy to inculcate fear, patriotism, and an unreflective support for government policy. So too was the charge that terrorist attacks would be more likely under a Kerry administration because he was weak on defense, since "weakness attracts those who are waiting to do America harm."[81]

A central feature of the campaign was the effort to link the president's personal faith with the destiny of the nation. This included a conscious effort to inculcate a belief among conservative Christians that Bush was God's choice for the White House.[82] The message, in effect, was that God was on our side in the fight against terrorism and, by implication, on the Republican side in the presidential campaign. The extensive use of churches as a mechanism of political mobilization—as well as the use of internet prayer ministries such as the "Presidential Prayer Team" and "Pray the Vote"—were significant in promoting this view and in bolstering Evangelical turnout.[83] So, too, was the kind of conservative populism that had defined earlier Republican campaigns. Bush, for example, invoked many of the same themes and ideas associated with Quayle's 1992 critique of the "liberal elite" in order to attack Kerry as culturally inauthentic. Kerry's service in Vietnam was similarly disparaged by groups linked to the Bush campaign, and even Kerry's faith came under attack. The Republican National Committee, for example, mailed voters in Arkansas and West Virginia a notice that accused Democrats (and Kerry) of preparing to ban the Bible.[84] Conservative Catholic Bishops also threatened to withhold communion from elected leaders who were not sufficiently anti-abortion, a controversy that directly affected Kerry and other Catholics in the Democratic Party leadership. The Republican Party was also successful in placing local ballot initiatives on gay marriage in eleven states—including swing states such as Ohio. These initiatives were a key factor in turning out a large conservative Christian vote and perpetuating a perception that the electorate was divided between "believers" and "unbelievers."[85]

The Bush campaign of 2004 can be seen, then, as the latest iteration—and the culmination—of the Nixon strategy of positive polarization.[86] By depicting its Democratic opposition as hostile to religion, Republican strategists were able to build a conservative majority based on an exclusive vision of religion and national identity. Although the specific issues varied to a limited extent, they always involved the core concerns of religion, patriotism, and free market capitalism. Party operatives also perpetuated a nationalist ideology that stigmatized dissent as un-American and readily conflated religion with national security and the state. The danger of this trend, as Niebuhr had warned many years earlier, was its tendency to blur "genuine faith with national[ist] ideology."[87] This type of religious politics, moreover, differs from the more ecumenical understanding of civil religion by fostering divisions instead of commonality. By consciously linking conservative religion with administration policies, the Bush campaign continued to polarize American society and fan the flames of sectarian division for its own political gain.

This strategy succeeded once again in 2004, but the politicization of religion was wearing thin. The deep, and largely artificial, divisions that this generated were an obstacle to effective governance and ultimately undermined the goal of creating a permanent Republican majority. So, too, did the empowerment of conservative religious activists and their exclusive vision of American society. The influence of cultural conservatives on such issues as stem cell research and medical ethics—culminating in the federal government's intervention in the question of whether to terminate Terri Schiavo's life support—was a particular liability. This debate alienated libertarians and economic conservatives alike. It also contributed to a perception that the Republican Party was controlled by ideological extremists who were out of step with the American mainstream. The xenophobia associated with an exclusive vision of American nationalism was also manifest in the debate over immigration reform. In this context, national security and fear of minorities fueled an anti-Mexican backlash in 2005 and 2006. The stigmatization of Hispanics, however, estranged a key demographic that might otherwise have been attracted to the Republican Party. It also contributed to the homogenization of the party, as members of a various minority populations—Arab, Mexican, African-American—were alienated by the rhetoric and policies of the Bush administration and its nativist supporters.

There was also a growing sense among many cultural conservatives after 2004 that they were being used for political ends. This was evident in a book published by a former deputy director of the Bush administration's Office of Faith-Based and Community Initiatives, David Kuo. The book argued that the administration never took the work of the office seriously and that its specific projects were driven by political considerations. Moreover, Kuo noted that political operatives like Karl Rove denigrated Christian Conservatives leaders in private—referring to them as "the nuts"—while relying on their political support to keep Republicans in office. Kuo felt that there was a steep price to be paid, spiritually, for the kind of politicization of religion in which the White House was engaging. As Kuo notes in his book, "By so passionately pursuing politics, Christians have alienated everyone [who differs with them politically]. . . . [Consequently,] the name 'Jesus' doesn't bring to mind the things he said he wanted associated with his followers—love for one another; love for the poor, sick and imprisoned; self-denial; and devotion to God. It is associated with anti-abortion activities, opposition to gay rights, the Republican Party, and tax cuts."[88]

These criticisms were echoed by other Christian leaders, who were aware of the instrumental manipulation of religion by party leaders. For example, Randy Brinson, a Christian activist and founder of Redeem the Vote, noted in a 2006 interview that "the power structure in the Republican Party is too entrenched with big business. It's not with Evangelicals—they're a means to an end."[89] Other Christian activists echoed this complaint, noting that Republican Party leaders talk a good game, but "when it comes down to it, what they are mostly interested in are defense issues and business issues."[90] Richard Czick, former president of the National Association of Evangelicals (NAE), reinforced the point, noting that whenever religious and business interests collide, it is the business community that wins "every time."[91] The disconnect between the pursuit of power and the values that such power was meant to extol was heightened by the various scandals that plagued the Republican Party throughout the Bush era. These included the fundraising scandals associated with Republican lobbyist Jack Abramoff, who was a key associate of House Republican leaders and helped funnel money from Washington lobbyists into Republican campaign coffers. It also included the sex scandal involving Congressman Mark Foley and a number of male pages. The Abramoff scandal was particularly hurtful because he used Christian groups (and former Christian Coalition director Ralph Reed) to further the interests of gambling casinos that Abramoff represented. The disaffection among the different factions of American conservatism and disgruntlement with Republican record in office led to the Democratic gains in the 2006 congressional elections. It also shaped the 2008 presidential elections.

## Barack Obama and the Return of Civil Religion

The 2008 election marked the end of the Republican revival. The goal of creating an enduring conservative majority was dealt a major setback in the 2006 midterm elections—where both House and Senate went Democrat—and collapsed in 2008. This turn of events was due in no small part to the Republican Party's record in office. The failures of the Bush administration in Iraq, its inability to reign in government spending, and the ineffectual response to Hurricane Katrina in 2005 all helped to discredit the administration and its congressional allies. There was also a demonstrable gulf between Republican rhetoric and its members' actions. Not only had those in positions of authority failed to abide by their core commitments to fiscal responsibility and moral rectitude, they also appeared to be either incompetent or untrustworthy. The resurrection of the religious left also played a role in ending Republican dominance. This was evident in Barack Obama's presidential bid, which successfully challenged the Republican Party's claim on religious and cultural authenticity. Obama's candidacy was defined by a religious idealism that informed his centrist, and liberal, politics. His approach to religion also helped to unify disparate elements of American society, reflecting a more traditional conception of American civil religion.

The 2008 presidential campaign was once again informed by the longstanding debates in America over both religion and society. This was evident in a public forum hosted in August of that year. The two candidates, Senator John McCain and Senator Barack Obama, met in an Evangelical church in California to discuss their views on religion. They were hosted and interviewed by the Reverend Rick Warren, pastor of Saddleback Church (where the event was held) and author of *The Purpose-Driven Life*. In his opening remarks to the Saddleback Forum, Warren spoke of the need of the American people to understand the religious "world view" of the candidates in order to understand their politics. The significance of the debate was twofold. First, it highlighted the centrality of religion, and particularly theologically conservative religion, for American politics. In this regard, the forum demonstrated how influential—and mainstream— Evangelical Christianity had become in the previous three decades. Both candidates subsequently sought to convey an image of themselves as religious and, hence, culturally authentic leaders by affirming the centrality of Jesus Christ in their life and work. The second key feature of the forum was the dichotomous understanding of Christian tradition that the two candidates embodied. Even though both affirmed their commitment to an Evangelical interpretation of Christianity, Obama interpreted the tradition in a manner consistent with the Social Gospel teachings of American religion, while McCain saw in Christianity a basis for his conservative politics.

Ironically, it was the McCain campaign that struggled with the religious issue. Like George H. W. Bush, John McCain was not a conservative Christian, and he had even alienated this wing of the party in his 2000 bid for the presidency. During a campaign speech in February 2000, McCain chastised televangelists Pat Robertson and Jerry Falwell as agents of intolerance and argued that "intolerance by any political party is neither a Judeo-Christian nor an American value."[92] He went on to note that faith, properly understood, "unites and never divides." These statements created a deep reservoir of distrust and animosity between McCain and the stalwarts of the Christian Right. This was reflected in comments by the Reverend James Dobson, founder of Focus on the Family, who in 2008 said, "I would not vote for John McCain under any circumstances."[93] McCain subsequently sought to reach out to other conservative Christians, including Pastor John Hagee, a televangelist from San Antonio, Texas, in an effort to repair relations with the religious right—a choice that ultimately proved counterproductive, due to Hagee's anti-Catholic beliefs. It is also why McCain's performance at the Saddleback forum was especially important for his candidacy.

McCain's choice of Sarah Palin as the vice-presidential candidate reflected another effort to court the cultural conservatives of the Republican Party. Palin was a wildly popular choice among the party base and helped to rally conservative Christians behind McCain's bid. She was a member of a Pentacostal church in Alaska, and her position on abortion, gun rights, and other key social issues were in tune with the religious right. She supported teaching creationism in schools, opposed gay marriage, and was consequently seen as a fellow traveler among Evangelicals. As Richard Land, president of the Southern Baptist Ethics and Religious Liberty Commission, noted in an August 2008 interview: "She's one of us."[94] Palin's selection also helped to resurrect the culture wars, which had been in eclipse during the primary season. As such, the McCain campaign consciously chose a strategy of right-wing populist mobilization in the general campaign.

A central feature of the McCain-Palin alternative was a particular vision of American nationalism and the country's role in the world. Their understanding of the war on terror as defined by moral absolutes—and as a conflict against an irredeemable and evil Islamic extremism—was indistinct from that of the Bush administration. As McCain noted in the Saddleback forum, "We're facing the transcendent challenge of the twenty-first century, radical Islamic extremists. . . . We're going to defeat this evil and the central battleground is Baghdad, Mozul and Iraq." Palin reiterated this theme in the vice-presidential debates when she noted that "these [people] hate America and hate what we stand for, with our freedoms, our democracy, our tolerance, our respect for women's rights." These comments reflected a very superficial understanding of the Islamist challenge yet were invoked to provide the kind of priestly affirmation of the American system that informed previous Republican administrations and campaigns. It was an approach that readily conflated religion, state, and Republican policies while at the same time questioning the Democrats' patriotism, faith, and commitment to national security.

The central problem with this strategy in 2008 was that the conservative ideology associated with the Bush administration had been largely discredited, especially among centrist Republicans. The Iraq War, in particular, was enormously unpopular, and the ability to spark fear in the electorate by invoking the specter of terrorism on American soil no longer seemed credible outside of the conservative base. Moreover, the idea of a culture war simply did not resonate in the way it had in earlier years. After eight years of Republicans in the White House—and fourteen years running both houses of Congress—these campaign themes simply did not seem to correlate with reality. Moreover, the economic crisis that emerged in the summer of 2008 had a profound impact on the general campaign. The economic problems sweeping the country greatly diminished the salience of cultural issues for working families who were fearful of losing jobs and homes. As the economic downturn turned into a full-scale financial crisis, the hot-button issues of earlier years—abortion, gay marriage, gun rights—simply paled in comparison to the question of which candidate could more effectively handle the economic crisis at hand. Economic considerations, not culture, became a primary basis of voting for many Americans.

The Obama campaign also had a sophisticated understanding of religion and readily invoked its own religious themes. This was evident at the Democratic National Convention, in the emphasis on Joe Biden's Catholic roots in working-class Pennsylvania, and in the discourse of the presidential candidate. Like Clinton before him, Obama spoke with an easy familiarity of biblical teachings and a sincere conviction that resonated with voters. In doing so, he was able to minimize the salience of divisive social issues and offer an alternative reading of the Judeo-Christian tradition that emphasized social justice, tolerance, and ecumenism. Obama was also able to shed the idea of the Democratic Party as uneasy with religion and of being invariably tied to an exclusive vision of secularism. In a 2006 speech, for example, Obama noted that it is a mistake to disregard the influence of faith in individuals' lives. More the point, society should not "ask believers to leave their religion at the door before entering into the public square." Rather, Obama argued that it was necessary to find a compromise that can reconcile faith with the realities of a religiously diverse political community. To this end, "a sense of proportion should also guide those who police the boundaries between church and state."[95]

Obama's message in 2006 found expression in the 2008 campaign. Its power was rooted in its pragmatism and in Obama's ability to expand the relevance of religion to issues such as poverty, stewardship of the planet, and foreign policy. In terms of domestic politics, Obama recognized both the power of faith and the challenges of religious pluralism to American political life. In many respects, Obama was returning to the central challenge of this country: how to accommodate a deeply religious population that finds little agreement on either theology or politics. In this regard, Obama's ideas on religious tolerance reflected the kind of ecumenism inherent in the understanding of secularism as nondiscrimination. Whether influenced by the ideas of the Founders or not, his vision of religion and society mirrored the religious compromise that was at the heart of the American Constitution. Obama's religious message, then, was imbued with ideas of equal treatment and nondiscrimination in matters of faith. It was at once reverential and tolerant. It was also distinctly modernist, reflecting the liberal consensus of the years after World War II. His ideas on religion and politics were closer to those of Reinhold Neibuhr than those of Jerry Falwell. They were also very much in keeping with America's tradition of civil religion and entailed a rejection of the kind of exclusive religious nationalism that had defined the Reagan-Bush era. It was this alternative that proved more persuasive on Election Day.

## Conclusion

The 2008 elections demonstrate the limitations of an exclusive religious politics. Although the effort to use religion and culture to mobilize populist sentiment—and to distract the electorate from economic considerations—was effective for a number of decades, the contradictions inherent in the strategy ultimately bred its own demise. Nixon's Southern Strategy was enormously successful in fostering a political realignment in the country—especially by winning over Democratic voters in the South—but at the cost of the liberal wing of the Republican Party. This realignment proved to be a liability for both George H. W. Bush and John McCain in their respective bids for the presidency. Neither candidate was seen as authentic among the conservative base, and their efforts to invoke culture war issues came off as disingenuous. The transformation of the party, moreover, precluded the creation of a permanent Republican majority. As movement conservatives became more influential, they created an environment within the party that was ideologically rigid, intolerant, and hostile to the concerns of centrists. The xenophobia associated with the war on terror and the debate over immigration policy also alienated key segments of American society. The divisive nature of the party's religious politics, in short, precluded the kind of ideological inclusiveness necessary for a ruling coalition.

The ideological rigidity of the Bush administration's economic and foreign policies also contributed to the party's demise. Its embrace of an unregulated free market created an enormous amount of social dislocation and, ultimately, the financial crisis that overshadowed the 2008 campaign. Moreover, the Bush administration's ill-conceived invasion of Iraq destroyed its image of responsible leadership. The ideological fusion of God, flag, and country may have been useful in marketing the administration's policies, but it set the stage for the kind of imperial overreach that is the hallmark of great powers in decline. The tendency to see religion as a justification, not as a moral benchmark, was central to this failure. Blinded by a misguided sense of mission, the Bush administration pursued policies that abrogated the principles for which it ostensibly was fighting. Instead of promoting individual freedom and democratic norms, the religious nationalism of the Bush era was used to sanction a bid for imperial dominance and a set of policies that were morally dubious at best. By seeing the nation as an end in itself—and informed by religious purpose—the Bush administration engaged a foreign policy that was both "unchecked and unbalanced."[96]

The politicization of conservative religion also had an impact on Christianity in this country. By linking state authority with Evangelical Christianity, state actors such as Ronald Reagan, George W. Bush, and Richard Nixon redefined notions of cultural authenticity, fostering a perception that Evangelical denominations offered a more genuine rendering of Christian tradition than their liberal counterparts. In this way, state actors empowered conservative Christian activists and validated their exclusive vision of religion and society. Again, this is not to argue that the religious politics and culture wars of recent years were simply the result of elite manipulation. Rather, the central claim here is that the resurgence of the Christian Right was not simply the spontaneous reaction of a religious population to the modernizing tendencies of a secular elite. On the contrary, the active manipulation of ideas and activists by Republican Party operatives was a central feature of the rise of religious fundamentalism. The dominance of Evangelical Christianity in American public life, in short, cannot be separated from the efforts of state actors to use theologically conservative interpretations of religion to sanction a conservative political agenda.

As in India, however, the excesses associated with the manipulation of illiberal religion prompted a course correction and the resurrection of a more centrist politics. The Obama presidency thus embodies a return to the type of civil religion more common in the mid-twentieth century, one that gives social justice and concern for the poor greater priority than divisive cultural issues. This alternative understands the Judeo-Christian tradition as informing America's values, not providing a license for unrestrained action. To this end, the emphasis is on the latter half of John Winthrop's famous statement regarding the providential covenant of American nationalism—abiding by Judeo-Christian principles—not upon the claim of chosen status or providential mission. As such, the 2008 presidential election once again illustrated the ongoing competition between inclusive and exclusive visions of both religion and society. Moreover, much like 1992, the 2008 election reasserted the priority of economic considerations over cultural issues as a basis of voting. This helped diminish the salience of divisive wedge issues and allowed the Obama campaign to offer both a religious and an economic alternative. The outcome of this last presidential election, however, does not mean that the messianic strain of American religious nationalism is relegated the past. That would be a misreading of American history. Rather, the 2008 election demonstrated that questions about the proper role of religion in American public life—and how to define the nation—remain unresolved, as perhaps they always will be.

# Religious Politics Reconsidered

The global resurgence of religion and its influence on modern politics remain topics of keen interest. Much of the contemporary research, however, continues to view this trend in largely dichotomous terms: either as a religious phenomenon or as simply a matter of politics. The first of these two perspectives sees the revivalism of recent years as an organic expression of humanity that has emerged autonomously within traditional populations to reshape the political life of countries around the globe.[1] Religion, from this perspective, is a causal variable emanating from below and driving world events. The materialist alternative, on the other hand, sees religion as a vernacular for articulating political purpose and not as a causal force in its own right. The real issue from this second view is politics, not religion. There is, of course, a good deal of truth to both views. Religion is an innate feature of the human condition and has an autonomy that is not readily controlled. Conversely, the contemporary revival is driven by material considerations and the socioeconomic deprivation that breeds extremism and discontent. There is, however, a third factor as well. The continuing relevance of religion to modern politics is also due to the fact that many find utility in promoting religion within the public sphere. This is true whether religion is used to mobilize popular sentiment behind an existing pattern of social order or if religion is invoked to transform it. It is also true whether religion is used to sanction the policies of the modern nation-state or to restrain government action. The real question, then, is which interpretation of religion is being promoted, and to what end?

If religion is reshaping modern politics, the converse is also true: its politicization has changed religion. The effort by political actors—and particularly state elites—to promote one interpretation of religion at the expense of others has greatly influenced the internal debates over religious interpretation. It has also contributed to the proliferation of religious ideologies. This is evident in each of the cases of this book, in which exclusive variants of religious tradition were conflated with nationalist or communal ideologies and mobilized for explicitly political ends. By invoking not just religion but an illiberal variant of their respective traditions, mainstream political actors greatly influenced popular perceptions about which understanding of religious tradition—literal or modernist, inclusive or exclusive—was the more legitimate and the more culturally authentic. The ramifications of this instrumental manipulation of religion, moreover, have been far-reaching. The politicization of religion has divided societies along religious and ethnic lines and denigrated the idea of religious tolerance (both within and between traditions). It has also led to a common perception that illiberal renderings of religion are somehow more valid or true than their liberal counterparts. This marks a sharp break with the mid-twentieth century, when modernist or liberal understandings of religion were predominant and state actors tended to eschew the exclusive religious ideologies associated with modern religious fundamentalisms.

The changing orientation of state elites away from secularism and toward religion helps to explain these trends and why exclusive interpretations of religion emerged so forcefully in the political life of three ostensibly secular societies. Despite the common assumptions that the contemporary resurgence of religious politics represents a popular rejection of state-led secularization or that it is the result of a failed modernity project, the cases of this study indicate a more nuanced explanation. Rather, the ideological transformation of this period involved the active promotion of religion by state actors as a means of mobilizing popular support behind their respective claims to rule. This is surprising in part because it was state actors who were at one time the primary opponents of the kind of exclusive religious ideas associated with fundamentalist movements. This orientation toward religion changed, however, as state elites abandoned commitments to an inclusive vision of social order, choosing instead to "ride the tiger" of an exclusive religious politics.[2] This shift was very much a part of an antileftist discourse and, in many parts of the world, part of the Cold War dynamic. Conservative religion was promoted in the United States, the Middle East, and South Asia in large measure because it was seen as a bulwark against the influence of socialism and leftist ideologies.

It is certainly not that illiberal interpretations of religion are a new phenomenon, nor are the debates over the proper relationship between religion and political authority. On the contrary, these debates have persisted for some time. Moreover, the organizations and ideologies associated with religious fundamentalisms were active for much of the twentieth century and have long been involved in struggles to define the nation. What changed in recent years was the context. By coopting fundamentalist groups instead of opposing them, ostensibly secular state elites helped to normalize what had, in many instances, been perceived as "the idiot fringe of defeated conservatism."[3] Mainstream political actors subsequently brought exclusive visions of religious nationalism back into the ideological mainstream, making them more palatable to societies that were perceived at the time as increasingly secular. In this way, state actors helped to confer—whether intentionally or not—a degree of legitimacy on conservative religious activists. The changing orientation of state actors helps to explain how in each of the cases under consideration illiberal religion found a home among the modern institutions of nation and state.

## Religious Politics Reconsidered

The turn toward exclusive interpretations of religion by ostensibly secular state elites raises two important and related questions: why was the commitment to secular norms so readily displaced, and why was the attraction of exclusive (as opposed to inclusive) versions of religion so strong? As to the first issue, loyalty to liberal ideas—and the relegation of religion to the private sphere—proved less compelling in each of the cases during the 1970s and 1980s than the compulsion of religious sectarianism. Some would argue that this reflects the limits of loyalty to a public sphere shorn of religious imagery or the continuing appeal of certitude in a world defined by socioeconomic change.[4] These are important and valid points. However, there is more to the answer than just these two issues. Here, the cases are instructive. In each instance, religion was (and is) central to the construction of collective, and particularly national, identities. Hence, religion was invoked to activate or appeal to the ethnic or religious loyalties of key constituencies. Moreover, religion is important because it provides the moral framework in which modern politics functions. Religion provides a sense of belonging to a larger community and attachment to the institutions that govern society. More to the point, it provides a language for political action and lends a timeless quality to institutions that are, in truth, modern social constructs. Hence, arguments over the legitimacy of modern states—as well as the critique of such states—are frequently articulated in a religious vernacular.

This leads to the second issue. It was not just religion that was being promoted but exclusive interpretations of religion. Why was this? There are two answers indicated by the cases. One is that the inherent communalism inherent in the very idea of the nation state—the tendency toward a homogenizing ideology of unity—more readily conforms to exclusive visions of religion than do their liberal counterparts. In other words, the communalism inherent in exclusive interpretations of religion fit more readily with the ideological requirements of the modern state than does the ambiguity of liberal religion. Very much related to this are the certitude offered by illiberal religion and the utility that such an unquestioning faith can provide for modern political actors. Second, the role of state elites in promoting one vision of religion and society as opposed to the other is crucial. If the first point deals with the inherent tendencies—and tensions—within both religion and society, the second point involves human agency and choice. As the cases illustrate, the embrace of communalism was not preordained or determined by the nature of the state. On the contrary, there was ongoing tension between liberal and illiberal visions of the nation, and this was a defining feature of the politics of all three societies. Moreover, the active role of state elites in the debates over how to define the nation proved critical to the success of liberal renditions of religious politics in the mid-twentieth century and of illiberal interpretations in the latter part of the twentieth century. This helps to explain, then, the transition from a benign expression of civil religion to a more assertive religious nationalism. Although both visions of society are latent in the idea of the nation-state, the actions of state leaders had an important bearing on which of the two would emerge as dominant at any given point in time.

As the cases indicate, one cannot assume that an exclusive vision of religion and society is somehow more natural, more authentic, or ultimately more effective. Nor do the cases argue that the resurgence of religious politics is *simply* a matter of elite manipulation. On the contrary, what this volume illustrates is the interactive and the variable nature of the entire process. Religion is a potent force, and it has been alternately used for both good and ill by political actors. Moreover, religion can provide an inclusive basis to social life or justify an exclusive (and often violent) chauvinism. Implicit in this variability are assumptions about human nature and the continuing tension between humankind's better impulses and its more aggressive ones. The instrumental manipulation of illiberal visions of religion by political leaders, then, reflects a willingness to pander to the baser instincts of the majority community. Instead of appealing to a more virtuous reading of religion—one that unifies diverse communities instead of dividing them—the appeal to an illiberal version of religious tradition had the clear intention of polarizing the population along communal lines. The intent was also to promote the interests of one community (or one section of a community) at the expense of others.

Interestingly, in the two cases where there is democratic accountability— India and the United States—the appeal to communal chauvinism had clear limits. Although there was obviously a visceral resonance in both cases to the rhetoric of religious nationalism, the excess to which this phenomenon led— division, rancor, persecution, war—generated its own backlash. The result was a return to moderation and a widespread revulsion of extremist politics. This was evident in the outcome of the Indian elections in 2004 and 2009 and the corresponding repudiation of the BJP's record in office, and it was evident in the Republican Party's electoral defeats in 2006 and 2008 in the United States. In both instances, there was a return to a more centrist politics and a distancing of many political actors from the inflammatory rhetoric of earlier years, even if only temporarily. Strategists such as Karl Rove saw in right-wing populism the makings of a permanent majority, but the strategy ultimately precluded such an outcome. An exclusive religious politics may have been an effective means of gaining power, but it did not provide a viable basis for governing. On the contrary, the division and polarization on which this strategy was based had an enormously deleterious effect on public discourse and hamstrung government. More to the point, in both cases the party's cultural politics alienated the centrist voters that were essential to its continued rule. In both India and the United States, then, the perception that these political parties were dominated by extremists greatly undermined their ability to forge an enduring coalition and adversely affected their fortunes at the polls. This last point provides a reason for hope with regard to the inherent appeal and practicality of tolerance. Even if the discourse in both countries continues to be informed by a religious vernacular, it increasingly eschews the hatefulness of religious intolerance and bigotry, since it simply does not play well with the moderate center.[5]

Two other theoretical implications of this book are worth mentioning. First, contemporary religious politics do not reflect a struggle between the forces of progress and modernity, nor does religious revivalism represent an antimodern traditionalism. Although this typology has superficial appeal, it is ultimately misleading. To begin with, neither the state nor modernity has ever been entirely secular. As each of the cases illustrate, states and state actors have always invoked some form of religious narrative in the context of a nationalist or communal discourse. Although at times this was inclusive—and consistent with a secular vision of nondiscrimination—at other times it was highly exclusive and coupled with a messianic vision of national purpose. Similarly, modernity has never been defined exclusively by Enlightenment norms of reason, tolerance, and inclusion. On the contrary, there are multiple paths to modernity, and they are just as likely to be sectarian and exclusive in orientation as cosmopolitan and inclusive. This again, is because the traditional beliefs that underpin modern politics are themselves defined by ambiguity. Consequently, differences over religion are reflected in competing visions of social life and competing visions of modernity. The conservative religious ideologies that emerged so forcefully in recent years, then, do not represent a return to some timeless notion of tradition but rather are a modern example of the time-honored practice of linking religion to political authority.

Second, the book validates the claim that religions (or particular religions) are in no way monolithic or defined by an unchanging set of values. On the contrary, as the cases illustrate, each religious tradition is characterized by a variety of competing interpretations—progressive and conservative, liberal and illiberal—and these divisions offer competing notions of both religious authority and the construction of modernity. What is at issue in each case, then, is a twofold struggle. The first involves a reinterpretation of a given religious tradition for the modern era—one rooted in revelation or in reason—while the second involves the application of these ideas to a political setting. Should particular religious ideas and identities define the institutions of nation and state, or can a politics of primordial compromise be found? How, in short, ought modernity—and the nation—be constructed? The debates over secular as opposed to religious conceptions of moral order are the means by which these questions are resolved, as they pit competing visions of both religious tradition and modernity against one another. What transpires in each case, then, is that state and opposition compete for political power, with each side seeking to leverage a particular interpretation of their shared tradition for political "gain within their own internecine conflict."[6] Neither state nor opposition, however, are wedded to particular interpretations of religion; rather, this varies over time and reflect differing goals.

## Comparing the Cases

There are several patterns common to each case that warrant elaboration. The first of these is the historical tension between religious politics and secular conceptions of moral order. In each case, the acceptance of a secular vision of social order was based in large measure on a desire to provide the kind of primordial compromise that Geertz argued was essential for constructing an inclusive basis of political life in religiously plural societies. This was evident in the founding consensus of both India and the United States as well as in Nasser's Arab Nationalism. It is also evident in the origins of religious tolerance in seventeenth-century Europe. The inherent diversity of multiethnic, multireligious societies precluded—at least in the eyes of dominant elites—a close association of state authority with one particular interpretation of religion. This provided the basis for religious tolerance and for the promotion of a conception of the nation that was explicitly secular in orientation. In this context, secularism was understood as nondiscrimination in matters of religious belief, not as hostility to religion. As such, the secular order precluded a close link between civil status and religious identity and represented a more viable alternative to the kind of communalism associated with ethnic or religious nationalisms.

Despite the sentiments of those who were hostile to any form of religious expression in the public sphere, religion remained a common feature of national life during the modernist era of the 1950s and 1960s. During this period, liberal or "modernist" interpretations of religion tended to be predominant—at least at the national level—and were perceived as consistent with the requirements of economic and political development. This trend was reflected in the more liberal and overtly secular conceptions of order that characterized each of the cases in this volume. Conservative groups and discourse existed, not least among the elites of the old order. However, the advocates of a theologically conservative religion did not have the kind of political support that they currently enjoy. This was due in large measure to the opposition of national leaders at the time to the political agenda of traditional elites and the chauvinistic tendencies

of fundamentalist religion. What changed in each case, then, was the orientation of state actors toward illiberal interpretations of religious tradition and the
related effort to coopt and promote conservative or communal beliefs as a basis
of national authority.

A second common pattern was that the pivotal figures in the religious transformation of each case tended to be pragmatic politicians who used religion in a
largely instrumental fashion. These key state actors were not necessarily defined
by their religious beliefs but rather recognized the utility of manipulating religion for political gain. Indira Gandhi, Anwar Sadat, and Richard Nixon are not
typically associated with religious politics, but they were clearly complicit in
the promotion of exclusive religious ideas. This instrumental use of religion,
however, was not something that could be readily controlled. Their actions created an opening for groups and actors that more fervently embraced the ideals
of religious communalism and that were defined more explicitly by religious
purpose. The policies of these ostensibly secular state elites, in sum, created
a political environment that was more overtly religious and accommodating
to majoritarian tendencies. It should not be surprising, then, that the national
leaders and activists who later emerged were more clearly constituted by their
religious faith (or communal beliefs) than were the initiators of the trend.[7]

In the case of Sadat and Mrs. Gandhi, moreover, this instrumental manipulation of religion had dire consequences. The politicization of religion was intended to cultivate a degree of quiescence and greater obedience to state authority. The assumption was that conservative religion would support a politics of
the status quo. This was fundamentally mistaken. Their policies did not take
into account the potential radicalism of extreme forms of religious belief. It
also did not account for the possibility that theologically conservative forms
of religion would indeed support certain ends of government and oppose others. More to the point, these various state elites did not foresee the agency of
religious activists and the unwillingness of the latter to play a role assigned to
them by others.

The inability of state leaders to control the forces they had unleashed is applicable to other instances of contemporary religious politics as well. Perhaps
the best example is modern Pakistan.[8] Over much of the past thirty years, Pakistan's intelligence services, known as the Inter-Service Intelligence (ISI), provided support (military, financial, and political) for Islamist militancy. This was
evident during the 1980s, when the ISI was the main conduit for funding the
*mujahedin* in Afghanistan during their war with the Soviet Union. The ISI also

supported the Taliban government, helping it come to power in Afghanistan in the mid-1990s. Similarly, the ISI helped to create and fund other militant groups, such as Lashkar-e-taiba, Jaish-e-Mohammed, and the Afghan Taliban. These militant organizations operated—and continue to operate—from Pakistani territory and have increasingly come to have interests in conflict with those of the Pakistan government. Although these militant groups were once seen as a tool of Pakistan foreign policy, they are clearly no longer under the control of any official organization. Like the Islamist groups in Egypt, the militant movement in Pakistan has taken on a life of its own that now threatens its former patron. Leaders such as Zia al-Huq may have seen Sunni fundamentalism as a useful means of building popular support among the majority population, but the country has paid a steep price for these policies in terms of sectarian division, violence, and instability.

It is important to note that the rise of Islamist militancy in South Asia was not simply the product of the Pakistani intelligence services. Rather, the governments (and intelligence services) of Saudi Arabia and the United States were very much involved in providing the financial and military support that launched the international *jihadi* movement. Again, at the time, support for Islamist militancy was seen as a necessary means of countering the Soviet influence in Afghanistan and of fighting the Cold War. The promotion of conservative religion by pro-Western governments was driven, then, by a variety of strategic considerations, including the belief that Sunni fundamentalism could serve as a bulwark against both the influence of the Soviet Union and against the resurgent Shi'ism of the Iranian Revolution. The unintended consequence, of course, is that external support from the United States and Saudi Arabia helped to strengthen the Islamist movement and the proliferation of loosely connected Islamist militant groups worldwide. This set the stage for the spread of Islamic militancy throughout the Middle East and North Africa during the 1990s, the creation of al-Qaeda, and, ultimately, to the events of September 11.

Similar trends, though not as extreme, were evident in Israel and Turkey as well. Throughout Israel's brief history, secular governments provided various accommodations to the ultra-orthodox Haredim. This was done in part to secure their allegiance but also to develop the Jewish character of the state. Government accommodation to religion included state funding for *Yeshivas* (centers of Jewish teaching), exemption from military service, and, ultimately, support for religious settlements on the lands captured in the 1967 June War.

The state has also recognized the ultra-orthodox wing as the authentic inter-preter of religious tradition, giving this trend a disproportionate influence on religious and cultural matters at the expense of other, reform-minded, inter-preters of Judaism. The secular left, in short, contributed to the growth of the religious right, a force that came to have significant political influence with the rise of the Likud Party and other, more explicitly religious political parties, such as the Shas Party. Similarly, in Turkey, Islam was promoted in the 1980s by the government as a bulwark against the political left. After the 1980 military coup, those with leftist sympathies were purged from positions of influence. At same time, religious education was reintroduced into the public school systems, mosques were built with state funds, and Turkish nationalism took on religious overtones. These policies came to fruition under Turgut Özal, leader of the Conservative Motherland Party (ANAP) and prime minister from 1983 to 1989. During his tenure, religion was tied to a program of economic liberalization and a politics of the status quo. Although the military sought to reverse this trend in the 1990s, the earlier policies had changed Turkish society in a manner that set the stage for the rise of the Islamist Refah Party and, later, the Justice and Development Party (AKP), which came to power in 2005.

A third, and related, pattern evident in each of the cases is the association of illiberal interpretations of religion with the phenomenon of right-wing pop-ulism. In each instance, exclusive interpretations of religious tradition were in-voked to mobilize popular sentiment along communal, not class, lines. As the cases in this study illustrate, the use of religion by conservative political actors was intended to develop a cultural or religious basis to state authority and to cul-tivate popular acceptance for policies that supported an existing, and hierarchi-cal, pattern of social order. The problem that conservative elites faced was how to get poor people to vote for (or otherwise support) policies that favor the eco-nomic and political interests of the few. The answer they hit upon was through appeals to religion and culture. In each case, the invocation of religion and communal appeals were part of a broader effort to redirect anxiety and socio-economic despair away from criticisms of capitalism or state policy and toward some other, more convenient target. Hence, the ills of society were typically linked to an overt secular square that had purged religion (and, hence, morality) from public life or to a "liberal elite" that placed the interests of minorities ahead of the majority population. Such popular animosity was also directed at minor-ity populations themselves—portrayed as either antinational or a danger to the majority community—or to rival countries. This mode of cultural mobilization was evident in the Indian case, in which religion was invoked to counter caste mobilization, and in the program of positive polarization in the U.S. case.

Finally, a fourth pattern of note is the loss of ideological commitment in each case. Political campaigns in both India and the United States, for example, increasingly favor marketing strategies and steer clear of substantive political debate. The corresponding emphasis on social issues, then, embodies a distracting discourse that is used to mobilize niche constituencies and is not intended to provide a program for governance. Divisive social issues, moreover, are commonly used to undermine, not encourage, genuine dialogue on matters of national concern. This has bred what Dionne has referred to as "a politics of false choices."[9] It has also contributed to a competitive populism. In this context, political elites tend *not* to defend secular norms and identities or minority populations. Rather, political actors of all stripes have largely embraced the politics of religious exclusivity lest they be perceived as culturally inauthentic. This is particularly evident in Egypt, where the Mubarak regime has chosen not to defend secular norms or liberal Islam in the face of the Islamist challenge. Rather, the regime has promoted its own vision of conservative religion as a means of blunting the Islamist critique. As a result, both the Islamist opposition and the state now appeal to a Salafist-oriented Islam in order to strengthen their competing claims for political power.

## Constructing and Deconstructing the Clash of Civilizations

It is clear that religion remains an important force in modern politics. Although Huntington perceived this new era as one of religious conflict between "civilizations"—each defined by competing value systems—the cases indicate that the real divisions lie *within* the different traditions themselves. This is evident in the ongoing debates over religion and culture that inform the struggle to define the nation. In each of the three cases, there are longstanding controversies over whether or not secular norms of nondiscrimination are consistent with the religious tradition of the dominant community. In Egypt, this dynamic pits Islamic activists and members of the official religious establishment against liberal and secular Muslims. Similarly, within the Hindu tradition, liberal and secular Hindus are very much at odds with members of the Sangh Parivar over both the nature of their tradition and the implications for social life. And despite Huntington's claim that Western civilization is defined by the tolerance of diversity, the internal debates within the American tradition over both religious interpretation and American nationalism illustrate that it, too, is divided over such core issues as the basis of religious authority and the merits of tolerating diversity and dissent.

This last point warrants elaboration. The Huntington thesis and the Bush administration consistently argued that the West is defined by its commitment to the Enlightenment norms of an open society, but experience argues to the contrary. The policies developed to pursue the war on terror featured infringements on individual liberty, increased government secrecy, and overt hostility to dissent. These are not the characteristics of an open society but rather are more typical of the ethnic nationalisms of the closed society. This trend, moreover, was not limited to the politics of the Bush era or the politics of the United States. On the contrary, a central feature of each case in this book was the promotion of an illiberal interpretation of both religion and society by political actors who sought to associate their interests with religious and national purpose. By promoting illiberal religious ideologies—and conflating religion and nationalism—state elites helped to construct the kind of conflict of which Huntington had warned. In each instance, the promotion of conservative populism was intimately associated with the kind of religious nationalism that perceives external groups and internal enemies as existential—and imminent—threats. Consequently, any action taken by state actors on behalf of the nation was argued to be legitimate by its very definition. These assumptions took on new life in the aftermath of 9/11, justifying the Bush administration's pursuit of a war on terror in a manner that was commonly perceived as a religious war.

There are, however, key differences between Huntington's predictions and what unfolded in the post-9/11 era. The conflict between the United States and its Islamist opposition was never about fundamental values. Rather, it was between countries and groups increasingly defined along communal or religious lines. In other words, the emerging dominance of religious nationalisms in the United States, the Middle East, and elsewhere defined these conflicts in religious terms. Hence, it is not that different civilizations reflect differing values or ideals but rather that each society succumbed to the allure of religious communalism in its various guises. The Bush administration's response to the tragedy of 9/11 was not, in short, informed by Enlightenment values but rather embodied an opportunistic assertion of power that was motivated by a sense of vengeance, grief, and Providential mission.

The events surrounding 9/11 are interesting in part because they had such an important influence on internal debates within the United States over religion, politics, and the conception of the nation. It also highlights the way in which *intra-communal* debates over social and political life were complicated by the fact that they were occurring in the context of *inter-communal* conflict. In other words, debates over social order were greatly affected by inter-group relations, particularly in societies in which differing groups are defined by their respective religious identities. The communalization of politics in one society, in short, helps to instill a corresponding communalism in other societies. This is abetted in no small part by the tendency of religious extremists and political hardliners in one nation or community to strengthen and inflame their counterparts in other nations or communities. This dynamic is also complicated by inter-state conflicts, wherein the cultural ties of minority populations to external powers contribute to a belief that these groups are suspect or otherwise have divided loyalties.

The perception of amorphous threats to the nation in all three cases of this book, then, provided a license for persecuting individuals and minorities in their respective societies. It also sanctioned—at least in the popular mind—the willful violation of international human rights norms. This tendency reflects a deification of the nation—and, hence, the state—and the corresponding demonization of those who are seen as opposing the national interest (whatever that may be). Similarly, those who advocate a liberal, or inclusive, vision of social life are commonly criticized by hardline nationalists as unpatriotic or as otherwise insufficiently committed to the defense of the nation. Secularism in this context is subsequently seen as either immoral, because it does not give sufficient deference to the dominant forms of religion in public life, or as treasonous, because it places the interests of minority communities on the same level as those of the majority community.

Although religion and the discourse of tradition are used to justify such policies, the modes and purposes to which they are deployed are a byproduct of the modern nation-state. The state's preoccupation with security and the promotion of nationalist homogeneity has stigmatized dissent and minority groups as antinational and sanctioned a variety of military and police actions against perceived enemies, both internal and external. This tendency has helped to normalize intolerant interpretations of religion and a belief that members of other religious traditions are by definition hostile to the community in question. This has, in each of the cases of this book, also led to the marginalization (and stigmatization) of liberal religious and political ideas. Again, the dominance of an illiberal religious communalism reflects not a return to tradition but a resurgence of exclusive modes of modern politics. The irony is that the religious politics that unfolded during the post–Cold War period—and the view that this embodies a clash of civilizations—are not about differing values or beliefs but rather are about warring tribes, with each group believing that God is on its side.

Whether the election of Barack Obama in the United States or the turn away from extremism in India heralds a new era of tolerance in modern politics remains to be seen. Putting the genie of religious communalism back in its bottle is no small task. Ironically, the success of such an effort—and the hope of redemption—may be found in religion itself. The liberal religious tradition offers an opportunity for tolerance and a basis for a political life defined by non-discrimination. This is not, moreover, a foreign imposition or an alien modernity to be foisted on reluctant societies. Rather, the basis for an inclusive social order can be found in the liberal interpretation of the religions in each of the three cases in this volume. This point underscores the fact that religion can be a source of unity and peace and need not be a source of conflict. The issue, though, is whether the modern institutions of political life—and the political actors who shape these institutions—are willing once again to embrace the theologically liberal interpretations of their respective traditions. Or will they remain trapped in the communal discourse of an exclusive religious politics and, hence, remain mired in conflict and division? On these questions, only time will tell.

# Notes

## Introduction

*Epigraph*: Michael Sells, "Pilgrimage and 'Ethnic Cleansing' in Herzogovina."

1. Cited in Gilles Kepel, *Muslim Extremism in Egypt: The Prophet and the Pharoah* (Berkeley: University of California Press, 1993), p. 192.

2. See, for example, Mark Juergensmeyer, *Global Rebellion: Religious Challenges to the Secular State, from Christian Militias to al-Qaeda* (Berkeley: University of California Press, 2008). Similar arguments about religious activists and modernity can be found in Michael Mazarr, *Unmodern Men in the Modern World: Radical Islam, Terrorism, and the War on Modernity* (New York: Cambridge University Press, 2007).

3. By illiberal religion I am referring to interpretations of religious tradition that place an emphasis on scriptural literalism, conservative morality, and an exclusive claim on religious truth.

4. For a discussion of these trends in Malaysia and Pakistan, see Seyyed Vali Reza Nasr, *Islamic Leviathan: Islam and the Making of State Power* (New York: Oxford University Press, 2001). On Turkey, see M. Hakan Yavuz, *Islamic Political Identity in Turkey* (New York: Oxford University Press, 2003). On Sudan, see Francis Deng, *War of Visions: Conflicts of Identities in Sudan* (Washington, DC: Brookings Institution Press, 1995). On Sri Lanka, see David Little, *Sri Lanka: The Invention of Enmity* (Washington, DC: United States Institute of Peace, 1994).

5. In this book, I use *religious fundamentalisms*—admittedly a contentious term—to refer to those religiously inspired political movements that are defined by a commitment to a more central role of conservative or illiberal interpretations of religion in political life. The defining feature of fundamentalisms is the combination of religious and political motivations, which accounts for their dynamism and appeal. See Gabriel Almond, Scott Appleby, and Emmanuel Sivan, *Strong Religion: The Rise of Fundamentalisms around the World* (Chicago: University of Chicago Press, 2003).

6. "Liberal" in this context is used narrowly, to identify patterns of society that place a premium on individual liberty and are otherwise consistent with Enlightenment norms.

7. I am indebted to Zoya Hasan for both her terminology and her thoughts on this transformation. See Zoya Hasan, "Changing Orientation of the State and the Emergence of Majoritarianism in the 1980s," in *Communalism in India: History, Politics, and Culture*, ed. K. N. Panniker (Delhi: Manohar, 1991).

8. I am indebted to Ahmer Nadeem Anwar, Delhi University, and David Little, Harvard University, for their thoughts on this topic.

9. Religion is defined here as "a complex of socially prescribed beliefs and practices relating to a realm of reality conceived as sacred." Gianfranco Poggi, *Forms of Power* (Malden, MA: Polity Press, 2001), p. 63.

10. Secularism is here defined narrowly, as a political doctrine that prescribes the separation of religious authority and political authority. This can be interpreted alternately as an hostility to religion, as official state neutrality, or as an inclusiveness that tolerates all religion in the public sphere. These distinctions are elaborated in chapter 1. See also Charles Taylor, "Modes of Secularism," in *Secularism and Its Critics*, ed. Rajeev Bhargava (Delhi: Oxford University Press, 1998).

11. Liberal or "modernist" understandings of religion are defined by their tendency to read scripture as metaphor and not literal truth. They employ reason as a guide for interpreting religion and are more inclined toward religious pluralism. More on these distinctions are found in chapter 1. Salafist Islam is a literal reading of the tradition that looks to the early Muslim community as an example of piety. The term literally means "of the ancestors."

12. A literalist, or Salafist, rendering of Islam based on the teaching of Mohammed Ibn Abd al-Wahhab.

13. See Karl Popper, *The Open Society and Its Enemies*, vols. 1 and 2 (Princeton: Princeton University Press, 1971).

14. R. Scott Appleby, *The Ambivalence of the Sacred: Religion, Violence, and Reconciliation* (New York: Rowman and Littlefield, 2000), p. 27.

15. The reference is to Clifford Geertz, "The Integrative Revolution," in *Old Societies and New States: The Quest for Modernity in Asia and Africa*, ed. Geertz (Glencoe, IL: Free Press, 1963).

16. See James Mahoney and Dietrich Rueschemeyer, eds., *Comparative Historical Analysis in the Social Sciences* (New York: Cambridge University Press, 2003).

17. I am deeply indebted to David Little and Scott Appleby for their work in this field and for their theoretical insights, from which I have drawn heavily in writing this book.

18. Geertz makes a similar argument about what he refers to as "ideological re-traditionalization" in Geertz, "Ideology as a Cultural System," in *Ideology and Discontent*, ed. David Apter (New York: Free Press, 1964).

19. For an overview of the "secular-integralist" debate of the 1990s, see Alexander Flores, "Secularism, Integralism, and Political Islam: The Egyptian Debate," in *Political Islam: Essays from Middle East Report*, ed. Joel Beinin and Joe Stork (Berkeley: University of California Press, 1997).

20. Nabil Abdel Fattah, Al-Ahram Centre for Political and Strategic Studies, in conversation, August 5, 2000.

21. For more on the religious narrative of American nationalism, see Robert N. Bellah, "Civil Religion in America," in *Beyond Belief: Essays on Religion in a Post-Traditionalist World* (Berkeley: University of California Press, 1991).

CHAPTER ONE: Reinterpreting Modern Religious Politics

1. Peter Berger, "The Desecularization of the World: A Global Overview," in *The Desecularization of the World: Resurgent Religion and World Politics*, ed. Berger (Washington, DC: Ethics and Public Policy Center, 1999).

2. Notable among these are Martin Marty and Scott Appleby, eds., *Fundamentalisms*

*Observed* (Chicago: University of Chicago Press, 1991) and other volumes in the Fundamentalisms Project; Ted Jelen, *The Political Mobilization of Religious Beliefs* (New York: Praeger, 1991); Ted Jelen and Clyde Wilcox, *Religion and Politics in Comparative Perspective: The One, the Few, and the Many* (New York: Cambridge University Press, 2002); and Bruce Lawrence, *Defenders of God: The Fundamentalist Revolt against the Modern Age* (Columbia: University of South Carolina Press, 1995).

3. See, for example, Mazarr, *Unmodern Men.*

4. See also Norman Podhoretz, *World War IV: The Long Struggle against Islamofascism* (New York: Doubleday, 2006). This view is similarly evident in Lawrence Wright, *The Looming Tower: Al-Qaeda and the Road to 9/11* (New York: Vintage Books, 2006).

5. Juergensmeyer, *Global Rebellion*; and Berger, "Desecularization of the World." See also Mark Juergensmeyer, *The New Cold War? Religious Nationalism Confronts the Secular State* (Berkeley: University of California Press, 1993).

6. Juergensmeyer, *Global Rebellion*, p. 2.

7. See Robert Kaplan, *Balkan Ghosts: A Journey through History* (New York: Vintage Departures, 1993). See also Kaplan, "Looking the World in the Eye," *The Atlantic Monthly*, December 2001.

8. Samuel Huntington, "The Clash of Civilizations," *Foreign Affairs*, Summer 1993, p. 68. Huntington goes on to argue that "the next world war, if there is one, will be a war between civilizations," p. 82.

9. Norman Podhoretz, *World War IV: The Long Struggle against Islamofascism* (New York: Doubleday Press, 2006).

10. See, for example, the writings of Robert Spencer and Daniel Pipes.

11. See Norman Podhoretz, "Defending Freedom," *Commentary*, November 2005.

12. Roxanne Eubens, *Enemy in the Mirror: Islamic Fundamentalism and the Limits of Modern Rationalism* (Princeton: Princeton University Press, 1999), p. 6.

13. Quoted in "Marines Suffer Heavy Losses in Iraq," *Washington Post*, April 7, 2004.

14. See, for example, Sayyid Qutb, *Milestones* (Cedar Rapids, IA: Mother Mosque Foundation, 2000); Hasan al-Banna, "The New Renaissance," in *Islam in Transition: Muslim Perspectives*, ed. Donohue and Esposito (New York: Oxford University Press, 1982); and Mohamed El-Hachmi Hamdi and Hasan al-Turabi, *The Making of an Islamic Leader: Conversations with Hasan al-Turabi* (Boulder, CO: Westview Press, 1998).

15. The antisecular nature of this critique is also reflected in the ideology of Hindu nationalism, particularly in the writings of Hindu communalists such as V. D. Savarkar and M. S. Golwalker. See chapter 4 for a more thorough discussion of this aspect of the debate.

16. For more on this point, see Olivier Roy, *Secularism Confronts Islam* (New York: Columbia University Press, 2007).

17. See, for example, Steve Coll, *Ghost Wars: The Secret History of the CIA, Afghanistan, and Bin Laden, from the Soviet Invasion to September 10, 2001* (New York: Penguin, 2004).

18. See Podhoretz, *World War IV*; and Wright, *Looming Tower.*

19. See Mark Tessler, "The Origins of Popular Support for Islamist Movements," in *Islam, Democracy, and the State in North Africa*, ed. John Entelis (Bloomington: Indiana University Press, 1997). This argument is similar to Norris and Inglehart's claim that there is a strong correlation between the lack of human security and the continuing strength of religious belief. They also argue that high levels of existential security drive

the secularization process. Pippa Norris and Ronald Inglehart, *Sacred and Secular: Religion and Politics Worldwide* (New York: Cambridge University Press, 2006).

20. "Fundamentalisms arise or come to prominence in times of crisis, actual or perceived. The sense of danger may be keyed to oppressive and threatening social, economic or political conditions, but the ensuing crisis is perceived as a crisis of identity by those who fear extinction as a people or absorption into an overarching syncretistic culture to such a degree that their distinctiveness is undermined in the rush to homogeneity." Marty and Appleby, eds., *Fundamentalisms Observed*, pp. 22–23.

21. Saad Eddin Ibrahim, "The Changing Face of Islamic Activism," in *Egypt, Islam, and Democracy: Twelve Critical Essays* (Cairo: American University in Cairo Press, 1996). Ibrahim distinguishes, however, between the motivations of the different waves of Islamic activism; while one was driven by anomie, later waves were influenced by the unmet expectations in the postrevolutionary era.

22. Paul Lubeck, "Globalization and the Islamization Movement: Explaining Communal Conflict in Muslim Majority States," Working Paper 6.1, Center for German and European Studies, University of California. March 1995.

23. Craig Calhoun, "The Radicalism of Tradition: Community Strength or Venerable Disguise and Borrowed Language?" *American Journal of Sociology* 88, no. 5 (1983): 886.

24. A related analysis can be found in Huntington's *Political Order in Changing Societies*, which argues that the mobilization of social forces generated by economic growth itself creates instability, as political institutions are slow to accommodate new constituencies. In short, Huntington argues that "it is not the absence of modernity, but the efforts to achieve it which produce political disorder." Samuel P. Huntington, *Political Order in Changing Societies* (New Haven: Yale University Press, 1968), p. 41.

25. Lubeck, "Globalization and the Islamization Movement," p. 7.

26. Here one must distinguish between the political economists and the sociologists, since the latter do address the issue of why religion emerges as a basis of political mobilization. This is particularly true of Egyptian sociologist Saad Eddin Ibrahim, who demonstrates quite ably how and why the changing material context has influenced changes in religious thought. The materialist perspective, however, does not necessarily explain why it is religion that has become the basis of such activism and not some other ideological resource (although, admittedly, sociologists such as Ibrahim do address this issue).

27. This is the basis of Thomas Frank's inquiry into the Christian Right. See Frank, *What's the Matter with Kansas? How Conservatives Won the Heart of America* (New York: Metropolitan Books, 2004).

28. Walker Conner, *Ethnonationalism: The Quest for Understanding* (Princeton: Princeton University Press, 1994), p. 46.

29. This point is made by Dwight B. Billings and Shaunna L. Scott in "Religion and Political Legitimation," *Annual Review of Sociology* 20 (1994): 186.

30. Jose Casanova, *Public Religions in the Modern World* (Chicago: University of Chicago Press, 2004).

31. Appleby, *Ambivalence of the Sacred*, p. 27.

32. See David Little, "Religion and Global Affairs: Religion and U.S. Foreign Policy," *SAIS Review: A Journal of International Affairs* 18, no. 2 (1998): 25–31. See also Fouad Ajami, "The Summoning," *Foreign Affairs*, September/October 1993.

33. A different way of phrasing this point is offered by Aziz Huq, University of Chi-

cago. Huq notes that "there are two parallel conflicts which intersect: the clash within a religion and the clash between an entrenched government power and its opposition." What transpires in each case, then, is the intersection of these conflicts, with each side seeking to leverage a particular interpretation of their shared tradition for political "gain within their own internecine conflict." Aziz Huq, in correspondence.

34. I am indebted to the Rudolphs for their insights on this topic. See Lloyd I. Rudolph and Susanne H. Rudolph, *The Modernity of Tradition: Political Development in India* (Chicago: University of Chicago Press, 1967).

35. Casanova argues that the secularization thesis was the only theory to attain truly paradigmatic status among social scientists and was "intrinsically interwoven with all the theories of the modern world and with the self-understanding of modernity." See Casanova, *Public Religions*, p. 18.

36. Although this theory was largely descriptive in nature, in the post–World War II period it was also prescriptive, since economic and political progress were seen as requiring a diminution of religious belief.

37. See Yilmaz Esmer and Thorlief Pettersson, eds., *Measuring and Mapping Cultures: Twenty-Five Years of Comparative Values Surveys* (Boston: Brill, 2007). See also www.world valuessurvey.org.

38. The state is here understood as the governing institutions of society. This derives from Joel Migdal's definition of a state as "an organization composed of numerous agencies led and coordinated by the state's leadership (executive authority) that has the ability to make and implement the binding rules for all the people as well as the parameters of rule making for other social organizations in a given territory, using force if necessary to have its way." Migdal, *Strong States and Weak Societies: State-Society Relations and State Capabilities in the Third World* (Princeton: Princeton University Press, 1988), p. 19.

39. Hasan, "Changing Orientation of the State," p. 152. See also Sumantra Bose, "'Hindu Nationalism' and the Crisis of the Indian State: A Theoretical Perspective," in *Nationalism, Democracy, and Development: State and Politics in India*, ed. Sugata Bose and Ayesha Jalal (New York: Oxford University Press, 1999), p. 149.

40. See, for example, Anthony Smith, "The Sacred Dimension of Nationalism," *Millennium: Journal of International Studies* 29, no. 3 (2000): 791–814.

41. Anthony Marx, *Faith in Nation: Exclusionary Origins of Nationalism* (New York: Oxford University Press, 2003), p. 197.

42. Max Weber famously defined a state as a "compulsory political association with continuous organization [whose] administrative staff successfully upholds a claim to the monopoly of legitimate use of force in the enforcement of its order . . . within a given territorial area." Weber, *The Theory of Social and Economic Organizations* (New York: Free Press, 1947), p. 154.

43. Ideology, in this context, is the "schematic image of social order" that political actors use as a guide to manage the social environment. See Geertz, "Ideology as a Cultural System."

44. Robert Bellah, *The Broken Covenant: American Civil Religion in Time of Trial*, 2nd ed. (Chicago: Chicago University Press, 1992), p. 176.

45. Little, *Religion, Order, and Law: A Study in Pre-Revolutionary England* (Chicago: University of Chicago Press, 1984), pp. 6, 7.

46. This is what Wuthnow refers to as "moral order": "the values and norms that reg-

ulate and legitimate social institutions." See Robert Wuthnow, *Meaning and Moral Order: Explorations in Cultural Analysis* (Berkeley: University of California Press, 1987), p. 1.

47. Appleby, *Ambivalence of the Sacred*, p. 173. See also Little, *Religion, Order, and Law.*

48. This is reflected in Berger's discussion of religion and social legitimation in *The Sacred Canopy: Elements of a Sociological Theory of Religion* (Garden City, NY: Anchor Books, 1967) and in Vanaik's discussion of cosmization/nomization in Achin Vanaik, *The Furies of Indian Communalism: Religion, Modernity, and Secularization* (New York: Verso, 1997).

49. "Now, therefore, if ye will obey my voice indeed, and keep my covenant, then ye shall be a peculiar treasure unto me above all people: for all the earth is mine. And ye shall be unto me a kingdom of priests, and a holy nation." Exodus 19:5–6, cited in Conor Cruise O'Brien, *God Land: Reflections on Religion and Nationalism* (Cambridge: Harvard University Press, 1988), p. 5.

50. David Little, "Belief, Ethnicity, and Nationalism," in *Nationalism and Ethnic Politics* 1, no. 2 (Summer 1995): 284.

51. For more on this understanding of communalism, see Bipan Chandra, *India's Struggle for Independence, 1857–1937* (New Delhi: Penguin Books India, 1989), ch. 31.

52. See David Little, "Religion, Nationalism, and Human Rights," *The Annual of the Society of Christian Ethics*, 1997.

53. Popper, *Open Society and Its Enemies*, vol. 1.

54. Judith Lichtenberg, "How Liberal Can Nationalism Be?" *Philosophical Forum* 28 (Fall/Winter 1996–97): 69.

55. Anthony Smith, *National Identity* (Reno: University of Las Vegas Press, 1991), p. 13.

56. These distinctions are not uniform, however. For example, Calvinist beliefs are theologically conservative but tend to eschew a close link between religion and state.

57. Geertz, "Integrative Revolution."

58. David Apter, "Political Religion in the New Nations," in *Old Societies and New States*, ed. Geertz, p. 80.

59. Geertz, "Integrative Revolution," p. 157.

60. The appeal of this type of religious nationalism was commonly associated with the reactionary backlash produced by rapid social change. It was particularly widespread among members of dominant communities—particularly elites—who were marginalized by such change. In Popper's view, the appeal of the closed society was precisely this type of backlash—what he referred to as the "strain of civilization"—generated by the individualism inherent in open democratic societies. The retreat into totalizing ideologies, then, represented for Popper a "revolt against civilization." Popper, *Open Society and Its Enemies*, vol. 1, p. 4.

61. For a discussion of these different understandings of secularism, see Vanaik, *Furies of Indian Communalism*, esp. ch. 3. See also Rajeev Bhargava, ed., *Secularism and Its Critics* (Delhi: Oxford University Press, 1998).

62. See T. N. Madan, "Secularism in its Place," and Ashis Nandy, "The Politics of Secularism and the Recovery of Religious Toleration," both in *Secularism and Its Critics*, ed. Bhargava. See also William E. Connolly, *Why I Am Not a Secularist* (Minneapolis: University of Minnesota Press, 1999).

63. David Little, in correspondence.

64. An alternate typology would add a third variable distinguishing between genu-

inely "pluralist" as opposed to simply inclusive notions of religion, the distinction being whether alternative viewpoints are genuinely embraced as opposed to simply tolerated. This threefold typology of inclusive, exclusive, and pluralist is offered by Diana Eck and referenced in Appleby, *Ambivalence of the Sacred*, p. 15.

65. Again, counterexamples such as Roger Williams notwithstanding, the overall pattern is reflected in the cases of this volume.

66. This includes the early Congress Party under Nehru or the "civil religion" of Franklin Delano Roosevelt, John Kennedy, and Bill Clinton.

67. Examples include the Indian Nationalist Movement under Gandhi and the American Civil Rights Movement under Martin Luther King.

68. This includes the regimes of Sadat and Mubarak and the religious nationalisms of Ronald Reagan and George W. Bush.

69. This includes, most notably, the Islamist opposition movements in Egypt and elsewhere in the Middle East and North Africa, the Christian Right in America, and the Hindu communalists in India.

70. In India, members of the RSS and other communalists perceived themselves as this vanguard and, thus, as the only "true Indians." See John Zavos, *The Emergence of Hindu Nationalism in India* (New Delhi: Oxford University Press, 2000). Similarly, in Egypt, it was the membership of the Muslim Brotherhood who saw themselves in this role.

71. Daniel Lerner, *The Passing of Traditional Society: Modernizing the Middle East* (New York: Free Press, 1965). See also Donald Smith, *India as a Secular State* (Princeton: Princeton University Press, 1963). I am indebted to Raj Mohan and Sujit Dutta for their comments on the progressive nature of modernity in the mid-twentieth century.

72. This was due, in part, to the continuing relevance of religion on a personal level, particularly in those societies in which there was no significant change in living standards or education levels for the majority of the population. See Ibrahim's work, particularly "The Changing Face of Islamic Activism," and Norris and Inglehart, *Sacred and Secular*.

73. Rudolph and Rudolph, *Modernity of Tradition*, p. 8.

CHAPTER TWO: The Rise and Decline of Egyptian Secularism

1. Migdal, *Strong Societies and Weak States*. The term *Islamic activism* refers to the phenomenon commonly referred to as Islamic fundamentalism, political Islam, or Islamism. While there is some debate over the proper use of these terms, I use *Islamist* and *Islamic activist* interchangeably to reference those individuals and groups associated with the broader phenomenon typically referred to as Islamic fundamentalism.

2. Imam al-Ghazali summed up his suspicion of political rulers as follows: "Three kinds of relations are possible with princes, governors, and oppressors. The first and worst is that you visit them. Somewhat better is the second whereby they visit you; but best of all is the third in which you keep your distance so that you neither see them, nor they see you." Abu Hamid Al-Ghazali, *Ihya' 'Ulam al-Din, Book 14: Kitab al-Halala wa al-Haram*, cited in Mullaney Francis Cabrini, *The Role of Islam in the Hegemonic Strategy of Egypt's Military Rulers (1952–1990)*, unpublished dissertation, Harvard University, 1992, p. 120.

3. Nabil Abdel Fatah, *Quran and Sword: State-Religion Conflict in Egypt* (Cairo: Mabooli Books, 1998; in Arabic).

4. For a good summary of this period, see Alaf Lutfi Al-Sayyid Marsot, *A Short History of Egypt* (Cambridge: Cambridge University Press, 1998).

5. See Sami Zubaida, "The Quest for the Islamic State: Islamic Fundamentalism in Egypt and Iran," in Zubaida, *Islam, The People, and the State: Essays on Political Ideas and Movements in the Middle East* (New York: I. B. Taurus, 1995).

6. See Richard Mitchell, *The Society of the Muslim Brothers* (New York: Oxford University Press, 1969), esp. chs. 8 and 9. See also Ibrahim Abu-Rabi, *Intellectual Origins of Islamic Resurgence in the Modern Arab World* (New York: State University of New York Press, 1995), ch. 3.

7. Alaf Lutfi Al-Sayyid Marsot, *A Short History of Egypt* (Cambridge: Cambridge University Press, 1998).

8. The "six principles" of the revolution were the end of imperialism, the end of feudalism, limits on monopoly capitalism, the establishment of social justice, the building of a powerful army, and the institutionalization of democracy.

9. Maye Kassem, *Egyptian Politics: The Dynamics of Authoritarian Rule* (Boulder, CO: Lynne Rienner Press, 2004), p. 13.

10. Nasser's approach to dealing with the communists fluctuated between repression and limited cooperation. After an initial suppression of the Communist Party and the labor movement in the early 1950s, a period of rehabilition and collaboration was initiated in 1961, reflecting the regime's closer ties to the Soviet Union. See Hamid Ansari, *Egypt, The Stalled Society* (Cairo: American University in Cairo Press, 1986), p. 92.

11. For more on this "ruling bargain," see Kassem, *Egyptian Politics*, p. 13.

12. Ibrahim Ibrahim, "Religion and Politics under Nasser and Sadat," in *The Islamic Impulse*, ed. Freyer Barbara Stowasser (Washington, DC: Center for Contemporary Studies, 1987), p. 125.

13. Some of the leading Arab Nationalists were Christian, such as Michel Aflaq, who was one of the founders of the Arab Ba'ath (Renaissance or Rebirth) Party, a pan-Arab party whose offshoots came to power in Syria and Iraq in 1963.

14. Michael Gilsenan, "Popular Islam and the State in Contemporary Egypt," in *State and Ideology in the Middle East and Pakistan* (New York: Macmillan, 1988), ed. Fred Halliday and Hamza Alavi, p. 171.

15. Between 1952 and 1962, the government built or helped fund upwards of fifteen hundred mosques and virtually doubled the personnel levels in government mosques. See Anwar Alam, *Religion and State: Egypt, Iran, and Saudi Arabia* (Delhi: Gyan Sagar Publications, 1998), p. 87.

16. The Brotherhood was a critic of the Egyptian monarachy and of British influence in Egypt. Its guiding ideology, developed by al-Banna, focused on defending Islam from the influence of Western ideas. It also embraced political action to achieve its religious goals. The Brotherhood was formally banned in December 1948. Weeks later, members of its military wing assassinated the prime minister, which prompted the king's security agents to assassinate al-Banna in February 1949.

17. It has been argued that "the RCC contained officers who were either full members or sympathetic to the fundamentalist cause" and that a number of them had close contacts with the Brotherhood prior to 1952, including both Sadat and Nasser. See Ansari, *Egypt, The Stalled Society*, p. 82; and Mitchell, *Society of the Muslim Brothers*.

18. Albert Hourani, *Arabic Thought in the Liberal Age: 1798–1938* (New York: Cambridge University Press, 1991), p. 353. This debate is also discussed in Nadav Safran,

*Egypt in Search of Political Community: An Analysis of the Intellectual and Political Evolution of Egypt, 1804–1952* (Boston: Harvard University Press, 1961). For more background on both Kalid and Abd al-Raziq, see also Leonard Binder, *Islamic Liberalism: A Critique of Development Ideologies* (Chicago: University of Chicago Press, 1988).

19. Safran, *Egypt in Search of Political Community*, p. 235.

20. The full quotation from al-Ghazzali is: "Seldom, if ever, has Islam needed the state more than today—not merely because the state is an integral part of it, but also because Islam is threatened with extermination in a world where only the strong can survive." Cited in Safran, *Egypt in Search of Political Community*, p. 236.

21. Safran, *Egypt in Search of Political Community*, p. 237.

22. Rubin, *Islamic Fundamentalism in Egypt*, p. 12.

23. Members of the Brotherhood deny involvement in the assassination attempt, arguing that it was a ploy by the police to give the state an excuse to crack down on the Brotherhood.

24. This coincided with a purge of dissident officers in the army and the faction of the RCC led by President Naguib, who had advocated a return to liberal democracy in lieu of the continued military rule.

25. Tamir Moustafa, "Conflict and Cooperation between the State and Religious Institutions in Contemporary Egypt," *International Journal of Middle East Studies* 32 (February 2000): 5.

26. The court and educational systems had previously been divided into private, Islamic, and national systems. The reform of the *sharia* courts and of Al-Azhar were designed to end this separation and to bring both under the control of the state. See Jakob Skovgaaard-Peterson, *Defining Islam for the Egyptian State: Muftis and Fatwas of the Dar al-Ifta* (New York: Brill Press, 1997), p. 184.

27. Malika Zeghal, "Religion and Politics in Egypt: The Ulama of al-Azhar, Radical Islam, and the State (1952–54)," *International Journal of Middle East Studies* 31, no. 3 (August 1999): 374.

28. Moustafa, "Conflict and Cooperation," p. 7.

29. See Malcolm Kerr, *The Arab Cold War: Gamal Abd Al-Nasir and His Rivals, 1958–1970* (New York: Oxford University Press, 1971).

30. Gilsenan, "Popular Islam and the State," p. 175.

31. Gilsenan, "Popular Islam and the State," p. 167.

32. Fouad Ajami, *The Arab Predicament: Arab Political Thought and Practice since 1967* (New York: Cambridge University Press, 1992), p. 32.

33. Ajami, *Arab Predicament*, p. 74. There was also a "technological explanation," which argued that Egypt's scientific underdevelopment was the basis of the defeat. Consequently, a thorough modernization of Egyptian society based on scientific and technological development was necessary to avoid similar failures in the future. See Nazih N. M. Ayubi, "The Political Revival of Islam: The Case of Egypt," *International Journal of Middle East Studies* 12, no. 4 (December 1980): 489.

34. The term is one used by Beattie in his delineation of the ideological currents of the Nasser regime, which he divides among "regime leftists," "regime centrists," and "regime rightists." Sadat fit in the "rightist" camp. See Kirk J. Beattie, *Egypt during the Sadat Years* (New York: Palgrave, 2000).

35. See Ansari, *Egypt, The Stalled Society*.

36. The regime's new political philosophy was embodied in Sufi Abu Talib, *Our*

*Socialist Democracy: The Ideology of the May Revolution* (Cairo, 1978). The book was commissioned by Sadat in 1975 and written by the president of Cairo University. For more on both Abu Talib and this text, see Beattie, *Egypt during the Sadat Years*, pp. 168–72.

37. In one speech before the National Assembly, Sadat remarked: "I want us to return to the village source, to our origin. . . . I want the constitution to take this into account, not only for the sake of the villages, but so that the whole of Egypt should take shape in the way and become a single village." Cited in Marie-Christine Aulas, "State and Ideology in Republican Egypt: 1952–82," in *State and Ideology in the Middle East and Pakistan*, ed. Halliday and Alavi, p. 149.

38. The number of government-controlled mosques increased from 3,000 to 7,000 under Sadat's rule. The total number of mosques grew from roughly 15,000 mosques in the mid-1960s to 27,000 mosques in 1980. These statistics come from Egypt's Central Agency for Public Mobilisation and Statistics, cited in Alam, *Religion and State*, p. 96. Alam also notes that the government actively wooed popular sheikhs, either giving them land or helping to finance the construction of new mosques.

39. For more on this rapprochement, including the contents of the six-point agreement between Sadat and the Muslim Brotherhood, see Nemat Guenena and Saad Eddin Ibrahim, *The Changing Face of Egypt's Islamic Activism*, unpublished manuscript submitted to the U.S. Institute of Peace, September 1997. See also Ali Eshmawy, *The Secret History of the Muslim Brotherhood Movement* (Cairo: Dar al-Hilal, 1993). Leaders of the Brotherhood were also involved in drafting sections of the 1971 constitution and were allowed to participate in parliamentary elections, although not as a registered party.

40. Carrie Rosefsky Wickham, *Mobilizing Islam: Religion, Activism, and Political Change in Egypt* (New York: Columbia University Press, 2003), p. 33.

41. See Beattie, *Egypt during the Sadat Years*, pp. 97–106.

42. Gilles Kepel, *Muslim Extremism in Egypt: The Prophet and the Pharaoh*, trans. Jon Rothschild (Berkeley: University of California Press, 1986), p. 139.

43. Mohamed Heikal, *Autumn of Fury: The Assassination of Sadat* (London: Andre Deutsch, 1983), pp. 133–34. See also Kassem, *Egyptian Politics*, pp. 140–45.

44. Abdel Monem al-Fatooh, in conversation, July 22, 2002.

45. Farid Zahran, in conversation, July 20, 2002. On the distribution of weapons to Islamist students, see Heikal, *Autumn of Fury*.

46. Saad Eddin Ibrahim, in conversation. See also Guenena and Ibrahim, *Changing Face*, p. 31.

47. Nadia Ramses Farah, quoted in Kevin Dwyer, *Arab Voices: The Human Rights Debate in the Middle East* (Berkeley: University of California Press, 1991), p. 67.

48. Mary Anne Weaver, *A Portrait of Egypt: A Journey through the World of Militant Islam* (New York: Farrar, Straus and Giroux, 1999), p. 91.

49. Malika Zeghal, "Religion and Politics in Egypt," p. 381.

50. Cabrini, *Role of Islam*, p. 169.

51. Patrick Gaffney, *The Prophet's Pulpit: Islamic Preaching in Contemporary Egypt* (Berkeley: University of California Press, 1994), p. 85.

52. There was a doctrinal difference between the two groups, however. One felt that the society had been led astray by a corrupt leadership and that a coup d'état was sufficient to set Egypt back on the right track. Takfir wa Hijra, seeing both society and state as beyond redemption, however, advocated complete isolation from the society at large.

An influential book dealing with these issues, *The Neglected Duty*, was published in 1982 by Mohamed Abdel al-Salam al-Farag, a member of the Jihad militant group.

53. Saad Eddin Ibrahim argues that this reflects a general trend. Younger Islamic activists are more inclined to violence, while older Islamists are more accommodating. This reflects both experience and a recognition that militancy is of only limited usefulness. In conversation, July 3, 2000.

54. The basic division is one of tactics, not ends. While all the Islamists argue for an Islamic state and society, they differ on how to accomplish that. The accomodationists tend to advocate a "bottom-up" approach and work within the system to cultivate greater religiosity in society. Those who advocate violence take a "top-down" approach, seeking to seize control of the state in order to Islamicize society.

55. Mary Ann Weaver quotes Hosni Mubarak as saying that Sadat was "responsible for the formation of al-Gama'a," the primary militant group of the 1990s. Weaver, *Portrait of Egypt*, p. 165.

56. Nabil Abdel-Fattah, *Veiled Violence: Islamic Fundamentalism in Egyptian Politics in the 1990s* (Cairo: Khattab Press, 1994), p. 49.

57. Moustafa argues that the state's domination of Egypt's religious institutions contributed to the resurgence of radical groups, since such groups perceived official Islam as tainted by political expediency. Moustafa, "Conflict and Cooperation," p. 10.

58. This view was expressed by a bishop in the Orthodox Coptic Church during an interview with the author in July 2002.

59. Saad Eddin Ibrahim, *The Copts of Egypt* (London: Minority Rights Group International, 1996), p. 18.

60. It should be noted that there are a number of different sects within Coptic Christianity, including Coptic Catholics, Evangelicals, and other denominations.

61. During consideration of the 1971 constitution, Islamic conservatives had proposed making *sharia* the sole source of legislation.

62. Hopwood, *Egypt: Politics and Society, 1945–1990* (New York: Routledge, 1991), 3rd ed., p. 117.

63. This body was called the Supreme Muslim Council and was created in November 1979. See Alam, *Religion and State*, p. 102.

64. Moustafa, "Conflict and Cooperation," p. 8.

65. David Sagiv, *Fundamentalism and Intellectuals in Egypt, 1973–1993* (London: Frank Cass, 1994), p. 60.

66. See Johannes J. G. Jansen, *The Neglected Duty: The Creed of Sadat's Assassins and Islamic Resurgence in the Middle East* (New York: Macmillan, 1986).

67. Farag Foda, a secular writer assassinated in 1992, cited in Fouad Ajami, *The Dream Palaces of the Arabs: A Generation's Odyssey* (New York: Pantheon Books, 1998), p. 206.

68. Fouad Ajami, *Dream Palaces*, p. 206.

69. Zeghal, "Al-Azhar and Radical Islam," p. 382.

CHAPTER THREE: The Islamization of Egyptian Politics

1. Members of al-Jihad planned to capture the radio and television building in central Cairo and broadcast news of the uprising. This would signal other members of the organization that the plan was in effect. The failure to capture the building, however, kept many of the cell leaders in the dark and out of the fight.

2. Cited in Sullivan and Abed-Kotob, *Islam in Contemporary Egypt: Civil Society vs. the State* (Boulder, CO: Lynne Rienner Press, 1999), p. 81.

3. Abdel-Fattah, *Veiled Violence*, p. 19.

4. These crises remain a defining feature of contemporary Egypt. See, for example, Michael Slackman, "Dreams Stifled, Egypt's Young Turn to Islamic Fervor," *New York Times*, February 17, 2008, A1.

5. Muhammad Faour, *The Arab World after Desert Storm* (Washington, DC: U.S. Institute of Peace Press, 1993), p. 55.

6. Gehad Auda, "The Normalization of the Islamic Movement in Egypt from the 1970s to the Early 1990s," in *Fundamentalisms and the State*, ed. Martin E. Marty and R. Scott Appleby (Chicago: University of Chicago Press, 1994), p. 390. Auda reiterated these themes during two discussions in Cairo during the summer of 2002.

7. Abdul Fatooh and al-Erian in conversation, September 22 and October 12, 2002, respectively.

8. For a comprehensive treatment of this movement, see Rosefsky Wickham, *Mobilizing Islam*; and Geneive Abdo, *No God but God: Egypt and the Triumph of Islam* (New York: Oxford University Press, 2000).

9. Nabil Abdel Fatah, Al-Ahram Centre, in conversation, July 21, 2002.

10. Gehad Auda has argued that this modus vivendi was "the hallmark of Mubarak's style of democratization: it aimed at consolidating the mainstream through creating consensus among political actors on the need to avoid involvement in de-stabilizing actions against the government." Auda, "Normalization of the Islamic Movement," p. 388. These ideas were reiterated in conversation with the author during the summer of 2002.

11. This was targeted at the NGOs that were engaging in relief activities during the earthquake but was subsequently used by the regime against Saad Eddin Ibrahim for his support from the European Union to monitor the 2000 elections.

12. See Sullivan and Kotob, *Islam in Contemporary Egypt*; Weaver, *Portrait of Egypt*; and Caryle Murphy, *A Passion for Islam: Shaping the Modern Middle East: The Egyptian Experience* (New York: Scribner, 2002).

13. Cited in Murphy, *Passion for Islam*, p. 75.

14. These were the basic themes articulated by Abd al-Salam Farag, a leading ideologue of al-Jihad, and Sayyid Qutb. See Jansen, *Neglected Duty*.

15. For more on this trend, see Coll, *Ghost Wars*. See also Mary Anne Weaver, "Blowback," *Atlantic Monthly*, May 1996.

16. Mohamed al-Salah of *Al-Hayat* newspaper, in conversation, Cairo, October 2, 2002.

17. Caryle Murphy cites "several hundred" in *Passion for Islam*, p. 74, while Mohamed al-Salah of *Al-Hayat* put the number at between 3,000 and 4,000 Egyptians. Salah, having recently completed a book on the Afghan Arabs, provided the number in conversation, Cairo, October 2, 2003. A former head of Pakistani intelligence estimated the total number of Afghan Arabs (from all countries in the Middle East) that participated in the war at 30,000.

18. Robert Oakley, former ambassador to Pakistan, cited in Scott W. Hibbard and David Little, *Islamic Activism and U.S. Foreign Policy* (Washington, DC: U.S. Institute of Peace Press, 1997), p. 76.

19. Abdel Rahman eventually received a visa to the United States. He was later con-

victed in a U.S. court for his involvement in the first attack on the World Trade Towers in the early 1990s.

20. While many of the Islamists complained of the "moral laxity" of foreign tourists, the primary intention was to deprive the Egyptian government of foreign exchange. It is estimated that the tourist industry earned about $3.3 billion annually at this time.

21. Estimates of casualty figures for these years can be found in Guenena and Ibrahim, *Changing Face*, p. 58. In 1993, roughly 330 people died in the violence, equally distributed among civilians, Islamists, and the security forces, with 1,100 wounded, the vast majority of which (700) were civilian.

22. Lawyers Committee on Human Rights, *Escalating Attacks on Human Rights Protection in Egypt* (Washington, DC: Lawyers Committee, 1995).

23. See Human Rights Watch, *Annual Report*, 1994. A former member of al-Jihad who was interviewed for this project spent eight years in jail without a trial or any charges being formally brought against him.

24. This included Abdel Harith Madani, a lawyer who was killed in police custody in April 1994.

25. See Rosefsky Wickham, *Mobilizing Islam*; and Abdo, *No God but God*.

26. This announcement was made in December 1992, about the same time as the incursion into Imbaba.

27. Sheik Mansour al-Rifai Obeid, head of the Mosques Administration of the Ministry of Religious Endowments, referenced in Human Rights Watch, *Annual Report*, 1994. Only 30,000 of the country's 170,000 mosques were at that time under direct control of the Ministry of Religious Endowments.

28. Murphy details the activities and final end of Talaat Mohammad Yassin Hammam, one of the senior leaders of al-Gama'a al-Islammiyya. See *Passion for Islam*, ch. 5.

29. Ajami, *Dream Palaces*, p. 202.

30. This claim was made by Interior Minister Alfi, who was replaced after the Luxor attack in 1997.

31. See "Interview with Islamic Group Leaders on Recent Revision of Their Ideology," *Al-Musawar*, June 21, 2002.

32. These figures are documented by the Egyptian Organization for Human Rights; others estimate the number of political prisoners from this time at between 15,000 and 30,000.

33. This reflected an earlier critique offered by Sheik Gad al-Haq (then the mufti, later the sheikh of al-Azhar) of al-Jihad's violent manifest, *The Neglected Duty*, in the aftermath of the Sadat assassination. Abdalla Kamal, "Intellectual Map of Azhar Reveals Diversity," *Ruz al-Yusef*, March 25, 1996.

34. See Julie Taylor, "State-Clerical Relations in Egypt: A Case of Strategic Interaction," presented at the American Political Science Association Annual Meeting in Washington, D.C., September 2000.

35. The analogy to "white ants" was offered by Robert Springborg in the Summer of 2002, who was then the director of the American Research Center in Egypt. He was referring to the manner in which sympathizers of the Muslim Brotherhood had come to influence key institutions of the state from within, such as the Ministry of Education, Al-Azhar, and even the judiciary. In conversation, June 18, 2002.

36. The Muslim Brotherhood also contributed money to Al-Azhar to build schools

and institutes in return for the right to select the teachers. See Kamal, "Intellectual Map of Azhar."

37. The Islamists, criticizing the official religious establishment as being too closely tied to the state, offered their own interpretations of Islam.

38. Zeghal, "Al-Azhar and Radical Islam," p. 389.

39. Moustafa, "Conflict and Cooperation," p. 12.

40. See Steven Barraclough, "Al-Azhar: Between the Government and the Islamists," *Middle East Journal* 52, no. 2 (Spring 1998).

41. Walid Khazziha, American University of Cairo, in conversation, October 20, 2002.

42. Ajami, *Dream Palaces*, p. 202.

43. See Judith Miller, *God Has Ninety-Nine Names: Reporting from a Militant Middle East* (New York: Simon and Schuster, 1996), p. 71. The Saudi influence in Egyptian culture and politics was reiterated by Tahseen Bashir in conversation with the author, July 2000.

44. In a very interesting discussion of these issues, Rutherford associates this position—or at least that advocated by the more moderate wing of the Islamist movement—with a communitarian, not a totalitarian, vision. This may be true among the "Islamic constitutionalists," but even their belief that the state ought to enforce religious belief and practice remains fundamentally illiberal. See Bruce Rutherford, *Egypt after Mubarak: Liberalism, Islam, and Democracy in the Arab World* (Princeton: Princeton University Press, 2008).

45. The proceedings of this debate can be found in *Misr Bayn al Dawla al Diniya wa al Madaniya* [Egypt: Between Religious State and Civil State] (Cairo, 1992). The Islamist position was represented by Muhammad Imara, Mamoun al-Hodeiby of the Muslim Brotherhood, and Sheikh Muhammad al-Ghazzali of Al-Azhar. On the other side was Farag Foda, the founder of *al-Tanwir*, and Muhammad Ahmed Khallafa. The debate was significant because it was the first and last such debate hosted in a public forum. It was shortly after this that Farag Foda was gunned down by Islamic militants outside his home in Cairo.

46. See Fauzi M. Najjar, "The Debate on Islam and Secularism in Egypt," *Arab Studies Quarterly* 18, no. 2 (Spring 1996): 21.

47. He prefers the term *civic* or *humanist* as opposed to *secular* and sees himself as "working for a civic society." Many of his ideas are influenced by Sufist thought. In conversation, September 18, 2002.

48. Muhammad Said al-Ashmawy, *Islam and the Political Order* (Washington, DC: Council for Research in Values and Philosophy, 1994), p. 11. Originally published in Arabic as *Al-Islam al-Siyasi* [*Political Islam*] (Cairo: Dar Sina, 1987).

49. Al-Ashmawy, in conversation. See also Carolyn Fluehr-Lobban, ed., *Against Islamic Extremism: The Writings of Muhammad Sa'id al-Ashmawy* (Gainesville: University of Florida Press, 1998). This perspective is reflected in other writers, such as Sayed Mahmoud al-Quimni.

50. Al-Ashmawy, in conversation, September 2002.

51. Fu'ad Zakariya, cited in Flores, "Secularism, Integralism, and Political Islam," p. 91.

52. As Farag Foda asked in a public challenge to a Sheikh al-Ghazali, "Which of the contemporary Islamic states, Iran or the Sudan, would you want us to take as a model?" Cited in Najjar, "Debate on Islam and Secularism," p. 4.

53. See Flores, "Secularism, Integralism, and Political Islam," p. 85.

54. When Abd al-Raziq made this point in 1925, he was accused of unbelief and dismissed from al-Azhar.

55. Cited in the published proceedings from the 1992 Cairo Book Fair debate between secularists and Islamists, *Egypt: Between Religious State and Civil State* (Cairo, 1992). These sentiments were echoed in the author's interview with al-Hodeiby in September 21, 2002, prior to his elevation to supreme leader.

56. The quotation is from Egyptian columnist Muhammed Sid Ahmed, cited in Kevin Dwyer, *Arab Voices: The Human Rights Debate in the Middle East* (Berkeley: University of California Press, 1991), p. 63. These remarks were echoed by several participants in a conference at Cairo University on the "Clash of Civilizations" in October 2002.

57. For more on the mechanics of this process, see Gregory Starret, *Putting Islam to Work: Education, Politics, and Religious Transformation in Egypt* (Berkeley: University of California Press, 1998).

58. Saad Eddin Ibrahim, in conversation, July 17, 2002, Cairo, Egypt.

59. The Committee for Research and Publication (CRP) is a subsidiary of the Islamic Research Academy. The process for banning books is irregular, with cases often being referred to the "Censorship Police" or to the state security apparatus. See Salwa Ismail, "Religious Orthodoxy as Public Morality: The State, Islamism, and Cultural Politics in Egypt," *Critique*, Spring 1999, p. 38. See also, Egyptian Organization of Human Rights, *Freedom of Opinion and Belief: Restrictions and Dilemmas*, Cairo, 1994.

60. The ruling was State Council Fatwa no. 58/1/63, which can be found in Egyptian Organization of Human Rights, *Freedom of Opinion and Belief*. See also Abdel Sattar al-Tawaka *"Ayna yaqaf ulema al-azhar?"* [Where Do the Ulema of al-Azhar Stop?] *Ruz al-Yusef*, April 1994.

61. Samir Amin, "Pluralism Spurs Innovation," *Al-Ahram Weekly*, April 1994.

62. The *fatwa*, from which this quotation is drawn, was issued by Judge Tarik al-Bishri, a noted Islamic scholar and vice chair of the State Council. Egyptian Organization of Human Rights, *Freedom of Opinion and Belief*, p. 26.

63. Egyptian Organization of Human Rights, *Freedom of Opinion and Belief*, p. 27.

64. William Mann, "Novelist's Blasphemy Conviction Shakes Egypt's Writers," Associated Press, January 8, 1992. Hamed's publisher and printer, also charged in the case, were designated "blasphemers."

65. See footnote 56.

66. George N. Sfeir, "Basic Freedoms in a Fractured Legal Culture: Egypt and the Case of Nasr Hamid Abu Zayid," *Middle East Journal*, Summer 1998, p. 406.

67. Al-Ashmawy, in conversation, September 19, 2002, Cairo, Egypt.

68. The reference is to Mamoun al-Hodeiby and is cited in "Islamic Scholars Demand Waiving Immunity from Al-Ashmawy and Confiscating his Books that Malign Islam," *Al-Nour, Arab Press Review*, January 29, 1992.

69. The reference is to former National Assembly deputy Sheikh Yusef al-Badry, quoted in *al-Nour, Arab Press Review*, January 29, 1992.

70. "Writer Condemns Confiscation by Police," Associated Press, June 1996.

71. Ismail, "Religious Orthodoxy as Public Morality," p. 40.

72. Egyptian Organization for Human Rights, Press Release, May 1, 1997.

73. Max Rodenbeck, "Witch Hunt in Egypt," *New York Review of Books*, November 16, 2000, p. 39.

74. The motivations behind this riot, however, were mixed. One journalist who spoke with some of the students involved said that much of the unrest was targeted at the poor living conditions at the university. Hossam al-Hamalawi, *Cairo Times*, in conversation, October 2002, Cairo, Egypt.

75. Saleh is the author of *The Season of Migration to the North* [*Mawsim al-Higra ila ash-Shamal*] (London: Heinemann, 1970), trans. Denys Johnson-Davis. Several human rights groups issued a joint statement depicting the affair as a "fascist attack against freedom of expression." The statement (in Arabic) is available through the Cairo Institute for Human Rights Studies.

76. Max Rodenbeck, "Witch Hunt in Egypt," p. 38.

77. Max Rodenbeck, "Witch Hunt in Egypt." The quotation is from the report by the Islamic Research Academy of Al-Azhar.

78. Mona Anis, "Intellectuals' Dilemma," *Al-Ahram Weekly*, May 11–17, 2000.

79. Hamid Suleiman, "Sirr al-hajoom ala al-Azhar" [The Secret Attack on al-Azhar], *Akher Sa'a*, April 20, 1994.

80. Fatemah Farag, "Re-Drawing the Line," *Al-Ahram Weekly*, August 3–9, 2000, p. 4. Farag quotes the editor-in-chief of *Sawt al-Azhar* (The Voice of Al-Azhar) as saying, "Those who want to be atheists can do so . . . but they do not have the right to publish such ideas."

81. As one official from the Coptic Church noted, "The Government says the right things, but continues to act in opposition to its statements." This is what he referred to as the "theatre game." In conversation, July 2002, Cairo, Egypt.

82. There is dispute over the size of the Coptic population. Government figures place the number at 6 million, or roughly 5% of the population, while Coptic activists claim a much higher figure, around 10 million. Independent sources place it at 7 to 8 million.

83. "International Religious Freedom Report 2001, Egypt," U.S. Department of State, www.state.gov/drl.

84. Mahmoud Nahkleh, in conversation, October 14, 2002, Cairo, Egypt.

85. Alberto Fernandez, "In the Year of the Martyrs: Anti-Coptic Violence in Egypt, 1988–1993," paper presented at the Middle East Studies Association Annual Meeting, San Francisco, California, November 18–20, 2001.

86. The reference is to a headline in *El-Kiraza*, the Coptic Church's official magazine, cited in Nadia Abou El-Magd, "The Meanings of Al-Kosheh," *Al-Ahram Weekly*, February 3–9, 2000.

87. "Kosheh File Re-Opened," *Al-Ahram Weekly*, March 20–26, 2003.

88. "Kosheh File Re-Opened."

89. Quoted in Nadia Abou El-Magd, "The Meanings of Al-Kosheh," *Al-Ahram Weekly*, February 3–9, 2000.

90. Several Coptic activists interviewed for this project emphasized a common set of themes: that they were "strangers in their own land," and that they sought "genuine equality."

91. The program "Essence of Life," for example, is run on state television and presents converts to Islam to discuss their choice of "the right path." See *2004 Report on International Religious Freedom*, U.S. Department of State.

92. Dina Al-Howega, CEDEJ, in conversation, October 8, 2002, Cairo, Egypt.

93. The quotation was from a 21-year-old protester. Cited in Nadia Abou El-Magd, "Unprecedented Show of Coptic Anger," *Al-Ahram Weekly*, June 21–27, 2001.

94. Cited in Nadia Abou El-Magd, "Beyond the Slur," *Al-Ahram Weekly*, June 28–July 4, 2001.

95. Samir Ruca, CEOSS, in conversation. August 25, 2002, Cairo, Egypt.

96. Faculty member from the University of Cairo, in conversation, Cairo, Egypt, Fall 2002.

97. See Lila Abu-Lughod, "Dramatic Reversals: Political Islam and Egyptian Television," in *Political Islam*, ed. Beinin and Stork.

98. For a discussion of the "civil society" alternative to both extremism and authoritarianism, see Judith Miller, "The Challenge of Radical Islam," *Foreign Affairs* 72, no. 2 (Spring 1993). See also Hibbard and Little, *Islamic Activism and U.S. Foreign Policy*.

99. Anthony Lake, "Remarks Presented at the Washington Institute for Near East Policy," Washington, D.C., May 17, 1994.

100. "Tahaallif al-Azhar wa al-Ikwan dad Moutimir Bekeen" [Alliance between Azhar and the Brotherhood against the Peking Conference], *Al-Wasat*, September 3, 1995.

101. The governor of Cairo dissolved the board of directors of the Front and allowed the sheikh to appoint his own people to an interim board. An administrative court ruling reversed the order, but Tantawi prevailed on appeal. See Mona El-Nahhas, "Dissolved Board Wins Legal Battle," *Al-Ahram Weekly*, May 13–19, 1999.

102. Nabil Abdel Fatah, in conversation, Cairo, Egypt, July 21, 2002.

103. Muhammad Sayyed Tantawi, interviewed in *Al-Rai Al-Aam*, cited in Y. Yehosua, "Cairo Conference Calling for Reform Raises the Ire of the Egyptian Religious Establishment," *Middle East Media Research Institute*, October 22, 2004.

104. Mohamed Sayed Tantawai, cited in Youssef Rakha, "Mohamed Sayed Tantawi: An Abstract Contention," *Al-Ahram Weekly*, October 6–12, 2005.

105. Interview with Michelle Dunne, U.S. State Department, Cairo Embassy, June 5, 2002, Cairo, Egypt. See also *International Religious Freedom Report*, U.S. Department of State, December 2004.

106. "Egypt Cracks Down on Breaking Ramadan Fast," Al-Arabiya News Channel, September 21, 2009.

107. Rutherford's discussion of Islamic constitutionalism is extremely helpful in understanding the rationale behind the intervention of the state in religious matters. See Rutherford, *Egypt after Mubarak*, chs. 3 and 6.

108. Hossam Bahgat, "Al-Azhar Is Wrong, But the State Is the Real Culprit," *The Daily Star*, September 23, 2004.

109. Mustafa Kamal Al-Sayyid, University of Cairo, in conversation, July 2000.

110. United Nations Development Programme, *Arab Human Development Report, 2002: Creating Opportunities for Future Generations* (New York: United Nations Publications, 2002).

111. An Egyptian scholar, in conversation with the author, October 2002.

CHAPTER FOUR: The Rise and Decline of Indian Secularism

1. See Hasan, "Changing Orientation of the State."

2. I am indebted to Pasha Anwer, Delhi University, for his comments on this issue.

3. It is best to avoid drawing analogies to Christian history, since there was no Hindu

orthodoxy or establishment to be reformed. Rather, there was a caste structure and a tradition (*sampradaya*, literally "that which is handed over"), which were interpreted in various ways. See John Zavos, *The Emergence of Hindu Nationalism in India* (New Delhi: Oxford University Press, 2000), p. 42.

4. For a discussion of the early revivalist movements in the Islamic world, see John L. Esposito, *Islam and Politics*, 3rd ed. (Syracuse: Syracuse University Press, 1984).

5. See Gyanendra Pandey, *The Construction of Communalism in Colonial North India* (New Delhi: Oxford University Press, 1996), p. 236.

6. T. W. Holderness, *Peoples and Problems of India* (London, 1911), p. 127, cited in Mushiral Hasan, *Nationalism and Communal Politics in India, 1885–1930* (New Delhi: Manohar, 2000), p. 3.

7. Chandra distinguishes between "liberal" and "extreme" variants of religious communalism. See Bipan Chandra, *India's Struggle for Independence, 1857–1947* (New Delhi: Penguin, 1988), ch. 31.

8. See Hasan, *Nationalism and Communal Politics*, pp. 180–81.

9. These categories, for example, did not account for religious tendencies that had both Hindu and Islamic roots (such as Bhakti or Sufist cults) or many of the sub-caste designations (*jati*). See Stuart Corbridge and John Harriss, *Reinventing India: Liberalization, Hindu Nationalism, and Popular Democracy* (Cambridge: Polity Press, 2000).

10. Chandra, *India's Struggle for Independence*, p. 401.

11. For more on these distinctions, see Bruce Graham, *Hindu Nationalism and Indian Politics: The Origins and Development of the Jana Sangh* (Cambridge: Cambridge University Press, 1991). Although Graham uses different labels for each of these groups, the basic distinction is the same. A similar differentiation of the pre-Independence Hindu community is made by Bipan Chandra, although he uses the terms *secular nationalist, liberal communalist,* and *extreme communalist.* See Chandra, *India's Struggle for Independence,* chs. 31–33.

12. Motilal Nehru, for example, argued in his 1928 presidential address that religion's influence on Indian politics was wholly detrimental and that "Complete divorce of one from the other is the only remedy." Cited in Hasan, *Nationalism and Communal Politics,* p. 253.

13. See Rudolph and Rudolph, *Modernity of Tradition.*

14. As Madan Mohan Malaviya remarked, "If the Hindus made themselves strong and the rowdy section among the Mahomedans were convinced they could not safely rob and dishonor Hindus, unity would be established on a stable basis." Cited in Walter Anderson and Shridhar Damle, *The Brotherhood in Saffron: The Rashtriya Swayamsewak Sangh and Hindu Revivalism* (Boulder, CO: Westview Press, 1987), p. 29.

15. Although the Mahasabha was an independent entity, its members worked within the Congress and served in leadership positions until the split between the two occurred in 1937.

16. Christophe Jaffrelot notes that he modeled himself on the Italian nationalist Mazzini. Jaffrelot, *The Hindu Nationalist Movement in India* (New York: Columbia University Press, 1996), p. 26.

17. Savarkar's definition of a Hindu includes those who are tied to the ancestry of ancient India and who identify India as both their fatherland and their homeland. This would rule out Muslims and Christians but not Buddhists, Sikhs, or Jains. See Savarkar, *Hindutva: Who Is a Hindu?* (New Delhi: Hindi Sahitya Sadan, 2003), esp. pp. 83–116.

18. See Marzia Casolari, "Hindutva's Foreign Tie-Up in the 1930's: Archival Evidence," in *Economic and Political Weekly,* January 22, 2000.

19. Jawaharlal Nehru in *Link,* May 24, 1970, p. 15, quoted in Jaffrelot, *Hindu Nationalist Movement,* p. 51. The reference to fascism is meant to emphasize the corporate nature of social organization, not necessarily fascism's emphasis on the state.

20. Hasan, *Nationalism and Communal Politics,* pp. 173–74.

21. Hasan cites a letter written to Mohamed Jinnah from a League supporter criticizing the Jamia Millia Islamia. As the writer contends: "If this factory for Hinduising Muslims is allowed to continue its evil work, real Islam will soon disappear from India. The great killings like the one in Bihar grieve us most profoundly, but they do not kill Islam. They rather revive it to some extent. But the slow and secret poison of the *Jamia Millia Islamia* will soon kill Islam, and will make every Muslim a mere 'show-boy' of the Hindus. This is the cleverest plot so far designed for the destruction of Islam in India." Mushirul Hasan, *Legacy of a Divided Nation: India's Muslims since Independence* (London: Hurst and Co., 1997), pp. 240–41.

22. This was premised on the fact that the League's membership was composed only of Muslims. See Farzana Shaikh, "Muslims and Political Representation in Colonial India: The Making of Pakistan," *Modern Asian Studies* 20, no. 3 (1986): 543.

23. The Muslim League captured 108 out of 485 seats set aside for Muslim constituencies.

24. Fazlul Haq, speaking at a special session of the Muslim League in Calcutta in 1938, cited in Deepak Pandey, "Congress-Muslim Relations 1937–39: 'The Parting of the Ways,'" *Modern Asian Studies* 12, no. 4 (1978): 635.

25. Hasan, *Legacy of a Divided Nation,* p. 77.

26. In the 1946 election, for example, the vote in favor of the League and the creation of Pakistan was characterized as a "vote for Islam." Chandra, *India's Struggle for Independence,* p. 436.

27. See Sudipta Kaviraj, "A Critique of the Passive Revolution," in *State and Politics in India,* ed. Partha Chatterjee (Delhi: Oxford University Press, 1997).

28. Gandhi's vision for India's future economic development emphasized a village-based agrarian economy and did not favor the industrial development that Nehru and others proposed.

29. It is important to keep in mind that this emphasis on social reform petered out by the mid- to late 1950s. See Chatterjee, ed., *State and Politics in India,* introduction.

30. Jawaharlal Nehru, cited in Bipan Chandra, Mridula Mukherjee, and Aditya Mukherjee, *India after Independence: 1947–2000* (New Delhi: Penguin, 2000), p. 48.

31. It is this interpretation of secularism that is the basis of Ashis Nandy's and T. N. Madan's critique of Indian secularism referenced in chapter 1. See Rajeev Bhargava, ed., *Secularism and Its Critics* (Delhi: Oxford University Press, 1998).

32. This legislation would have standardized Hindu family law provisions and applied a uniform civil code to all Hindus, regardless of caste or sect, but was never passed into law.

33. Pakistan had sent troops into Kashmir on the eve of Independence, and the Hindu communalists advocated a more forceful response than Nehru was prepared to undertake.

34. See Graham, *Hindu Nationalism and Indian Politics.* See also Andersen and Damle, *Brotherhood in Saffron,* p. 50.

35. For a discussion of Godse's ties to the Mahasabha and the RSS, see A. G. Noorani, *Savarkar and Hindutva: The Godse Connection* (New Delhi: LeftWord Books, 2002).

36. See Gopal Godse, *May It Please Your Honour: Statement of Nathuram Godse* (Pune, India: Shri Gopal Godse, 1977), pp. 66–67, 97–117.

37. Nehru expressed his views in this way: "We have a great deal of evidence to show that the RSS is an organization which is in the nature of a private army and which is definitely proceeding on the strictest Nazi lines, even following the technique of organization." J. Nehru, *Letters to Chief Ministers 1947–1964*, vol. 1, ed. G. Parthasarathi (New Delhi: Oxford University Press, 1985), cited in Jaffrelot, *Hindu Nationalist Movement*, p. 87.

38. Golwalker wrote: "If you with Government power and we with organized cultural force combined, we can eliminate this menace [of communism]." Cited in Anderson and Damle, *Brotherhood in Saffron*, p. 52.

39. Romila Thapar, a leading Indian historian and emeritus professor at Jawaharlal Nehru University, argues that the popular history of the Somnath Temple is largely inaccurate. Situated as it is near the ocean, the damage to the temple was more likely the result of erosion than wanton assault. Moreover, the relations between the Hindu community and Muslim traders were both close and profitable. In conversation, July 28, 2003, New Delhi, India.

40. Cited in Peter Van der Veer, "Ayodya and Somnath: Eternal Shrines, Contested Histories," *Social Research* 59, no. 1 (Spring 1992): 91.

41. The issue of funding was also resolved by an agreement that the funds for the restoration would be raised privately and that public funds would not be used. Romila Thapar, in conversation, July 2003, New Delhi, India.

42 Nehru was concerned that Tandon had "become to large numbers of people in India some kind of a symbol of this communal and revivalist outlook and the question rises in my mind: Is the Congress going that way also?" Letter from Nehru to Tandon, August 8, 1950, cited in Graham, *Hindu Nationalism and Indian Politics*, p. 25.

43. See letter from Nehru to Patel, August 27/8, 1950, in Das (ed.) *Sardar Patel's Correspondence 1945–50 (Ahmedabad: Navajivan Publishing House, 1971)*, ed. Durga Das, p. 221.

44. The law was the Representation of the People Act, cited in Jaffrelot, *Hindu Nationalist Movement*, 104.

45. The reference is to an argument made by S. P. Jookerjee, the leader of the Mahasabha, in Jaffrelot, *Hindu Nationalist Movement*, p. 103.

46. The politicization of the Ayodhya mosque started in 1949, when two idols appeared in the sanctuary. See A. G. Noorani, "The Babri Masjid–Ram Janmabhoomi Question," *Economic and Political Weekly*, November 4–11, 1989.

47. This disparity was the result of a "first past the post" electoral system.

48. Sarvepali Gopal, *Jawaharlal Nehru: A Biography* (Cambridge: Harvard University Press, 1984), vol. 3, p. 173.

49. Jaffrelot, *Hindu Nationalist Movement*, p. 133.

50. Other states, including Madya Pradesh, passed similar laws around the same time.

51. Jaffrelot describes this situation in the following terms: "The Hindu nationalists seemed to be held in a vice-like grip by the 'Congress system.' On the one hand, in the states . . . Congress traditionalists appropriated some of their arguments; on the other,

Nehru was denouncing them at the Centre in the name of the Secular state." Jaffrelot, *Hindu Nationalist Movement*, p. 165.

52. This represented an effort to remodel Hinduism along the lines of the "Semitic" religions, whose strength was seen as deriving from their unity and centralization of authority. As Jaffrelot argues, this reflected a strategy of stigmatization and emulation. See Jaffrelot, *Hindu Nationalist Movement*, p. 201.

53. Kaviraj, "Critique of the Passive Revolution," p. 70.

54. These included the Communist Party of India (CPI), the Akali Dal (Sikh), the DMK (Caste), and the Muslim League.

55. This included the Swatantra Party and the Samyukta Socialist Party (SSP).

56. This guerilla movement was organized by a militant faction of the Communist Party (the Naxalites) in the late 1960s and early 1970s. The peasants took land reform into their own hands and seized property, burned records of ownership, and killed the landlords.

57. James Manor, "Parties and the Party System," in *India's Democracy: An Analysis of Changing State-Society Relations*, ed. Atul Kohli (Princeton: Princeton University Press, 1988), p. 70.

58. Sunil Khilnani talks about this as a central feature of Indira's ability to marginalize the traditional party bosses. See Khilnani, *The Idea of India* (New York: Farrar, Straus and Giroux, 1997), pp. 44–45.

59. Sudipta Kaviraj, "Indira Gandhi and Indian Politics," *Economic and Political Weekly*, vol. 21, September 20–27, 1986, p. 1702.

60. The statement is from J. P. Narayan, quoted in Bipan Chandra, *In the Name of Democracy: JP Movement and the Emergency* (New Delhi: Penguin, 2003), p. 73.

61. This was made explicit by Morariji Desai, a leader of Congress (O), who stated: "We intend to overthrow her, to force her to resign. For good." Cited in Chandra, *India after Independence*, p. 252.

62. Indira Gandhi cited in Chandra, *In the Name of Democracy*, p. 76.

63. See K. N. Seth and N. N. Bhardwaj, "Sanjayvad: A Study of the Phenomenon That Defeated Congress," *Secular Democracy* 1 (April 1977). See also Ian Jack, "Sanjay's Untold Story," *The Sunday Times* (London), March 6, 1977.

64. Congress (I) captured 351 of 525 seats, or roughly 65% of the seats in the lower house of the parliament. See Harold Gould, "The Second Coming: The 1980 Elections in India's Hindi Belt," *Asian Survey* 20, no. 6 (June 1980).

65. See Rajni Kothari, "The Emergency in Perspective," in Kothari, *State against Democracy: In Search of Human Governance* (New Delhi: South Asia Books, 1988), p. 275.

66. See Paul Brass, "National Power and Local Politics in India: A Twenty-Year Perspective," in *Caste, Faction, and Party in Indian Politics, Vol. I: Faction and Party*, ed. Brass (New Delhi: Chanakya Publications, 1984).

67. Paul Brass, "The Punjab Crisis and Unity of India," in *India's Democracy*, ed. Kohli, p. 175.

68. Kothari, *State against Democracy*, p. 246.

69. I am indebted to Kumkum Sangari, a fellow at the Nehru Library and Professor at Delhi University, for her thoughts on this topic, particularly concerning the connection between Hindu nationalism and antileftist sentiments. In conversation, September 26, 2003, New Delhi, India.

70. This included the inauguration of a VHP temple in Haridwar in 1983.

71. Ravi Nair, South Asian Human Rights Centre, in conversation. This point was reiterated by Neera Chandoke, University of Delhi, who noted that Indira was greatly influenced by a close associate, Dhirendra Brahmachari, who had an influential ashram in Delhi and a television show on which he lectured on yoga. In conversation, September 2003, New Delhi, India.

72. Indira Gandhi, cited in "Congress (I) and Minorities," *Economic and Political Weekly*, December 15, 1984, p. 2098.

73. "Congress (I) and Minorities," p. 2098.

74. Kothari, "Communalism: The New Face of Indian Democracy," in *State against Democracy*, p. 247. The reference is to a speech she gave in Garwal.

75. See Aaron Klieman, "Indira's India: Democracy and Crisis Government," in *Political Science Quarterly* 96, no. 2 (Summer 1981). See also Manor, "Parties and the Party System."

76. See Sumantra Bose, "'Hindu Nationalism' and the Crisis of the Indian State," in *Communalism in India: History, Politics, and Culture*, ed. K. N. Panniker (Delhi: Manohar, 1991), p. 121.

77. Anderson and Damle, *Brotherhood in Saffron*, p. 231.

78. Manor, "Parties and the Party System," p. 81.

79. Kothari describes this strategy as a shift from considering politics as a coalition of diverse interests to one of mass mobilization. The key, he argues, was focusing on the "Hindu heartland [where] a majority of the people are located." Kothari, *Politics and the People: In Search of a Humane India*, vol. 2 (New Delhi: Apex, 1989), pp. 486–88.

80. Pradeep Nayak, *Politics of the Ayodhya Dispute* (New Delhi: South Asia Books, 1993), p. 20.

81. Mark Tully and Satish Jacob, *Amritsar: Mrs. Gandhi's Last Battle* (London: Jonathan Cape, 1986), p. 12.

82. Jaffrelot, *Hindu Nationalist Movement*, p. 327. Jaffrelot also notes that "just at the stage when the BJP appeared to be moderating its use of Hindu nationalism, the will of the authorities to uphold secularism began to weaken," p. 315.

83. "BJP Goes Hindu?" *Hindustan Times*, February 14, 1985.

84. "Rajiv's India, RSS and BJP," Editorial in *The Janata Annual*, 1985, reprinted in *Muslim India*, March 1985, p. 140.

85. Ashis Nandy, Trivedy, Mayaram, and Yagnik, *Creating a Nationality: The Ramjanmabhumi Movement and Fear of the Self* (Delhi: Oxford University Press, 2003), pp. 17–18. See also Asghar Ali Engineer, *Communalism and Communal Violence in India: An Analytical Approach to Hindu Muslim Conflict* (New Delhi: South Asia Books, 1989).

86. See Manoj Joshi, *The Lost Rebellion: Kashmir in the Nineties* (New Delhi: Penguin, 1999).

87. Ali Asghar Engineer, in conversation, August 11, 2003, Bombay, India.

88. Raja Mohan, *The Hindu*, in conversation, October 2, 2003, Delhi, India.

89. For a full account of the early support of Bhindranwale by Sanjay Gandhi and former Congress chief minister of the Punjab, Zail Singh, see Tully and Jacob, *Amritsar*. See also Kuldip Nayar and Khushwant Singh, *Tragedy of Punjab: Operation Bluestar and After* (New Delhi: Vision Books, 1984); and Sarab Jit Singh, *Operation Black Thunder: An Eye Witness Account of Terrorism in Punjab* (New Delhi: Sage Publications, 2002).

90. See Ashutosh Varshney, "Contested Meanings: India's National Identity, Hindu

Nationalism, and the Politics of Anxiety," in *Daedalus: Journal of the American Academy of Arts and Sciences*, Summer 1993.

91. See Brass, "Punjab Crisis and Unity of India," pp. 182–83.

92. A negotiated agreement on these issues was reportedly turned down by Mrs. Gandhi, to the surprise of both government and Akali Dal negotiators. The explanation offered is that the terms of an accommodation would have been unacceptable to other states in the region. Conceding the transfer of land (including Chandrigarh) would have also been perceived either as a sign of weakness or as an indication that Mrs. Gandhi was favoring the interests of minority populations over those of the majority. A virtually identical agreement was accepted by her son Rajiv a few years later.

93. Ranbir Vohra, *The Making of India: A Historical Survey* (Armonk, NY: M.E. Sharpe, 2000), p. 251. G. Balachandran argues that the communalization of politics in the Punjab allowed "Mrs. Gandhi and the Congress leadership to play the ethnic/religious card in the guise of upholding secularism and 'national unity.'" Balachandran, "Religion and Nationalism in Modern India," in *Unravelling the Nation: Sectarian Conflict and India's Secular Identity*, ed. Kaushik Basu and Sanjay Subrahmanyam (New Delhi: Penguin Books India, 1996), p. 122.

94. Dipankar Gupta, "The Communalising of the Punjab, 1980–85," *Economic and Political Weekly*, July 13, 1985, p. 1187.

95. The issue is whether Bhindranwale was primarily a religious figure giving voice to Sikh discontent, or whether he was directly responsible for the violence that characterized the era. As Brass argues, most of the reporting on this era support the latter contention, though there is some truth to the former. For more on this debate, see Brass, "Punjab Crisis and Unity of India," pp. 189–90.

96. Singh, *Operation Black Thunder*, p. 52.

CHAPTER FIVE: Embedding Communalism in Indian Politics

1. "The Patriots Have It," *Economic and Political Weekly*, December 22–29, 1984, p. 2137. This theme was echoed by Romesh Thapar, "The Rajiv Party and the Hindus," *Economic and Political Weekly*, December 7–15, 1984, p. 2105.

2. Tully and Jacob, *Amritsar*, p. 7.

3. A common refrain was that the "Sikh should be taught a lesson, Hindu tolerance should not be mistaken for weakness." See "Our Skin-Deep Secularism," *Hindustan Times*, November 10, 1984.

4. People's Union for Democratic Rights (PUDR) and People's Union for Civil Liberties (PUCL), *Who Are the Guilty? Report of a Joint Inquiry into the Causes and Impact of the Riots in Delhi from 31 October to 10 November, 1984* (Delhi: PUDR/PUCL, 1984), p. 3.

5. PUDR/PUCL, *Who Are the Guilty?* p. 1.

6. "A Time to Choose," *Frontline*, December 15–28, 1984, p. 9. The lack of substance for these attacks is similarly echoed in James Manor, "Parties and Party System," p. 83.

7. "Rajiv Blames Opposition for Punjab Agitation," *The Hindu*, December 4, 1984, p. 11.

8. The BJP leaders responded by noting that "it was the Congress (I) which brought Bhindranwale to the center state of Punjab politics," creating the problem of Sikh militancy. BJP General Secretary L. K. Advani, cited in "Opposition Objects to PM's

Remarks in UP," *The Hindu,* December 3, 1984, p. 9. See also "Congress (I) Created Punjab Problem Says Opposition," *The Hindu,* December 22, 1984.

9. "Congress (I) Digs Out Past Incidents," *The Hindu,* December 14, 1984, p. 9.

10. "Rajiv Talks of Threats on Country's Border," *The Hindu,* December 3, 1984, p. 9.

11. "Rajiv Blames Opposition for Punjab Agitation."

12. The headline of the advertisement was "Will Another War Be the Last War in the Life of Free India?" in *The Hindu,* December 5, 1984, p. 6.

13. "Stunning Verdict: Cover Story," *Frontline,* December 29, 1984–January 11, 1985, p. 10.

14. Congress (I) party advertisement, *The Hindu,* December 15, 1984.

15. Cited in "Akali Leader Objects to Making Punjab a Poll Issue," *The Hindu,* December 15, 1984.

16. Manor, "Parties and the Party System," p. 88. Manor's article provides an insightful commentary on the election and on Congress's shift in strategy.

17. The state assembly was dissolved in 1983 and direct rule of the province by the central government was established. Article 357 of the Indian Constitution gave the central authorities this right. See "President's Rule in Punjab," *Economic and Political Weekly,* October 8, 1983.

18. Asghar Ali Engineer, "Introduction," *The Shah Bano Controversy,* ed. Engineer (Bombay: Orient Longman, 1987), p. 1.

19. For more on these issues, see Pradeep Nayak, *The Politics of the Ayodhya Dispute: Rise of Communalism and Future Voting Behavior* (New Delhi: Commonwealth Publishers, 1992).

20. The government initially supported the court decision but reversed itself after poor electoral results in several by-elections. See Zoya Hasan, "Religion and Politics in a Secular State: Law, Community, and Gender," in *Politics and the State in India,* ed. Hasan (New Delhi: Sage Publications, 2000).

21. Vishnu Hari Dalmia, president of the VHP, cited in "Interview," *Frontline,* October 14–27, 1989, p. 19.

22. Nandy et al. *Creating a Nationality.*

23. Seema Mustafa, "Uttar Pradesh Government Took Sides in Ayodhya Dispute," in *Babri Masjid/Ram Janambhoomi Controversy,* ed. Asghar Ali Engineer (Delhi: Ajanta Books, 1990), p. 117, cited in Bose, "'Hindu Nationalism' and the Crisis of the Indian State," p. 127. In a 1990 interview, Syed Shahabuddin, a leading Muslim activist, noted that "It was [Indira Gandhi] who really re-opened the Babri Masjid issue. . . . And of course, her son was the beneficiary. He inherited this. And in 1986 on February 1, when the lock was opened, there is no doubt in my mind that that order of the district judge of Faizabad was a contrived order. The entire scenario was written by the government. It was done as a matter of state policy. Thus a monster was raised which grew and grew and has come to the present stage." In Nandy et al., *Creating a Nationality,* p. 38.

24. "No Role in Ayodhya, Says Arun Nehru," *The Statesman,* August 17, 1989, The article also notes that "Mr. [Arun] Nehru is widely believed to be responsible for the reopening of the shrine," a position reiterated by Manishankar Aiyer, MP, in conversation, October 11, 2003, New Delhi, India.

25. Asghar Ali Engineer of the Center for the Study of Secularism in Society noted

that Arun Nehru was the driving force behind the Ayodhya issue and had advised Rajiv Gandhi on this matter. In conversation, August 11, 2003, Bombay, India.

26. See Mohan Sahay, "Buta Singh's Reported Green Signal to VHP," *The Statesman*, Delhi, October 26, 1989, p. 1.

27. A. G. Noorani, "The Babri Majid–RamJanmabhoomi Affair," *Economic and Political Weekly*, November 4–11, 1989. p. 2461.

28. Rajiv Gandhi, cited in Ambikanand Sahay, "Faizabad Hindus Move Towards Congress (I)," *The Statesman*, November 10, 1989.

29. "PM's Ayodhya Speech Ridiculed," *The Statesman*, November 5, 1989. He was reported to have also said that people should take pride in being Hindu, a clear reference to the majoritarian communalism of the VHP.

30. "A Traumatic Situation," *Frontline*, October 14–27, 1989, p. 14.

31. Quoted in Malini Parthasarathy, "Divide and Win: Spotlight on Communalism," *Frontline*, October 14–27, 1989, p. 17.

32. The significance of the Babri Masjid had been augmented by the airing of the Ramayana between January 1987 and August 1988, in serialized form, on state-run television. This production depicted the Lord Rama as a militant hero and a national symbol. In this way, "the so-called secular state became the principal vehicle by which the Ayodhya movement was placed before the Indian public." Corbridge and Harriss, *Reinventing India*, p. 190. See also Victoria Farmer, "Mass Media: Images, Mobilization, and Communalism," in *Contesting the Nation: Religion, Community, and the Politics of Democracy in India*, ed. David Ludden (Philadelphia: University of Pennsylvania Press, 1996).

33. Mahant Awaidyanath, cited in Kanchan Gupta, "Shilanyas Ceremony Begins," *The Statesman*, November 10, 1989.

34. In testimony before the Liberhan Commission in 2001, V. P. Singh noted that the Congress (I)'s efforts were intended to undermine talks between the Janata Dal and the RSS to resolve the issue. News of a possible settlement reached the Congress leaders, who then "proposed to allow shilanyas by the VHP." Quoted in Naunidhi Kaur, "Ayodhya: Of Ayodhya and the Congress," *Frontline*, December 8–21, 2001.

35. Amartya Mukhoadhyah, "Electoral Strategies of the Congress (I), the CPI (M), and Communalism," in *Religion, Politics, and Communalism: The South Asian Experience*, ed. Rakhahari Chatterji (New Delhi: South Asian Publishers, 1994), p. 73.

36. "A Rude Shock to Congress (I)," *The Statesman*, November 12, 1989. Bukhari spoke on behalf of his father, the Shahi Imam of the *Jama'a Masjid*.

37. "A Rude Shock to Congress (I)."

38. Sibal Dsgupta, "Gujarat Muslims Against Cong (I)," *The Statesman*, November 22, 1989.

39. Jaffrelot, *Hindu Nationalist Movement*, p. 382.

40. Having won 88 seats in Parliament in 1989, the BJP had become the third-largest party in India. In 1991, it increased its share to 120, making it the second-largest party in India.

41. For an analysis of the political economy of communalism in India, see Corbridge and Harriss, *Reinventing India*. See also Sumantra Bose, "'Hindu Nationalism' and the Crisis of the Indian State."

42. Edward Desmond, "Storm over India," *New York Review of Books*, May 14, 1992.

43. See Joshi, *Lost Rebellion*, p. 31.

44. "The Patriotism Stakes," *Economic and Political Weekly*, September 4, 1999.

45. Sumantra Bose, "'Hindu Nationalism' and the Crisis of the Indian State," p. 146.

46. A VHP publication called *Angry Hindu: Yes, Why Not?* argued for an "aggressive assertion of Hindu power to avenge the wrongs inflicted on them by Muslims in the past." Nandy et al., *Creating a Nationality*, p. 54.

47. "What does Secularism Mean?" *Indian Express*, October 28, 1990; and "When Can the Court Decide?" *Times of India*, October 31, 1990, cited in Nayak, *Politics of the Ayodhya Dispute*, p. 196.

48. For a thorough discussion of the symbolic elements of the Rath Yatra, see Richard Davis, "The Iconography of Rama's Chariot," in *Contesting the Nation*, ed. Ludden.

49. The VHP was also organizing other processions, known as *Ram Jyoti Yatras*, at the same time.

50. Nandy et al., *Creating a Nationality*, p. 123.

51. Nandy et al., *Creating a Nationality*, p. 42. The authors note that that the local press in Uttar Pradesh blamed either the Muslims or the state government for the violence: "Never was the violence or the crisis traced to inter-party competition; the press chose to depict it as a confrontation between the people and the government," p. 44.

52. Jaffrelot notes that there was a strong correlation between incidences of violence and the rise in votes for the BJP (particularly among scheduled caste voters). See Jaffrelot, *Hindu Nationalist Movement*, pp. 447–48.

53. As Jaswant Singh, an MP from the BJP, remarked, "You cannot make political soufflé rise twice from the same recipe." Cited in Nandy et al., *Creating a Nationality*, p. 166.

54. From the BJP's white paper on the Ayodhya issue, cited in Naunidhi Kaur, "Ayodhya: Echoes of a Demolition," *Frontline*, March 16–29, 2002.

55. Kaur, "Ayodhya: Echoes of a Demolition," p. 187.

56. One VHP billboard in Bombay warned: "There will no longer be any pleas, just war . . . and the battle will be bloody and terrible." See "Ayodhya: The Shiv Sena's Game," *Frontline*, August 4–17, 2001.

57. R. Padmanabhan, "Communalism: The Shiv Sena Indicted," *Frontline*, August 15–28, 1998.

58. Praveen Swami, "Srikrishna Commission: A Searing Indictment," *Frontline*, August 29–September 11, 1998.

59. Swami, "Srikrishna Commission." In a submission to the Libheran Commission—a government panel set up to investigate the circumstances surrounding the destruction of the Ayodhya Mosque—the All-India Muslim Personal Law Board (AIMPLB) accused the central government of vacillating "for political considerations" in the period before and after the destruction of the mosque. In the written submission, it noted, "The Board feels that the Central Government is guilty of misfeasance/nonfeasance in discharging its public and Constitution duties." It also accused the BJP-led government of Uttar Pradesh of having "direct complicity" in the destruction of the mosque. Reported in "AIMPLB Blames Congress Government for Demolition of Disputed Structure," March 8, 2004, *India Express*.

60. See Venkitesh Ramkrishnan, "A Case Demolished: The Politics of an Investigation," *Frontline*, December 17, 1993, pp. 20–21.

61. A. G. Noorani, "Retreat of Reason: And No Amends in Sight," *Frontline*, December 17, 1993, p. 20.

62. Kum Kum Sangari, in conversation, September 2003.

63. Asghar Ali Engineer, "Communal Darkness in Shining India," *Economic and Political Weekly*, February 28, 2004.

64. Romila Thapar, for example, was removed from the former board for her views on historical matters. The BJP was also rewriting bylines of exhibits in the National Museum and packing various boards and university grants commissions with Hindutva supporters.

65. Kum Kum Sangari, Nehru Memorial Library fellow, in conversation, September 26, 2003, New Delhi, India. Part of the danger, according to Sangari, was that these tactics were undermining institutions that were central to India's open society and that these institutions "will crumble long before free speech goes."

66. Jaffrelot, "The BJP at the Centre," in *The BJP and the Compulsion of Politics in India*, ed. T. B. Hanson and Jaffrelot (New York: Oxford University Press, 1998), p. 366.

67. The immediate provocation came when a number of activists harassed the Muslim vendors on the train platform.

68. "We Have No Orders to Save You: State Participation and Complicity in Communal Violence in Gujarat," *Human Rights Watch Report*, May 2002, p. 1.

69. "We Have No Orders," p. 1. See also Nandini Sandar, "A License to Kill: Patterns of Violence in Gujarat," in *Gujarat: The Making of a Tragedy*, ed. Siddharth Varadarajan (New Delhi: Penguin, 2002).

70. "We Have No Orders," p. 1.

71. Praveen Swami, "Saffron Terror," *Frontline*, March 16–29, 2002.

72. Jan Bremen writes on the link between the economic decline and the "lumpenization" of the proletariat, and how it tied into the BJP's mobilization in the spring of 2002. See Jan Breman, "Communal Upheaval as Resurgence of Social Darwinism," *Economic and Political Weekly*, April 20, 2002.

73. Breman, "Communal Upheaval."

74. Dionne Bunsha, "Hindutva's Triumph," *Frontline*, December 21, 2002–January 3, 2003.

75. Remarks by Prime Minister Atal Biharri Vajpayee in Goa, April 12, 2002, reprinted in Varadarajan, ed., *Gujarat*, p. 451.

76. "An Endorsement of BJP Policies," interview with Chief Minster Narendra Modi, *Frontline*, December 21, 2002–January 3, 2003.

77. See Rama Lakshmi, "In Indian Election, Hate Is Part of the Platform," *Washington Post*, December 11, 2002. Ironically enough, the candidate's last name was Patel.

78. "An Endorsement of BJP Policies." The Congress (I) Party's candidate in Godhra was Rajendra Singh Patel.

79. Venkitesh Ramakrishnan, "Congress Resurgence," *Frontline*, May 26–June 1, 2009.

CHAPTER SIX: The Rise and Decline of American Secularism

1. Bellah, "Civil Religion in America."

2. Russell Richey and Donald Jones, introduction, *American Civil Religion* (New York: Harper and Row, 1974), ed. Richey and Jones, p. 10.

3. Bellah, "Civil Religion in America," p. 168.

4. See Kevin Phillips, *The Emerging Republican Majority* (New Rochelle, NY: Arlington House, 1969).

5. John Winthrop, cited in Bryan LeBeau, *Religion in America to 1865* (New York: New York University Press, 2000), p. 38.

6. For a personal biography of Williams, see Edwin Gaustad, *Liberty of Conscience: Roger Williams in America* (Grand Rapids, MI: William B. Eerdmans, 1991).

7. See Frank Lambert, *The Founding Fathers and the Place of Religion in America* (Princeton: Princeton University Press, 2003), ch. 3.

8. Isaac Kramnick and R. Larence Moore, *The Godless Constitution: The Case against Religious Correctness* (New York: W.W. Norton, 1997), p. 56.

9. Other colonies, such as Maryland, similarly embraced a formal separation of church and state.

10. Lambert, *Founding Fathers*, p. 161.

11. The quotation is from Edmund Burke's defense of religious tests for public office holders in England. Cited in Kramnick and Moore, *Godless Constitution*, p. 80.

12. There were also differing modes of "establishment" that were proposed in these early debates, including the designation of Christianity or Protestant Christianity as the official religion in lieu of any one particular sect or denomination.

13. Article 6, Section 3 of the Constitution also contains a ban on religious tests for national office holders.

14. Lambert, *Founding Fathers*, p. 238. It should noted that these clauses did not apply to states, which did have various forms of establishment and bans on clergy in politics until the early 1800s. Aziz Huq, University of Chicago, in correspondence.

15. Hutcheson argues that the importance of republican institutions was a third element to the Calvinist-deist synthesis. See Richard Hutcheson, *God in the White House: How Religion Has Changed the Modern Presidency* (New York: Macmillan, 1989), pp. 18–20.

16. Richard Pierard and Robert Linder, *Civil Religion and the Presidency* (Grand Rapids, MI: Zondervan, 1988), p. 57.

17. Bellah, "Civil Religion in America."

18. Abraham Lincoln, The Gettysburg Address, cited in Bellah, "Civil Religion in America," p. 177.

19. The references are to Lincoln's second inaugural speech, in which he depicted the war as divine retribution for America's failings. In the speech, Lincoln says: "He gives to both North and South this terrible war as the woe to due to those by whom the offense [of slavery] came."

20. James Davison Hunter, *Culture Wars: The Struggle to Define America* (New York: Harper Collins, 1991), p. 83.

21. For a good discussion of the Scopes Trial, see Garry Wills, *Under God: Religion and American Politics* (New York: Simon and Schuster, 1990), ch. 9.

22. Franklin Roosevelt, Campaign Address, Cleveland, Ohio, November 2, 1940.

23. Franklin Roosevelt, Annual Message to Congress, January 4, 1939.

24. "Rise of Religion in US Analyzed: Churches Council Finds Gain in Revival, but Its Moral Effect is Questioned," *New York Times*, October 21, 1956. See also Will Herberg, *Protestant-Catholic-Jew: An Essay in American Religious Sociology* (Chicago: University of Chicago Press, 1960), ch. 4.

25. Wuthnow, *The Restructuring of American Religion* (Princeton: Princeton University Press, 1988), ch. 3.

26. Harry Truman, Inaugural Address, January 20, 1949.

27. Harry S. Truman, Remarks at the National Convention of the Augustana Lutheran Church, June 7, 1950.

28. James Reston, "Eisenhower Opens 'Crusade' Amid His Boyhood Scenes: General Hews to Old-Fashioned Revivalist Line with Appeal to Frugality, Honesty," *New York Times*, June 5, 1952, p. 17.

29. Dwight Eisenhower, cited in "Eisenhower Links Religion, Freedom," *New York Times*, October 17, 1949, p. 20.

30. Dwight Eisenhower, cited in "President Sees Editors: Tells Them Communism Can Be Beaten through Religion," *New York Times*, August 10, 1953, p. 12.

31. Cited in Hutcheson, *God in the White House*, p. 51.

32. Cited in Will Herberg, *Protestant-Catholic-Jew*, p. 84.

33. Pierard and Linder, *Civil Religion and the Presidency*, p. 191.

34. The quotation is from an editorial in the Christian Century, cited in Wuthnow, *Restructuring of American Religion*, p. 41.

35. Douglas MacArthur, *Revitalizing a Nation: A Statement of Beliefs, Opinions and Policies Embodied in the Public Pronouncements* (Washington, DC: Heritage Foundation, 1952), cited in Pierard and Linder, *Civil Religion and the Presidency*, p. 191.

36. Senator Joseph McCarthy, cited in Philip Jenkins, *A History of the United States* (New York: St. Martin's Press, 1997), p. 239.

37. Postwar Conservatism, known as "Fusionism," integrated these three strands of conservative thinking into a new intellectual movement. For more on the history of the early conservative movement, see George Nash, *The Conservative Intellectual Movement since 1945* (New York: Basic Books, 1976).

38. Ellen Schrecker, *The Age of McCarthyism: A Brief History with Documents*, 2nd ed. (New York: Palgrave, 2002), p. 13.

39. Percy Greaves, "Economic Equality," *Christian Economics*, January 27, 1953, cited in Sara Diamond, *Roads to Domination: Right-Wing Movements and Political Power in the United States* (New York: Guilford Press, 1995), p. 99.

40. See Peter Viereck, "The Revolt against the Elite," and Daniel Bell, "The Dispossessed," both in *The Radical Right*, ed. Daniel Bell (Garden City, NY: Anchor Books, 1964).

41. Godfrey Hodgson, *American in Our Time: From World War II to Nixon, What Happened and Why* (New York, Random House, 1978), p. 43.

42. Bell, "The Dispossessed," p. 5.

43. See F. B. Schick, "Americanism Seminars and the Communist Challenge," *Western Political Quarterly* 15, no. 2 (June 1962). Schick notes that one such meeting, held in the Hollywood Bowl in Los Angeles, attended by twelve thousand people, was televised to an audience of more than four million.

44. Statement of Senator Fulbright, *Congressional Record*, August 2, 1961, p. 14,433.

45. Cabell Phillips, "Right-Wing Officers Worrying Pentagon," *New York Times*, June 18, 1961, p. 1.

46. Bell, "The Dispossessed," p. 7. For more on these seminars and the controversy surrounding them, see Jonathan Schoenwald, *A Time for Choosing: The Rise of Modern American Conservatism* (New York: Oxford University Press, 2001), ch. 4.

47. Cited in George Dugan, "Presbyterian Hits New Anti-Red Cult," *New York*

*Times*, May 30, 1953, p. 16. The address was to the 165th General Assembly of the Presbyterian Church.

48. Dugan, "Presbyterian Hits New Anti-Red Cult."

49. Reinhold Niebuhr, interview with Mike Wallace, ABC Television, April 27, 1958.

50. Rienhold Niebuhr, *Moral Man and Immoral Society: A Study in Ethics and Politics* (Louisville, KY: Westminister John Knox Press, 1960), p. xviii.

51. Richard Hofstadter depicts these forces not as conservative in a Burkean sense but rather as pseudo-conservative, a rejection of America's "liberal" consensus. See Hofstadter, "The Pseudo-Conservative Revolt" (1955) and "Pseudo-Conservatism Revisited: A Postscript" (1962) in *Radical Right*, ed. Bell, chs. 3 and 4.

52. John F. Kennedy, Inaugural Address, January 1960, cited in Bellah, "Civil Religion in America," p. 172.

53. Bellah, "Civil Religion in America," p. 169.

54. One of the more significant pieces of social legislation adopted during this period was that which created Medicare, a health insurance plan that provides universal coverage for the aged.

55. The full quotation runs, "We are confronted primarily with a moral issue. It is as old as the scriptures and is as clear as the American Constitution. . . . If an American, because his skin is dark . . . cannot enjoy the full and free life which all of us want, then who among us would be content to have the color of his skin changed and stand in his place? Who among us would then be content with the counsels of patience and delay?" John F. Kennedy, cited in David Leege, Kenneth Wald, Brian Krueger, and Paul Mueller, *The Politics of Cultural Differences: Social Change and Voter Mobilization Strategies in the Post-New Deal Period* (Princeton: Princeton University Press, 2002), p. 111.

56. Lyndon Johnson, quoted in Bellah, "Civil Religion in America," p. 181.

57. Phillips discusses the shifting trend in liberalism from New Deal economic populism—which provided support for farmers, unions, social security, and education—to Great Society liberalism, which became more centered on "social engineering" and which subsequently lost the Democrats "the support of poor whites," particularly in the South. See Phillips, *Emerging Republican Majority*, p. 206.

58. Phillips, *Emerging Republican Majority*, p. 31. See also Charles Colson's comments on Nixon's efforts to reach out to evangelicals and Catholics as a key part of the "Southern strategy" in William Martin, *With God on Our Side: The Rise of the Religious Right in America* (New York: Broadway Books, 1997), pp. 97–98.

59. Phillips, *Emerging Republican Majority*, p. 206.

60. The states that Wallace won included South Carolina, Georgia, Alabama, Mississippi, and Louisiana. For an analysis of the 1968 vote, see Alan Otten, "Politics and People: Voting Patterns," *Wall Street Journal*, December 20, 1968.

61. Arlen Large, "In the South, Events Close in on Nixon," *Wall Street Journal*, September 18, 1969.

62. "The Republican Outlook," *New York Times*, August 11, 1968, p. E10.

63. Spiro Agnew, quoted in Richard Lyons, "Agnew: HHH 'Squishy Soft,'" *Washington Post*, September 11, 1968. For a summary of the Republican Party platform and its policy on Vietnam, see "Return to Tradition," *New York Times*, August 6, 1968, p. 36.

64. Senator Everett Dirksen's keynote address to the convention dwelt almost exclusively on this theme. See Max Frankel, "Campaign Issues Take New Direction," *New York Times*, July 1, 1968, p. 12.

65. Leege et al., *Politics of Cultural Differences*, p. 17.

66. The statement is from an NAACP official, quoted in Thomas Johnson, "Negro Leaders See Bias in Call of Nixon for 'Law and Order,'" *New York Times*, August 13, 1968, p. 27.

67. Edward Brooke, cited in Lyons, "Agnew: HHH 'Squishy Soft.'"

68. Nixon had been catapulted to fame by his position on House Un-American Affairs Committee (HUAC), particularly for his involvement in the Alger Hiss case. It was this high-profile conservative activism that had earned him the vice-presidential position on Eisenhower's ticket.

69. The phrase "silent majority" was first used by Richard Nixon in a televised speech on the Vietnam War. See Richard Nixon, "Address to the Nation on Vietnam," November 3, 1969.

70. Charles Henderson, *The Nixon Theology* (New York: Harper and Row, 1972), p. 106.

71. Richard Nixon, Inaugural Address, January 20, 1969.

72. As a Nixon campaign strategist noted, "We have to be very clear on this point: that the response is to the image, not to the man. . . . Politics is much more emotional than it is rational, and this is particularly true of Presidential politics. People identify with a President in a way they do with no other public figure. Potential presidents are measured against an ideal that's a combination of leading man, God, father, hero, pope, king, with maybe just a touch of the avenging Furies thrown in." Cited in Joe McGinniss, *The Selling of the President 1968* (New York: Trident Press, 1969), pp. 193–94. Referenced in Bernard Donahue, "The Political Use of Religious Symbols: A Case Study of the 1972 Presidential Campaign," *Review of Politics* 37, no. 1 (January 1975): 62.

73. See Lowell Streiker and Gerald Strober, *Religion and the New Majority: Billy Graham, Middle America, and the Politics of the 1970's* (New York: Association Press, 1972), p. 62. Graham did endorse Nixon in the 1972 campaign.

74. Cited in Henderson, *Nixon Theology*, p. 29.

75. Billy Graham, cited in Edward Fiske, "The Closest Thing to a White House Chaplain," *New York Times Magazine*, June 8, 1969.

76. Fiske, "Closest Thing."

77. Richard M. Nixon, Remarks at Dr. Billy Graham's East Tennessee Crusade, May 28, 1970. See also Randall King, "When Worlds Collide: Politics, Religion, and Media at the 1970 East Tennessee Billy Graham Crusade," *Journal of Church and State* 39, no. 2 (Spring 1997).

78. Streiker and Strober, *Religion and the New Majority*, p. 71.

79. Leege et al., *Politics of Cultural Differences*, p. 17.

80. Pierard and Linder, *Civil Religion and the Presidency*, p. 219.

81. Leege et al., *Politics of Cultural Differences*, p. 116.

82. Donahue, "Political Use of Religious Symbols," p. 51.

83. George McGovern, cited in Donahue, "Political Use of Religious Symbols," p. 51.

84. See Leege et al., *Politics of Cultural Differences*, p. 115.

85. E. J. Dionne, *Why Americans Hate Politics* (New York: Touchstone Books, 1991), p. 202. Dionne goes on to note: "What is so odd in retrospect is that Nixon was polarizing American politics at the very moment when he was depolarizing all the important

political issues." This, in turn, meant that American politics would come to be defined a series of "false choices" surrounding cultural and racial politics, pp. 202–3.

86. Kevin Phillips, "How Nixon Will Win: A Republican Takes to the Soapbox," *New York Times*, August 6, 1972.

87. Kenneth Briggs, "Ford, in Appeal to Evangelists, Stresses His Religious Faith," *New York Times*, October 10, 1976, p. 42.

88. President Gerald R. Ford, cited in Kenneth Briggs, "Ford, in Appeal to Evangelists," p. 42.

89. E. J. Dionne, *Why Americans Hate Politics*, p. 205.

90. The term is coined by Kevin Phillips in *American Theocracy: The Peril and Politics of Radical Religion, Oil, and Borrowed Money in the 21st Century* (New York: Viking Press, 2006), p. 179.

91. Jimmy Carter, Remarks at the National Prayer Breakfast, January 18, 1979.

92. Jimmy Carter, "The Crisis of Confidence," speech delivered on July 15, 1979.

93. Carter, "The Crisis of Confidence."

CHAPTER SEVEN: Religious Nationalism in the Reagan-Bush Era

1. Leege et al., *Politics of Cultural Differences*, p. 122. The authors call the effort to create a more explicit secular order the "Third Disestablishment," which "displaced the protestant ethic as the authoritative model of personal conduct." See also Phillip Hammond, *Religion and Personal Autonomy: The Third Disestablishment in America* (New York: Columbia University Press, 1992).

2. Leege et al., *Politics of Cultural Differences*, p. 122.

3. Rev. James Kennedy, cited in Kenneth Briggs, "Evangelicals Debate Their Role in Battling Secularism," *New York Times*, January 27, 1981, p. A12.

4. George Gilder, cited in Lewis Beman, "A Capitalist Manifesto from the New Right," *Business Week*, December 29, 1980.

5. This "religion gap" became pronounced in the 1980s and 1990s. It distinguishes between those who attend church on a regular basis and those who do not. There is a case that the best marker for party identification is degree of religiosity, not membership in one denomination or another. See Laura Olsen and John Green, "The Religion Gap," *PS: Political Science and Politics*, July 2006.

6. Ronald Reagan, speech to the Religious Roundtable in Dallas, Texas, August 22, 1980.

7. Ronald Reagan, cited in Martin, *With God on Our Side*, p. 214.

8. The basis of this strategy was articulated in the "Black Book," a document drafted by longtime Reagan pollster Richard Wirthlin. See Lee Edwards, *The Conservative Revolution: The Movement That Remade America* (New York: Free Press, 1995), p. 219.

9. Ronald Reagan, cited in Howell Raines, "Reagan Backs Evangelicals in the Political Activities," *New York Times*, August 23, 1980, p. 8. See also Robert Marus and Greg Warner, "Reagan Political Years Paralleled Right's Rise," *The Christian Century*, June 29, 2004, p. 11.

10. Martin, *With God on Our Side*, p. 217.

11. For an account of this meeting, see Jerry Falwell, *Falwell: An Autobiography*

(Lynchburg, VA: Liberty House, 1997), ch. 14. See also Edwards, *Conservative Revolution*, pp. 196–99.

12. James Guth, "The Politics of the Christian Right," in *Religion and the Culture Wars: Dispatches From the Front*, ed. John Green, James Guth, Corwin Smidt, and Lyman Kellstedt (New York: Rowan and Littlefield, 1996), p. 13.

13. Haynes Johnson, *Sleepwalking through History: America in the Reagan Years* (New York: Doubleday, 1992) p. 196.

14. Ronald Reagan, Remarks at the Annual Convention of the National Association of Evangelicals in Orlando, Florida, March 8, 1983. For more on the speech, see Frances Clines, "Reagan Denounces Ideology of Soviet as Focus of Evil," *New York Times*, March 9, 1983, p. A1.

15. Reagan, Remarks at Annual Convention of the National Association of Evangelicals.

16. Reagan, Remarks at Annual Convention of the National Association of Evangelicals.

17. Charles Austin, "Divided Evangelicals Avoid a Policy Stand on Nuclear Freeze," *New York Times*, March 12, 1983, p. A7.

18. The exchange occurred during testimony before the House Foreign Affairs Committee, cited in Anthony Lewis, "What Kind of Country Are We?" *New York Times*, May 17, 1981, p. E23.

19. Charles Jones, "Re-nominating Ronald Reagan: the Compleat Politician at Work," in *The American Elections of 1984*, ed. Austin Ranney (Durham, NC: Duke University Press, 1985).

20. The ERA actually passed Congress in 1972 but failed to win passage in a sufficient number of state assemblies. It was reintroduced in 1982 after a ten-year time limit for passage had elapsed.

21. Jeffrey Hadden and Anson Shupe, *Televangelism: Power and Politics on God's Frontier*, cited in Johnson, *Sleepwalking through History*, p. 197.

22. Ronald Reagan, Remarks at the Annual Convention of the National Religious Broadcasters, January 30, 1984. Referencing his support for a constitutional amendment on school prayer, Reagan further noted, "If we could get God and discipline back in our schools, maybe we could get drugs and violence out."

23. Ronald Reagan, Remarks at a Nevada Republican Party Fundraising Luncheon in Las Vegas, Nevada, February 7, 1984. See also Lou Cannon, "The Lord Seems to Have Been Tapped as Reelection Chairman," *Washington Post*, February 13, 1984, p. A3.

24. Ronald Reagan, Remarks at an Ecumenical Prayer Breakfast in Dallas, Texas, August 23, 1984.

25. Ronald Reagan, Remarks at a Spirit of America Festival in Decatur, Alabama, July 4, 1984.

26. I am indebted to Craig Mousin, director of the Center for Church State Studies at DePaul University School of Law, for his thoughts on this topic.

27. John Winthrop, cited in Bryan LeBeau, *Religion in America to 1865* (New York: New York University Press, 2000), p. 38.

28. Jerry Falwell, addressing the National Right to Life Convention, cited in Robert Inderman, United Press International Wire Service, June 8, 1984.

29. Carolyn Sudeth, associate director of public liaison for the White House, cited

in Marjorie Hyer, "Evangelical Broadcasters Define Role in Politics," *Washington Post*, February 4, 1984, p. B6.

30. Lou Cannon, "The Lord Seems to Have Been Tapped," p. A3. See also Steven Tipton, "Religion and the Moral Rhetoric of Presidential Politics," *The Christian Century*, October 31, 1984, pp. 1010–13.

31. Senator John Danforth, cited in T. R. Reid, "Prayer Bill Foes Attack 'Election-Year Religiosity,'" *Washington Post*, March 7, 1984.

32. Walter Mondale, cited in Milton Coleman, "Mondale Warns against Mixing Politics, Religion," *Washington Post*, August 28, 1984, p. A4.

33. Cited in Juan Williams, "The Religious Merges with the Political in Reagan's Campaign," *Washington Post*, March 6, 1984, p. A3.

34. T. R. Reid, "Prayer Bill Foes Attack 'Election-Year Religiosity.'"

35. To be clear, what was happening was a realignment among elites while party identification diminished at the grassroots level. See James Wilson, "Realignment at the Top, Dealignment at the Bottom," in *American Elections of 1984*, ed. Ranney.

36. Leege et al., *Politics of Cultural Differences*, p. 118.

37. George Bush, cited in Leege et al., *Politics of Cultural Differences*, p. 301.

38. See Wills, *Under God*, ch. 5.

39. George Bush, quoted in Sidney Blumenthal, *Pledging Allegiance: The Last Campaign of the Cold War* (New York: Harper Perennial, 1991), p. 264.

40. Dan Quayle, Address to the Commonwealth Club of California, May 19, 1992.

41. Dan Quayle, "Remarks to the Southern Baptists' Convention," Indianapolis, Indiana, June 9, 1992.

42. For more on the debate about the nature of this "culture war," see Rhys Williams, ed., *Culture Wars in American Politics: Critical Review of a Popular Myth* (New York: Aldine De Gruyter, 1997) and Green et al., eds., *Religion and the Culture Wars*. See also Hunter, *Culture Wars*.

43. George Bush, Remarks to the Knights of Columbus Supreme Council Convention in New York City, August 5, 1992. For more on the speech, see Andrew Rosenthal, "Bush Jabs at Rival's Morals, Saying Values Are Besieged," *New York Times*, August 6, 1992, p. A20.

44. George Bush, Remarks to the Knights of Columbus.

45. Jerry Falwell, cited in "A Republican God?" *Christianity Today*, October 5, 1992.

46. Patrick Buchanan, 1992 Republican National Convention Speech, Houston, Texas, August 17, 1992.

47. Bill Clinton, cited in Gwen Ifill, "Clinton Says Foes Sow Intolerance: Asserts That GOP Is Trying to Create Religious Split," *New York Times*, September 12, 1992, p. A1.

48. Letter issued by National Council of Churches, August, 1992, cited in "Using 'God' in the Campaign Is Blasphemy, Clergymen Say," *New York Times*, August 30, 1992, p. 31.

49. Despite the importance of economic issues in the 1992 election, Kellstedt et al. note that the results point to a continuing ethno-religious realignment in the electorate. The division, however, is based on degree of religious belief, not type. In other words, those with strong beliefs tend to vote Republican, and those who are less committed—or explicitly secular—tend to vote Democrat. This reflects a degree of cultural polarization in society and the ongoing tensions within different denominations between "modern-

ists" and "traditionalists." See Lyman Kellstedt "Religious Voting Blocs in the 1992 Election," In Green et. al., eds., *Religion and the Culture Wars*.

50. Kellstedt, Green, Guth, and Schmidt, "Has Godot Finally Arrived? Religion and Realignment," in *Religion and the Culture Wars*, ed. Green et al., p. 295.

51. See David Frum, "Sex, Lies, and Public Virtue," *The Weekly Standard*, February 23, 1998, p. 27. See also Noemie Emery, "The Clinton Legacy: Morality Turned Upside Down," *The Weekly Standard*, August 10, 1998, p. 21.

52. Rabbi Eric Yoffie, president of the Union of American Hebrew Congregations, cited in Gustav Niehbur, "Defining Moral Failings, Both Private and Public," *New York Times*, October 10, 1998, p. B8.

53. George W. Bush, remarks delivered at Bob Jones University, South Carolina, February 2, 2000, reprinted in *Washington Post*, March 6, 2000, p. A6.

54. George Bush, cited in Tony Carnes, "A Presidential Hopeful's Progress," *Christianity Today*, October 2, 2000, p. 62. Bush's comments were relayed by Rev. Robison; the full quotation reads, "I've heard the call. I believe God wants me to run for President."

55. George Bush, cited in Larry Witham, "Heart-Changing Faith Is Guidepost for Bush," *Washington Times*, July 23, 2000, p. C1.

56. Chuck Colson, cited in Lauri Goodstein, "Bush Uses Religion as Personal and Political Guide," *New York Times*, October 22, 2000, p. A1.

57. Senator Joe Lieberman, quoted in Ceci Connolly, "Taking the Spirit to the Stump, Lieberman Urges 'Place for Faith in Our Public Life,'" *Washington Post*, August 28, 2000, p. A1.

58. Senator Joe Lieberman, quoted in Spencer Hsu, "Lieberman Urges Moral Awakening: Vice Presidential Nominee Vows to Purge Cultural Pollution," *Washington Post*, October 25, 2000, p. A10.

59. Senator Joe Lieberman, quoted in Connolly, "Taking the Spirit to the Stump."

60. Lieberman, quoted in Hsu, "Lieberman Urges Moral Awakening."

61. The request came in the form of a letter to Senator Lieberman by the Anti-Defamation League. Cited in Gustav Niebuhr, "Lieberman Is Asked to Stop Invoking Faith in Campaign," *New York Times*, August 29, 2000, p. A19.

62. For the religious overtones of this transformation, see Tony Carnes, "Bush's Defining Moment," *Christianity Today*, December 12, 2001, p. 38.

63. For more on the "call to war," see J. Bottum, "A Nation Mobilized," David Tell, "The End of Illusion," and Robert Kagan and William Kristol, "A War to Win," in *The Weekly Standard*, September 24, 2001.

64. George W. Bush, President's Remarks at National Day of Prayer and Remembrance, The National Cathedral, Washington, D.C., September 14, 2001.

65. George W. Bush, "We Will Prevail in War on Terrorism," reprinted in *New York Times*, November 9, 2001, p. B6.

66. President Bush first used this term in 2005, though it had become a common refrain among neoconservative commentators. See President George Bush, Remarks to the National Endowment for Democracy, October 6, 2005. See also Podhoretz, *World War IV*.

67. George W. Bush, Remarks at National Day of Prayer and Remembrance.

68. Phillips, *American Theocracy*, p. 207.

69. Podhoretz, "In Praise of the Bush Doctrine," *Commentary*, September 2002, p. 21.

70. See, for example, Bin Laden's 1998 fatwa, in Raymond Ibrahim, *The Al-Qaeda Reader* (New York: Broadway, 2007).

71. Many saw in the revived "God Talk" a sign that "relativism seems obsolete, . . . postmodernism [has expired], . . . and God is back." Tony Carnes, "Bush's Defining Moment," *Christianity Today.*

72. J. Denny Weaver, "Responding to September 11—and October 7 and January 29: A Real World Pacifist Response," paper presented at the Symposium on Religion and Politics, Calvin College, Grand Rapids, Michigan, May 2002, p. 1.

73. Statement by Methodist Bishops, in "Methodists Critique the War Effort," *New York Times,* November 10, 2001, p. B6.

74. James Childress, University of Virginia, cited in Bill Broadway, "War Cry from the Pulpit: Some Fear Mix of Patriotism, Religion in Bush's Vow to Rid World of Evil," *Washington Post,* September 22, 2001, p. B9.

75. Jerry Falwell, "God is Pro-War," posted on www.worldnetdaily.com, January 31, 2004.

76. See Charles Marsh, "Wayward Christian Soldiers," *New York Times,* January 20, 2006.

77. General William Boykin, quoted in "The General Who Roared," *New York Times,* October 22, 2003, p. A22. See also Tom Teepen, "A Sectarian Stew Pot," Cox News Service, October 27, 2003.

78. See John Yoo, *The Powers of War and Peace: The Constitution and Foreign Affairs after 9/11* (Chicago: University of Chicago Press, 2006).

79. Andrew Bacevich and Elizabeth Prodromou, "God Is Not Neutral: Religion and U.S. Foreign Policy after 9/11," *Orbis,* Winter 2004, p. 43.

80. For a commentary on the Bush campaign's use of the terrorist threat in its strategy, see Mark Danner, "How Bush Really Won," *New York Review of Books,* January 13, 2005.

81. George Bush, cited in Richard Stevenson, "Bush Attacks Kerry as Weak on Security," *New York Times,* October 23, 2004, p. A13. Interestingly, Bush's father made a similar comment in the 1988 campaign: "Weakness and ambivalence lead to war. Weakness tempts aggressors. Strength stops them. I will not allow this country to be made weak again." George W. Bush, Acceptance Speech, Republican National Convention, August 18, 1988.

82. For a discussion of the conservative Christian view of the election, see Deborah Caldwell, "Did God Intervene? Evangelicals Are Crediting God with Securing Re-Election Victory for George W. Bush." Posted on www.beliefnet.org, November 5, 2004.

83. For a discussion of these prayer ministries and the controversy over their sectarian nature, see Ken Walker, "The Politics of Prayer," *Christianity Today,* August 2004, p. 26.

84. The flyer sent out in Arkansas encouraged turnout among conservative Christians by stating: "If you don't vote—if you stay away from the polls—the Bible [will be] banned." Reprinted in the *Congressional Record,* September 30, 2004, p. S10015.

85. For an analysis of the significance of the gay marriage issue to the Christian Right and the extensive mobilization surrounding it in the autumn of 2004, see Bob Smietana, "Church Militant," *Christianity Today,* October 24, p. 22.

86. For two competing views of the implications of the 2004 elections, see Garry Wills, "The Day the Enlightenment Went Out," *New York Times,* November 4, 2004,

p. A25; and David Neff, "Post-Election Faith at Work," *Christianity Today*, December 2004, p. 5.

87. Jim Wallis, "Dangerous Religion: George Bush's Theology of Empire," *Sojourners Magazine*, September–October 2003, p. 20.

88. David Kuo, *Tempting Faith: An Inside Story of Political Seduction* (New York: Free Press, 2007), p. 261.

89. Randy Brinson, cited in Amy Sullivan, "When Would Jesus Bolt?" *Washington Monthly*, April 2006.

90. Rod Dreher, a conservative columnist with the *Dallas Morning News*, quoted in an interview with Krista Tippett, on *Speaking of Faith*, a nationally syndicated radio program produced by American Public Media, October 9, 2008, available at http://speakingof faith.publicradio.org. Dreher went on to note that it was frustrating to see "how easily people like me—religious conservatives—fall into line."

91. Richard Czick, cited in Sullivan, "When Would Jesus Bolt?"

92. John McCain, February 28, 2000, Virginia Beach, Virginia.

93. James Dobson, cited in Bob Unruh, "Dobson says 'No Way' to McCain Candidacy," January 13, 2007, available at www.wnd.com/news/article.asp?ARTICLE_ID=53743, accessed January 4, 2010.

94. Richard Land, cited in Adelle Banks, "Evangelicals Pleasantly Surprised with McCain's Choice," Religious News Service, August 29, 2008.

95. Barack Obama, remarks before the "Call To Renewal Speech," Washington, D.C., June 26, 2006. For more on this speech, see Peter Boyer, "Party Faithful: Can the Democrats Get a Foothold on the Religious Vote?" *The New Yorker*, September 8, 2008.

96. Frederick A. O. Schwartz and Aziz Z. Huq, *Unchecked and Unbalanced: Presidential Power in a Time of Terror* (New York: New Press, 2008).

## Conclusion

1. See, for example, John Micklethwait and Adrian Wooldridge, *God Is Back: How the Global Revival of Faith Is Changing the World* (New York: Penguin, 2009).

2. The reference is to Nasr's characterization of Zia al-Huq's efforts to coopt Sunni fundamentalism in the 1980s. See Vali Nasr, *Islamic Leviathan*.

3. Bose, "'Hindu Nationalism' and the Crisis of the Indian State," p. 152.

4. See, for example, Gabriel Almond, Scott Appleby, and Emmanuel Sivan, *Strong Religion: The Rise of Fundamentalisms around the World* (Chicago: University of Chicago Press, 2003).

5. On a related note, it is instructive to recognize that Egypt's authoritarian political structure has become quite reliant on an exclusive Islamist discourse and is not as amenable to the kind of change seen in the other two cases.

6. Aziz Huq, University of Chicago, in correspondence.

7. I am indebted to Pasha Anwar of Delhi University for his thoughts on this topic.

8. See Vali Nasr, *Islamic Leviathan*.

9. Dionne, *Why Americans Hate Politics*, introduction.

# Index

Lightning Source UK Ltd.
Milton Keynes UK
UKHW042357291121
394787UK00001B/45